Africa — A Modern History (1800–1975)

J. O. Sagay
D. A. Wilson

AFRICANA PUBLISHING COMPANY
A division of Holmes & Meier Publishers, Inc.
NEW YORK

First published in the United States of America 1980 by
Africana Publishing Company
A division of Holmes & Meier Publishers, Inc.
30 Irving Place,
New York, N.Y. 10003

Copyright © 1978 by J. O. Sagay and D. A. Wilson
Illustrated by Reproduction Drawings

Originally published by Evans Brothers Limited 1978

Library of Congress Cataloging in Publication Data

Sagay. J. O.
  Africa, a modern history, 1800–1975
  Includes index.
  1. Africa . . History . . 19th century. 2. Africa . . History . .
1884–1960. 3. Africa . . History . . 1960–
I. Wilson, Derek A., joint author. II. Title.
DT28.S23 1979 960 79-16594
ISBN 0-8419-0542-8
ISBN 0-8419-0543-6 pbk.

Printed in Great Britain

Contents

Acknowledgements

The publisher's thanks are due to the following who have photographs on the pages indicated:

Africana Museum, Johannesburg for the photographs on pages 48, 142, 154, 155, 153;
Bodleian Library for the photographs on pages 42, 80, 118, 121, 126, 128, 137, 232, 233, 234, 247, 248, 408;
British Museum for the photograph on page 295;
British Airways for the photograph on page 22 (top);
J. Allan Cash for the photographs on pages 2, 6, 31, 43, 46;
Camera Press for the photographs on pages 264, 314, 323, 330, 333, 335, 336, 351, 379, 388, 402, 416, 417;
Daily Express for the photograph on page 336;
Daily Herald for the photograph on page 342;
Daily Sketch for the photograph on page 382;
De Beers Consolidated Mines for the photograph on page 152;
Edinburgh University Publications for the photographs on page 304;
Elliot and Fry for the photograph on page 259;
Fox Photos for the photograph on pages 401, 414;
Foto Tadema Sporny for the photographs on pages 1, 28;
Hulton Picture Library for the photographs on pages 17, 19, 33, 34, 164, 237, 309, 319, 325, 340, 341, 377, 395, 398;
Imperial War Museum for the photograph on page 267;
Horniman Museum for the photograph on page 22;
Kenneth King for the photograph on pages 369, 373;
Kenya Information Service for photograph on page 167;
Dr A. V. King for two photographs on page 1;
E. D. Lacey for the photograph on page 315;
Longmans for the photograph on page 132;
Mansell for the photographs on pages 13, 18, 71, 100, 111, 176, 197, 201, 205, 206, 228, 298, 408;
MacMillan Memorial Library, Nairobi, for the photograph on page 261;
Mary Evans Picture Library for the photographs on pages 181, 187, 191, 199, 274, 276;
McQuitty International Inc. for the photograph on page 322;
National Portrait Gallery for the photograph on page 275;
Nigerian Information Service for the photograph on page 351;

Popperfoto for the photographs on pages 33, 210, 245, 247, 281, 291, 320, 321, 327, 328, 339, 372, 376, 385, 388, 391, 392, 399, 401, 412, 414, 415;
Sunday Telegraph for the photograph on page 40;
Tommy Photo for the photograph on page 225;
United Nations for the photograph on page 311.

Note:
Historical names are used for lakes, etc. except in a present-day context.

The word 'African' has a very limited value. It may apply to someone who speaks any one of the hundreds of languages and dialects spoken on the continent. He may be a devout Muslim from Marrakesh; a Coptic Christian from Ethiopia; a pygmy hunter-gatherer from the Congo forest; a Maasai herdsman with a contempt for modern city life; a sophisticated, Western-educated businessman from Lagos. He may live on the plains, in the forest, by the sea or in the desert. His staple diet may be meat or fish or maize or cassava. He may live at sea-level or at 2,000 metres. Africa is a diverse continent and its people are equally diverse.

For this reason it is no easy matter to write a brief history of the whole continent. In this book we have had to select in each region those peoples and events that we think we should write about. Inevitably, there is much that we should have liked to say but could not for lack of space. We state this at the beginning so that students will realize that the following pages only contain a *selection* from the history of Africa since 1800. There is much more for the reader who is interested in the history of the continent to study and discover.

Africa is richly varied in almost every way—geologically, climatically, racially, linguistically, culturally. Are there then no themes, no patterns of development that hold good for the entire continent, or large areas of it, and which will help us to understand what was happening in different places? Indeed there are, and the purpose of these first few pages is to survey the major events in broad outline, to build up a framework of history to which the more detailed information that comes later in the book can be attached.

(a) Mandinka woman

(b) Swaziland warrior

(c) Libyan Arab

(d) Hausa musician

(e) Xhosa woman

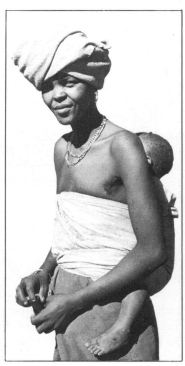
(f) Tembu woman

For thousands of years Africa was a sparsely populated continent. This meant that when one area became over-crowded, or over-farmed, or the supply of water or game animals dwindled, some of the people could move to find new homelands. Therefore, periodic migration has always been a feature of life in Africa. This does not mean that all parts of Africa are suitable for settlement. Look at the map below right. You can see that broadly speaking there are three types of country in Africa: forest, desert and grassland. There have always been people living in the deserts and forests but most Africans have preferred the temperate grassland belts where a variety of crops can be grown, where there is an abundance of game animals to hunt and where domestic beasts can be pastured. If you look at the second map you will see that most of the main population movements have been migrations through grassland belts.

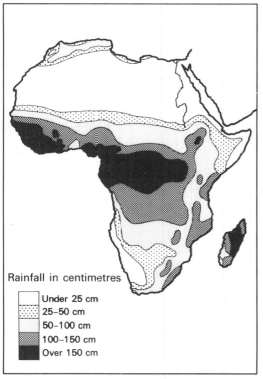

Rainfall in centimetres

- Under 25 cm
- 25–50 cm
- 50–100 cm
- 100–150 cm
- Over 150 cm

Rainfall in Africa

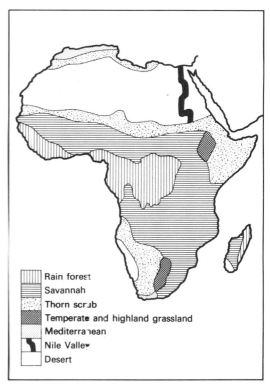

- Rain forest
- Savannah
- Thorn scrub
- Temperate and highland grassland
- Mediterranean
- Nile Valley
- Desert

Vegetation in Africa

3

The most massive and complex migration was that of the Bantu peoples who now make up most of the inhabitants of central, southern and eastern Africa. The word 'Bantu' refers to the basic language spoken by these people. (We generally distinguish between different groups of Africans on linguistic grounds.) The first Bantu-speakers (known as 'proto-Bantu') lived either to the north or south of the Congo forest. These people obviously thrived and multiplied rapidly, so some had to move out. They moved in all directions but were careful to skirt inhospitable areas such as the forest to the north and the desert to the south. They spread throughout most of eastern Africa and many groups were still on the move in 1800. Sometimes the Bantu were confronted by more powerful peoples who were also migrating. In East Africa, for example, the Kamba, Kikuyu, Pogoro and others encountered Galla and Somali herdsmen travelling from the direction of the Horn of Africa. They therefore turned westwards again, only to be confronted by the powerful Maasai and had to settle in the forested Kenya Highlands. They were thus still very much on the move throughout most of the nineteenth century. At the other end of the continent the Nguni found their south-ward migration blocked by European settlement. Population pressure built up until in the 1820s the serious conflict known as the *Mfecane* took thousands of men, women and children back into Central and East Africa. Some of the peoples who stood in the path of Bantu expansion were too weak to resist. Such people as the Saan and Khoi of southern Africa had to move into areas of sparse vegetation on the fringes of the Kalahari desert.

Migrations in North Africa were, in part, inspired by religion. From about A.D. 700 waves of Muslim Arabs had swept along the north coast conquering or absorbing the local Berber peoples. They completely eradicated North African Christianity which had flourished in many centres, such as Alexandria, since the first century A.D. The story was the same in the Nile valley. But in the mountains of Ethiopia powerful Christian kingdoms resisted the Muslim advance and continued to do so right down to the nineteenth century, as we shall see.

Islam crossed the Sahara to West Africa along the trade routes, but because the desert took two months to cross large-scale migration or invasion was out of the question. However, a similar religious migration did occur in West Africa. The

Fulani pastoralists gradually spread eastwards from their homelands in Senegambia through the western Sudan, taking their fervent Islamic faith with them and sometimes enforcing it on the peoples among whom they settled.

Much of the history of nineteenth-century Africa is concerned with the continued expansion or decline of large political units which had been established earlier. We must therefore consider these states briefly, starting with North Africa and working southwards. After the Muslim invasions of the eighth, ninth and tenth centuries Egypt remained united with Arabia and Syria, but to the west, in what the Arabs called the Maghrib, there were several independent kingdoms. In the sixteenth century the Ottoman Turks took over the leadership of the Muslim world and brought all North Africa, except Morocco, under their control. By 1800 the fires of Turkish zeal had died. Though the Ottoman Sultan was still recognized as overlord, the governors of Algiers, Tunis, Tripoli and Egypt had become hereditary rulers. They derived their wealth from trans-Saharan trade and piracy in the Mediterranean.

Islam had spread up the Nile valley and in the sixteenth century the powerful Funj Sultanate was established along the lower reaches of the Blue Nile, with its capital at Sennar. Islamic settlements were also established along the Red Sea coast. Under pressure from all sides the Empire of Ethiopia shrank and fell into political chaos. By 1800 the four major kingdoms that made up the Empire were in a state of almost continual warfare and there was no universally recognized emperor. The Church was, however, a unifying factor.

To the west lay the states of Darfur, Wadai and Kanem-Borno. All were nominally under Muslim rule but all had large pagan populations. The trans-Saharan trade so vital to these states was frequently interrupted by internal conflict or war with neighbours.

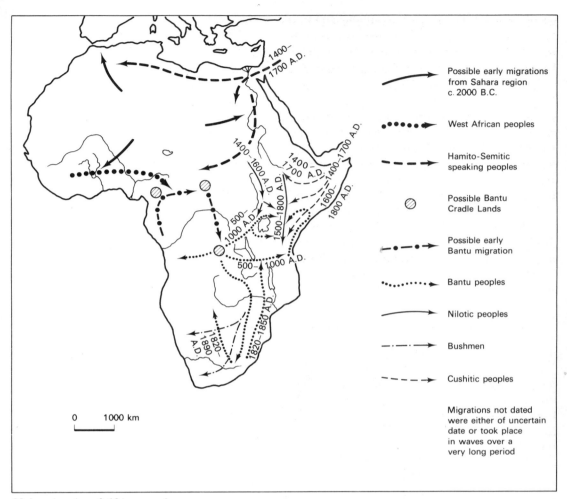

Major migration of African peoples

The most powerful of the forest states of West Africa were Asante and Oyo. The Asante from their capital at Kumasi had established control over all the Akan people and their neighbours. The Alafin of Oyo ruled over a confederacy of Yoruba states. Both Asante and Oyo derived much of their wealth from the slave trade with European agents at the coast.

The most important states of Central Africa were the Lunda empires of Mwata Yamvo and Kazembe and the Rozwi Confederacy. Mwata Yamvo came into existence about 1600 when a powerful Luba prince established himself on the lower Lulua and began to create a powerful state by conquest. By the early eighteenth century the Mwata Yamvo's empire had become too unwieldy and the ruler handed over the eastern part to his governor, the Kazembe. Both empires were at their height in 1800. In the sixteenth century an area roughly the same as modern Rhodesia came under the control of a dynasty whose rulers took the title *Changamire*. They ruled a confederacy of Rozwi kingdoms, and enjoyed great power and wealth, mostly derived from gold mines. They built impressive stone buildings, the ruins of which can still be seen today in such places as Great Zimbabwe, the ancient Rozwi capital.

In the days before well-built roads and powered vehicles, long journeys through Africa were extremely difficult. For foreigners unused to Africa's climate and with no resistance to tropical diseases, penetration of what became known as the 'Dark Continent' was almost impossible. In Arabia, Asia and

Foreign influence

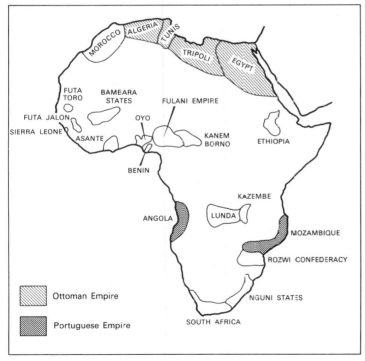

Major political units of Africa c. 1800

Europe many legends and fables were told about Africa. For thousands of years the continent had provided learned men with at least one great puzzle—the source of the mighty river Nile. But by 1800 no foreigner had ever successfully ventured to the heart of Africa in an attempt to discover the truth. The most successful travellers had been Arab merchants who made regular trips from their bases on the north coast across the Sahara to the grasslands of the Sudan.

Trade, however, had brought many foreigners to the coasts of Africa. Africa produced two commodities which were in great demand in other parts of the world—ivory and slaves. Some regions (such as the Rozwi Empire and the Volta basin) also

Old Portuguese fort Zanzibar

produced gold. For merchants and captains prepared to risk the journey and the African climate, great profits were to be made from trade in these commodities. As time went by the foreigners set up fortified settlements on the coast.

On the eastern side of the continent the Arabs were the first to arrive. The entire coastline from the Zambezi to Cape Guardafui was drawn into the thriving commercial life of the Indian Ocean. In settlements like Mogadishu, Zanzibar and Mombasa the Arabs intermarried with the local people to form the Swahili race. In the sixteenth century the Portuguese reached this part of Africa and forced the Arabs out of the area south of Cape Delgado. For the next three hundred years the Portuguese exercised precarious rule at a few bases on the coast, such as Mozambique and Sofala. They even established bases at Sena and Tete on the lower Zambezi. But, though a large area of East-Central Africa was claimed for the Portuguese crown and though occasionally Portuguese pioneers ventured far into the interior, Portuguese rule looked more impressive on maps than it was in reality.

The same was true of Portuguese activity on the western coast of Central Africa. Portuguese ships reached this area in the mid–fifteenth century, and they established a foothold by conquering the Kingdom of Kongo and other coastal states. From their bases at Luanda and Benguela the Portuguese made forays into the interior. They established relations with trading peoples such as the Ovimbundu and Mbangala, who brought them goods from the far interior. Half-caste agents and, occasionally, Portuguese led trading expeditions to the interior but Portugal's African 'allies' effectively kept the markets and routes closed to them.

On the coast of West Africa the situation was more complex. Here, merchants lured by the slave trade had come from many countries of Europe and the Americas to establish bases. The map shows all the principal foreign ports on this stretch of coast.

The Dutch colony in South Africa began as a trading post but by 1800 had become a European settlement. The first post was established at Cape Town in 1652 by the Dutch East India Company which wanted a port where merchant ships travelling to and from the East could obtain supplies and repairs. Soon potential farmers began to move into the interior in search of farmland. They clashed with the local Saan and Khoi but took whatever land they wanted. Slaves were imported to work

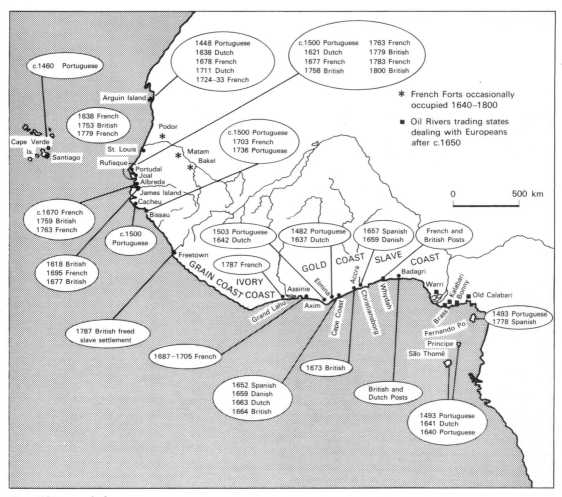

West African trade forts

on the farms but some of the settlers (who were known as 'Boers', the old Dutch word for farmers) were already enslaving Africans. In 1795, as a result of a European war, Cape Colony was taken over by the British. Although the Dutch regained the colony from 1803 to 1806, it reverted to Britain thereafter.

That, then, is a 'bird's-eye view' of Africa as it appeared in 1800. Now we must see how the African peoples and their invaders changed the situation during the next one hundred and seventy years.

Peoples of North Africa   Chapter 2

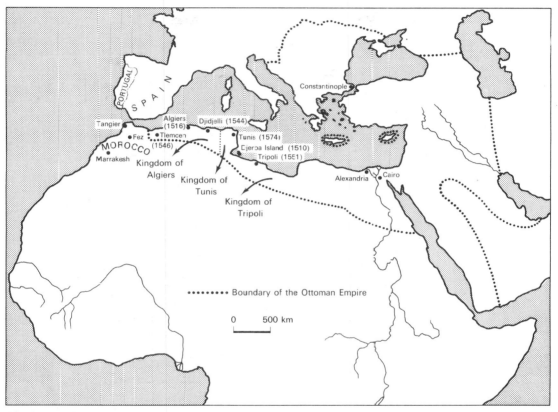

The Ottoman Empire in North Africa

The first area we are going to study is the large part of Africa
north of the grassland belt (approximately north of the 15°N
parallel). Geographically the area falls into three quite distinct
parts: the Sahara, populated only by a few nomadic peoples,
the north-coast belt, which has a much larger population as
well as long-standing links with Europe and the Middle East,
and the mountainous country of Ethiopia (formerly known as
Abyssinia), peopled by many independent groups of people.

First, we shall consider Egypt and the Sudan, then the states of the Maghrib, then Ethiopia and Somalia, and finally the desert peoples.

The history of Egypt, as one might expect, has many similarities with the lands of the Maghrib to the west. As we saw in the first chapter, all these lands, except Morocco, were part of the Ottoman Empire and were, in theory, ruled from Constantinople. In fact, because of the gradual decline of Ottoman power and prestige, the local representatives of the Sultan held the real authority in each state. Throughout the nineteenth century the story of North Africa is concerned largely with three main themes: the continued decline of Ottoman power; the growth of European influence; and the attempts by the coastal states to control areas of land further south, along the Nile and the trans-Saharan trade routes. All these features appear quite clearly in the history of Egypt and the Sudan.

Egypt

In 1798 a European war between France and England affected Egypt. The French dictator, Napoleon Bonaparte, seized control of the country in order to block England's trade routes to India and the East. Napoleon failed because his enemies had superior sea power and could control the Mediterranean, and in 1801 the remaining French soldiers were withdrawn. But this brief occupation altered the history of Egypt because it challenged the power of the Mamluks, brought Muhammad Ali to Egypt and introduced the Franco-British rivalry that eventually led to the colonization of the country.

The Mamluks were a military caste recruited in the distant corners of the Ottoman Empire and used to govern Egypt. For over five hundred years they had dominated the local people, levied harsh taxes and ruled as a group of powerful foreigners having no dealings with the Egyptians. In 1798 the Mamluk army had not suffered a serious defeat for nearly three hundred years. Then, at the Battle of the Pyramids, they confronted one of the greatest generals of all time, Napoleon, and the well-armed, well-disciplined French troops. The result was total defeat for the Mamluks.

Now the Egyptians, and particularly their religious leaders, the sheikhs, realized that Mamluk power could be challenged. So did an ambitious young Ottoman officer, Muhammad Ali.

Battle of the Pyramids

The Life of Muhammad Ali

1769	Born in Macedonia (now northern Greece)
1787	Served with an Albanian regiment in the Ottoman army
1800	Arrived in Egypt to fight against the French
1805	Seized power in Cairo
1806	Appointed Ottoman Governor of Egypt
1807	Suppressed a Mamluk revolt
1811	Finally destroyed Mamluk power
1820–4	Conquered the Sudan
1832–3	Conquered Syria
1839–40	Reconquered Syria
1840	Treaty of London. Muhammad Ali lost Syria but became hereditary Viceroy of Egypt and established a new royal dynasty
1849	Died

13

He arrived in Egypt at the head of a regiment of Albanian troops to fight against the French. But the conflict was soon over and political chaos followed the French departure. Groups of Mamluks struggled for power under the leadership of their *beys*, and the sheikhs were plotting the overthrow of the Turks. Muhammad Ali aimed to gain supreme power for himself.

By giving the support of his Albanian troops first to one party, then another he achieved his goal. By 1805 the chief Imam had been deposed and Muhammad Ali was the most powerful man in Cairo, the Egyptian capital.

Muhammad Ali based his power on the support of the Egyptian people. He pretended to be a leader who would deliver them from the Mamluks. But the Mamluks, though divided into various factions, were still strong. In 1811 he disposed finally of the Mamluk threat by inviting all their important men to a banquet in Cairo. As they were leaving the city afterwards Muhammad Ali had them trapped in a narrow passageway where concealed soldiers fired at them and massacred three hundred.

The new dictator of Egypt genuinely wished to develop the country and make life better for its people. He took over control of farmland, improved irrigation and introduced new farming methods. He encouraged the growth of industry and developed trade with Christian Europe, which had been discouraged by the Mamluks. He replaced the corrupt and oppressive taxation system of his predecessors with one that was more efficient and less severe. He introduced a new currency. He brought European advisers in to assist him in commercial and military matters.

At the same time Muhammad Ali launched several military campaigns. Between 1811 and 1818 his armies were employed in Arabia helping the Ottoman Sultan destroy the power of the Wakhabis and other Arabian tribes. The pacification of Arabia led to an increase of overland trade from Egypt and Ethiopia to the Red Sea coast. Muslim pilgrims could once again travel in safety to the holy city of Mecca. European travellers going to India and the East began to use the overland route through Egypt (Alexandria–Cairo–Suez and thence by ship down the Red Sea). All this brought to Egypt increased prosperity and a new international prestige.

When the army returned from Arabia Muhammad Ali sent it against the Sudan. There were many reasons for this campaign quite apart from Muhammad Ali's imperial ambition. He believed that gold was to be found in the Sudan. He knew that black slaves could be obtained there. These he wanted for his various building and agricultural projects and also for his army. He had built up a purely Egyptian army with the help of French professional soldiers. The despised Egyptian peasants had for centuries not performed any military service. Muhammad Ali forced thousands of them into the army. Although they served well in Arabia he did not think very highly of them. He planned to make up a black slave army which would have a loyalty only to himself. He also wanted to bring as much of the Red Sea coast as possible under his control. The last reason for Muhammad Ali's interest in the Sudan was that a band of Mamluk refugees had settled in the northern part of the country. They were terrorizing the peoples of the area and were a threat to Egypt.

Muhammad Ali

In 1820 a double attack was launched. One column moved towards the Funj Sultanate of Sennar while the other invaded Kordofan. Both were successful. The Funj Sultanate was in decline and offered no resistance to the invaders. The Governor of Kordofan gave battle outside his capital of El-Obeid but his army was no match for the Egyptians. The Egyptians gained little from the victory. The land and people were very poor. There was no gold. Most of the people were Muslims, so could not be enslaved. The soldiers suffered greatly from disease and from the unpleasant climate. Potential slaves were only to be found in the lands further south, beyond a vast region of marshland and floating vegetation known as the Sudd. Muhammad Ali's officers satisfied themselves with capturing what slaves they could and imposing harsh taxes on their new Sudanese subjects.

The result was, by 1822, widespread revolt. The Sudanese refused to pay taxes, and attacked Egyptian garrisons. Muhammad Ali's son, Ismail, was murdered by rebels at Shendi. The Egyptians responded by massacring hundreds of Sudanese. Most of the outbreaks were successfully put down and in 1824 a new administrative centre was set up from which the Egyptians could control their new conquests. It was called Khartoum.

In terms of power Muhammad Ali had become a greater man than his master, the Ottoman Sultan. The Turkish ruler was gradually losing control of parts of his empire, particularly

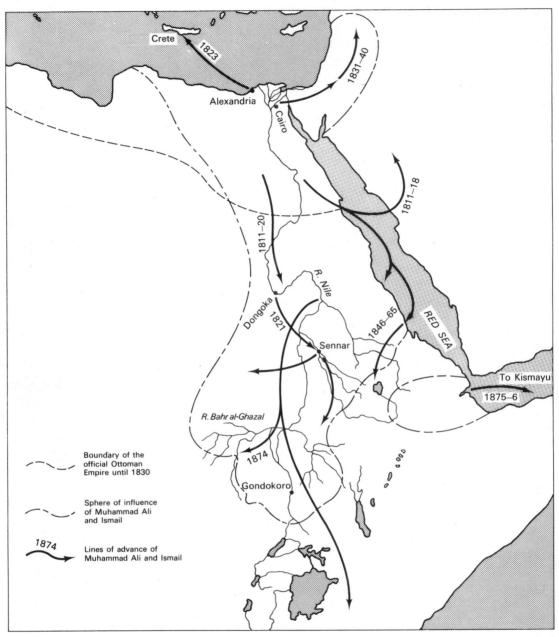

Egypt and the Sudan 1820–1880

Boundary of the official Ottoman Empire until 1830

Sphere of influence of Muhammad Ali and Ismail

1874 Lines of advance of Muhammad Ali and Ismail

Crete 1823

1831–40

1811–18

1811–20

Dongoka 1821

R. Nile

Sennar

1846–65

RED SEA

To Kismayu

1875–6

R. Bahr al-Ghazal

1874

Gondokoro

Alexandria

Cairo

south-eastern Europe (the Balkans). In 1824 Muhammad Ali sent a large force to Greece to help the Sultan suppress a Balkan revolt. Unfortunately for him Russia, France and Britain joined the conflict on the side of their fellow Christians and in 1827 the Egyptians suffered a serious defeat. The Sultan had promised to appoint Muhammad Ali Governor of Syria and Palestine in return for his aid. Now, alarmed at the Egyptian ruler's power, he went back on his word. What Muhammad Ali could not get by agreement he took by force. By 1833 the disputed territory was in the hands of Egyptian armies and the Ottoman Sultan had to recognize Muhammad Ali as Governor. But in 1839 an army was sent from Constantinople to drive the Egyptian rulers out. Muhammad Ali's forces not only repelled this invasion; they pushed the Ottoman troops back into Turkey and threatened to attack the capital, Constantinople. Now the leading governments of Europe agreed that Egypt had become too powerful. In 1840 Muhammad Ali was forced to give up Syria and Palestine but he was recognized as hereditary ruler of Egypt (under the Sultan), and his family remained in power for over a century. At the same time Britain occupied Aden on the eastern coast of the Red Sea to prevent Egypt controlling the short route to India. Furthermore, Muhammad Ali had to agree to limit the size of his army. All these points were included in the 1841 Treaty of London.

The last eight years of Muhammad Ali's life were less adventurous. Though an old man (he was over eighty at the time of his death in 1849) he continued to rule Egypt and the northern Sudan firmly. With the aid of his western advisers, schemes dear to his heart, such as the establishment of cotton and sugar growing and the increase of the amount of land under the plough, prospered. He was a dictator but his rule was largely beneficial for Egypt. He was succeeded by Abbas who added little to the achievements of his grandfather and was murdered after a reign of five years, from 1849 to 1854. The reigns of the next two Viceroys, Said and Ismail, were far more important.

Muhammad Said was a weak man. He was dominated by his European advisers. In order to boost trade he encouraged Europeans to come to Egypt and establish industries and businesses. Because of the generous terms offered, Frenchmen, Italians, Greeks, Britons and Germans flocked to Cairo and other towns. They invested money in the country. They

Muhammad Said

17

prospered. So, for a time, did Egypt. But Said's policies laid the foundation of future problems. He borrowed a great deal of money from European banks and he helped to establish in Egypt a large group of wealthy and powerful foreigners.

One foreigner who made an impression on Said was Ferdinand de Lesseps, a French diplomat. He had re-examined an old idea that it would be possible to connect the Mediterranean and the Red Sea by a canal, thus creating a short seaway link between Europe and the East. De Lesseps gained Said's permission to form a company which would finance the building and running of the canal. He formed his company largely with French capital and in 1859 with Egyptian forced labour he began to dig the Suez Canal.

Digging the Suez Canal 1869

Said died before the canal was completed but he did see the completion of one important project, the linking by railway of Alexandria, Cairo and Suez (1856–7). Said was succeeded by his nephew Ismail. Ismail, like Muhammad Ali, wanted to make Egypt a thriving, modern nation. He had ideas for the creation of fine cities and the development of agriculture, industry and commerce. Unfortunately he did not understand financial affairs. During a reign of sixteen years, from 1863 to 1879, he plunged himself and his country deep into debt.

If we consider Ismail's achievements the first we must mention is his winning of independence from Turkey. In 1863, at his accession, he was granted control of the Red Sea ports of Suakin and Massawa. Four years later the Ottoman Sultan gave Ismail the title of Khedive and with it considerable freedom as a representative of his country in international affairs. The opening of the Suez Canal in 1869 enormously increased the importance of Ismail and Egypt.

The Khedive Ismail

Cairo replaced Constantinople as the most important diplomatic centre of the eastern Mediterranean region. Foreign governments competed to win Ismail's favour, and the number of Europeans in Egypt doubled. With foreign money which he borrowed on a large scale, regardless of the consequences, Ismail carried out a massive programme of building and improvements. Nearly two thousand kilometres of new railway track were laid. Hundreds of irrigation schemes were begun. The port of Alexandria was modernized. Major centres were linked by telegraph. Thousands of schools were built. Ismail also spent a lot of money on impressive displays of wealth—palaces, public buildings, entertainment of important visitors.

Like his grandfather Ismail had imperial ambitions. He extended Egyptian control of the Red Sea coast and claimed (after 1870) to rule the entire coastline from Suez to Cape Guardafui. On the middle Nile he employed a powerful slave and ivory trader, Zubeir, to extend Egyptian frontiers. In 1874 Zubeir overthrew the Darfur Sultanate and added another large area to Ismail's empire. The Khedive wanted to establish Egyptian authority over the entire length of the White Nile, and employed several British officers to lead the attack on the southern Sudan. In 1869 Stanley Baker was sent up the Nile to establish Ismail's authority beyond the Sudd. In three years Baker fought his way through to Gondokoro and planted the Egyptian flag there. Apart from the difficulties of the country, Baker had to face the hostility of local rulers and also of the powerful ivory and slave traders who resented any challenge to their independence. Pushing on southwards Baker attempted to annexe Bunyoro and Buganda. He returned to Khartoum in 1873, claiming to have added the vast area of the Equatoria Province to Egypt. However, only in a few places did Egyptian officials have any real authority. Baker's successor, Charles Gordon, had slightly more success during his brief governorship, from 1874 to 1876. He installed garrisons at several posts on the upper Nile south of Gondokoro. Expeditions against Ethiopia met with still less success.

Unfortunately for Ismail, all his grand schemes had to be paid for. Apart from foreign loans and Sudanese ivory the only source of government revenue was taxation. Ismail's Egyptian and Sudanese subjects were taxed to the limits of their endurance—and still the government was in debt. In 1875 the Khedive was forced to offer for sale his majority shareholding in the Suez Canal Company. The shares were bought by the British government (for £4 million) to prevent the canal falling into the hands of France, Britain's rival.

Still Ismail's financial position grew worse. The European bankers and businessmen who had lent their money so willingly now grew alarmed and demanded help from their own governments. At last Britain and France decided to intervene jointly in Egypt's affairs. In 1878 Ismail was forced to accept within his government advisers from the two countries to help him to reorganize Egypt's finances. Ismail resented this threat to his independence and after a few months, he dismissed his advisers. The Europeans now showed their real power. They persuaded the Ottoman Sultan to depose Ismail in favour of his son, Tawfiq. The new ruler was completely controlled by Europeans, who now largely took over the government. From that time onwards the important decisions concerning Egypt were made, not in Cairo, but in London and Paris.

The Sudan

The Sudan has two quite distinct regions, the Muslim, Arabized North and the African South. They are divided by the tract of marshland and floating vegetation known as the Sudd, which is almost impenetrable. For decades the Sudd protected the peoples of the upper Nile from invasion from the north.

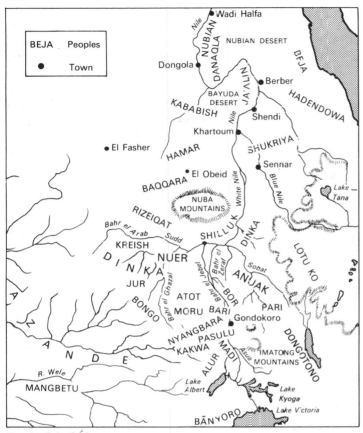

People of the Sudan

Groups who could not resist the Funj sultans and did not wish to be incorporated in an Islamic empire withdrew southwards through the marshland. The Nuer even made the barrier more effective by deliberately floating vegetation downstream.*

The southern region is inhabited by many groups of Nilotic and Sudanic peoples. Little is known about the history of these peoples before the Egyptian and European invasions of the second half of the nineteenth century. Some, like the Nuer, were pastoralists. Others, such as the Azande, practised shifting agriculture and hunting. Nowhere was settled life

*This vegetation, known as the 'mother of wool plant', forms large floating islands. It collects around river bends and other obstructions and can create blockages several kilometres long.

The Sudd

Azande pot

possible. In most communities the clan was the important social and political unit, though the Azande were ruled by kings. There were clashes between clans and between peoples but no group was ever large enough or strong enough to establish lasting dominion over its neighbours.

To the north, much of the Nile valley was under the control of the Funj Sultanate, a Negro Muslim state that had been in existence since the sixteenth century. By 1800 it had little real power. The Funj sultans had never mastered the Dinka and Shilluk peoples and by this time they exercised only a loose control over the Arab and African communities of the middle Nile valley from their capital at Sennar. Funj trade had been badly affected by disturbances in Arabia and along the African Red Sea coast. These had almost completely blocked the pilgrim route from the central Sudan to Mecca and shut off the Sultanate from valuable supplies of slaves, ivory and copper. By 1800 Kordofan, to the west, had fallen under the control of Darfur. In Sennar real power lay in the hands not of the sultans but of the army commanders.

Darfur and Wadai were wealthy trading states of the savannah. They raided southwards to obtain slaves from among the peoples of the forest fringe and by 1800 Darfur was exporting over 5,000 slaves annually to Egypt. They obtained copper from the region of Hofrat an-Nahas. They were not reliant on trade routes to the Nile and the Red Sea but dealt directly with Egypt and North Africa by the trans-Saharan caravan route from El Fasher to Asyut known as the *Darb al Arbain* (the Forty Days Road). These states had absorbed Islamic influences from their trade contacts to the north. Their official religion was Islam but, like other states of the central and western Sudan, they did not follow the teachings of the Prophet Muhammad in all purity. Strong elements of the old pagan religions of the area remained.

Between 1820 and 1880 this whole area came under Egyptian influence. This invasion from the north involved two kinds of men: the official representatives of the Egyptian Viceroy and independent traders seeking ivory and slaves. But these two groups were not completely separated, for sometimes, as we shall see, the Viceroy employed traders in his service and some slave dealers conquered fresh territory or demanded tribute in the name of the Egyptian government.

The Egyptian invasion of 1820, as we have seen (page 15), had two 'prongs'. One, under the leadership of Muhammad Ali's son, Ismail, struck deep into Funj territory. The second 'prong' of the invasion under the command of Muhammad Bey Khusraw, the Viceroy's son-in-law, advanced on Kordofan in mid-1821. He defeated the Sultan of Darfur's army at Bara and set up a new administration at El Obeid. The people, who had merely exchanged one conqueror for another, did not resist and the Sultan made no move to reconquer his territory. But the Viceroy did not have the men or money for further conquest and for many years an uneasy peace existed between Darfur and Egypt.

Khartoum, the new administrative centre of the Egyptian Sudan, grew in sixteen years from a tiny fishing village to a city of over 20,000 inhabitants. It was the establishment of Khartoum as a large market and commercial centre that made possible the massive exploitation of the southern Sudan. Sudanese, Egyptian and Turkish traders led expeditions up the Nile to raid the Shilluk, Dinka and Nuer for slaves. All the healthy males were despatched to Egypt for military service while most of the women went via Suakin to the harems of wealthy Muslims in other lands. Official slave raids also took place. Egyptian army detachments made frequent expeditions into the mountains south of Sennar and El Obeid returning with as many as 5,000 captives at a time. The soldiers were given half the slaves they captured to sell for their own personal profit.

Africa has suffered much over the centuries from slave traders but some of the worst of all the dealers in human flesh were the Khartoumers who ravaged the Sudan between 1839 and 1883. Muhammad Ali sent three expeditions up the Nile between 1839 and 1841. These penetrated the Sudd and reached almost as far as Gondokoro. Muhammad Ali had hoped that they would discover valuable mineral deposits. What they did discover was almost as important — large herds of elephant. Now there was a rush to exploit the area. European businessmen financed well-equipped expeditions. Official and unofficial Egyptian raiding parties were assembled, their ranks filled from the prisons and gutters of Cairo and Khartoum.

Every means was used to obtain ivory and slaves. At first the traders only encountered people living near the river, the Shilluk, Nuer and Bari. With trade goods such as beads and cloth they bought ivory from the Nilotics, who had no use for it. But as the numbers of traders increased, the situation changed. They had to travel further in search of ivory. The Khartoumers armed their allies with guns and encouraged them to raid their neighbours to take tusks and slaves by force. This led to a disastrous increase of inter-community warfare. The merchants' allies soon tired of the cheap trade goods brought from the north; they demanded cattle as the price of their ivory. So the Khartoumers began to raid peaceful villages in order to get cattle. They attacked Sudanese settlements, not caring whether they killed the villagers or not. Survivors were taken as slaves; anything valuable was looted; cattle were stolen to pay for ivory. The wealthier traders established permanent fortified posts on the upper Nile well beyond the range of Egyptian administration, where their greed, cruelty and contemptuous treatment of the Africans were subject to no laws or controls. So a network of routes and posts was built which in turn encouraged more traders to enter the area. Most of them were small traders who could not compete in the ivory trade and so confined themselves to the easier business of slave dealing. By 1860 an Austrian diplomat at Khartoum could report to his superiors, 'there are no longer merchants, but only robbers and slavers on the White Nile'. Raiders also entered the country from Ethiopia and the Somali coast. Probably, during the 1870s, some 50,000 slaves each year were exported from the Sudan.

One of the most notorious and certainly the most successful

of these traders was al-Zubeir Rahma Mansur (usually known as Zubeir or Zubeir Pasha). His story also illustrates the complex relationship that existed between the Egyptian government and the slavers. Zubeir was a Sudanese Arab who spent most of his early life in Khartoum. He made his first trading journey in 1856 and the following year started his own business. He made a profit of £1,000 from his first batch of ivory and slaves. This he invested in boats, men and guns for a major expedition to the land beyond the Sudd. Here he made a marriage alliance with the powerful Azande chief, Tikima, and built a trade post (*zeriba*) called Deim Zubeir. He trained and armed a large slave army and by a combination of trading and raiding acquired a considerable horde of ivory. He became increasingly involved in inter-community warfare and, indeed, he encouraged conflict for his own purposes. By 1866 he had made himself master of most of the Bahr al-Ghazal.

Zubeir

In 1869 the Khedive Ismail decided to extend Egyptian administration over the Bahr al-Ghazal. This brought his agents directly into conflict with Zubeir, a conflict which the imperial forces lost. Ismail did not want to withdraw from the southern Sudan so he made an agreement with Zubeir. In 1873 the notorious slaver was appointed Egyptian Governor of Bahr al-Ghazal. He immediately decided to extend his territory—with or without permission from Cairo. He invaded Darfur, defeated the Darfur army, captured El Fasher and killed the Sultan. The Khedive was delighted to have his territory extended at little cost to the treasury, and promoted Zubeir to the rank of pasha. From El Fasher, Zubeir attacked Wadai and forced the Sultan to pay tribute. But the Khedive thought that Zubeir was becoming too powerful. When Zubeir paid a visit to Cairo in 1876 he was detained in honourable captivity.

It soon became obvious that Egypt could not control the Sudan. The vast area was full of resentful people and deposed rulers, and it was ruled harshly but inefficiently by officials and traders who were usually squabbling among themselves. In 1877 a revolt in Darfur was only suppressed with difficulty. The next year Sulaiman, Zubeir's son, angry at the government's treatment of his father, rebelled. The Governor of the Sudan was now a British soldier, General Charles Gordon. He had travelled throughout Equatoria extending Egyptian authority and strengthening the garrisons and was now based at Khartoum as the Khedive's agent. He believed that Egypt must keep control of the Sudan to prevent it slipping back into anarchy and uncontrolled slave trading. In 1879 Gordon sent an expedition against Sulaiman which was successful but Egyptian rule in the Sudan was still precarious and dependent on isolated garrisons.

Tripoli

In Tripoli* a ruler similar in many ways to Muhammad Ali had appeared at the beginning of the eighteenth century. This

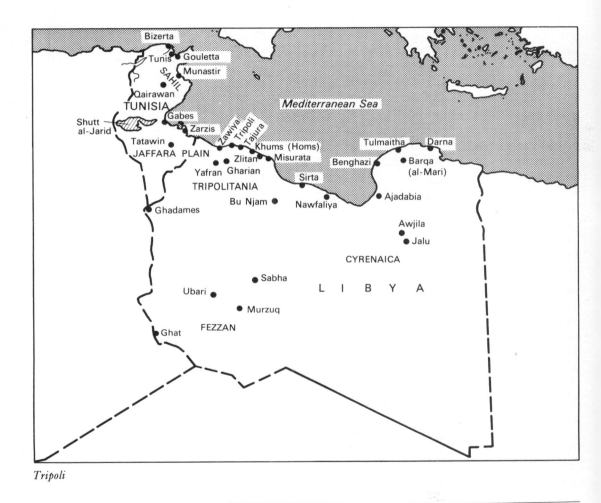

Tripoli

---

* By 'Tripoli' here we mean an area covering about half of present-day Libya. The Qaramanli pashas had established their authority over Tripolitania, Fezzan and Cyrenaica.

was the ambitious soldier Ahmad Qaramanli, who overthrew the Governor, slaughtered his supporters, forced the Ottoman Sultan to recognize him as a virtually independent pasha and established a dynasty. At the beginning of the nineteenth century Tripoli was under the rule of the very able Yusuf Qaramanli. He reopened the trans-Saharan trade route to Kanem-Borno which had been closed by strife in the Sudan. In 1811 he conquered Fezzan and established a governor in Murzuq.

Another source of revenue to the crown in the early years of Yusuf's reign was piracy. His warships attacked Mediterranean shipping belonging to countries that had not paid Yusuf for 'protection'. This piracy hastened European intervention in Tripoli. In 1803 the United States of America, in retaliation for attacks on their shipping, attempted to install a rival as ruler of Tripoli. The activities of the British and French navies destroyed the profitability of piracy in the later part of Yusuf's reign.

Like the rulers of Egypt, Yusuf had to take increasing notice of the Europeans. The British Consul, James Warrington, was particularly influential. He encouraged European explorers, introduced some of the benefits of European technology to the Pasha's subjects and persuaded Yusuf to agree to the stationing of a British vice-consul at Murzuq. Warrington became a trusted adviser of the Pasha. He represented other European states which had no consul in Tripoli and he regarded himself as the protector of all Christians in the country. Trouble arose when the French attempted to challenge Warrington's position. Yusuf Qaramanli in attempting to maintain good relations with everyone was accused by Warrington of plotting with France the murder, in 1826, of a British explorer, Major Laing. In 1830 the Pasha was forced, by threat of naval bombardment, to make a treaty with the French, who had just invaded Algiers.

Yusuf's troubles now increased rapidly. Loss of revenue from piracy and the decline of the slave trade under European pressure placed him in financial difficulties. He had to debase the coinage and impose heavy taxes but these measures lost him the support of his people. His subordinates despised him because he seemed to be merely a tool of the foreign consuls. The conquered tribes of the desert became restless and were encouraged by the British Consul to rebel. In 1831 they liberated Fezzan. Yusuf borrowed money from European

financiers who now began to demand repayment. In 1832 the Tripolitanian peoples revolted under the leadership of Yusuf's nephew, Muhammad Qaramanli. They were supported by the British. The French gave their help to Yusuf's declared heir, Ali. In 1835 the Ottoman Sultan sent a small force under the command of Najib Pasha, who overthrew the Qaramanli dynasty, reasserted direct Ottoman rule and installed himself as Governor (*Wali*).

By 1842 Najib had reconquered Fezzan but Ottoman rule there was largely confined to the immediate vicinity of the desert garrisons. Trans-Saharan trade, which had suffered as a result of the disturbances, revived and from 1850 over 2,500 slaves were shipped from Tripoli every year. Under British pressure the Sultan, in 1848, forbade his officials to take part in the slave trade and in 1857 slavery was abolished in Tripolitania, but these measures made little impact on the evil traffic through the port of Tripoli.

The Ottoman government in Constantinople was anxious to prevent Tripoli becoming independent once more. The *walis* were kept under careful control and were changed frequently.

Furthermore, Cyrenaica was placed under the rule of its own governor who had only partial responsibility to the Governor of Tripoli.* The Cyrenaican authorities in Benghazi made little attempt to reconquer the hinterland. This area soon fell under the control of the Sanusiyya Brotherhood. This was a Muslim order founded in 1837 by an Algerian, Sidi Muhammad bin Ali al-Sanusi. On his return from pilgrimage to Mecca he settled in Benghazi where, in 1843, he established the headquarters of the Brotherhood.

The Brotherhood had great influence among some of the inland peoples, especially the Jibara and Harabi bedouins. Sidi Muhammad and his followers instructed large numbers of disciples who were sent even further afield to form new cells. In this way the Sanusiyya Brotherhood spread southwards over a large area of the Sahara and particularly along the

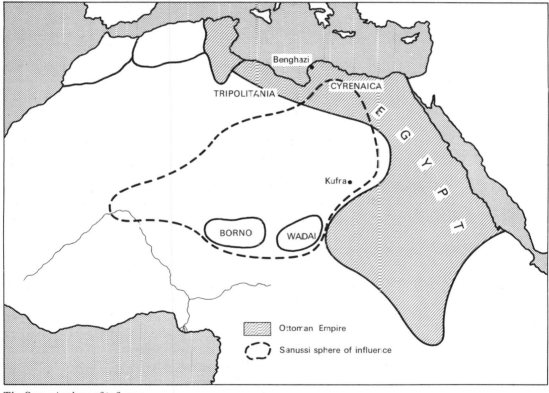

The Sanussi sphere of influence

---

*The two provinces were separated completely in 1879.

Benghazi-Kufra-Wadai trade route. In 1859 the headquarters of the order (now under the leadership of Sidi Muhammad's son, Sayyid al-Mahdi) was moved to Kufra.

The Sanusiyya soon became much more than a religious order. They were the only controlling and unifying force in the province. They settled disputes between the desert tribes. They organized resistance to the spread of French influence in the Sahara. They established administrative centres where culture and religion flourished. The Ottoman authorities recognized the power of the Sanusiyya. In 1856 the Sultan exempted them from taxation and allowed them to administer the areas under their control. After the separation of Cyrenaica and Tripolitania, in 1879, the authority of the Brotherhood was complete and beyond the bounds of the province they exercised influence in Wadai, Borno and as far west as the middle Niger.

Tunisia

To the west of Tripoli lay the ancient Muslim kingdom of Tunisia. Its main centres were Tunis, the capital and principal port, and the religious capital, Qairawan, which lay at the end of the important caravan route from Hausaland and Kanem-Borno, via Agades and Ghat. The ruler of Tunisia was the bey and, by 1800, the Husainid dynasty had established itself firmly on the throne. Tunisia was another Ottoman state where the Sultan's rule was a formality. The main threat to the position of the beys came from Tunisia's powerful neighbour Algiers.

Hammuda Bey, who ruled until 1813, was a strong and wise leader who firmly established the administration of the country and resisted Algerian interference. Three times—in 1807, 1808 and 1811—Tunisia was invaded by her neighbour. Three times Tunisia shook off the invaders. Unfortunately Hammuda's successors were not so able. During the reigns of Mahmud (1814–24) and Husain (1824–35) foreign influence in Tunisia grew. European pressure put a stop to piracy and severely restricted the slave trade. With these important sources of revenue removed, the beys had to impose harsh taxes, which had a bad effect on the loyalty of the people. When the French invaded Algiers in 1830 (see page 33) they made a treaty with the Bey of Tunis to ensure his neutrality. The Bey was delighted to help the French against his old enemy and as a reward the victorious French made one of his relatives

Bab-el-Bhar, Old Gateway in Tunis

Governor of the Algerian Province of Constantine.

After the French conquest of Algiers and the Ottoman reconquest of Tripoli, Tunisia was hemmed in by powerful neighbours. The Sultan made persistent attempts to assert more control over the beys. At such times the Tunisian rulers looked to the French for help to maintain their independence but they also had to be on their guard against French attempts to seize Tunisian territory. To help preserve his country's independence Ahmad Bey (1837–55) recruited and equipped a large army. This cost a lot of money as did the magnificent palaces the Bey built for himself. The people were taxed to the limit of their endurance and when this failed Ahmad borrowed heavily from European financiers. Soon the pattern of events we have already noticed in Egypt appeared in

Tunisia: the government fell more and more heavily into debt; the foreign money-lenders and their consuls grew more and more powerful.

The Europeans pressed for and obtained economic, judicial and political reforms. In 1860 a new constitution was introduced which transferred some of the Bey's powers to a Supreme Council. The opposition of the country's corrupt officials, who benefited personally from the old system, brought this constitutional experiment to an end after four years. In 1864 a rebellion against the Bey's cruel taxation system was only put down with foreign help.

By 1866 government finance was on the point of collapse. Tunisia's foreign creditors stepped in and after long negotiations an International Financial Commission was set up in 1869 on which the French, Italians and British were represented. The Commission took over the organization of government finance. Before long it was interfering in other government departments. The Bey was now seriously alarmed and, in 1871, Muhammad al-Sadiq Bey placed his country firmly under Ottoman sovereignty and accepted from the Sultan the title of pasha.

Such action could delay but not prevent Tunisia's final showdown with the Europeans. For four years the country enjoyed peaceful development and stability under the extremely able Prime Minister Khair al-Din. The financial situation improved, railways were built, taxation was reduced, new agricultural measures were introduced, and state schools were founded. But Khair al-Din also tried to restrict the influence of the European consuls and this brought about his downfall. Under foreign pressure, the Pasha sacked his Prime Minister in 1877. Immediately the old pattern of financial recklessness, extortionate taxation and increasing foreign pressure reappeared. For over three years the Pasha tried to control the rivalries of the French, Italian, British and Turkish governments. In April 1881 the French cut across all the diplomatic wranglings by invading Tunisia. They forced Muhammad al-Sadiq to sign the Treaty of Bardo, which virtually turned Tunisia into a French protectorate.

Algeria

The Regency of Algiers was another nominally Ottoman territory under the control of a military dictator called the dey, who ruled with the help of a Turkish army. The country was divided into three provinces (Constantine, Tittari, Oran) and its administrators were interested in little more than the preservation of peace and order and the collection of taxes. Under such government trade and agriculture could hardly flourish. Normally the deys' authority did not extend far beyond the walls of the regional capitals, and in the countryside the governors ruled through the local Arab and Berber chiefs. Religious leaders of the Sufi orders also exercised considerable influence in the remoter areas.

Like other states of the Maghrib, Algeria suffered as a result of growing European activity in the Mediterranean. Piracy was brought under control and foreign consuls were established in Algiers. Algeria developed particularly close ties with France and supplied that country with wheat during the last years of the eighteenth century when France was at war. Unfortunately this led to the development of bad relations between the two states and the ultimate conquest of Algeria.

The Dey, Abdul-Hamid II

At the root of the trouble was France's failure to pay for the wheat. Debts incurred between 1793 and 1798 had still not been settled by 1827, despite demands and protests by the Dey. On 29 April 1827 matters came to a head when, at the end of a heated interview between Husain Dey and Consul Pierre Deval, the Dey struck the Frenchman across the face with his fly-swatter. The French government demanded a public apology for this insult. The Dey, urged on by the British Consul, refused. A senseless quarrel now developed in which neither side would give way. No one in Algeria imagined that this clash would lead to invasion but the government in Paris was in difficulties and certain ministers decided that a foreign conquest would win them popular support. So in May 1830 an army left the French port of Toulon, its declared intentions being to avenge a diplomatic insult, suppress piracy and abolish slavery by means of a brief occupation. All the important coastal towns fell quickly and the Dey surrendered in July, signing away his sovereignty to France.

But the occupation did not turn out to be a brief affair. There were two main reasons for the permanent colonization of Algeria—the activities of the French General Clauzel and the resistance of the interior peoples. Immediately after the invasion no civilian government was set up and no official policy for Algeria laid down. Clauzel, therefore, made his own plans for the newly acquired territory. He confiscated land and allocated it to French settlers. The number of settlers

Abd-el-Kader

33

Revolt of Abd-el-Kader 1845

grew steadily and they were soon strong enough to oppose successfully any anti-colonial policies decided on in Paris. The French Governor-General in Algiers, needing the support of the settlers in his continuing struggle with the Algerians, could only follow policies acceptable to the colonists.

In the interior, the French faced unexpectedly strong and united resistance. At its head was the Sheikh of the Qadiriyya Brotherhood (the largest Sufi order), Muhyi al-Din, but the military leader of the movement was his son, Amir Abdul Qadir. Many nomadic peoples joined in the *jihad* (holy war) launched by Muhyi al-Din against the French and their allies. Abdul Qadir, by surprise raids from his mountain strongholds, restricted the Europeans to the coastal plain. In 1834 General Desmichels, the French military commander in Oran, signed an agreement recognizing the Amir's control of the western part of the coastal plain. But the French continued to try to break Abdul Qadir's power. In a disastrous attack on Constantine in 1836 they lost over a thousand men. The following year they signed the Treaty of Tafna which defined more closely the extent of Abdul Qadir's territory.

As the struggle continued, proving costly to the French in men and money, it became more and more difficult for the newcomers to withdraw. Instead they introduced more colonists and officials to strengthen their hold on the area under control. They built roads and public buildings. They introduced taxes. They turned mosques into churches. And they prepared for fresh conflict with Abdul Qadir. Meanwhile the Amir strengthened his position by winning other tribes to his cause, either by agreement or conquest. Unfortunately he could not unite all Algeria's people. The powerful Tijaniyya Brotherhood, rivals of the Qadiriyya, refused to join the Amir's forces. After their defeat in battle by Abdul Qadir they joined forces with the French. The sectarian and tribal divisions of Algeria undermined the nationalist movement and made Abdul Qadir's ultimate downfall inevitable.

War broke out again in 1839. In the first phase of the fighting, nationalist forces drove their opponents back to the gates of Algiers. The French were now faced with a choice between withdrawal and complete conquest of Algeria. They chose the latter. Under a new leader, General Bugeaud, the army of occupation renewed the conflict with great vigour and cruelty. By a campaign of terror that involved burning undefended villages, stealing cattle, murdering prisoners and destroying crops, the French succeeded in frightening many of Abdul Qadir's allies into submission. In 1843 the Amir had to retreat into Morocco. He was pursued by his enemies who forced the Moroccans to agree not to shelter the outlaw. Abdul Qadir fought on, in Algeria and Morocco, until 1847 when he was captured and imprisoned in France. In 1852 he was released and spent the rest of his days in Damascus.

The end of the war brought a flood of new settlers into Algeria. By 1848 there were 109,000 colonists as opposed to 25,000 in 1839. Immigration continued steadily under French government sponsorship and the number of settlers trebled between 1848 and 1880. During this time they also gained effective control of the whole of Algeria, which, by 1880, was organized almost entirely for the benefit of the colonists. In November 1848 Algeria was declared a French territory and citizens were allowed to elect representatives to the Paris parliament. This created two clearly distinguished classes—the privileged French citizens and the unprivileged Muslim Arab subjects. Between 1863 and 1870 the French Emperor Napoleon III tried to change this situation. He believed that France had a responsibility for the well-being

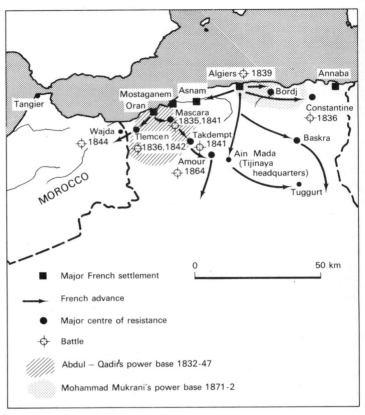

Resistance to French rule in Algeria

and development of *all* the people of Algeria. He arranged
for the full recognition of tribal lands, encouraged the
preservation of Islamic culture and established the right of
the Arabs to equal protection at law.

All this alarmed the settlers but they could do little except
obstruct the local officials as much as possible—until 1871.
In that year Napoleon III's government was overthrown and
France suffered a humiliating defeat in a war with Germany.
In Algeria there were two immediate results; the settlers
grasped their opportunity to dominate the political life of the
colony, and the majority population grasped their opportunity
to stage a large-scale revolt. Ever since 1847 there had been
resistance to colonial rule. The Muslim Arabs hated the
Christian French, and armed uprisings were frequent
(see map) but the rebellion of 1871 was the greatest mass
movement since the days of Abdul Qadir. Its leader was

Muhammad Mukrani, who had been a minor official in the pay of the French. Many foreign troops had been taken away to fight a war in Europe. The rebellion spread rapidly and soon involved over a third of the indigenous people. Mukrani was killed in battle in May 1871 but the conflict continued for another year. It cost the lives of over 2,500 Frenchmen and a much greater number of Muslims.

Morocco in the nineteenth century

The rebellion was a disaster for the people of Algeria. The settlers persuaded the new government to enforce strict control over Muslims and an enormous fine was imposed on several communities. Their lands were taken away and either given to settlers or sold back to their original owners. The Muslims were denied education and any participation in the administration. French became the only official language.

Islamic law courts were closed. The influence of Muslim religious leaders was deliberately undermined. Devout Muslims were prevented from making the pilgrimage to Mecca. In fact the French settlers aimed at cultural, as well as economic and political domination.

Morocco

Of all the states of the Maghrib Morocco was the furthest from the centres of Ottoman power and the closest to Europe. Much of the land was ruled by Berber chiefs who acknowledged the spiritual authority of the Sultan in Fez but refused to pay taxes. For most of the time royal authority did not extend much beyond a region bounded by Fez, Marrakesh and the Atlantic coast. On the north coast, Ceuta and Melilla were occupied by Spain. Morocco was difficult to control for other reasons. Ever since the Moors had been thrown out of Spain centuries before, the Moroccans had hated Europeans, yet almost all the country's overseas trade was with Europe. Morocco exported wheat and gold dust across the Mediterranean. The southern caravan routes, along which came gold dust and slaves from the western Sudan, were still important so that however much the Sultan wished to impose his will on the Berber chiefs he could not risk disturbing the peace to such an extent that the trade routes were closed.

Mawlay Sulaiman (1792–1822) and Mawlay Abdul-Rahman (1822–59) restricted as far as possible all trade with Europe, and would not allow European merchants to set foot outside the towns of Tangier, Rabat, Tetuan and Mogador. All European consuls were confined to Tangier and knew little or nothing about events in the country. Barbary pirates continued to obtain refuge in Moroccan ports long after their other havens had been blocked as a result of European diplomatic pressure.

The French occupation of Algeria put an end to Moroccan isolation. In 1830 Mawlay Abdul-Rahman sent troops into Algeria to help resist the aggressors. The troops were withdrawn after two years, having achieved very little. When France threatened reprisals the Sultan had to turn to a rival European power, Britain, for support. The British government, anxious to keep control of the Strait of Gibraltar and to assist the growing British commercial community, was glad to become Morocco's protector. When Abdul Qadir was pursued onto Moroccan territory by a French army in 1844 Mawlay

Abdul-Rahman sent a Moroccan force to drive the intruders out, but the home army was soundly defeated at Isly (near Oujde). The Sultan's defeat weakened both his international reputation and his authority within the country.

The French were now able to extort trading concessions from the Sultan. As French commercial activities increased so did those of their British and other rivals. The Sultan found himself being used as a weapon in the diplomatic warfare of the European powers. In 1856 Mawlay Abdul-Rahman was forced to open his territory to European traders. But Spanish authorities were dissatisfied with the terms of the treaty and decided to improve their position in Morocco by force. In 1860 a small Spanish army seized Tetuan. To buy off the invaders, the new Sultan, Mawlay Muhammad, had to give Spain more coastal territory, sign a new commercial treaty with the invaders and pay a large sum of money. This finally broke Morocco's independence. The government had to obtain British help to persuade Spain to modify her demands and even then the treasury had to borrow heavily abroad to pay the Spaniards. The Sultan was forced to levy harsh taxes. This and the Spanish victory stirred up a major rebellion in the mountains south of Wazzan.

Between 1860 and 1880 foreign activity in Morocco increased steadily. Europeans came not only to trade but also to farm. Consular protection was given to Moroccan citizens working for Europeans, thus placing them beyond the Sultan's laws. Mawlay Hasan (1873–94) tried to restore the authority and independence of the government. He built up a new army with European weapons and instructors. He reorganized the administration and he created a more efficient taxation system. But all these reforms came too late. It was only a matter of time before Morocco was swallowed up by European colonialists.

Ethiopia and Somalia

The area we now have to consider consists of the mountainous Ethiopian Highlands and the long desert coastline from Massawa to Mogadishu. At the beginning of the nineteenth century the whole region was in a state of political and economic decline. The Red Sea was plagued with pirates. The caravan routes that brought trade goods and pilgrims from the Sudan to the ports were virtually closed. Somali herdsmen of the coastal plain were steadily using up the scant vegetation and were spreading further inland in search of pasture. Under similar pressures the Galla were pushing into what is now northern Kenya and the lands of the Ethiopian borders. The great Ethiopian Empire was much weaker than it had once been. Galla pressures and internal disintegration had reduced its borders. The collapse of central government had led to the emergence of a number of independent kingdoms of which the most powerful were Tigre, Amhara, Shoa and Lasta. The leaders of these four states competed for the imperial title for, though the Emperor had ceased to have much power, the Ethiopians still attached much importance to the title.

Most of the Red Sea ports were under the nominal control of the Ottoman Sultan. In effect they were ruled as petty trading and pirate states by their amirs. Their prosperity had dwindled with the increased activity of Somali and Galla raiders in the interior. They were, however, still active, and the local Somali, though they were quite likely at any time to attack the towns, used them regularly as trading centres. The towns could

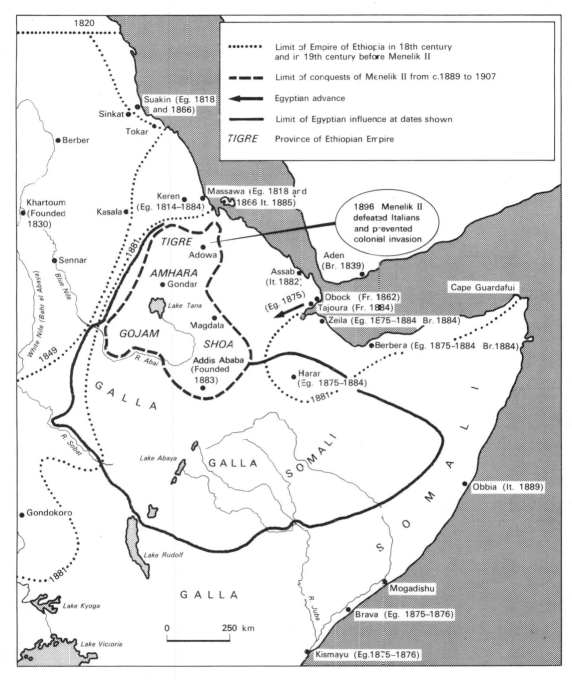

Legend:

- •••••• Limit of Empire of Ethiopia in 18th century and in 19th century before Menelik II
- ▬ ▬ ▬ Limit of conquests of Menelik II from c.1889 to 1907
- ◀▬▬ Egyptian advance
- ▬▬▬ Limit of Egyptian influence at dates shown
- *TIGRE* Province of Ethiopian Empire

1820

Suakin (Eg. 1818 and 1866)

Sinkat

Tokar

Berber

Khartoum (Founded 1830)

Kasala

Keren (Eg. 1814–1884)

Massawa (Eg. 1818 and 1866 It. 1885)

1896 Menelik II defeated Italians and prevented colonial invasion

Sennar

TIGRE

Adowa

AMHARA

Gondar

Assab (It. 1882)

Aden (Br. 1839)

Cape Guardafui

Lake Tana

(Eg. 1875)

Obock (Fr. 1862)

Tajoura (Fr. 1884)

Zeila (Eg. 1875–1884 Br. 1884)

GOJAM

Magdala

SHOA

R. Abai

Addis Ababa (Founded 1883)

Harar (Eg. 1875–1884)

Berbera (Eg. 1875–1884 Br.1884)

White Nile (Bahr el Abaya)

Blue Nile

1849

1881

G A L L A

1881

Lake Abaya

G A L L A

S O M A L I

Obbia (It. 1889)

R. Sobat

Gondokoro

Lake Rudolf

1881

S O M A L I

Mogadishu

G A L L A

R. Juba

Brava (Eg. 1875–1876)

Lake Kyoga

0   250 km

Lake Victoria

Kismayu (Eg.1875–1876)

Ethiopia and Somalia in the nineteenth century

defend themselves, as Zeila showed in 1821 when its inhabitants drove off an Egyptian attack.

Harar, to the south of Ethiopia, was a larger state than the coastal towns. It was the successor of the ancient Islamic Sultanate of Adal. But internal discord and the activities of the Galla had reduced its size and prosperity. The town of Harar itself was well fortified and set amidst fields and plantations. It was an important market centre for goods from the coast, Shoa, and the interior, and for the local Galla and Somali. The relationship that existed between the Amir and the local peoples is not an easy one to understand. The Galla attacked traders, destroyed crops and raided the Amir's territory up to the very gates of Harar. Yet many Galla chiefs, recognizing the traditional authority of the Amir, accepted Islam, copied several aspects of the court life of Harar, and their people regularly traded in its market. A similar relationship existed between the kings of Shoa and their Galla neighbours.

Harar was, and had always been, an important centre of Muslim teaching and worship. Christian Ethiopia was thus surrounded on three sides by the forces of Islam. After the southward expansion of Egypt, Ethiopia was completely surrounded and her total collapse seemed only a matter of time. From 1827 Egyptian and Sudanese forces extended their control over more and more of the territory on Ethiopia's north and west borders. The Viceroy of Egypt tried for many years to gain control of the Red Sea coast, and its valuable ports. Massawa and Suakin were occupied briefly by Egypt in 1818 and leased from the Turks in 1846. It was not until 1866 that the Egyptian government was able to obtain permanent possession of these towns. In 1821 an Egyptian attack on Zeila was, with difficulty, beaten off by the ruler of the town. The Egyptians were not the only people interested in the Red Sea coast. In 1839 Britain acquired a protectorate over Aden, to safeguard the short route to India. Thus when, in 1846, Egypt tried to establish her control right along the coast as far as Cape Guardafui, the local rulers had a powerful ally and were able to resist successfully. Later, as we shall see, France and Italy also developed interests in the area.

The expansion of Egypt and Ethiopia's Muslim encirclement had two important effects in the mountain empire: they encouraged trade and they forced Ethiopians to realize the necessity of unity. As we have seen, one result of Egypt's

Emperor Teodros II

42

Church of St George at Lalibela, Ethiopia

conquest of the Sudan was the revival of commerce on the
caravan routes to the Red Sea coast. Ethiopian merchants
benefited from this. Through their warfare with the Galla and
Sidama the Ethiopians were able to obtain many slaves. By
the middle of the century they were sending over 7,000 slaves
a year to the coast.* Other exports of importance were ivory,
which entered Ethiopia from the south-west, gold from Enarya
and musk which was obtained from the civet cat. Commercial
revival led directly to political revival because it enabled
rulers to buy guns. In the 1830s a period of political and economic expansion in Shoa enabled the merchants of that
kingdom to by-pass Harar and trade direct with Tajoura.

---

* This is only a very rough estimate. The total probably fluctuated
widely. One British observer in the closing years of the century
saw a slave caravan that took four days to pass through Mandara.
He estimated that this one caravan contained 12,000 slaves.

43

About 1840 a man called Kassa began to make himself notorious in north-western Ethiopia as a brigand chief of great audacity and success. He enriched himself and his men by raiding caravans. He obtained guns and considerably increased the size of his personal following. He defeated some of the powerful rulers of the area and became a king himself. He had enormous ambition. He decided to reunite Ethiopia under his leadership and restore the glory of the Empire. After years of warfare he achieved his aim and was crowned as the Emperor Teodros II in 1855.

Teodros was a nationalist fanatic who set himself and his people impossible aims. He believed himself divinely appointed not only to unite Ethiopia, but to crush the power of Islam, conquer the Sudan and overrun Egypt. In pursuing his aims he achieved much. He crushed all opponents to the central government. He recruited and equipped a large army. He imposed heavy taxes to pay for the army and public works. He employed European advisers. But in time the regional kings and some of the Emperor's own officials grew to resent Teodros's tyranny and looked for an opportunity to overthrow him. It came in 1867 when the Emperor, by imprisoning two British diplomats, provoked a prompt military reaction. A force was despatched from England. It landed at Zula (south of Massawa) and made its way into the mountains. Had Teodros been able to rely on the loyalty of his people the British might have been massacred before they had marched many days, but they were helped on their way to Magdala. There in March 1868 Teodros committed suicide rather than fall into the hands of his enemies. The British released the prisoners and withdrew.

After the short reign of Tekle Giyorgis (1868–72) two great men confronted each other for control of Ethiopia—Kasa of Tigre and Menelik of Shoa. Kasa managed to get himself crowned as Emperor Yohannis (or John) IV but his rivalry with Menelik continued until an uneasy peace was made between the two men in 1882.

Yohannis needed internal peace because his country was now faced by a major threat. The Khedive Ismail of Egypt was planning a full-scale invasion of Ethiopia and the coast. Naval expeditions captured Zeila and Berbera in 1875. Another force succeeded in overwhelming Brava and Kismayu far down the Somali coast but was forced to withdraw when the protests of the Sultan of Zanzibar were supported by European powers. From Zeila an Egyptian army marched inland and seized Harar. Ismail hoped to benefit from the conflict between Yohannis and Menelik. He ordered a force to march from Tajoura to Shoa, there to link up with Menelik's men for an onslaught on the Emperor's strongholds. However, the expedition was ambushed by the Somali and massacred. Nevertheless, Ismail was determined to subdue Ethiopia. A small but well-equipped army was despatched from Massawa. In November 1875 it encountered the main Ethiopian force at Gundet and was destroyed. The Khedive's reaction was to send a larger army. This came face to face with Yohannis's troops at Gura in March 1876. The ensuing battle lasted for three days but then the Egyptians were forced to withdraw. Egypt made no more attempts to conquer the empire of the mountains.

Victory strengthened Yohannis's position at home. He did not make Teodros's mistake of trying to bully all the kings into submission. Instead he tried to obtain their co-operation. He settled conflicts within the Ethiopian Church. He thus brought to Ethiopia a greater degree of unity and stability than it had known for a very long time. In so doing he prepared the way for his even greater successor, Menelik.

When we come to consider the peoples of the Sahara we find that, though nomadic, they tend to be concentrated along the ancient caravan routes. Controlling the western trade route from Morocco through the salt lands of Taghaza and Taodeni, through southern Mauretania to Timbuktu were the Moors, a mixture of Arabs, Berbers and Negroes. In the centre, a Berber group called the Tuaregs or the 'People of the Veil' (a name given to them because they wore a veil which consisted of a long strip of cloth wound round the head so as to form a hood, covering the mouth and nose) controlled the Timbuktu–In Salah–Gadames–Tunis or Tripoli route as well as the Hausa–Tripoli route through Ghat. The eastern route, the Chad–Tripoli route through the Fezzan was in the hands of the Tibu, the people of Tibesti.

None of these peoples was organized into states. In the desert, we can talk only of bands consisting mostly of the members of a clan with their dependants and slaves who, faced with a climate that made agriculture difficult, tried the best means of conserving what little they could obtain to live. Because they were in the lines of communication between

Peoples of the Desert

North Africa and West Africa and because they knew the routes across the desert, they acted as guides. Caravans that passed through their territory and refused to obey their commercial conditions were pillaged. Sometimes, the gangs went to attack other places of commercial promise, such as the salt mines of other communities.

This did not mean that there were no settled communities. Among the Moors, although there were many such bands, there were also communities engaged in the gum trade. At the end of the eighteenth century, two powerful Moorish states of Trarza and Brakna had been firmly established. Among the Tuaregs, Aïr had a sultan who lived in the large town of Agades. Among the Tibu, those who lived round the areas of large salt deposits such as Bilma had developed a state system.

Tuareg tribesmen, Libya

Since these people lived mostly in the oases which needed to be defended against intruders, much importance was attached to the warrior class which often formed the highest rank of the nobility. The Moors were a mixture of Arabs, Berbers and the indigenous black community. The Arabs, or those who could claim Arab ancestry, formed the warrior class. The Berbers in the Moorish territories who had been forced to submit to the Arab invaders, became second-class citizens. The Tuaregs, who were themselves Berbers, were not prepared to accept Arab domination, so there were conflicts between the two racial groups. The Tibu were also confronted with the Arab threat, to which was added that of the Tuaregs. When they were invaded, they took refuge in mountain fortresses.

Among the Moors, just below the warrior class was the priestly class of marabouts, which was responsible for the religious affairs of the state, burying the dead, arranging marriages and engaging in commerce. There were marabouts among the Tuaregs and the Tibu, but they were not so prominent a group. This is mainly because most of the Tuaregs and Tibu were animists. The marabouts and the warriors in the Moorish settlements were often different clans and the training of each group followed different lines. Since Islam was a strong force, the marabouts played an important part in the state.

Apart from the nobility, from whom the rulers were chosen, there were the common people or vassals. The Zenague or Berbers formed the bulk of this class among the Moors. They paid tribute and were allowed to follow the higher classes to collect gum. For this, however, they had special permission and they were given some of the gum they collected. They joined the army as volunteers with the hope of plunder. As soon as the waters receded, they went to the banks of the rivers to sow millet. They had flocks of sheep which provided them with milk and meat, and with their agricultural products they paid their tribute. Although they had few rights, they were free men.

At the lowest social level were the slaves, most of whom were captured in war. The slave was the property of his lord. Once a slave had been accepted into a household, he was rarely sold again. He did most of the work, collecting gum and planting crops for his overlord, whether Arab, Zenague, Tuareg or Tibu. Slaves did the mining in the terrible desert salt mines where they were sometimes allowed to starve to death before provisions came.

At the beginning of the nineteenth century there were already in existence powerful Moorish emirates in Ardrar, Trarza, Brakna and Tagant. Of these the most important were Trarza and Brakna. The rivalry between the two began in the eighteenth century when one of the greatest of the Moorish rulers, Mohammed Mokhtar (1766–1800), was on the Brakna throne. In a famous battle against the Trarza king, Eli Kouri, he not only successfully routed the Trarza forces, but killed Eli Kouri (1786).

The Moors of Trarza and Brakna were thus fairly settled in 1800 when our story begins. Mohammed Mokhtar's son, Sidi Eli I (1800–18), was not as forceful a character as his father. He was particularly noted for his friendship with the French, with whom his father had signed a treaty in 1786. Through his efforts, the conflict between the Tukolor State of Futa Toro and the French was settled and a treaty signed in 1806. Sidi Eli, however, did not live long enough to make any real difference to the welfare of his people. He was succeeded by Ahmeddou (1818–41) who was the first emir of Brakna to experience French ambition in the Senegal area after Colonel Schmaltz, Governor of Senegal, had explored the left bank of the Futa Toro and had followed that in 1818 by moving to Galam and establishing commercial and military outposts along the river. When in May of the following year the French bought the lower basin of the river Senegal from Amar Boye, King of Walo, it was clear that war with France was inevitable (see pages 80–82).

The Moorish Emir of Trarza was the overlord of Walo and, naturally, he could not accept French sovereignty over Walo territory. But Trarza was not in a position to fight at this stage because she was engaged in one of those dynastic disputes that often followed the death of an African ruler. Mohammed Mokhtar had been appointed as regent to take charge of the country while his nephew, Sidi Ali, was a minor. Mohammed Mokhtar was a wise and brave man and by bribing the people, especially the chiefs of the tribe, he obtained power for himself. In this he probably had the support of the French.

Sidi Ali was not prepared to allow this. At the age of thirty, he claimed the throne and when this was refused, he decided to fight for it. In the first encounter, he was successful and this increased the number of his supporters. Mokhtar now pursued him with fury and obtained the help of the Braknas. He already had 400 princes or great vassals and 800 tributaries or slaves. The King of the Braknas sent him 2,000 foot soldiers and with this force, despite the fighting ability of Sidi Ali, the legitimate ruler was defeated, captured and put to death.

If Mohammed Mokhtar thought that the struggle was over, he was wrong. Sidi Ali's son, M'Hammet Ould Eli Kouri, continued the struggle. This time, the usurper had the support of the French Governor of Senegal, Colonel Schmaltz. With comparative peace restored, especially after the end of hostilities between Trarza and Wolof, Mohammed Mokhtar was in a position to stop the French from acquiring the Walo territory. In this enterprise he had the support of the Brakna Emir Ahmeddou. In 1819, the Trarza crossed the Senegal, pillaged Walo and burnt down many villages, carrying away a hundred prisoners. The French sent forces after them to put a stop to such raids. But this policy of fighting against the Moors disrupted the gum trade, so the French looked for other ways to restore peace to the area. By 1820, the French government was no longer prepared to tolerate the policy of expansion which Governor Schmaltz was introducing at very great expense and he was recalled.

One reason why the French authorities in Senegal were anxious to have control of Walo was that they were interested in setting up cotton, indigo and groundnut plantations so that they would not have to depend wholly on the gum trade. It was for this reason that Louis XVIII, King of France, had entrusted the colonial administration to a Bordeaux ship-builder, Pierre Barthelemy Portal, who worked out the plan for developing and expanding the French possessions. Portal chose Schmaltz for the Senegal post because of the Colonel's experience in Java. The hope was that if the plantation experiment succeeded, French farmers would begin to settle in the area.

There were many reasons why the experiment failed. The first was that the sandy shores of the Senegal were not suitable for cotton and indigo; it was semi-arid and suitable only for groundnuts, which the Africans themselves were already growing. The Senegalese trading community was not interested in taking up agriculture; nor were the Africans interested in the scheme. For cotton to succeed, the price in France would have to be doubled. Apart from all this, Baron Jacques François Roger who succeeded Schmaltz soon found that harassment by the Moors was increasing and that the treaties signed with them to safeguard the plantations were never respected. The position of the Moors was clear: no foreign establishment was to be allowed in the hinterland to interfere with the sovereign rights of the people over their land. The establishment of plantations by the French would disturb the gum trade on which the Moors depended. Foreigners were to be allowed to trade and nothing else. By 1826, the whole experiment had come to an end and Baron Roger resigned as Governor of Senegal.

In 1827 Ahmeddou I was still the ruler of Brakna. All the treaties he had signed with the French were of no avail. Before Baron Roger left, he made clear his distrust for this Moorish leader when, on 28 August 1824, he had stated that Ahmeddou, the chief of the Brakna, was greedy and untrustworthy. He advised that the Moorish chief should be listened to and that all his proposals should be accepted with a promise of rich compensation in case of success. He warned that nothing should ever be given to him in advance. It was clear that the French were so blinded by their own interests that they did not see the logic in the action of the Moors who were being expected to sell their sovereignty for trifling gifts.

In 1827 the French were confronted by a new leader in Trarza — Muhammad le-Hbib. His priority was regaining of the Walo territory. To strengthen his claim, in 1833 he married a Walo heiress, Princess Diombot. He signed new treaties, aware of the military and naval strength of the French, he agreed treaties which he knew he would not keep.

In a treaty of 1817 between Britain and France the latter had been given the whole of the Senegal area. The French now imposed strict controls on trade. The 1817 treaty had been signed without consulting the local rulers who were determined to trade with whatever nation they wished. They resented the French monopoly which enabled the foreigners to fix the price they would pay for the gum brought to the coast by the Moors. The easy way of breaking this monopoly was to open the trading post of Portendick and trade with the British. When they tried to do this the French reacted immediately by blockading the port. The Trarza fought back by raiding French positions in Senegal. Attacks and counter-attacks marked the relationship between the French and the Moors until Louis Faidherbe was appointed Governor in 1854. In 1858 he inflicted a heavy defeat upon the Trarza.

West African societies I: peoples of the savannah

Chapter 3

Most of the people of West Africa are Negroes. They have, however, been joined in the northern part by immigrants from the north, especially the Berbers and Arabs brought either by persecution or by trade along the trade routes to produce a mixed people, the Fulani, who are to be found all over West Africa today. Some Arabs who have preserved their racial characteristics are still to be found. The Berbers, the Tuaregs and the Fulani represent the Hamitic group. In Equatorial Africa, most of the people are Bantu. We shall only be able to deal here with those groups that had the greatest influence on the history of West Africa as a whole.

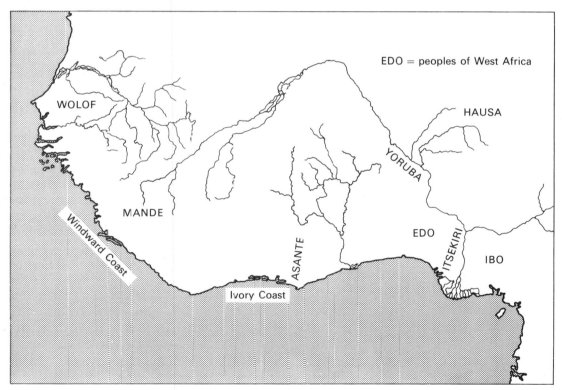

Some important peoples of West Africa during the nineteenth century

Fulani

The Senegambian peoples and states

There had been peoples living between the Senegal and the Gambia long before 1800 who had been faced with the pressure from Moors in the north, from Europeans in their settlements along the Atlantic seaboard and in the east from waves of Mandes. In the north, some of them had been absorbed into the Moorish states. We have seen how the Moors claimed control of Walo, south of the Senegal. Walo was one of the states that formed part of the Wolof peoples. South of the Wolof peoples were the Serer and in the east of the Wolof territory lay the Futa Toro, the country of the Tukolor. The largest single group was the Mande. In all these lands we also find Fulani groups which like the Tukolor played an important part in the history of West Africa in the nineteenth century.

We have grouped all these peoples together because they had a similar form of government. They were all ruled by kings

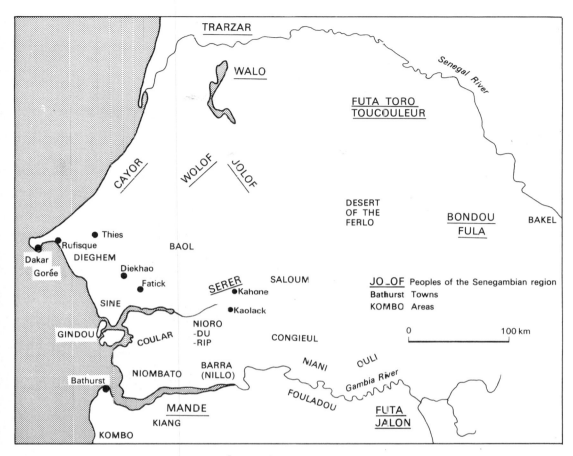

Senegambian peoples

who, even though their powers were limited, were greatly respected by their subjects. The kings were chosen from among a group of ruling families, the heads of which were territorial lords or provincial governors who had the powers in the provinces that the king had over the whole of the country. In the states where Islam had not taken over, the king had ritual functions to perform, mainly concerned with ancestor worship.

Although the king and his important chiefs and ministers were responsible for the legislative, executive and judicial functions of the state, local government was in the hands of district officials called *alkalis* who were appointed by the kings. These collected tribute, levied duties on travellers and merchants, presided over the local assemblies in which the king consulted his people, assigned rights to land, recruited

Wolof people

age-groups for public works and performed local judicial functions. They were also responsible for ritual duties connected with the ancestors.

Along the western Atlantic coast, well watered by the rivers that have their sources in the Futa Jallon hills, are several peoples who have for centuries occupied the banks of these rivers, some fishing and others farming. First are the Wolofs who live along the Senegal. They produced salt which was in great demand in the interior. They were the first group of African peoples to have contact with Europeans and, at the same time, they were well placed to gain from Arab and Berber influences. There were five Wolof states virtually independent of each other: Walo, Salum, Kayor, Baol and Joloff. Of these, Kayor, which was situated on the Atlantic, had, under the rule of Damel Amari Ngene-Ndela-Jumba (1790–1809), become one of the most powerful states among the Wolofs. He resisted Islam even though he allowed Muslim priests (marabouts) to remain in the state. He put down a marabout revolt in Kayor and he was so powerful that when his country was invaded by the Tukolor of the Futa Toro under Almamy Abd-al-Qadir, he successfully routed the Tukolor forces and captured the Almamy himself. He left a prosperous country to his nephew, Birayma Faatma-Tyuub (1809–32), who began a process of territorial expansion after he had beaten off another marabout revolt. Soon after this, the King ordered an attack on the Wolof state of Baol which he conquered and incorporated in his own kingdom.

South of the Wolof peoples and occupying the territory between the rivers Salum and Gambia was the largest group of the West Atlantic peoples, the Serer, a mixed group having Mandinka and Wolof connections. Probably Mandinka migrants had set up states in the area and had extended their influence over the Serer peoples. There were two Serer states, Sine and Saloum. Sine was smaller and more centralized. In Saloum, there was a larger community of Wolof and Tukolor peoples. Saloum was therefore stronger than Sine even though the power of its king (*bur*) was far more restricted than that of Sine. Because for some time Saloum was under the power of Joloff, there came to be established four Joloff chiefdoms over which the Bur Saloum had only partial control. After the people had thrown off the Joloff yoke, they were able, because of their advantageous economic position, to establish a buoyant economy and then gain control as far south as the Mandinka state of Niumi from which they took tribute until the end of the eighteenth century. The extent of Saloum jurisdiction could be seen in a map of Mungo Park, the British explorer, which placed the whole area along the mouth of the Gambia under the Bur Saloum. So powerful was the Bur Saloum in the eighteenth century that he was always able to send messages to the foreign factors resident and trading in the Niumi ports of Albreda and Jellifry.

A marabout

At the beginning of the nineteenth century, therefore, the Serer, taking advantage of their economic position, were powerful enough to act as buffer states between the spreading Wolof peoples in the north and the equally spreading Mandinka peoples from the south.

The Mande peoples and states

Of all the peoples who have exercised great influence on the whole of West Africa, there is none more important than the Mande who originated from Manding and expanded in all directions. As early as the thirteenth and fourteenth centuries, some Mande groups had taken Islam to Hausaland in present-day northern Nigeria. Why were the Mande peoples so adventurous? The most important reason was the need for salt. The earliest movement was probably the Soninke (a Mande group) thrust to the north, where they met Berber and Arab

Mande movement

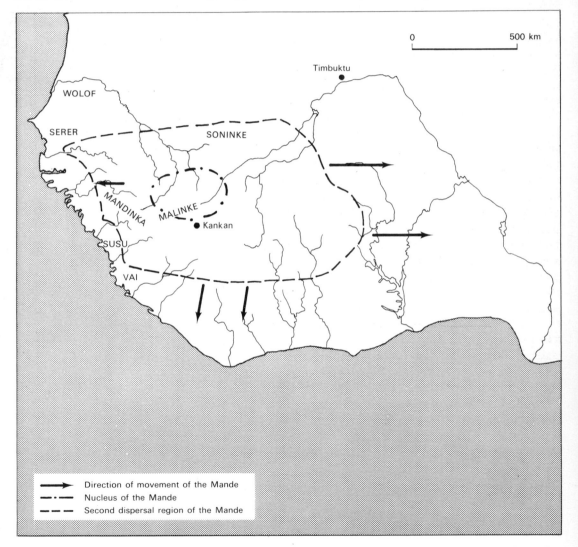

groups (the Moors) who brought salt from the mines of Taghaza, N'Teret in southern Trarza, Sebka d'Ijil, and Taodeni which they came to exchange for gold obtained in Bambuk (Wangara). The quest for salt also led to expansion southwards to the shores of the Great and Little Scarcies. Mande groups, the Susu, the Limba, Korankos and Vais occupied present-day Sierra Leone. Another group, the Mandinka, occupied the banks of the Gambia and pushed northwards to form the aristocracy among the Serer. Salt-making along the banks of the Gambia and the Senegal encouraged migration to the territories. The search for gold took the Mande to the banks of the Caramance, dislocating life there. They absorbed some of the inhabitants like the Banhuns and the Casangas who have now almost lost their identity. The Mande probably forced the Papels to find refuge in the islands of the Geba estuary while the Balante, Manjaco and Brame were driven into the unhealthy coastal lands. As the gold in the west became scarcer, new mines had to be found and this brought links with the Asante of Ghana and other members of the Akan hinterland.

Apart from the search for gold, which took the Mande far and wide, there was also a constant search for agricultural land. The lands fringing the great rivers Niger, Gambia, Senegal, Caramance, Gorubal, the Great and Little Scarcies and the Volta were rich. The rivers provided easy communication as well as fish. The higher lands and the savannah grass encouraged cattle-rearing.

Mandinkas of Upper Niger

Another factor which caused the Mande to spread over a wide area was the frequent religious and political upheavals in the western Sudan. Kingdoms rose and fell and Islamic revolution followed Islamic revolution. State boundaries expanded and contracted and those who lost power were constantly on the move. So new Mande communities were born. The new settlement would form the nucleus of a city-state which expanded to incorporate other settlements.

The Mande states occupied important economic points. After the appearance of the Europeans at the coast, the trade routes along the Sahara were no longer as important as the coastal ports. So the Mande established new commercial links with the coastal belt while at the same time retaining control of the areas of mineral wealth. The Mande language was understood throughout much of the western Sudan and Mande merchants could be found arranging the caravans

57

which traded from one state to another. They established large trading communities in different states. There were fourteen river kingdoms occupied by the Mande. The most important were: Niumi (Barra), which had an excellent economic position along a section of the Gambia unchoked by mangrove swamps and controlled many trade routes; Baddibu which, although lacking the strategic position of Niumi, was a good place for the growth of groundnuts and was soon to become a flourishing Islamic centre; and Oulli bounded by Walli on the west, the Gambia on the south, the river Walli on the north-west and Bondou on the north-east, which was rich in tobacco, cotton, vegetables and corn, and had an impressive capital, Medina.

The rival Bambara states of Segu and Kaarta

The two Bambara states of Segu and Kaarta were at first one military state. The divisions of the country occurred in the mid-nineteenth century as a result of a dynastic feud. At the beginning of the nineteenth century, two powerful kings ruled

Bambara girls

in these states: Mansong (1783–1808) in Segu and Dece ou Dece-Koro (1789–1802) in Kaarta. Of the two, the more determined was Mansong who was jealous of the growing prosperity of Kaarta.

Unlike Segu, Kaarta had internal enemies. Prominent among these were the Djiavara who took every opportunity to revolt against the Kaartans. Externally Kaarta was faced with the threat of the Muslim states of Bondu and Futa Toro. In 1817, the Kaartans attacked Bondu, destroying the capital, Fatteconda. From this time, Kaarta went from strength to strength until the 1840s when the Djiavara revolted.

Segu also remained powerful even after the death of Mansong when his son, Da, took over in 1808. Like Kaarta, there were no succession problems and after Da, other sons of Mansong came to the throne. Although the Bambara of Segu were animists, Islamic influence was already present in the state. This was probably because of trade with the Muslim centre, Djenne.

The Hausa

The well-watered lands enclosed by the lower Niger, the Benue, the Shari, the Logone and Lake Chad felt the influence from the north. When the Tuaregs occupied Aïr, they pushed the Hausa people southwards. It is sometimes claimed that the Hausa are a mixture of Berber and Negro peoples. There were originally seven Hausa states, often called Hausa Bakwai: Daura, Kano, Rano, Katsina, Zazzau (Zaria), Gobir and Biram. Then the Hausa extended their influence over some other southerly and westerly territories of which Kebbi, Zamfara and Yauri were important. Gobir was the most northerly of the states and formerly occupied the Aïr territory from which they were pushed by the Tuaregs. From early times, the different Hausa states were ruled by chiefs (*sarki*) who ruled with the aid of state officials, mostly provincial governors and feudal lords, who were bound when called upon to provide armies for the defence of the state. The nobility (at least those who held high offices of state) could depose unpopular rulers. The states were independent of one another and there was no guarantee that if one was attacked, the others would send help. Yet the wealth of some of the states could not but attract the envy of their neighbours.

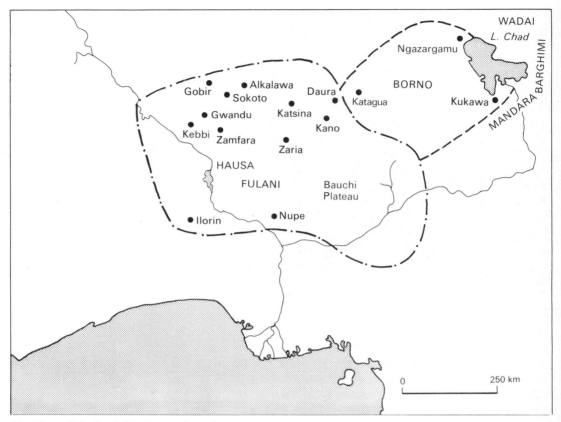

The Hausa-Fulani and Chadian peoples and states

Borno-Kanem

This is one of the oldest kingdoms in West Africa. At the beginning of the nineteenth century the capital was N'gazargamu. There were marked frontiers of the much reduced kingdom at the beginning of the nineteenth century. On the west, it extended to Zinder in the present-day Niger Republic, and Bahr-el-Ghazal was the north-eastern limit. The Mandara mountains formed the southern limit while the Hausa states lined the western frontier.

At the beginning of the nineteenth century, Borno was only a shadow of its former self. The Mai (king) remained the ruler of the kingdom but had to balance the interest of the princes, the free nobility and the military officers. All these were represented in the council of state. But the most powerful force in the country consisted of the three great officers of

Herd of elephants near Lake Chad

state who formed the bulwark of national defence: there was
the Kiaghama or ruler of the south who was the commander of
the army, the Yerima, the Governor of Yeri, who had to defend
the state against the attacks from the north (especially from
the Tuaregs), and the Galadima with his capital at Nguru,
who defended the state against the Hausa in the west. Of
all these wardens, the Galadima, who lived outside the capital,
easily became an overmighty subject. We shall return to the
history of Borno-Kanem when we come to consider the
jihadist movement in the central Sudan (see page 70).

(see page 70)

The State of Wadai

East of Borno lay the equally important kingdom of Wadai.
Wadai had been an Islamic state ever since the overthrow of
the Tunjur dynasty in the seventeenth century. There was,
however, the constant fear that either Darfur or Borno would
bring back the Tunjur and as a result of this, the new rulers of
Wadai continued to pay tribute to these two states.

One of the most powerful kings of this Islamic state was
Abd al-Karim (1803–13). During the reign of his father,
Islam had suffered a reverse because the King had put to
death many of the clerical class. Urged by the need to recover
the state for Islam, and at the same time punish his father for

ill-treating his mother, Abd al-Karim had taken the opportunity of his father's absence on campaign outside the kingdom to revolt. He killed his father in 1803 and seized power.

Abd al-Karim has been acclaimed the wisest king in this part of Africa. He quickly consolidated his position. So powerful did he become that soon he was invited to aid Borno in her encounter with Baghimi and enriched himself by the act, acquiring clothes, coral and silver which he carried away in five camel loads (equal to about eight thousand kilograms). Instead of helping Borno, he helped himself to the territories of Baghimi which he made a tributary state to Wadai.

Until the reign of Abd al-Karim, there was no direct route from North Africa to his country that did not pass through the Fezzan. Whenever there was trouble in the Fezzan, Wadai, like many of the states in the Chad basin, starved. What Abd al-Karim did was to turn his attention to direct trade with Egypt through Benghazi. This meant access to the Nilotic Sudan and a new awakening of Islam in his country.

Understandably, Borno was deeply hurt by the action of the Wadai king who was aware of this. He collected a large army to attack Borno before he could be attacked himself, and it was during this preparation that he suddenly collapsed and died in the tenth year of his reign, leaving the throne to his son Yusuf Kharifain (1814-29).

The Tukolor and Fulani jihads

Many rulers who were unable to bring the remote parts of their kingdoms under control believed that spiritual power could be supplied by the marabouts. The marabouts were learned men who understood the techniques of government and could use their knowledge to the advantage of the ruler. Since they were regarded as holy men whose charms could preserve the ruler from harm, they were allowed to travel freely from place to place.

Although there were marabout groups among the Moors and among the Mande and Hausa and Kanuri-Kanembu peoples, marabout revolutionaries seemed more dominant among two racial groups in West Africa, the Tukolor and the Fulani. The rulers of these peoples often found themselves accepting some of the religious practices of the peoples over whom they ruled. Strict marabouts taught that a Muslim state must be kept pure. A ruler who refused to rule in accordance with the Koran should be overthrown. In the case of the Tukolor rulers, it had been found by 1776 that the

Denianke dynasty was unable to give effective leadership to stop the constant invasion of their territory by the Moors of Trarza. The Fulani living in Mande, Hausa, Kanuri and Adamawa were also discontented.

In Hausaland and Borno, they were forced to pay taxes and tribute which they regarded as unfair. To this was added the fact that the Fulani tended to think themselves superior to those by whom they were held in subjection. Fulani marabouts who were attached to the courts tried to get the rulers to introduce Islamic reforms. If they failed, they found that their movements among the people were restricted, so they considered themselves justified in raising the standard of religious revolt. Obviously, the leaders of those movements were deeply religious men, but it could not be said that their followers had the same religious zeal. The love of plunder and wealth, the desire for political power went hand in hand with racial and political issues.

In the eighteenth century, there were Islamic revolutions in the Tukolor country, Futa Toro, in the Mande country of Bondu and in the Mande country of Futa Djallon. At the beginning of the nineteenth century, the Islamic states of Futa Toro, Futa Djallon and Bondu seem to have lost their original zeal for spreading Islam. Mungo Park reported that the Almamy of Bondu, although head of a Muslim state, was not himself a Muslim. At the beginning of the nineteenth century, only Tukolor still had an effective leader, Abd-al-Qadir, who ruled the country firmly. The main reason why these Islamic governments failed to be effective was that no clear rules governed the succession to the throne.

While the Muslim states of the western Sudan were facing their succession problems the Fulani of Hausaland were producing an ardent scholar called Shehu (sheikh) Uthman dan Fodio who, while he was in the service of the ruler of the Hausa state of Gobir, had formulated in his mind an idea of what a true Islamic state should be. He believed that power should never be given to anybody who seeks it. He believed in consultation in government. He was against tyranny and commended justice and good works. All these he believed were not to be found in the Hausa states, where orphans and widows were denied justice. There should be four ministers in every government, a *waziri* or chief adviser to the monarch, a *qadi* enforcing Islamic law, a chief of police for the maintenance of law and order and a collector of taxes.

In about 1781 he was appointed tutor to the son of Bawa, the Sarki (king) of Gobir. Fortunately for him, Bawa was prepared to accept criticism, but when he died (1801) his son Nafata realized that Uthman had more prestige and following than himself. So although he had once been a student of Uthman he passed a series of laws to make further conversion to Islam difficult. Uthman could not tolerate these laws. He preached against taxes and impositions and this brought him the support of cattle-owners who hated the *jangali* or imposition on cattle. As a scholar he had the support of many of the learned men, both Fulani and Hausa. Nafata could not take effective steps to stop the mounting support of the Shehu before he died in 1802.

He was succeeded by Yunfa, Nafata's son and another of the Shehu's former pupils. But teacher and former pupil soon found themselves in opposing camps. Yunfa did not want to take directions from the clerical class. He threw one of the Shehu's disciples into prison. The Shehu released him without the ruler's authority. In anger, the Sarki decided to stop the Muslim movement. He arranged to kill Uthman secretly, but the plan leaked out, thus increasing the sympathy that many people had for the great teacher. In 1804 Uthman withdrew from Gobir to Gudu. Shortly afterwards he declared a *jihad* (holy war) against the Habe rulers.

Shehu Uthman dan Fodio was a holy man and he confined himself to the purification of religion. He established himself in a new settlement near Sokoto, from which his supporters, who obtained flags from him, marched against the different Habe rulers. The main direction of the jihad was left in the hands of his equally learned son, Bello. When the Shehu died, in 1817, the Fulani Empire that his followers had established had already been divided between his son Bello and his brother Abdullahi. Bello from his headquarters of Sokoto had the east, while Abdullahi, had the west and established himself in Gwandu. When Abdullahi died Bello became sole leader as Sultan. The Sultanate of Sokoto was a confederation of Islamic emirates acknowledging the spiritual leadership of the Sultan. It is sometimes known as the Fulani Empire.

The administration of the Empire followed the old provincial lines of the Habe states. Each successful Fulani leader who conquered a territory replaced the Habe sarki, as emir, so that there were emirs of Kano, Katsina, Zaria, etc. In the beginning these emirs were closely supervised from Sokoto

Sokoto in 1854

and Gwandu. Since they were in charge of the provinces or emirates, it was their duty to see that the Maliki laws were operated. New offices were created within the emirates, some of which were borrowed from Borno. There were the waziris who became the chief advisers of the emirs. At the same time, judicial officials were appointed called qadis. These manned the courts to guarantee fair play and decide civil and criminal cases according to the Koran. Certain concessions were made to some Hausa practices such as land tenure and taxation. Arabic became the language of administration and schools were built to teach it.

When Bello was visited by the British explorer, Hugh Clapperton, in 1824, he was then, according to Clapperton, 'a noble looking man, forty-four years of age, although much younger in appearance, five feet ten inches high, portly in person, with a short curly black beard, a small mouth, a fine forehead, a well-shaped nose, and large black eyes. He was dressed in a light blue cotton robe, with white Muslim turban, the shawl of which he wore over the nose and mouth in the Taurick (Tuareg) fashion.'

Bello was a warrior who was faced with constant revolts and incursions by both Arabs and Tuaregs. In order to create a more stable empire he ordered guns from Europe. He also asked for a British consul to be appointed and a physician sent. He was a learned man interested in knowing details of

Kano wall in the nineteenth century

the world and he wanted Arabic books and maps to be sent to him.

During his reign, therefore, Islamic culture flourished, especially literature and politics. Treatises were produced on religion, morals and government. The Fulani Empire, because it had effective government, began to reap the fruits of trade. Kano became the chief centre of trade in the central Sudan, taking the place of the former Borno capital N'gazargamu. Caravans went to Asante in the west and Tripoli in the north, so that the Kano market had every conceivable article. Wealth poured into the emirates and, as we shall see later, corrupted many of the emirs.

One of the effects of the Fulani take-over in Hausaland was the attack on Borno. The main reason for this was that the Mai of Borno had always had the title of *Amir-el-Muminin*, Commander of the Faithful, which Shehu Uthman dan Fodio had assumed. Some of the Habe rulers had sought the help of the Mai of Borno against the Fulani and this had been given by Mai Ahmed, the ruler of Borno. During the first engagement, the Fulani were defeated and it then seemed that Borno, which claimed to be a Muslim state, had triumphed. But the success of the Fulani in the Habe states had opened the eyes of the Fulani in Borno to the need for action against their Kanuri overlords and they rose in support of their people in Hausaland. A second Fulani attack in 1808 brought them to the walls of the Borno capital N'gazargamu. At this stage, Mai Ahmed sought the help of Mohammed-el-Amin-el-Kanemi, one of the greatest of the Kanembu scholars.

El-Kanemi arrived with forces composed of Kanembu and Shuwa Arabs but only after the capital had been taken and the Mai expelled. He was able to drive away the Fulani from the capital and return Mai Ahmed there. Ahmed died soon after this and was succeeded by his son, Dunama. Unfortunately, Mai Dunama was not a military leader, so when the Fulani attacked again, he was driven for the last time from N'gazargamu, which was destroyed. Everything now pointed to the fact that only El-Kanemi could save Borno and reclaim the western frontier states and towns which had been taken over by the Fulani to form the emirates of Katagum and Hadeija which now owed allegiance to the Sultan of Sokoto. People believed that he had seen a vision for liberating the people, and his first campaign, in which, with a force of 400 men, he had defeated the Fulani who had a force of 8,000, was believed by his followers to be a miracle.

After El-Kanemi had succeeded in halting the Fulani invasion, he was invited by Mai Dunama to settle inside western Borno, so he founded a new capital for himself at Kukawa, in 1814, while a new but less splendid town, Mongonu, was reserved for the Mai who held his court there with due ceremony, but without power. El-Kanemi now took the title of Shehu. The charges that the Fulani leaders of Sokoto had made that Borno was not a Muslim state because she practised some pagan rites and that the law gave no protection to widows and orphans, affected the policy El-Kanemi adopted. Strict Muslim laws were observed, judges learned in Muslim law were appointed and the Shehu insisted that a strict moral code should be observed. Adultery and fornication were punished severely with many lashes of the whip. The hands of thieves were cut off.

There was a reorganization of the administration with the Mai as head of state, but not head of government. The traditional offices like those of the four wardens: the Galadima, the Kiaghama, the Yerima, and the Meestreema remained, even though most of their functions were transferred to trusted slaves appointed by the Shehu. The Shehu's court, not the Mai's, became supreme. Direct supervision of all the officials was done by the Digma. The old Council of State remained, but the Shehu relied more on the administrative officials directly appointed by him. These officials of slave origin, the Kachellas, were responsible for military campaigns when the Shehu was not leading his army in person.

Mai Dunama was, however, not prepared to have pomp without power, so he made arrangements with the Sultan of Barghimi for an invasion of Borno. Unfortunately for him, the letter with which the Sultan of Barghimi made arrangements for the attack was handed over to the Shehu. In the fight that followed, the Sultan of Barghimi, thinking that he was attacking the Shehu, killed Mai Dunama before he realized the mistake.

Shehu El-Kanemi gained from the succession dispute which followed. In 1817 he accepted Ibrahim as the next Mai on the condition that he agreed to receive a fixed payment from the treasury and allow the rest of the revenue to be used by the Shehu for the administration of the country. Kukawa became the administrative headquarters of Borno. There a palace was built for El-Kanemi and he became king in all but name. Soldiers were recruited from all parts to guard the town.

El-Kanemi spent most of his time between 1817 and 1830 suppressing civil disturbance and fighting to regain former territories belonging to Borno. In the north-west, the Manga people revolted and instead of fighting them to a finish, the Shehu cleverly won back the common people from the rebel chiefs after showing that he was capable of using force. The Warden of the West, the Galadima, rose in rebellion and was attacked and fled to seek the protection of Sokoto. He was dismissed from his post but when he later came to submit, he was pardoned. The wars between Borno and Barghimi lasted for many years and eventually the Shehu was forced to obtain the help of the Sultan of the Fezzan. Barghimi was defeated and raided only to rise again to continue the struggle until, in a final battle at Ngala, her army was almost wiped out. The fight against the Fulani, however, was not at all successful. From Adamawa came Fulani soldiers. A joint expedition by Borno and Kandara troops was defeated. In the west where the Galadima had found support from the Fulani, the Shehu himself led an expedition against Hadeija and Katagum and this was successful. But when he threatened Kano, the ruler of Bauchi collected an army and severely defeated the Borno forces, the Shehu only just managing to escape. He died in 1837.

El-Kanemi was succeeded by his son, Umar, who was forced to continue the double regency for some time. It was he who completed the elimination of the old Borno dynasty when Mai Ibrahim arranged with the Sultan of Wadai to invade Borno. The plan was discovered by the Shehu who had the Mai executed. The invasion came in 1846 and the Shehu's forces were routed at Kusseri. Borno seemed threatened on all sides. In the north, the rising power of Zinder under Ibrahim had remained unchecked. The raiding of the Tuaregs continued and the Shehu had been forced to obtain the help of a contingent of Hadeija cavalry in the encounter with Zinder. This was the opportunity taken by Mai Ibrahim to seek the help of the Sultan of Wadai. It was only a bribe that stopped the Sultan of Wadai from taking over Borno. The Sultan of Wadai had put Mai Ibrahim's brother, Ali, on the throne. He was defeated and killed and the Sefuwa dynasty

Mai Umar of Borno

came to an end. Shehu Umar now became undisputed ruler of Borno.

Once on the throne, he rebuilt the capital, Kukawa, as a twin city which was surrounded with a white clay wall. Inside and near the main gate was the daily market, a high street lined by the houses of the important personalities and flanked by a mosque, built in clay with a tower at its north-west corner. The Shehu himself had his palace in the eastern city.

As soon as he was rid of the Sefuwa dynasty, he appointed his own officials from among the supporters and slaves who had distinguished themselves. The post of waziri was firmly established as chief minister, and the holder of the post, Haj Beshir, was a trusted man whose father had lost his life in the battle of Kusseri. He was responsible for many of the appointments to high offices. One of such important appointments was to the military post at Biriri for the control of the western frontier. A slave who had distinguished himself at Kusseri, Kachella Kher-Alla, had the duty of defending the country from the attacks of the Tuaregs.

In 1853, a dispute arose between Umar and his brother, Abdurrahman, about the right to the throne. From Gujba, Abdurrahman raised an army and defeated Umar and his Waziri, Haj Beshir. Umar was exiled to Dikwa while the Waziri was tricked into returning, only to be executed. Abdurrahman ruled tyrannically for almost two years and in 1854 a counter-coup was staged which returned Umar to power. He remained on the throne until 1881.

The rest of his reign was noted for the military activities of his son, Yerima Bukar, who tried to gain back the pagan peoples of Nzirim and obtain the submission of the Musgu. He attacked Adamawa, marched against the Beddes, attacked Fika and Bauchi and tried to punish the people of Kusseri who had aided the Sultan of Wadai.

The Empire of Seku Ahmadu

While Shehu Uthman dan Fodio was turning the scattered Hausa states into the one vast Fulani Empire, the area of Masina where there were many people of different tribes was beginning to come under the influence of another Fulani preacher, Seku Ahmadu. Masina itself and the surrounding districts were inhabited by Muslim Fulani, Soninkes, Bambaras and Bozos, a whole collection of Islamized and animist peoples. Already, the influence of Uthman dan

Market place of Musgu

Fodio's jihad had been felt in the important trading posts of Djenne, Timbuktu and Segu and there was communication between the Fulani of Masina and Sultan Bello. Seku Ahmadu was himself inspired by the jihad of Uthman dan Fodio and he may have had the ambition of forming the different societies occupying the area into one large Fulani state in the way Uthman dan Fodio had done. He gathered round him many students. Soon the size of his movement frightened the Arma of Djenne and the ruler of the Bambara Kingdom of Segu. He was therefore expelled from the small village near Djenne, where he lived. When one of his scholars killed the son of the Ardo ruler of Masina, it was seen by the authorities as the beginning of an attack on the dynasty. This action provided the opportunity for the ruler to destroy the new movement. The number of Seku Ahmadu's followers had so increased that the Ardo ruler of Masina could not do this alone. He appealed to the ruler of the Bambara Kingdom of Segu for joint action. Seku Ahmadu, expecting this move, obtained a flag from Uthman dan Fodio who gave him authority to seize the Masina state and proclaim a jihad.

Between 1810 and 1815, Seku Ahmadu's military success was rapid and led to the establishment of a Fulani Empire which covered an area similar to that formerly covered by the

71

Mosque of Djenne on the Niger

Songhai Empire and controlled the bend of the Niger and its tributaries. During the early stages of his bid for power, Seku Ahmadu had allied himself with one of the most powerful chiefs of Masina called Mohammed Galaijo who himself was a Muslim and with this chief, he had spread his conquests far and wide. After the initial successes, however, Seku Ahmadu, claiming that he had obtained a flag from Uthman dan Fodio and that this empowered him to create a state in which he could exact tribute, insisted that Mohammed Galaijo should pay him tribute. Mohammed Galaijo refused. For three years the war between the two was fought furiously until Galaijo was overcome and fled from his home to find refuge at the court of Abdullahi of Gwandu.

Although Seku Ahmadu obtained a flag from Uthman dan Fodio, he did not submit his empire to rule from Sokoto. In fact, he soon began to regard his own movement as purer than that accepted by the heirs of Uthman dan Fodio, Abdullahi and Bello. He sent them messages threatening to punish them if they did not reduce the number of their wives to two and renounce their effeminate dress.

Seku Ahmadu founded a new capital which was called Hamdallahi. Djenne, the great Muslim cultural centre, also came under his control. Djenne was also an important port to

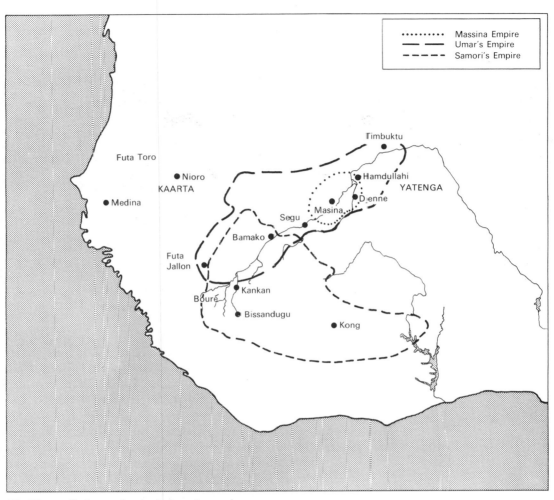

The Western Sudan empires in the late nineteenth century

which Moors, Mandinka, Bambaras and Fulani came to trade. Gold was sent there from the Kong country and from Bouré and in early times Djenne had been described as the land of gold. Slaves were bought in the Djenne market at the rate of 25, 30, or 40 thousand cowries each, according to their age. Calabashes and pots were made and sent to Timbuktu for sale. At first, Seku Ahmadu made Djenne his capital but he soon found that as a zealous disciple of the Prophet Muhammad, the great trade of the town interfered with his

Timbuktu

religious duties and this was why he moved to the new settlement of Hamdallahi.

Ahmadu then waged a relentless but unsuccessful war against the Bambaras of Segu, whom he wished to bring under his control. This series of invasions of Segu by the Fulani affected the commerce of Djenne because it interrupted communications with Yamina, Sansanding, Bamako and Bouré from where gold was brought and circulated in the interior. Trade was thus diverted to the entrepots of Yamina, Sansanding and Bamako.

The Fulani leader also had to deal with the Tuaregs who extended their power to Timbuktu and forced the Fulani to pay customs duties. Matters came to a head in 1826 when Gueladyo, his old enemy, took refuge in Timbuktu. This provided Ahmadu with a good excuse to bring under his control the great commercial centre of the western Sudan. The attack of 1826 was sudden and brought Timbuktu into the Fulani Empire of Seku Ahmadu.

Having acquired a vast empire spreading from Djenne to Timbuktu, Seku Ahmadu imposed a centralized administration using the village as the basic unit. The village heads, either directly or indirectly, became his representatives. Villages were grouped into units controlled by men who had been loyal to him from the beginning. Most of the important towns like Masina and Djenne were placed under the administration of his relatives. The chief responsible for the administration of a town, a group of villages, or even a village head, had the duty of collecting taxes, organizing recruitment for military service, keeping the highways in good repair, spreading Islam and administering justice. In the administration of justice, the chiefs were under the supervision of the qadis who had the power to review cases according to the practices of Muslim law.

State revenue was derived from tribute and from the booty acquired in war. Since there was a standing army, most of the booty belonged to the state. This was gathered as soon as the war was over. Seku Ahmadu received one-fifth, then two equal shares were granted: one went to the commander of the expedition and the other was allotted for buying back prisoners of war and helping some of the people to pay their debts. The rest was shared among the soldiers, the cavalry having twice the share of the foot soldiers. Other revenue came from fines, confiscations, estate duties, etc.

Seku Ahmadu was not a complete dictator: he had a legislative council of learned men and administrators who discussed all the issues that arose about the state and debated new laws before they were put into effect.

Seku Ahmadu was succeeded by his son Ahmadu II who reigned from 1844 to 1853. When Ahmadu II died there was a succession dispute which resulted in Ahmadu Ahmadu becoming the Imam. He could do nothing without the sanction of the forty-man Grand Council of the marabouts and was the representative of an assembly of Muslims whose interests he was bound to guard.

By now Timbuktu had become almost independent. There were many influential groups in the city. There was still the old family of the Moorish invaders, the *arma*. There were the Tuaregs. In 1831 the Kunta Arabs arrived under the leadership of the great Muslim scholar, Sheikh el Mukhtar. The Kunta Arabs and the Tuaregs worked together against the Fulani rulers of Masina so that in the year that Seku Ahmadu died, they succeeded in driving away the Fulani from Timbuktu. This was the beginning of a long conflict which threatened to destroy the commercial importance of the town. The walls of the city had been destroyed during the Fulani invasion of 1826, so its defences were weak.

The Fulani were, however, not interested in storming the city. They imposed a blockade instead. The city depended for its supplies and trade on the more fertile lands under the control of the Fulani. The supplies from Djenne were cut off and the town was short of corn. As a result of the constant intervention of the much respected Sheikh el Mukhtar, Seku Ahmadu had begun to relax the blockade when he died. His death was tactlessly greeted with joy by the Tuaregs and the Kunta, and this brought a sharp reaction from the Fulani Grand Council which at once tightened the blockade. Sheikh el Mukhtar appealed to the new Imam, Ahmadu II, but he was told that the Imam had no personal responsibility for the affair and that he would refer the matter to the Grand Council which refused to hear anything from the Kunta rebels.

The death of Sheikh Mukhtar in 1847 could not have come at a worse time for Timbuktu because it removed the one man who had international respect and who could continue to bargain with the Fulani. A succession dispute for the leadership of the Kunta Arabs began between Sheikh Sidi el Bekkay Ahmed who claimed to be the nearest relative, and the more legitimate claimant, Sheikh Sidi Hammada, a hermit. The struggle that followed was long and bitter and led to a state of anarchy which hastened the downfall of the city.

The fact that the choice of Sheikh el Bekkay was not acceptable to the Fulani leaders of Masina made them tighten their measures against Timbuktu. The city, which had been blockaded for three years already, was now in such a position that it was prepared to surrender to the Fulani unconditionally. The Tuaregs found that they were unable to go to the pastures on the left bank of the Niger so their herds perished. Many people began to doubt whether they were right to give Sheikh el Bekkay their support. Hunger made many decide to reject the leadership of Bekkay who, realizing that he was losing support, decided to go personally to the Fulani Imam, Ahmadu II. When he made a request to the Imam for an interview, the request was put to the Grand Council who refused it. Bekkay was not to be stopped by this and stealing secretly out of Timbuktu, he made his way to Hamdallahi. Informants had told the Fulani leaders what had happened and so, as he was about to enter the capital, Bekkay was met by thousands of cavalry waiting to lead him in.

All his requests, including permission to abandon his nomadic life and settle finally in Timbuktu, were turned down. He refused to swear an oath of allegiance to the Imam in the great mosque of Hamdallahi or send him soldiers. The political situation following this approach by Bekkay to the Fulani leaders was a compromise between the different parties:

> to the effect that Timbuktu should be dependent on the Fulbe (Fulani) without being garrisoned by a military force, the tribute being collected by two Kadis, one Pullo (Fulani) and the other Songhai, who would themselves decide all cases of minor importance, the more important ones being referred to the capital. But nevertheless, the government of the town, or rather the police, as far as it goes, is in the hands of one of the two Songhay Mayors, with the title of Emir, but who have scarcely any effective power, placed as they are between the Fulbe on the one side and the Tawarek (Tuareg) on the other, and holding their ground against the former through the two Kadis, and against the latter by means of the Sheikh el Bakay (Bekkay). Such is the distracted state of this town, which cannot be remedied before a strong and intelligent power is again established on this upper course of the Niger, so eminently favourable to commence.

We have seen that after the death of Ahmadu II on 27 February 1853 the Grand Council granted the succession to Ahmadu Ahmadu. The new Imam was unable to stop the decline at a time when the new Tukolor power under Al Hajj 'Umar was rising. Hamdallahi was invaded in 1862 and Ahmadu Ahmadu himself put to death. From this time on, the Tijani Brotherhood took over.

The Tijani Brotherhood and the Empire of Al Hajj 'Umar

A certain Muslim scholar, Ahmad al-Tijani, founded the Tijani order, or the Tijaniyya, in Fez about 1780. To this place, scholars and pilgrims went and were inspired. This movement reached the western Sudan through a Tukolor cleric from Futa Toro born in 1797, Al Hajj 'Umar ibn Salid. He travelled extensively and when he reached Mecca in 1825 he was given the leadership of the Tijani movement in the western Sudan. When 'Umar arrived in Sokoto, he married the daughter of Sultan Bello. Then he left to settle at Diagouku in the Futa Djallon from where he began to emphasize the need for reforms in the Fulani state of Futa Djallon, where the force of the earlier movement of the eighteenth century was spent. His movement became popular and attracted able and ambitious young men from the different groups and from all walks of life. For that reason he was expelled. He settled in Dinguiray and his reform movement became a jihad.

In his preparations against the forces opposing him, 'Umar was anxious to have the support of the European nations and to control the trade routes. While he had been at Diagouku he had made his followers work the land and trade for gold dust at Bouré. He used the gold to buy arms. He was thus in a position of economic and military strength to undertake his military campaigns, which began in 1852. He campaigned down the river Bafing where traditional religions were still believed despite centuries of Muslim contacts. The Mande principalities of Bambuk and Bouré, the centre of gold production in the western Sudan, fell and then, in 1854, he marched against Nioro, the capital of the Bambara state of Kaarta, which he placed under the administration of his faithful slave Mustafa. His movements further north were stopped when he came in conflict with the French. There were four reasons why he had to fight the French: they refused him arms and military support in his campaign against Futa Toro; they refused to pay tribute; French missionaries and traders were making converts for Christianity not only along the coast but also gradually in the interior; and they were arming some of the chiefs and had put them under their protection.

He had to destroy the French if he was to become overlord of the whole territory. He attacked the French fort at Medina in 1857. The French forces were strong and easily repulsed those of 'Umar. Having failed in the west 'Umar turned eastwards. There were two important pagan states which he planned to attack, Masina and the Bambara Kingdom of Segu.

At first, he tried to gain the support of the Kingdom of Masina. He appealed to Ahmadu III who, he thought, would willingly respond because he was a Muslim. He was surprised that Ahmadu showed no interest. 'Umar thus had to attack and capture Segu unaided. His victory spurred him to a more daring enterprise. He decided that Ahmadu III, by his failure to aid a fellow Muslim against a pagan state, had forfeited his right to the throne of Masina. If he could conquer Masina and build an African empire this might also stop the activities of the European powers which were beginning to dominate the coast. He therefore laid siege to the Masina capital, Hamdullahi. He captured it eventually in 1862 and in the same year he attacked and conquered Timbuktu.

The palace at Segu

'Umar did not depend on local risings. He wanted to create a vast, centralized, Muslim state. He liked to employ people who had had some form of European education. He therefore employed men from Sierra Leone and Senegal, who already had experience of European ideas and technology to employ their energies and skills in the creation of a modern African state. He encouraged traders of different nationalities. He established a class of civil servants, the Talibes, and these gave both military and administrative leadership. From his Tukolor supporters he appointed governors of provinces. The state was created on Islamic lines and he wanted to introduce strict Tijani principles. He prohibited alcohol and tobacco. This was probably what dampened the interest of the coastal educated classes who had seen in him the only hope of establishing a strong, modern state.

There were, however, conditions already making for decline in the empire. It was too large for any centralized administration at a time when communications were very poor. Some of the people hated the Tukolor governors who had been set over

General Faidherbe

them and most of the people disliked the new administrative and military classes. At the same time, the conflict with the French complicated matters for 'Umar. He had trouble with people living on the western frontiers and discovered that his new capital of Segu was too far inland for him to be able to control these areas fully.

Of all the things that could possibly bring conflicts with the French, the most important was the navigation of the Niger. French interests were expanding and the newcomers did not like the idea of a great African power controlling the major economic centres. The French Governor of Senegal, Louis Faidherbe, realized that 'Umar was too strong to be overthrown and tried to reach an agreement with him to make the caravan routes free from the Niger to the Senegal and to gain the concession of free navigation on the Niger up to Bamako. But before negotiations could start 'Umar faced a revolt of the Fulani of Masina aided by the Bambaras. His attempts at imposing the Tijani doctrine on a people who had accepted the Qadiri doctrine had met with strong opposition from the Fulani Muslims. In 1864 'Umar led his forces in person to quell the revolt, but in the fighting he lost his own life. His state was divided amongst his children.

The son who succeeded to the largest slice of the empire, including the capital, was Ahmadu. It took him ten years to put down rebellion led by his relatives and subordinates. He then turned his attention to the problems of expanding trade. He planned to open negotiations with the French so as to trade directly with Senegal. But between Senegal and Segu were the chiefs of Kaarta whose powers had increased since the various revolts. They made it difficult for traders to move through their territory to Senegal. Ahmadu had no alternative but to make arrangements with the British in the Gambia and Sierra Leone. These negotiations with the British offended the French, who were afraid of the British moving into the western Sudan. Colonel de L'Isle, Governor of Senegal, took action. In 1878 he decided to give military support to one of the great enemies of Ahmadu's government. This loyal supporter of the French, Dyouka Sambala of Khasso, attacked Niamodi, a ruler of a district called Logo which had thrown off Sambala's authority.

Ahmadu still did not seek a clash with the French. He sent his chief minister, Seydou Djeylia, to the French with the proposal that if they gave him aid in his fight to consolidate his empire, he would throw his markets open to them. Unfortunately for Ahmadu, this offer coincided with the French government's decision to build a Senegal railway. France's plans for internal penetration now definitely clashed with Ahmadu's interests. French aggression really began in 1879 when they built a fort at Bafoulabe in Ahmadu's territory. They began to look for territorial concessions which Ahmadu was not prepared to grant. He was not even prepared to accept a French resident ambassador unless he was an African Muslim. He emphasized the fact that the French must respect Tukolor sovereignty and independence. He was not interested in the railway project from the Senegal to the Niger. He detested the idea of the French introducing steamships on the Niger. He was afraid of French influence as it threatened the security of his realm. By 1880 war was inevitable.

While Ahmadu was struggling with the French, there was another brotherhood active in the Mandinka country. Unlike the empires of Uthman dan Fodio, Seku Ahmadu and 'Umar, the motives for the creation of the empire by Samori ibn Lafiya Toure were not purely religious. Samori was not a Muslim scholar or teacher, although he established an empire in which the only religion that was allowed was Islam. Probably his motives for establishing one religion were political and administrative, since Islam alone in the various regions of the western Sudan gave a concrete foundation for government. When he decided to take the title of Al-Mani in 1874, which made him both religious and political leader of a Muslim community, he was representing the Fulani national religion, which was always a contributing factor in Fulani relations. Samori ibn Lafiya Toure, however, was an efficient professional soldier who probably saw the weaknesses of the surrounding territories of the upper Niger and believed that it was possible to create from them a centralized and efficiently administered state which would be respected by and, if possible, work hand in hand with the other great Fulani empire. In 1873 he began a process that was to lead to the formation of a vast empire. This was the year in which he attacked and defeated Fa Modu, the chief of Kumadugu, and made his capital at Bissandugu. His initial success gave him confidence and within a short time he gained control over Toron, Konia and Wasulonke. Then in 1873 he gained a signal

The Empire of Samori Toure

victory over Kankan. Samori had thus established a military state which continued to expand, as each provincial military unit had the function of guarding the empire from external attack as well as undertaking wars for territorial expansion. He had a disciplined and well-equipped army. By 1880 he controlled an area extending from the upper Niger to the upper Volta. As well as power he had popularity. In the following years he was to prove himself a determined opponent to French expansion.

West African societies II: Chapter 4
peoples of the coast and forests

In the forest regions of West Africa, there had grown up for
centuries before 1800 powerful states such as the Mende and
Susu of Sierra Leone, the Kru and the Kpelle of Liberia, the
Akan states of Ghana, Dahomey, and, in the area of modern
Nigeria, Oyo, Benin, Warri and the Niger Delta states. Mande
influence was strong among the Sierra Leone states and those of
Ivory Coast and Liberia. Among the Akan states, although

The forest kingdoms

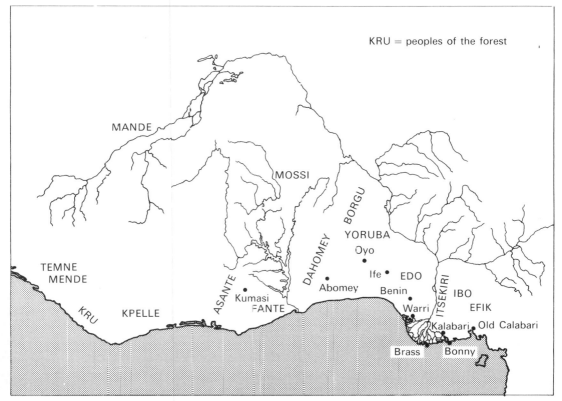

Forest peoples and states

Asante was a forest state with its own rich culture, there were Mande and Hausa influences in the capital, Kumasi. This arose from the trading connections between Asante and the more northerly peoples. South of Borgu was the Kingdom of Dahomey, often faced with invasion from the Yoruba Kingdom of Oyo, which in turn was under constant threat of Nupe and Benin raids. In the area of the Niger Delta, some states had been formed by immigrants from inland who took advantage of trade with European merchants to increase their hold as middlemen between the interior peoples and the Europeans. For instance, the Kingdom of Warri was established by an immigrant Benin aristocracy and Yoruba coastal settlers. The Efik states were created by immigrants from the north-east who moved into Iboland where they met the Ibos, left to settle among the Ibibio, and finally settled in the Calabar area, and from there their culture spread across the land between the Niger and the Cameroon mountains. The Oil Rivers states of Bonny, Kalabari and, later, Opobo were formed by the Ijaw and increased by Ibo and Efik immigrants.

One important feature of the forest states is that they were all monarchies. Each had a capital with outlying districts which formed the nucleus of the kingdom. Here the king and many of his influential chiefs lived. As other states were conquered, these were incorporated into the kingdom either as tributary states or as directly administered states with royal officials appointed by the central government. The king did not usually have unlimited powers. Apart from Dahomey, where there was an absolute monarch, most of the forest kingdoms such as Asante, Oyo and Benin had constitutions which contained careful checks and balances. The king could not be tyrannical because he was limited by his chief subjects and by age-old traditions.

In Asante, Dahomey and Benin, once the king had been installed as the symbol of the whole kingdom and the embodiment of the royal dynasty he could not be removed. There was no question of abdication. In Oyo, however, there was a provision in the constitution which ensured that the Oyomesi had the ultimate power of life and death over the king (*Alafin*). The chief minister (*Basorun*) had the duty of going once a year to the palace to divine whether or not the king was still on good terms with his spirit double (*Orun*) who was in heaven watching over the affairs of the kingdom. This was probably another way of asking whether or not public opinion was still favourable to the continuation of the reign. When the basorun concluded that the king was bad, he had the right to force the king to commit suicide.

The constitutions provided for councils of state composed of important traditional chiefs. In Dahomey the government was different because the state was founded to resist attacks from Oyo. Oyo, like other forest kingdoms, had tended to accept that father-son relationship which existed between the reigning king who was thus the occupant of the throne of the original ancestor and the major chiefs. In resisting the traditional links between the homeland of Allada and Oyo, the early Dahomey kings had created a new political pattern based on military rather than traditional force, and, since the king was himself a military leader, his power and personal prestige gave him greater respect than was enjoyed by the kings of the other kingdoms where the ruler did not play any personal military role. Thus it became possible to accommodate adventurers as citizens and establish a centralized administration.

The control of the army was always important during times of crisis. A successful military leader, because of the booty that he obtained during campaigns, could become very wealthy and by giving generous rewards could retain the loyalty of the troops. The Oyo constitution devised a means of checking the powers of the military leader, the *Are-ona-Kakanfo*, who had to go on a campaign at least once a year at the request of the king. The king (*Alafin*) could set him an impossible task as soon as he found that the military leader was becoming an over-mighty subject. The Benin kingdom did not concentrate all the military power in the hands of one leader. Military leadership was shared by the *Ezomo*, a hereditary Uzama chief who guarded the gateway from the Benin port into the city (he was also responsible for seeing to the ritual washing of foreigners' feet before they were allowed to enter the capital); the *Ologbosere*, the only hereditary town chief; and the *Imaran*, a palace chief. The kings of Dahomey were also military leaders and appointed their own generals, often from among the male descendants of previous kings. Sometimes military leadership was temporarily given to a powerful territorial chief whose support the king needed badly.

In most of the kingdoms there existed cults or secret societies which could make ritual demands of the king, the council of state, and the important chiefs. The cult discussed all the social and political problems of each reign and their meetings were secret. Although the kings had their representatives in some of the cults, they were themselves not always present at the meetings. Although the representatives of the council of state were members of the societies, they did not hold posts in them. All the cults also had important religious and judicial functions and dealt with such serious criminal offences as the shedding of blood, incest and arson. In their special groves the cults performed rites for the king and the community. The societies controlled law and order, provided a police force and public executioners.

Initiation into Ogboni cult

Whether the secret societies had inter-state rights, we do not know, but there was nothing to prevent the leaders of the societies in different states where the same cults existed from discussing matters of common interest. The members worked with the diviners. When any issue arose, the opinions of these diviners were sought and if it was considered that the omens did not favour a particular policy, that policy had to be dropped. Decisions did not need to be unanimous, but once taken, they were enforced strictly by the priesthood.

The area covered by modern Sierra Leone was the home of many peoples, prominent among whom by 1800 were the Mende and Temne. Most of the kings who had access to the coast were involved in the slave trade with European merchants and captains. But the establishment of the freed-slave colony of Freetown was to change the situation drastically. In 1787 the first attempt was made to found a settlement for British ex-slaves on land bought from coastal chiefs. The first attempt was a failure but the originators of the scheme persisted and by 1800 several thousand negroes from Britain and the United States of America were living and working at Freetown despite the opposition of local rulers and European slavers' agents.

Though the settlement survived it did not prosper and in 1808 the British government proclaimed Sierra Leone a crown colony. Freetown became the centre of government and also an important base for British anti-slave trade patrols. The British government obtained reciprocal search treaties with Portugal, France and Spain which gave her navy the right

Freetown in 1792

87

to search ships of these powers. Captains found in West African waters carrying slaves or slaving equipment were brought to Freetown for trial before a Court of Mixed Commission. Over the years thousands of slaves freed in this way were settled in Sierra Leone.

Sierra Leone and Liberia, the other freed–slave settlements (see page 91), were unique in that they were not true West African states. From the beginning European influences were strong and European ideas profoundly affected the political development of these countries. Christian missionaries were active among the Creoles of Freetown (the descendants of the freed slaves) and their neighbours. Primary schools were established and in 1827 the Church Missionary Society built the famous Fourah Bay College. (It began as a college for training African clergy but later became a university college.) Gradually there grew up a class of educated Africans, an élite who spoke good English and were literate in it.

Fourah Bay College

Under the colony's constitution, administration was in the hands of the Governor and the Executive Council who were responsible to the Secretary of State in England. For a long time educated West Indians were brought into the service but it was generally found that the Creoles preferred English to West Indian administrators. The West Indians who had come into the colony as professionals helped to rouse nationalist sentiments among the Sierra Leonians. Most of them were lawyers who wanted the people of Sierra Leone to share democratically in their government. In 1853 a Committee of Correspondence was formed in order to force the hand of Britain to grant representation. Since campaigns against colonial administration could not be effective without press support, one of the West Indian lawyers started his private newspaper, *The New Era*, which attacked the character of British administration in Sierra Leone.

These nationalist activities made it possible for the colony to start on the road towards democracy. In October 1863 a new constitution was granted. Although the Governor still had supreme powers and the Executive Council still consisted mainly of officials appointed by the Crown, there was a new Legislative Council comprising the members of the Executive

Freetown during second half of the nineteenth century

Council and a representative of the Sierra Leone people. Besides the Governor, who was President of the Legislative Council, the other members included the Chief Justice, the officer commanding the troops, the Colonial Secretary and the Queen's Advocate (all members of the Executive Council) plus three or four members nominated by the Governor, subject to the approval of the Colonial Office in London. It was mainly in order to gain both African and European merchant opinion that Charles Heddle came to represent the European trading community and a prominent liberated African merchant, John Ezzido, came to represent the African trading and the Sierra Leone community. Ezzido had come originally from Nupe and at an early age had been sold as a slave in Yoruba country. He was lucky: while he was being shipped to Brazil he was rescued and brought to Sierra Leone. He became a Methodist preacher and lay reader and as a result of the Methodist connection, in 1842 he was taken to England by the Reverend Thomas Dove, General Superintendent of the Wesleyan Mission. The good man of God introduced his liberated African to wholesale firms in England who then agreed to send him their articles for sale from his shop in Freetown. He was thus able to compete on a footing of equality with the Europeans. In 1844 he became an alderman in the Corporate Municipality of Freetown and in the next year was nominated mayor. When therefore Governor Blackhall, who himself had been a Member of Parliament, recommended the constitutional changes which brought in the amendment of the constitution in 1863, he arranged for the inactive Mercantile Association to be revived and elect a representative. At a meeting held on 8 December 1863 there were present fourteen Europeans, one Afro-West Indian and twenty Africans. Ezzido was elected by twenty-three votes.

In 1865 the Select Committee in urging a policy of withdrawal had emphasized the fact that the Africans should be taught to govern themselves. As a result of this, in 1872 there were in the Legislative Council, apart from the Governor and the Executive Council ex-officio members, only one nominated official (the Colonial Treasurer) and three unofficial African nominated members. The Legislative Council, however, was just an advisory body for discussing the actions of a powerful Governor. The unofficial African members could regard themselves as the voice of public opinion to criticize the actions of the colonial administration and to give support only to measures that were in the interest of the colony. One of the more active unofficial nominated members was Samuel Lewis who, in 1893, worked in and outside the Council for municipal reforms in the Municipality of Freetown. He continued to demand the spread of effective rule in the interior so that Sierra Leone would not remain a mere strip of coast, and he sought closer association with Liberia. It did seem that the road towards Liberia itself was open because the nationalists of the two countries could meet and influence each other. The most prominent of Liberian scholars, Dr Edward Wilmot Blyden, came to Freetown and wrote a series of nationalist articles in Sierra Leone newspapers. As education was increasing because of the activities of the missionaries, there was the need for a university since not all parents could afford to send their children to England. This was how Fourah Bay College came to be refounded in 1876 as an affiliated institution to Durham University in the United Kingdom. This institution became the training ground for West African educationalists and missionaries like Samuel Ajayi Crowther as well as administrators, politicians and lawyers.

The state of Liberia was founded in 1822 by the American Colonization Society. It was begun for the same reason that Sierra Leone was begun: to provide a home in Africa for freed slaves, in this case from the United States of America. It began as the small settlement of Monrovia built on land bought from local Kru chiefs.

Its problems were similar to those faced by Sierra Leone. It had to fight for existence against neighbouring rulers and foreign merchants with a stake in the slave trade. Its people had to work out a constitution for themselves. Political development was more rapid than in Sierra Leone, largely because of the strong traditions of democracy and freedom established in the land from which the Liberians had come, the United States of America. In its infancy the new state was administered by agents of the American Colonization Society but when the settlement ran into difficulties there was no question of the United States taking it over as a colony, for the American people were profoundly anti-colonial. The white officials of the Society tried to maintain their authority in the face of mounting opposition from the settlers. The settlers won the right to

Liberia

Monrovia

elect the members of the Governor's Advisory Council in 1828 and in 1841 the first black Governor, Joseph Roberts, was sworn in.

Liberia was now in a unique constitutional position. It was neither a colony nor an independent state. This fact enabled sea captains to avoid paying harbour dues and customs tolls. It encouraged criminals and outlaws to seek haven there. It invited foreign countries not to take the new state seriously. The British rulers of Sierra Leone were particularly contemptuous of Liberia and took every opportunity to 'put the Liberians in their place'. It was partly to rectify this situation that Roberts and many of his supporters agitated for independence. At the Monrovia Convention of 1847 a new constitution was agreed and the following year the independent Republic of Liberia came into existence.

The Asante Kingdom

The Asante nation at the beginning of the nineteenth century was a strong, centralized state covering a wide area. There were, however, challenges to her sovereignty from all directions, especially from the coastal peoples and the northern states of Gonja. The Asantehene (paramount king) of Asante at the beginning of the nineteenth century was Osei Bonsu (1800–24). Youthful and warlike, Osei Bonsu seemed fitted for a military career. He was aware of the cost of wars and, where possible, he preferred negotiated settlements, but was always prepared to accept challenges and was never known to falter in his determination to keep the nation one by putting down revolts. Asante prosperity depended on trade with the Mande and Hausa states and any threats to the trade routes brought out the Asante forces. The slave trade was a source of national wealth and, to this end, military expeditions to unfriendly states were designed to provide the country with human beings for sale. The Asantehene was only a few months on the throne when he decided to end the semi-independence of Gofan. The Gofan army was defeated, the King, a Muslim, was captured and died in the Asante camp having lost thousands of warriors dead or captured.

This victory over Gofan and the suppression later of a civil revolt in Gyaman showed that in Osei Bonsu, Asante had a king of great military stature. The result was that ambassadors came from neighbouring territories, including Abomey, Gonja and Dagomba, bearing presents and congratulatory messages. There might have been peace after this, but for the action of some Assin chiefs who drew Asante into conflict

Assin village

93

with the peoples of the coast and, through this, in 1805 with the British, who held several trading forts, or castles, at the coast. Assin was a tributary state and therefore subject to the decision of the Asante Council acting as the supreme court of the realm. In a dispute that came to the court, an Assin chief not only refused to abide by the decision of the Asantehene, but afterwards put some of the King's messengers to death before escaping to seek the protection of the Fante. Bonsu fought against the Fante, defeated them and pursued them to Anomabu where they placed themselves under the protection of the British Governor. An indecisive battle with the British and their allies followed, after which the Governor handed over one of the fugitives and confirmed Bonsu's rule over the Fante by right of conquest.

From this time until his death, Osei Bonsu came more and more into conflict with both the coastal peoples and the British. He kept his state well prepared for war. He launched many military expeditions to protect Asante's vital trade routes. He did all in his power to strengthen his control of the Akan states. Trusted chiefs were placed in Gyaman, Akwamu, Akim and Akwapim. Apart from Gonja and Dagomba which did not belong to the Akan group and so did not participate directly in the Asante wars, the greater part of present-day Ghana was under one form or another of political relationship with Asante. The different regions were either provinces, protectorates or tributaries.

But the Asantehene did not find it so easy to make good his claim to be ruler of the Fante. He launched three campaigns (1811, 1814, 1823) against the troublesome inhabitants of the coast and on each occasion he found himself in conflict with the British. On 21 January 1824 his warriors killed the British Governor, Sir Charles McCarthy, in battle. This led to severe reprisals in 1826 and the defeat of the Asante army at the battle of Dodowa.

Although the British forces had defeated the Asante, there was no peace, and trade continued to suffer. The British government wanted to abandon its Gold Coast forts altogether, but neither the merchants nor the Fante wished to see this part of West Africa handed over to the Asante. The British then decided to put the administration of the forts in the hands of a committee of three London merchants. The Charter of the Company carefully limited the areas to be administered; the Governor and the elected Council was to have jurisdiction of 'the forts, roadsteads and harbours thereunto adjoining, as well as the persons residing therein'.

It was under this Charter and in the disturbed situation on the Gold Coast that George Maclean came as Governor. He realized more than anybody else the necessity of reaching an agreement with the Asante who also were interested in the maintenance of peace. A treaty was therefore signed in 1831 which made Asante deposit 17 kg of gold as security and hand over two princes as hostages. The trade routes were to remain open and some evil practices like panyarring,* denouncing and swearing were to be discontinued. All the territories like Denkyera, Assin, and the coastal peoples which owed allegiance to Asante were to be given their independence. The British Governor was to be arbitrator in any inter-tribal dispute. This treaty kept the Asante and Fante at peace for over fifteen years.

As soon as Maclean assumed office, he saw that although he was a company agent and, therefore, that it was his main duty to make profits for the directors, he could not achieve this unless law and order were maintained. He knew that many of the troubles on the Gold Coast stemmed from the fact that most of the people could not get justice. He therefore established a court at Cape Coast Castle, his headquarters. His impartiality and the promptness with which he gave judgment appealed to the different peoples so that they brought their cases for settlement in his court. He thus expanded his jurisdiction over a people who were not British subjects. He got some of the chiefs to sit with him and he became familiar with native laws and customs. While Maclean was interested in stopping the slave trade, he was careful not to take any drastic measure against slavery.

In 1843, as a result of Maclean's work, another constitutional change occurred on the Gold Coast. The British government agreed to take over control of the Gold Coast from the Company. Commander Hill came over as Governor, while Maclean became a judicial assessor. Both British and African law came together in the legal system of the Gold Coast. The Africans did not realize that their states were losing their sovereignty. Maclean had ingeniously cleared the way

---

*Panyarring was the practice of seizing a relative or friend of a debtor and keeping him in prison until the debt was paid.

for British colonization without the African chiefs realizing it. His friendship with the chiefs disarmed them, and they were prepared to accept all British visitors in the same spirit in which they had accepted Maclean. Britain was establishing a virtual protectorate over the Gold Coast.

Commander Hill reached an agreement called the Bond with the Fante in 1844 which formalized the relationship between the Fante and the British. The position of the British made it easy for them to stop the slave trade and increase legitimate trade. The abolition of the slave trade made the position of the Danes on the Gold Coast unprofitable. They therefore agreed to sell their forts to the British, leaving Britain and Holland the only remaining European nations on the Gold Coast.

In 1852 a further step towards turning the Gold Coast into a protectorate was tried. The Governor summoned a 'Legislative Assembly' of chiefs empowered to vote taxes and make laws. The new body, which had no roots in tradition, only lasted until 1861.

The Asante were getting worried about the part the British were playing at the coast. They had lost the revenue that formerly came to them from the European forts as well as the traditional tribute from the coastal peoples. Their loss of Assin, Akim and Denkyera did not please them and they wanted an opportunity to strike back. The opportunity came in 1862, when a certain Kwasi Gyani found a gold nugget and kept it. This was a breach of Asante law and Kwasi Gyani fled to Cape Coast and there claimed British protection. Governor Richard Pine refused to send the fugitive back for trial. So the Asante army set out for the coast in March 1863 and defeated the combined African and British forces under the command of Major Cochrane. As the rainy season was approaching they retired.

The British had suffered a moral as well as a military disaster and had lost prestige among the coastal peoples, who found that their soldiers, who died in thousands from malaria, could not adequately protect them from the Asante. Worse was to follow; in 1864–5 a severe famine brought unprecedented suffering which the British could not relieve.

The British government, alarmed at the rising cost of administration on the Gold Coast, again decided to withdraw. They reduced their presence there by placing the Gold Coast under the jurisdiction of the Governor-General at Freetown.

English castle at Anamabu

By now some of the Fante chiefs were disillusioned with British protection and resentful of British power. They demanded a return to full independence. The move itself was led by John Aggrey, King of Cape Coast. He made it known that the British had at no time conquered the coastal peoples, who had only agreed to partnership with the British, and that the British could not exercise any rights, either political or judicial, without the consent of the people. The land, which in fact was stool land (i.e. land belonging to the nation), could not be alienated and so the British claim to the ownership of the land round the forts had no legal validity. He then insisted that the land round Cape Coast Castle belonged to the people and he was going to have it. To strengthen his position, he organized the chiefs on the coast to resist any attempt to persuade them to sign a treaty. King John Aggrey then called a meeting of the chiefs to draw up a strong protest on 5 September 1866. With their support he threatened rebellion. For this threat, the King was summoned by the administrator to appear before him at Cape Coast Castle. When he refused, Aggrey was seized and deported to Sierra Leone. The attempt to overthrow British jurisdiction quickly spread to other parts of the Gold Coast, especially Anamabu which did not want to abandon its local customs and traditions. The chiefs supported their king who wanted to maintain his judicial independence (the British Colonel Conran had recently released a criminal who had been imprisoned by the King).

Even in Accra, the leaders decided to find a solution to their problems without relying on the British. Frequent wars and disturbances had destroyed the importance of Accra and its trade, and the chiefs, urged on by the educated classes, wanted

Asante expedition and carriers waiting to be hired

to organize united resistance against the Asante. As a result
the Accra Native Confederation was formed.

But the great institution that sprang up to take concerted
action against the British and the Dutch was the Fante Confederation. This was created at a meeting in Mankessim in
January 1868. The main aim of the Confederation was to
achieve independence on the Gold Coast in line with the
constitution which the Sierra Leonian Dr J. Africanus B.
Horton had designed in his *Great principle of establishing
independent African nationalities*. He wanted the Gold Coast to
be divided into the Kingdom of Fante and the Republic of
Accra. But tribal jealousies made it impossible for the idealist
plan of the Confederation to work. The schemes of the Fante
Confederation failed because of fresh conflict with the Asante
which showed clearly how much the coastal peoples still
needed British protection.

Many raids were made on Fante and Denkyera territories
by the Asante during the reign of the Asantehene, Kofi

Karikari. When it became known in 1872 that the British had bought the Dutch forts, the Asante saw their only route to the coast blocked. They had always sold their slaves to the Dutch who transported them or used them as soldiers. This market had now ended. What particularly angered the Asante was the way in which Elmina Castle was traded by the Europeans without the consent of the Asantehene, for the land on which the castle stood belonged to Asante. At the same time, Asante had lost control of all the coastal peoples who had gained their independence through the military services of the British. Kofi Karikari now felt that the Asante must take the offensive to right all the wrongs they had suffered since the beginning of the century.

In 1873 at the beginning of their onslaught they met with little resistance. But even if Britain wanted to leave the Gold Coast, she could not condescend to be driven out by the Asante, so General Sir Garnet Wolseley was appointed military commander to deal with the Asante whose more than 20,000 fighting men threatened Elmina and Cape Coast Castle. He was completely successful in destroying Asante ascendancy, and in 1874 he decided to attack Kumasi itself. He occupied and destroyed the Asante capital. The Asantehene was made to sign the Treaty of Fomena. Representatives from Juaben, Bekwai, Kokoju, Kuntanase, Nsuta, Mampong and five smaller states also signed this treaty on 14 March 1874. In this treaty the Asantehene agreed to pay a war indemnity of 14,000 kg of gold, to renounce all allegiance from Denkyera, Assin, Akim and Adansi, to renounce all claims to Elmina and all payments made as a result of the lease of the ground on which the forts were built, and to withdraw all his forces from the south-west. The Asantehene also promised to keep the trade routes open and to keep a clear passage for traders from Kumasi to the river Pra. He was also requested to stop all human sacrifices in his domain. The Asantehene had no alternative but to agree to these humiliating terms.

This was the beginning of the break-up of the Asante Confederacy. Many of its tributary states now refused to take orders from a humiliated central government and began to feel themselves free to administer their own territories, since Asante did not seem to have the force to bring them back to their allegiance. It was only after the deposition of Kofi Karikari in September 1874 and the accession of Mensa Bonsu that the Asante people again had enough life in them

British fusiliers on Gold Coast

to force back one of these states, Juaben, to its traditional allegiance. Apart from getting the Asantehene to sign the Treaty of Fomena, the British took no steps to administer the territory, but the policy of withdrawal was no longer possible. The British government had to increase its jurisdiction over the coastal peoples in order to protect them from Asante. The power of the British government had to be increased and firmly exercised.

By Letters Patent issued on 24 July 1874 the Gold Coast forts and settlements were separated from the government of Sierra Leone and created into a colony. A Legislative Council was established on 6 August, and this body had the power to legislate for the whole of the Protected Territories which covered the territories between the rivers Pra and Volta. There was also an Executive Council to advise the Governor. Elements of English law were enforced by the Supreme Court Ordinance which introduced the English Common Law doctrines of equity and statutes of general application, although the courts of the chiefs were still allowed to operate under specified conditions. Arrangements were made for the collection of customs duties and it was accepted that taxes would have to be levied on the colony. On 12 September 1874 the British government proclaimed the Gold Coast a crown colony and, in 1876, they made Accra the capital.

Relations with Asante were not as harmonious as could have been expected after the destoolment of Kofi Karikari and the accession of Mensa Bonsu, whose position had been greatly strengthened by putting down the Juaben revolt. Because Britain could not afford to annex the whole of the Asante territory, she could not undertake measures calculated to destroy the only power that could maintain some order in the interior. Kumasi was rebuilt but the very fact that it had been burnt down before increased British prestige among the African tribes which, like Juaben, began to seek to be included in the protectorate that had been proclaimed over the coast. Mensa Bonsu on the other hand wanted to maintain the solidarity of the state. Asante was a military confederacy which could survive only if its military strength was preserved. He had brought back Juaben to its traditional allegiance and he next decided to reconquer Adansi, whose king Kwadwo Oben died in 1875. The Adansis in their attempt to remain independent of Asante control appealed to the British for protection. The Asantehene was told to respect the

Treaty of Fomena and he quickly stopped his military preparations.

The Asante could not keep the peace for long. Many of the chiefs were determined to regain the territorial strength and military glory of the Confederation. The Asante had not accepted defeat and continued to prepare for a final conflict with the British. When a refugee of the royal family of Gyaman called Owusu Tasiamandi fled to the Protectorate, the Asantehene sent messengers to bring him back. The British Governor refused to give up Tasiamandi. Many of the Asante chiefs wanted some drastic action taken, but the Asantehene kept the peace as he had done in the Adansi issue. He promised to pay an indemnity of about 560 kg of gold because he had received information of the vast military preparations on the coast. This was another Asante national humiliation. The war party became impatient. They tried to bring back Banda and Gyaman under Asante rule but were stopped by the Asantehene's submission to the arbitrations of the British Governor. British power was on the increase while that of Asante was in decline. People became disgusted with the 'peace at any price' methods of Mensa Bonsu and this coupled with his licentious temperament brought his deposition in February 1883. The war party was now in control of the state. But there for the moment we must leave the Asante story and look at the situation in some of the states to the east of the Volta.

The Yoruba States

The most important event in the West African forest kingdoms during the early nineteenth century was the collapse of the Oyo Kingdom. Its capital Oyo (now known as 'Old Oyo'), lying in the savannah, was favourably located for trade with the Hausa states. However, it was faced by the rising Nupe Kingdom and for some time Oyo kings were forced to find refuge in Borgu. A northerly frontier town was founded. This was Ilorin which became a garrison town in which the chief military officer of the kingdom, the *Are-ona-Kakanfo*, was stationed. In the east, the Kingdom continued to accept the river Ottun as its boundary with Benin, while westwards the kings of Oyo regarded the Allada king as a subordinate. Badagry was an Oyo port. When, therefore, Gezo, King of Dahomey, conquered Allada and began to expand his frontiers he refused to pay tribute to Oyo. Under the efficient financial administration of Da Souza, a European, trade increased and the coastal towns like Whydah began to do very well. The slave trade was very important to Dahomey and it has been calculated that during the reign of Gezo, the crown made as much as £60,000 a year from this trade alone. Da Souza became his financial adviser and customs agent at the port of Whydah with the title of Chacha. In 1818 Gezo declared Dahomey independent of Oyo.

The Dahomey capital, Abomey, became the centre of the political and ritual life of a community which was divided into three classes: the royals, the free citizens, and the slaves. The royals consisted of the descendants of the present and past kings of Dahomey who did no useful work and yet were maintained at the state's expense. The bulk of the people were free citizens who provided the state with civil, military and religious officials. Foreigners, such as Da Souza, could be recruited into the service of the state. The free citizens as well as the royals had slaves who did most of their work for them. Most of these slaves were foreigners as Dahomeyans could not be held as slaves. Those who became slaves because they were condemned for major crimes were sold and exported.

Since Whydah was the port with direct communication with the outside world, it had many markets which were supervised by the agents of the *Yovogan* (the port governor). It was easy from the proceeds of trade to know what amount each of the king's subjects, whether slave or free, should pay into the royal coffers. Taxes were fairly high; even one of Da Souza's slaves paid a large annual tax. This was a tax assessed on reputation, rank and income. Heavy duty was imposed on exports of palm oil and ivory and these were paid by the Dahomeyan merchants. All these dues were collected by the Yovogan, who was entitled to keep a proportion of all payments.

Da Souza became the middleman between Europeans and the Yovogan and between Europeans and King Gezo at a time when the British were trying to stop the slave trade. He did the supervision of trade for the Yovogan, while at the same time he gave personal advice to the King whom he supplied with European goods, especially firearms. In return for these services, he obtained trading privileges. Requests were made to him for goods and money during times of shortage. He died in May 1849.

Gezo, unlike the other rulers of the forest region, was the effective commander-in-chief of the armed forces even

Whydah, the sea port of Dahomey

though the actual direction of the campaigns was left to two important military officers, the *Migan* and the *Meu*. Gezo had usurped the throne, so needed a loyal bodyguard. He could not leave the whole military establishment in the hands of men who could not be trusted to defend him in time of need. This was why he reorganized the army, taking in more women than other kings had done. These were the famous Amazons who were led by military equivalents of the Migan and Meu, the She-migan or *Gundeme* and the She-meu or *Yewe*.

By the 1840s the Dahomey army was said to be 12,000 strong. Of this number 5,000 were women. There were 24,000 reserves who could be called up in an emergency. Muskets and cannons were provided and, without doubt, this was a fighting force sufficient to strike terror into the hearts of an enemy.

While King Gezo and his troops were raiding the towns eastwards and creating a vast kingdom which extended from Porto Novo and Savi in the east to Atakpame in the west, Dahomey was confronted by the rising power of Abeokuta. Under the leadership of Sodeke, the Egbas of Abeokuta were making a firm stand against the two Yoruba states of

Dahomey female soldiers

Ibadan and Ijebu. In the famous Owiwi war of 1832, the Egba, with the support of Ologun Adele of Lagos, had succeeded in routing Ijebu forces and thus opening a road to the port of Lagos which was becoming an important slave exporting centre. The Otta people who lived between Lagos and Abeokuta were defeated. The next Egba move was to attack and incorporate the Egbado towns into their kingdom in order to hold the Oyo caravan route to Badagry, a port that had become important to the Egba. Ijana and Ilaro were taken and the Egba moved westwards.

Sodeke took another step that was destined greatly to affect the history of the Bight of Benin: he invited missionaries and allowed the settlement of liberated slaves from Sierra Leone. The result was that Methodist and Anglican missionary societies set up churches in Abeokuta.

The growing power of the Egba and their alliance with the British greatly alarmed Gezo. In 1851 he sent an army of 12,000 under the leadership of General Akati to capture Abeokuta. Akati planned to surround the Abeokuta wall and take the town by storm but he met with fierce resistance from the Egba soldiers behind the walls. Then the front row of the Dahomeyan army foolishly tried to climb the walls. The attack was repulsed with heavy losses. In the ditches alone, the Egba counted about 1,200 dead bodies.

The Dahomey attack gave the missionaries an excuse for propaganda against both Dahomey and Lagos. The Church Missionary Society's African missionary, Samuel Crowther, made a personal appeal in Britain. As a result arms worth about £300 were given to the Egba and Commander Forbes, a British naval officer, was sent to Abeokuta to teach the people the best means of defence. Already John Beecroft, the British Consul for the Bights of Benin and Biafra, had an excuse for attacking Lagos: in 1845 Kosoko had deposed his uncle, Akitoye, as King of Lagos. The ex-king had appealed to the British to recover his throne. Kosoko realized the danger he was in. He obtained aid from Brazilian merchants for the defence of his town. On 7 December 1851 in order to force the kings of Porto Novo, Dahomey and Lagos to sign an anti-slave treaty, British warships commanded by Commodore Bruce blockaded all ports and places along the Bight of Benin except Badagry. Then Beecroft sent word to Kosoko that he was coming to Lagos for a conference with him. He thought that a show of force would make the king change his mind. He was wrong: Kosoko fought back. In the first encounter, the British navy suffered a set-back and was forced to withdraw. However, a strong British military and naval offensive soon conquered Lagos and on New Year's Day 1852 Akitoye was reinstated and signed an anti-slave trade treaty.

In 1853 a British Consul was appointed in Lagos. Missionaries began their activities and immigrants from Sierra Leone found their way to the town. In that year King Akitoye died and was succeeded by his son Dosunmu. Regarded as a British tool by many of his subjects, Dosunmu found it difficult to exercise any real authority. In 1854 the British agreed to recognize Kosoko as ruler of Palma and Lekki in return for his abandonment to all claims over Lagos. British trade increased in Lagos. It was soon obvious that Dosunmu had neither the power nor the will to protect British trade. He and his chiefs in fact opposed British control of affairs and the granting of land to foreigners, especially Sierra Leone immigrants. In September 1861 the British dropped the pretence of indirect rule in Lagos and they forced Dosunmu to sign a treaty of session granting the island of Lagos to the British Crown.

The British now had the problem of administering their new possession. There were still many people in England who were against the government's expansionist policy. Then there were also the problems of Lagos itself which was to be a new experiment in colonial administration. Domestic slavery still existed and had to be discouraged. The frontiers of Lagos were undefined. One of the reasons for the acquisition was French enterprise at Porto Novo, so it was necessary for the British to try to insulate Lagos from French penetration. At the same time the Yoruba wars in the interior posed their problems. Trade could only be carried on in an atmosphere of calm in the interior. There were people like the explorers Dr William Baikie and John Glover who had hoped that Lagos would become a great British base of operations for the interior. This meant that Lagos was to be the beginning of further

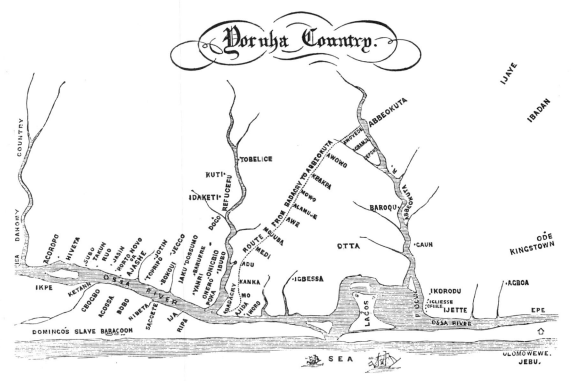

Nineteenth-century map of Yoruba country

expansion. The British administration also had to find out how best to incorporate the native institutions into the new government. With all these problems went also that of finance. The expense of administering this small but undefined territory was rising each year.

The men who had to face these problems were Governor Henry Stanhope Freeman and his assistant, Lieutenant John Hawley Glover. Slavery was dealt with by a series of compromise measures which ended the worse excesses of the system while avoiding the social chaos which would have resulted from total abolition. From the beginning both Freeman and Glover had to study the state of the finances. Since the cost of administration was rising, opportunities for more revenue had to be sought. There was only one obvious way of doing this; customs duties had to be imposed. But to what extent could they be imposed effectively? If the new tax was imposed in Lagos alone, the traders from the interior would use nearby ports. In order to obtain revenue Freeman annexed Palma and Lekki from Kosoko, as well as Badagry, and imposed a two per cent customs duty at Lagos, Palma, Badagry and Lekki. In order to guarantee trade with Lagos, the administration had to go to the length of granting protection to Ikorodu and bombarding Epe, in 1863. The ruler of Epe, Posso, suspicious of British intentions once Lagos had been taken over, may have been horrified by the secession of Palma and Lekki, so he got the support of Kosoko's followers in order to maintain a strong front against the British danger. In this, however, he fought a losing battle. The bombardment of his town was effective.

The extension of British jurisdiction to cover Epe, Lekki and Palma made the French realize that the British were trying to squeeze them out of the Bight of Benin and intended to annex the coast from Lagos to Cape St Paul. In July 1862 the agents of the French firm Victor Regis were able to get the ruler of Porto Novo to place his territory under French protection for fear of British invasion. The rivalry continued: the French extended their sphere to Appa to the west of Badagry; the British responded by incorporating Addo, Ipokid, Okeodan and Badagry. On 1 August 1863 the two European governments signed a convention to stabilize the situation at the coast. It lapsed when the French were forced by the local ruler to abandon Porto Novo. Glover now tried to take over the area from the French but he received no official backing. Indeed, he was ordered to confine his activities to Lagos and Iddo islands, the towns of Badagry, Palma and Lekki. He should maintain friendly relations with Okeodan, Addo and Igbessa but was not to seek protectorates over these territories.

Difficulties were, however, arising which were to have far-reaching effects on the administration of Lagos. The Yoruba wars of the interior had begun again. The trouble started in 1858, when Oba Atiba, the Alafin of Oyo, died. He was succeeded by his son, the Aremu Adelu. This was unconstitutional because the Aremu was expected to die with his father; so the Are of Ijaye refused to recognize him as Alafin. The traditional hostility between Ibadan, which had the Bashorun or Prime Minister, and Ijaye, which had the Are-ona-Kakanfo or Commander-in-Chief, made Ibadan support the Alafin. The immediate cause of the war was the refusal of a widow of Sake to pay tax to the Are, who sent for her to be arrested. She was defended by the Alafin who got the support of Ibadan. Ijaye was supported by Abeokuta. The Ijebu states, probably jealous of the new strategic position of Abeokuta, sided with Oyo and Ibadan and thus created a road for Ibadan to Lagos. Ibadan also sought the aid of Dahomey for this important encounter.

But there were deeper reasons for the civil war and they were so strong that the conflict lasted for nearly fifty years. Ibadan was ambitious to lead a new Yoruba empire. Ijaye resented the growing power of Ibadan. The Egba wanted to maintain their independence and their control of trade routes to the coast. The British needed peace in the interior if their new coastal colony was to prosper. Dahomey and Ilorin were always ready to intervene to extend their own territory. The situation was so complicated and the feelings on all sides so bitter that Consul Brand's attempt to make peace in 1860 failed. When Dahomey entered the war the British bombarded Porto Novo and planned to give military aid to the Egba. But at the same time British merchants were smuggling arms to Ibadan. With this help Ibadan was able to conquer Ijaye, in 1862. Ijaye's friends, the Egba, now turned against the British and their trading partners, the Ijebu.

In March 1865 Governor Glover intervened. He led an expedition into Egba territory and routed the Egba army before Ikorodu. This brought him immediate criticism from London, where the government complained that he had no reason to involve British men and money in 'native wars'. They ordered that the separate administration of Lagos should cease; it was to be administered from Sierre Leone as a first step to the restoration of independence.

But British withdrawal was no more possible here than on the Gold Coast. Trade could hardly expand unless there was peace. Once he had become committed and involved in the Yoruba war, Glover had to bring it to a satisfactory conclusion. Since the Egba were not cowed by their defeat this would be difficult. A group of educated Sierra Leone emigrants had formed the Egba United Board of Management in order to promote a European style African government in which both chiefs and educated Egba would be represented. This new move was headed by George W. Johnson who is generally known as Mr Secretary Johnson. Glover was intolerant of these self-appointed leaders of the Egba. The main reason for this was that in their attempt at increasing Egba revenues they had decided to establish customs posts for the collection of duties on articles between Lagos and Abeokuta. They were thus claiming sovereign rights which had to be respected by the Lagos colonial administration. This claim Glover was not prepared to accept. His intervention in their internal affairs annoyed the Egba and may have been one of the factors which contributed to the attack against Europeans (the Ifole) at Abeokuta on 13 October 1867, which was followed a year later by the expulsion of European merchants and missionaries. The whole Egba situation was further complicated by the death in 1868 of Regent Somoye, the Bashorun, and the succession dispute which followed. Sir Arthur Kennedy, the Governor of Sierra Leone, urged Glover, who was the administrator of Lagos, not to interfere.

But Glover was a determined imperialist. He believed it would be possible to turn Lagos into the main port of this part of Africa, handling a vastly increased amount of trade. In order to achieve this he had first to deal with the warlike surrounding states. First he tried, unsuccessfully, to open some of the trade routes by force. Having failed, he decided to attack the Egba source of arms, Porto Novo, and annex it. He placed an embargo on the arms trade with Abeokuta. He even attempted to close all the roads and forbid exports through Lagos. This roused the opposition of the British merchants, who complained about Glover to the Governor of Sierra Leone, who was already very concerned about the cost of Lagos politics. As a result, in 1870, Glover was sent home and thus was ended the period of unauthorized British expansion.

Meanwhile, the struggle in the interior continued. In 1877 Egba, Ijebu and Ilorin combined in an invasion of Ibadan and began another phase of the civil war which lasted for sixteen years.

Although Benin was in decline, it was still powerful enough to be respected. Like many of the West African states, Benin was weakened by succession disputes. In 1804, when Oba Obanosa died, there was a dispute between two claimants, Osemwede and Ogbebo. A bloody civil war followed which Ogbebo lost, but he did not want to be caught alive, so he hanged himself and burnt down the palace. The weakness in the capital brought revolt in the provinces. Osemwede, however, succeeded in bringing the various peoples under subjection. There was another succession dispute after the death of Oba Osemwede in 1848. At last Oba Adolo gained the upper hand but for a long time he was troubled by the raids of his rival's forces operating from Ishan. This was also the time when the rising power of Nupe, carrying the Fulani jihad southwards, and that of Ibadan, were beginning to be felt. The Niger-Ibo states were throwing off their allegiance, especially Abo and Onitsha which were growing as a result of the opening of the lower Niger to trade.

Benin was an inland kingdom with a port that had steadily declined in importance. Trade into Benin had to pass along the Benin River which was controlled by the Itsekiris of Warri who at the beginning of the nineteenth century were ruled by a powerful and tyrannical king, Olu Akengbuwa. Two ports had been opened by the Benin River for the collection of customs duties and there all European traders had to trade. Chief customs officials were appointed at Bobi and Eghoro and, in order to watch the traffic into the Benin port of Eghoro, the King built a small town called Reggio Town at the junction between the Ughoton Creek and the Benin River.

The frontiers of Warri and Benin were not well defined and commerce on the Benin River was so important to both that whenever a European merchant came, his wares were disputed by the two kingdoms. Warri did not have succession disputes

Ebony head of Oba of Benin

111

like Benin, but Olu Akengbuwa's harsh policies angered his chiefs. One of them, Uwangwe Uwakun, fled from the capital, Ode Itsekiri, to put himself under the protection of Oba Osemwede who later helped in installing him in Jakpa on the Benin River. Other chiefs left the capital also and settled along the Benin River where they founded small city-states.

Olu Akengbuwa gave one of his daughters to the King of Bonny in marriage, and the treaty led to an increase of trade between the two states. The dispute between him and Oba Osemwede continued. Although he had many children, at the end of his reign there was so much ritual murder involving his sons that it was difficult to decide who should succeed him. Constitutionally, his eldest son should have been king after him. Many of the chiefs were against his children because they feared a continuance of Akengbuwa's policies. Akengbuwa died in June 1848 and his two possible successors died within a few weeks. Thus the two great kings of Warri and Benin died in the same year.

The Niger Delta states

The slave trade had led to the migration of inland peoples to the Niger Delta. The competition for trade was keen and involved them in wars. Despite their different racial origins they all developed the same kind of state. The capital was at the mouth of a river and the state controlled a strip of territory running inland along the river. Canoes patrolled the rivers

Creek leading to Big Warri, capital of Warri Kingdom

bringing slaves and oil down from inland markets. These goods were then sold by the rulers and leading men to foreign traders. Each state was ruled by the 'House' system. These Houses were political as well as economic units each comprising a head, his children, his extended family and his slaves. The House had its own plantations worked by slaves. It had its trade connections. The status of the House depended on the ability of the head to bargain with the Europeans. The king of the state was always the head of one of the great Houses.

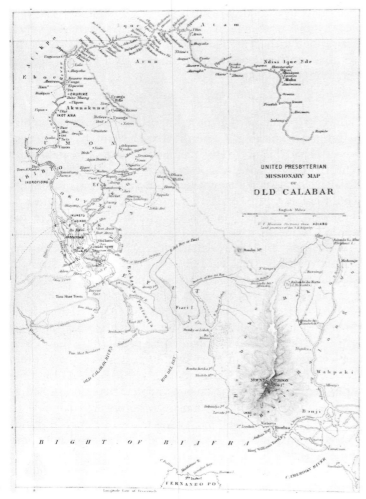

Nineteenth-century map of Old Calabar

The same kind of administration existed in all the Niger Delta states. These were Elem Kalabari, which controlled the trade of the river Sambreiro; Brass, which controlled the trade of the Middleton and other rivers; Bonny on the river Bonny; and Calabar on the Cross River. Trade was the major concern of these city-states. Although formerly noble birth had been essential for election to the headship of a House in Bonny and Brass, this was not always the case in the nineteenth century. In Elem Kalabari and Calabar many of the minor Houses had slaves who usurped power. The main reason for this change was that the nobles had tended to leave their trade in the hands of their slaves who gradually became wealthy and were able to buy their own trade canoes which were armed with cannons. The ability to trade and protect the members of the House against those of rival Houses became important qualifications.

Bonny

Bonny had become the most important commercial centre before the beginning of the nineteenth century. In fact, so powerful had this city-state become by the end of the eighteenth century, that the King was able (*c*. 1790) to attack and destroy Kalabari on two occasions. He compelled the inhabitants who were not put to death to take their merchandise to Bonny for sale. The Bonny King who did this was Perekule whom Europeans have called Pepple, a name that has stuck to the family, and the Kalabari ruler who was killed during the last raid was Amakiri. The result of this trial of strength was that Bonny was able to export as many as 20,000 slaves a year, about 16,000 of these slaves coming from the heart of Iboland where there were organized slave fairs. Bonny trade canoes, each of which was capable of carrying 120 persons, sailed for these fairs accompanied by drummers. Bonny war canoes were capable of carrying 140 persons each and often had a gun of large calibre mounted on the bow. At the time King Pepple died, it has been estimated that Bonny had as many as 20,000 inhabitants most of whom were traders.

Every favourable opportunity was taken by Pepple's grandson, King Opubo (1792–1830), to exhibit his wealth in pomp and pageantry. Trading relations with other states were made through dynastic marriages which provided the setting for the exhibition of wealth. Most of the King's wealth was derived from the slave trade. A great quantity of palm oil could be

A chief in his state canoe in Bonny during the nineteenth century

obtained in Bonny and the town was also one of the centres of salt production in the Niger Delta. Europeans paid for slaves, salt and palm oil with guns, powder, Manchester cloths, iron, crockery and other smaller articles.

Much of the trading was done, not by individuals, but by the House, the head of which had to ensure that there were enough large fleets of war and trade canoes. Since he was in charge of the finances and property of the House, he organized all its trade. He obtained credit in the form of an advance of goods which were sent for sale in the interior. The proceeds were used for buying the slaves, palm oil and ivory which the European merchants wanted. Houses could become bankrupt through mismanagement and the European merchants devised a system of certificates to ascertain the credit-worthiness of the heads of the Houses. These certificates the Bonny merchants always carried in wooden boxes hung round their necks, lest they should be lost in the event of the canoes capsizing. They were shown to captains with whom the Bonny traders wished to do business. As soon as the European merchants were satisfied with the credentials, they gave goods on trust. During the reign of Opubo, the palm oil which filled each cask did not cost more than two pounds in Bonny, but sold for ten times that in Britain to which about eight to ten thousand tons were sent annually from Bonny alone.

Although the export of palm oil was increasing, both King Opubo and his rivals preferred the trade in slaves to that of palm oil because trade in palm oil required much more capital than the trade in slaves. Huge trading canoes for transporting the oil to the coast had to be bought and manned by slaves. War canoes were also needed to protect the trade canoes. Palm oil trade was rather cumbersome as it involved the loading and unloading of casks. The Bonny people had made a lot of money from the slave trade and did not want to stop it. Opubo strongly resented British activity against the slave trade. He claimed that Bonny as an independent state was fit to dispose of her criminals and her prisoners of war as she thought fit and only people with ambitions to take over the jurisdiction of other states would behave in the way Britain was behaving.

Opubo was succeeded by a minor. His son Dappa Pepple was only thirteen years old at the time of the King's death in 1830. A minor could not rule Bonny, so a regent was appointed to take charge of the state until the boy came of age. Surprisingly, the next man in rank to this minor was an Ibo slave, Chief Madu, who had become the head of the House and who by his clever commercial policy had brought wealth to the House. Madu died in 1833 when the young prince was still a minor and he was succeeded by his son Alali.

Did Alali want to usurp the throne of Bonny which the constitution of the state denied to a slave? Whether he wanted to or not, his actions suggested it and Prince Dappa feared it. Alali treated the Prince with contempt. Soon he was involved in a conflict with the British over the slave trade. Britain had signed a treaty with Spain in 1835 which gave the British the right to search Spanish vessels for slaves and equipment used for the slave trade. When four Spanish ships were found in the port of Bonny, collecting slaves, without seeking the permission of the Bonny authorities, the British navy seized the Spanish ships. Alali regarded this action in Bonny's territorial waters as illegal, since Bonny was not a party to the

Anglo-Spanish treaty. Orders were given at once for the arrest of British merchants trading in Bonny. The British navy then intervened with the threat of force and Alali, under duress, signed a treaty, released the prisoners and guaranteed protection to British merchants.

Understandably, such a treaty signed with the naval guns pointing at the town of Bonny was unacceptable since Alali's claim that his policy was to protect the shipping of all foreign nationalities trading in his country was a legitimate one. The supposed treaty was not worth the paper on which it was signed. The slave trade continued in earnest.

In 1835 Dappa Pepple had come of age and was duly crowned even though the real power in the state was still held by Alali. The British action in 1836 drove Alali, who wanted to combine the slave trade with the trade in palm oil, into closer alliance with the Portuguese and the Spaniards. British merchants complained of ill-treatment. There is no doubt that Alali showed a commercial preference for other foreign traders rather than the British. Dappa Pepple saw in the continuing clash between the Regent and the British, an opportunity to overthrow his rival, so he intrigued with the British naval officers who overthrew the Regent in 1837. Dappa Pepple did not realize that by allowing a foreign power to interfere in the domestic affairs of his country, he was signing the death-warrant of independent Bonny.

It would be wrong to think that by his action Dappa Pepple had sold his country to the British. What he wanted was to adopt diplomatic tactics to seize power and bring back to the monarchy its former prestige. In this he was not successful. As the price of their support the British exacted from Bonny a treaty abolishing the slave trade.

But Dappa Pepple's position was far from secure. He dared not upset his British supporters, and his rival, Alali, continued to prosper. He maintained his authority until 1854. Then Alali took advantage of a dispute between the King and some British merchants to demand Dappa's deposition. He was successful and for several years the King and his family lived in exile in England. Even when, in 1861, Dappa was allowed to return he had little real authority. Power rested with the British Consul and the Bonny citizens he chose to support. After Dappa Pepple's death (1866) George Pepple became king.

Opobo

King Jaja of Opobo

Kalabari

At the same time Alali died and was succeeded by another Ibo slave, Jaja, as head of the Anna Pepple House. Jaja was an extremely shrewd trader and judge of men. When, in 1868, rivalry between the Manilla Pepple and Anna Pepple Houses flared up into armed conflict, he made a momentous decision. He decided to leave Bonny. As he was not a Pepple, his chances of becoming King of Bonny were remote. At a time when ships were being built to sail in shallow waters, there was no need for European vessels to stop at Bonny. He decided that it would be better for him to go and found a kingdom for himself near to the markets so that he could divert the trade from its traditional channels. He therefore established a new town, Opobo. Oko Jumbo, the head of Manilla Pepple House, made every attempt to bring him back to Bonny, but he was too late. Jaja had been able to persuade some of the European traders to shift their trading business from Bonny to his own territory. Jaja concentrated his activities on the Eboe and Qua markets while Oko Jumbo in Bonny now had the Okrika markets. The Anna Pepple House then settled in Opobo leaving Bonny to the Manilla House, and Opobo under Jaja replaced Bonny as the centre of trade along the Oil Rivers.

While the conflict in the canoe Houses in Bonny had resulted in the evacuation of one of them, in Kalabari, George Amakiri of Amakiri House was successful in establishing a position of pre-eminence in the Kalabari state over Will Braid and the Barboy House. Will Braid had tried to follow Jaja's example by taking a position in a fortified site at Ewofa in the Okpo-mbu-tolu area but he had not the power of Jaja and was forced to sign an agreement to return to Kalabari. But even then there was no peace. At last Will Braid moved and settled in Bakana. The Barboy group which did not support him founded Abonnema while the Amakari group settled first at Degema and later at Buguma. For a long time Bonny and Kalabari fought a series of wars over the acquisition of markets. European traders moved as members of the different towns also moved. The position of the European merchants became exceedingly difficult as matters were so unsettled. It was only with difficulty that the Consul was able to allocate spheres of activity to the different warring groups, and this was the time when French and German activity in the area was increasing. A halt would have to be put to these skirmishes if each group was not to gain the support of a different European power which would extort trading concessions from its ally.

It was already too late to stop the extension of British power. Britain was gradually consolidating her position in many areas of present-day Nigeria. Her commerce had expanded to such an extent on the Niger and in the Bight of Biafra that it was estimated that it had exceeded one million pounds annually. British commercial enterprise continued even when the government decided, because of the high cost involved, to stop naval escorts for vessels that sailed on the Niger. Occasional naval expeditions were in fact launched on the lower Niger to support the merchants and control native rulers who were forced to accept a virtual British monopoly of trade. In 1872 it was found necessary to transfer the British consulate from Fernando Po, which the Spaniards refused to sell, to Old Calabar, which now became the centre of British

Trading on the Niger

administration along the Bight of Biafra. The very fact that the consulate was brought to Old Calabar made it possible for the consuls to be around when minor reports came from the different states. This increased consular interference in native affairs. When the courts of equity were opened in Bonny, Kalabari and the other states, the only powers they had were to settle differences between the chiefs and the merchants. Gradually the function of the courts changed until they were exercising political authority over the kings who could not go to war without consulting the merchants in the courts. In 1873 the British regularized the sanctions of the courts by an Order in Council which empowered the Consul to inflict fines of up to £200 or twenty-one days imprisonment. The Consul also now had the power to banish any African rulers who went against the conventions of trade which they had signed. These powers were used by the consuls from time to time.

Peoples of South and Central Africa   Chapter 5

In the vast area south of the Congo forest three important events dominated the years 1800 to 1880, the Mfecane, the decline of the Lunda empires, and the spread of European settlement from the south.

Mfecane is an Nguni word meaning 'the time of trouble' or 'havoc' and it describes an upheaval that began among the Nguni peoples of south-east Africa and spread over about one fifth of the continent between 1820 and 1850. Its basic cause was over-population in the south-east. As we have seen, one characteristic of Bantu migration had been a south-eastward drift from the Congo watershed. Wave upon wave of migrants had filled up the area on both sides of the Drakensbergs with Sotho and Nguni peoples. The southward move had been finally stopped by Europeans spreading north-eastwards from the Cape. The result was increasing competition for control of land and water supplies. Then, in the early years of the nineteenth century a remarkable man, Shaka, the leader of a tiny Nguni group, the Zulus, made his people into a great fighting force. He conquered his neighbours and extended his territory ever farther. Other Nguni and Sotho leaders either had to become Shaka's subjects or lead their people in search of new lands to conquer. Thus Zulu expansion led to a sequence of conquests which extended thousands of miles into central and eastern Africa. It is this upheaval that is known as the Mfecane.

The Mfecane

Shaka, King of the Zulus

Shaka and the Zulus

Shaka was born about 1787, an illegitimate son of the Zulu Chief Senzengakona. The Zulus at this time numbered only about 2,000 people and they soon came under the control of the powerful Mthethwa ruler, Dingiswayo. Shaka and his mother were rejected by Senzengakona and the young man became one of Dingiswayo's warriors. He soon distinguished himself

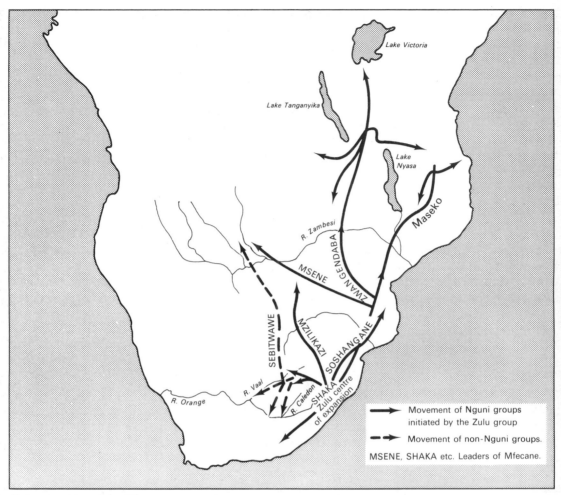

Zulu expansion and the Mfecane

as a brave and clever fighter and was made leader of a Mthethwa *impi* (regiment). Shaka won the friendship of Dingiswayo, who allowed him to return home after the death of his father, overthrow his half-brother and make himself the Zulu chief. Now he began to put into practice his own ideas about the training of soldiers and the waging of war. Each *impi* was trained, in its own separate camp, to high standards of bravery and loyalty. Shaka introduced the short, stabbing spear instead of the throwing spear and expected his men to engage in fierce, hand-to-hand fighting. He used spies and smoke-signals. In war he was a master of surprise, winning battle after battle by new and unexpected manoeuvres. He was ruthless in his dealings with conquered peoples, murdering their leaders, making them obey him completely and placing his own men as chiefs over them. In 1816 or 1817 Dingiswayo was killed in battle. Shaka murdered his successor and became ruler of the Mthethwa Empire, which he transformed into a Zulu Empire by forcing Dingiswayo's allies to swear support to himself and by placing his own supporters in all positions of authority.

The new state began to expand quickly. By 1820 Shaka controlled all the land east of the Drakensbergs between the Tugela and Pongola rivers. His armies raided still farther afield in search of cattle. The results were terrible. Groups of homeless people wandered the countryside. Some were taken into other communities. Some gave their allegiance to war leaders—dispossessed chiefs and princes who built up personal followings and trekked away from their conquered homelands in search of fresh territory. We are going to study the careers of seven of these leaders.

Zwangendaba and the Nguni

Zwangendaba was an officer in the army of Zwide, a powerful northern Nguni chief. In 1819 Shaka defeated Zwide and the latter's empire collapsed. Zwangendaba fled northwards with some of his warriors. For a while he lived with his people (who gradually increased in number as refugees from the south joined them) north of Delagoa Bay. In 1831 he was driven out by Soshangane, another Mfecane leader. He led his people and their herds north-westwards into the ancient empire of the Rozwi, whose capital was at Great Zimbabwe. Zwangendaba's followers were known as Nguni, though as time went by so many captives were added to Zwangendaba's horde that only a minority were real Ngunis. Peace and prosperity based on the gold trade reigned throughout the Rozwi Empire. The Shona were unused to the new style of warfare. They were swiftly defeated by the Nguni, and their leader, the Changamire, was killed. Great Zimbabwe and other towns were laid in ruins and one of Africa's great civilizations almost completely disappeared. Having completed their devastation, the Nguni moved northwards, crossing the Zambezi in 1835.

In what is now Zambia, Zwangendaba encountered peoples such as Kazembe's East Lunda and the Bemba, who could not be so easily conquered. He therefore concentrated

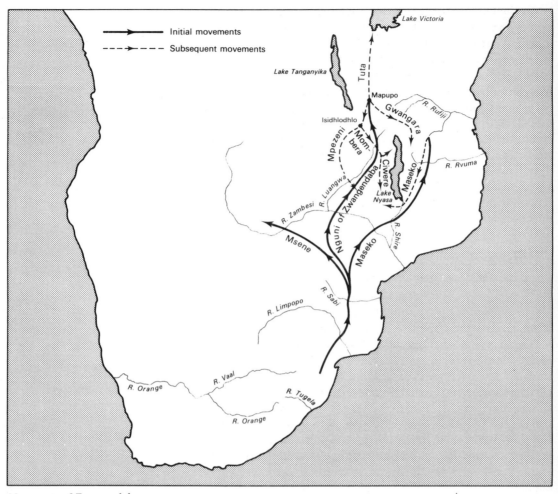

Movements of Zwangendaba

on attacking smaller and less warlike groups, and moving still northwards. At last he reached Ufipa between Lake Tanganyika and Lake Rukwa. Here, after defeating the Fipa, Zwangendaba died some time between 1845 and 1849.

The Nguni now split into five groups. Two of them, the Tuta and the Gwangwara, will be dealt with in chapter six. The others turned southwards and conquered parts of what are now eastern Zambia and Malawi. Mpezeni, one of Zwangendaba's sons, established control over a large part of the Nsenga who lived to the north of the middle Zambezi, where he continued to rule until the last years of the nineteenth century. Another of Zwangendaba's sons, Mombera, overthrew the Kamanga kingdom of northern Malawi (*c*.1855). There he settled but his power declined over the years as various sections of his people attempted to break away from Nguni control. The third group was led by Ciwere Ndhlovu, a Nsenga warrior who had been highly favoured by Zwangendaba. He led his followers to the southern end of Lake Nyasa. Here he established control of the Cewa living in the area. The wanderings of Zwangendaba and his successors form one of the more remarkable episodes in the whole history of Africa. The wanderings and conquests of the Nguni took some of them over five thousand kilometres before they reached new lands where they could settle.

Before we go on to discuss the career of the next great Mfecane leader we must say something about another Nguni group, the Maseko. Like Zwangendaba's people, they too moved northwards out of Nguniland and stayed for a while in Soshangane's territory. Like Zwangendaba's Nguni, they too were driven out in the early 1830s. Led by Ngware they crossed the lower Zambezi and entered the Shiré valley. Having terrorized the people of this area, they moved northwards passing to the east of Lake Nyasa. They battled with several Yao and Makua groups and finally settled around Songea in southern Tanzania in the early 1840s. A few years later they were joined by the Gwangwara from Ufipa. But the two groups fought and some of the Gwangwara murdered the new Maseko leader, Maputo. Most of the Maseko fled southwards, once more devastating the area east of Lake Nyasa. In the 1860s they settled in the Shiré Highlands. For many years they terrorized the settlements of this area and disrupted the trade of the lower Zambezi.

The Maseko Nguni

Soshangane's people are known as the Shangana, although the state founded by this great leader is called the Gaza Empire. As we have seen Soshangane settled to the north of Delagoa Bay in the 1820s. The ranks of his followers were swelled by refugees fleeing from the Zulus and it was the need for more territory that caused Soshangane to force out the Nguni. At the same time Soshangane was easily conquering

Soshangane and the Gaza Empire

the small decentralized societies of what is now Mozambique and overrunning the eastern parts of the Rozwi Empire. In 1833 he attacked the Portuguese town of Laurenço Marques. The following year he defeated a Portuguese army near Inhambane. In 1836 he destroyed the Sofala garrison and followed this up by bringing the Zambezi trading posts of Sena and Tete under his control. He controlled the rich trading life of this part of east-central Africa and his empire stretched from the Zambezi to the Limpopo. After Soshangane's death in the late 1850s the empire declined. The chief's successor, Mawewe, was deposed by another son, Mzila. Mawewe gained the help of the Swazi in a bid to regain the throne while Mzila employed Portuguese forces. Civil war and foreign interference continued for many years, and

Dance of Zulus collecting tribute from Portuguese

though Mzila continued to reign until his death in 1855 his land was not the strong, united empire he had inherited from his father.

Mzilikazi has gained the reputation of being the most ruthless and tyrannical of all the Mfecane leaders. He began his career as leader of one of Shaka's *impis* but in 1822 he quarrelled with his overlord and had to flee from Shaka's wrath. He took with

Mzilikazi and the Ndebele

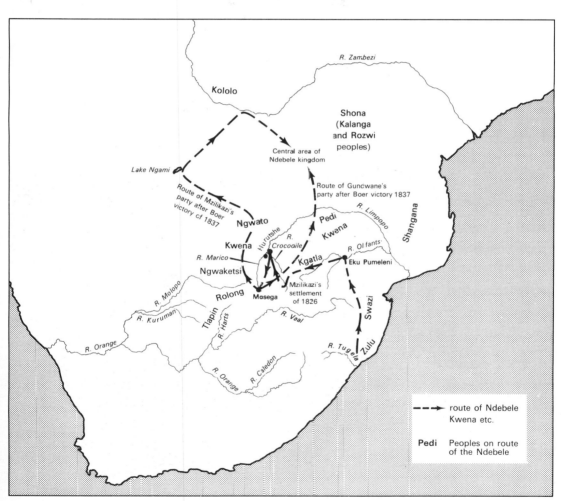

Wanderings of the Ndebele

him two or three hundred warriors and moved into the eastern Transvaal. By conquest and by giving refuge to others fleeing from the Zulus, Mzilikazi soon built up a large following of Nguni and Sotho people, who came to be known as Ndebele. But he was always having to move further and further in order to stay out of range of the Zulus. In 1832 the Ndebele settled near the source of the Marico and soon dominated some 80,000 square kilometres of the Transvaal. Four years later Boer farmers trekking inland from the Cape made alliances with some of Mzilikazi's enemies in the hope of driving the Ndebele out and taking their grazing lands. Mzilikazi struck the first blow, defeating the invaders at the battle of Vegkop (October 1836) and capturing their sheep and cattle. The following year the Boers struck back. In two battles at Maseko and by the Marico river, they inflicted heavy losses on the Ndebele. These defeats and fresh Zulu raids forced Mzilikazi to move again.

The Ndebele moved northwards and eventually settled in the region round modern Bulawayo in what had been the heart of the Rozwi Empire. Mzilikazi's warriors conquered

Mzilikazi receiving successful lion hunters

the peoples of the area, which came to be known as Matabeleland. The Ndebele's *impis* raided over a wide area and soon Mzilikazi ruled over a large territory between the Limpopo and the Zambezi, bordered only by the more powerful Boer and Griqua states, the Gaza Empire and the Kololo Empire. The Ndebele were always greatly feared but they became less warlike with the passing of time. Trade and agriculture flourished. European explorers and missionaries were welcomed. Many of them met and were impressed by Mzilikazi and were protected while in his territory. This remarkable leader died, an old man of more than seventy, in 1868.

The King's death was followed by a period of succession disputes and civil war. Eventually Lobengula won his father's throne. He reunited his people and ruled in peace for some years. He had to face the problem of increasing European interest in central Africa. More and more traders, missionaries and hunters came to his land and, though he continued his father's policy of hospitality, he grew more and more anxious about the real intentions of the white men.

Another remarkable Mfecane leader was Sebitwane. He belonged to a Sotho group called the Fokeng who lived west of the Drakensbergs. In 1822 his people were forced out of their homeland and Sebitwane led one of the groups which fled northwards across the Vaal. The Kololo, as the group came to be called, soon conflicted with Griqua and Ndebele forces and wandered back and forth for many years in an unsuccessful search for new lands. They journeyed via the Kalahari desert and Lake Ngami to the Zambezi. They crossed, and settled for a while near the river Kafue. Then they were challenged by an Ndebele force and Sebitwane decided to move again. Now he attacked the powerful Lozi kingdom which occupied the Barotseland flood plain. Here Sebitwane showed his great military skill. The Lozi expected to trap and destroy the Kololo in the low-lying, waterlogged land, but Sebitwane lured them away from their boats and it was their army that was destroyed. Eventually the Kololo were able to settle in a fertile land.

Sebitwane made a point of encouraging good relations between his people and the conquered Lozi. Peace and security settled on the land under his wise leadership. Two major Ndebele raids were driven off in the 1840s and thereafter

Sebitwane and the Kololo

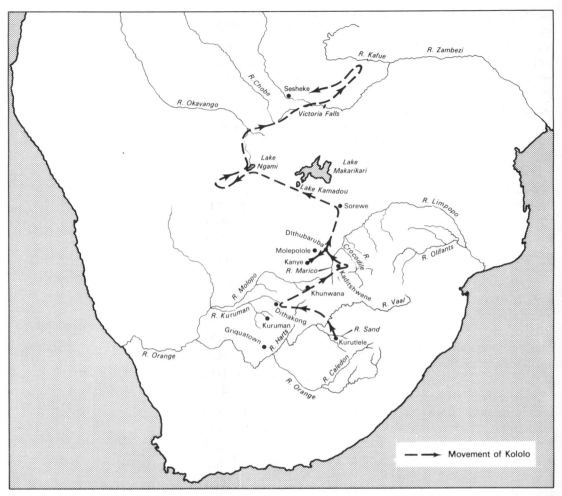

Wanderings of the Kololo

Mzilikazi ceased to trouble his old enemy. In 1851 Sebitwane received a visit from the most famous of all European explorers, David Livingstone, who later described him as 'decidedly the best specimen of a native chief I ever met'. Sebitwane died during the missionary's visit to his capital. Wise government died with him. His successor, Sekeletu, turned against the Lozi section of the population. In 1860 many Lozi left the kingdom to join their royal family in exile. Meanwhile, the Kololo were seriously weakened and their numbers reduced by malaria, a disease which flourished in the marshy lowlands. After Sekeletu's death in 1865 the Kololo were split by a succession dispute. The Lozi seized their opportunity. Under the leadership of their king, Sepopa, they invaded and reconquered Barotseland. Thousands of Kololo were massacred, many more were dispersed and Sebitwane's empire disappeared without trace. However, a small Kololo state did survive on the banks of the Shiré (in what is now southern Malawi). During his visit to Sebitwane Dr Livingstone hired some porters to assist him on his exploration of the Zambezi. In 1860 sixteen of these men decided to stay in the Shiré valley. They married local women and became the leaders of a small but powerful community which played an important part in the history of the region.

There were other great leaders whose wanderings did not take them as far as the warlords we have already considered. Such a man was Moshweshwe, the founder of modern Lesotho. When the Zulu storm burst, Moshweshwe was a young warrior, the son of a headman in the upper Caledon region. He was already famed for his bravery and wisdom, so that he was an obvious leader for many of the dispossessed Sotho of the early 1820s. Instead of wandering hundreds of miles in search of easy conquest and fertile land, Moshweshwe led his people into the mountains and at Thaba Bosiu found an impregnable natural fortress. By wise diplomacy rather than by warfare Moshweshwe extended his rule over neighbouring peoples and welded them into a nation which became known as the Basuto. When more powerful groups attacked his subjects he withdrew to Thaba Bosiu where they were safe. The hill fortress was never conquered; even raids by the mighty Zulus and Ndebele were driven off. Moshweshwe's wisdom is legendary. One example of it can be quoted. In 1831 the Basuto stronghold was attacked by the Ndebele. The invaders were successfully driven off. As they retreated Moshweshwe sent men after them with a present of cattle and the following message: 'Our master assumes that you must have been hungry to have attacked his people. He sends you these cattle so that you may eat and go in peace.' The Ndebele never raided Basutoland again.

Moshweshwe and the Basuto

Statue of Moshweshwe

Thaba Bosiu, the stronghold of Moshweshwe in 1834

By this time Moshweshwe had become the most important man in the area between the Caledon and Orange rivers. Soon he had to deal not only with brother African rulers but immigrant Europeans. To the newcomers he behaved with hospitality and wisdom. In 1833 he allowed Christian missionaries to begin work among his people. In 1835 he granted temporary grazing rights in his land to Boers trekking northwards. This, as we shall see later in this chapter, involved him and his people in a long conflict with the British and the Boers which ended in 1884 with Basutoland becoming a British colony.

Sobhuza and the Swazi

The last Mfecane leader we shall consider is Sobhuza, founder of Swaziland. In about 1815 he inherited a small northern Nguni chieftaincy which lay right in the path of Zulu expansion. In order to protect his people against more powerful neighbours Sobhuza expanded his state by conquest and reorganized his army. But this did not save him from serious defeats at the hands of his enemies. In 1817 he led his people into the mountains beyond the Pongolo river and there established a stronghold similar to Moshweshwe's. Many refugees fled to him for protection, and from these mixed origins was created the Swazi nation, which took its name from Sobhuza's successor, Mswazi (1836–75). By the middle

132

of the century the Swazi had become one of the most powerful Bantu groups in southern Africa. They were able, as we
have seen, to interfere in the affairs of the Gaza Empire. They
forced the Portuguese of southern Mozambique to respect
them. They allied with the trek Boers who began arriving in
the area in about 1845. In 1875 Mswazi's death was followed
by a succession dispute and from about this time British and
Boer agents began to compete for control of Swaziland.

Until the middle years of the nineteenth century the grasslands
to the south of the Congo forest continued to be dominated by
the two great Lunda states: the Lunda Empire of Mwata
Yamvo and the East Lunda Empire of Mwata Kazembe. Then,
in the next thirty years, these states collapsed completely.
There were three main reasons for this: succession disputes,
the emergence of powerful neighbours and the growth of
trans-continental trade. The last two reasons were inter-
woven, for it was largely as a result of commercial development
that powerful new states appeared.

The decline of the Lunda Empires

For almost a century the Lunda Empire had the advantage of
having only two rulers. Yaav ya Mbany reigned from 1760 to
1810 and Naweej II from 1810 to 1852. Both were strong and
ruthless tyrants. They successfully enforced the obedience of
their own people and of subject states. Their armies raided over
a wide area. During the reign of Naweej II, Imbangala and
Ovimbundu traders made frequent visits to the Lunda capital,
bringing firearms in exchange for ivory and slaves (Naweej
gave the traders permission to raid for slaves in parts of his
empire, and this made him very unpopular with many of his
own people).

Mwata Yamvo's Empire

Meanwhile changing trade patterns further west were creating new political and military forces. The quest for ivory and
slaves for the Portuguese market carried the leading Angolan
traders—the Imbangala and the Ovimbundu—ever further
into the continent. Rivalry between the two groups also
encouraged them to seek fresh sources far in the interior. By
the mid-century the Ovimbundu had gained the upper hand.
(About 1852 the first known trans-continental expedition was
completed by a party of Ovimbundu traders who reached
Mozambique.) At the same time Afro-Portuguese commerce

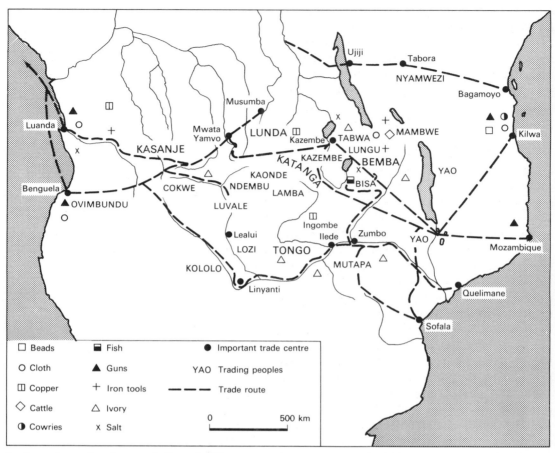

Lunda empires and trade routes in Central Africa

was affected by the declining demand for slaves. In 1822 the Portuguese coastal settlements were plunged by a revolution into eighteen years of political chaos. In the same year Brazil gained its independence. This meant that Angola no longer had a legal right to send slaves to Brazil (by an international agreement of 1815 Portugal limited the slave trade to her own territories). In 1836 Portugal declared the slave trade illegal. These facts, coupled with the mounting international anti-slavery pressure, led to a steady decline of dealings in human beings.

The Portuguese had to find new ways to make a profit out of Angola. They tried to develop new crops, with little success. They tried to compete directly with the Imbangala and take over some of their markets but were driven out by the African traders. They tried to increase their supplies of ivory (for which there was a growing world demand). It was in order to obtain more ivory for the Europeans that the Imbangala made a fateful alliance with the Cokwe. The Cokwe were a small community with a reputation as fine hunters. They made ideal trading partners for the Imbangala: in return for ivory they required guns, which the Imbangala could obtain from the Portuguese, and female slaves, which the Imbangala now found it difficult to dispose of elsewhere. So the Cokwe began to wander over a wide area far from their homeland. They came into contact—and conflict—with other people. They had guns, which made them a powerful enemy. By the acquisition of slave women—and children by these slave women—their numbers increased rapidly. All this amounted to the appearance of a large and warlike people. By the 1870s they had closed many trade routes to the Imbangala and Ovimbundu. They conquered most of the peoples who lived on their trade routes. By 1875 they were ready to challenge the mighty empire of Mwata Yamvo.

Cokwe ceremonial mask

The Lunda state was in no condition to offer serious resistance. For one thing its position in the very centre of the continent was a disadvantage. It lay at the end of trade routes from the east and west coasts so that its leaders could not easily acquire the guns and other important goods that brought wealth, power and prestige to African rulers. Better armed traders raided parts of the empire for slaves and ivory. As well as the Cokwe, Imbangala and Ovimbundu from the west there were Arabs from the north-east and Yeke and Bemba from the east. With strangers raiding freely in many areas it was difficult for the Mwata Yamvo to maintain the loyalty of his more distant subjects. Internal divisions further weakened the state. After the death of Naweej II rivals competed for the throne. Depositions, rebellions, assassinations and civil wars became common. Between 1857 and 1887 there were ten successive rulers.

In 1875 a contender for the Lunda throne, Mbumba, hired Cokwe warriors to help him overthrow Mbala II. From then on the Cokwe frequently interfered in Lunda affairs. In 1886 they drove the ruling Mwata Yamvo from his capital and sold the people of the town into slavery. For the next twelve years the empire was in Cokwe hands. When they were eventually overthrown their place was soon taken by the new colonial invaders. There were no more independent Mwata Yamvos.

Mwata Kazembe's Empire The situation was much the same in the East Lunda Empire. From 1805 to about 1850 the state was ruled by Kibangu Keleka, a powerful and enlightened king, who continued to expand the frontiers by conquest and who established important commercial links with the east coast. Kazembe dominated the Bisa who lived to the south-east of Lake Bangweulu. The Bisa were the most important link in Kazembe's trade chain. They brought imported goods from the peoples of the Zambezi valley and from the Yao who dominated most of the land east of Lake Nyasa. Kibangu Keleka was the first Kazembe to welcome Nyamwezi traders from beyond Lake Tanganyika and visitors from Angola. All these merchants brought him guns and other essentials in return for ivory and copper.

But Kazembe's trade routes could easily be disrupted. The expansion of the Bemba and the Nguni migrations seriously disturbed the area east of Kazembe's kingdom. By the middle of the century the Bemba had made themselves masters of the plateau. They controlled the Bisa, and goods that had once gone to Kazembe were now taken by the Chitimukulu (the Bemba paramount) and other Bemba chiefs. The Bemba also profited from trade with the Nyamwezi and the Arabs. We shall be thinking more about these merchants from the north-east later. They entered Central Africa in search of ivory, Katangan copper and slaves. Their routes to the south of Lake Tanganyika passed through Bemba territory and the Chitimukulu could impose his own terms on the passing caravans. He obtained guns from the traders which enabled him to fight off Nguni raids and maintain firm control of the plateau. Some Nyamwezi and Arab traders entered Lunda territory from the north. The two most important as far as the fate of Kazembe's empire was concerned were Msiri and Tippu Tip.

In 1856, when Kazembe VI, Cinyanta Mussona, had been two years on the throne, a Nyamwezi trader called Msiri arrived at the East Lunda capital and was given permission to settle in Katanga. There, he and his followers, the Yeke, traded with the local chiefs, and increased their numbers by immigration, slave-raiding and intermarriage. Soon Msiri had built up a state within a state. By conquest and treaty he attracted to himself the allegiance of many of Mwata Kazembe's people. He dealt with traders from the west, deflecting them from Mwata Kazembe's court to his own. He became so powerful that in 1865 the new ruler, Mwonga Nsemba (1862–70), had to seek his aid in suppressing a rebellion.

In the 1860s Arab traders, lured ever further inland by the quest for ivory, began trading to the west of Lake Tanganyika. They had a good supply of guns. They were ruthless in their dealings. They cheated and robbed chiefs of their stores of ivory. They destroyed villages. They forced warriors to hunt for them and chiefs to pay tribute. They pressed thousands of men and women into slavery. The most powerful and notorious of them all was Hamed bin Muhammed, better known by his nickname, Tippu Tip. In 1867 he travelled round the southern end of Lake Tanganyika and defeated the powerful Tabwa chief, Nsama. For months he traded and raided on the borders of Mwata Kazembe's kingdom.

Tippu Tip

Mwonga Nsemba was alarmed at the growing power of the Nyamwezi and the Arabs. In 1868 he killed all easterners in his territory and forbade traders to enter his dominions. Msiri, Tippu Tip and their colleagues responded by waging war on the East Lunda. In 1870 Mwonga Nsemba was defeated, driven from his capital and, at length, murdered by his own people. The East Lunda state now virtually collapsed. Rival Kazembes vied for power while Msiri became the effective ruler of most of the Empire.

Tippu Tip moved away to the north-west covering an enormous area of the eastern Congo up to the edge of the forest in his search for ivory. He subdued chiefdoms by force and trickery. Many rulers paid him tribute in ivory and he was able to send back to the coast enormous caravans laden with tusks. Early in the 1870s many of the other Arab traders recognized his authority and he became the uncrowned king of a vast area between Lake Tanganyika and the river Lomani.

Before we leave the story of nineteenth century Central Africa we must say something about one of the leading trading peoples of the area, the Yao. They controlled much of the land between Lake Nyasa and the coast and were thus well placed to partici-

The Yao

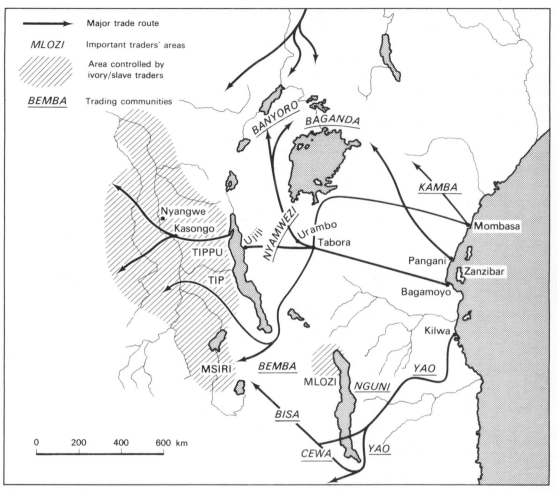

Area controlled by Arab traders

Legend	
→	Major trade route
MLOZI	Important traders' areas
/////	Area controlled by ivory/slave traders
BEMBA	Trading communities

pate in trade from the interior to Kilwa and to the lower Zambezi. With the growing demand for ivory and slaves in the nineteenth century the wealth of the Yao increased and their way of life changed. Ambitious young men set themselves up as traders and by slave-raiding built up large, personal followings. They raided other Yao groups as well as the communities of the lake shore and the Shiré Highlands. Some of these new leaders became very powerful indeed. The most famous of them was Mataka Nyambi. From his headquarters at Mwembe he ruled over an enormous area of

138

southern Yaoland. He is said to have had 600 wives and thousands of children.

Yao raids and the clashes between the Yao and the Maseko Nguni devastated almost the whole of the region between the Lake and the coast. Villages were deserted and farmland left unplanted. Men and women preferred to live in or near the fortified towns of the great chiefs where they were protected from raiders. Few traders, even the well-armed Arabs and Swahili, dared to cross Yaoland, because the local warriors were so fierce. One of the early European visitors described the Lake Nyasa region as 'one of the dark places of the earth, full of abominations and cruelty'. It has been estimated that over 20,000 men, women and children a year were taken from this area as slaves. The Yao were responsible for most of this traffic.

As a result of warfare on the continent of Europe Holland lost some of her overseas territories at the beginning of the nineteenth century. In 1806 Britain took over the small Dutch settlement of Cape Colony in order to protect her trade routes to the East and provide stores for passing ships. The new rulers found that they had inherited two kinds of subjects. There were the Africans who had lived in the Cape region for generations. These were mostly Saan hunters (Bushmen) and Khoi herdsmen (Hottentots) but the south-ward drift of Nguni and Sotho agriculturalists was soon to complicate the situation. There were also the Dutch settlers, or Boers. Many of them had been there for generations. They called themselves 'Afrikaners' and thought of themselves as independent from European control. They held beliefs that were quite opposed to the more modern political and religious ideals held by most Europeans. Their religion, represented by the Dutch Reformed Church, was a strict, puritanical faith based largely on the Old Testament. They believed that all coloured people were made by God inferior to whites. Black men were meant to serve white men. They could be enslaved, ill-treated, punished, even killed by their masters, for, being inferior creatures, the normal rules applying to relationships between human beings did not apply in dealings with Africans. There thus came to exist in South Africa three groups of people—Africans, British, Boers—and between them there was from the beginning a great deal of misunderstanding and

The spread of European settlement from the south

139

hatred. The situation became worse after 1811 when British settlers began to arrive in the colony. There were many clashes between these three groups during the nineteenth century.

The Xhosa Wars　The longest series of conflicts was the Xhosa Wars (sometimes called the 'Kaffir Wars' — *kaffir* is derived from an Arabic word meaning 'unbeliever' and was widely used for many years as a contemptuous term referring to Africans). There were nine Xhosa Wars in a hundred years. The dates are:

First Xhosa War	1779
Second Xhosa War	1789
Third Xhosa War	1799
Fourth Xhosa War	1811–12
Fifth Xhosa War	1819
Sixth Xhosa War	1834–5
Seventh Xhosa War	1846–7 (The War of the Axe)
Eighth Xhosa War	1850–3
Ninth Xhosa War	1877–8

The wars were basically border disputes between Boers, moving north-eastwards, and Xhosa, forced southwards by land hunger and population pressure. The first two wars were no more than clashes along the Fish river, the boundary between the colony and Xhosaland. The Dutch government at the Cape tried to remain impartial and refused to send large bodies of troops to crush the Africans. In 1799 the Boers at Graaff-Reinet rebelled against the newly established British government and tried to establish a tiny independent republic. While the Europeans were fighting among themselves the Xhosa chief, Ndlambe, united behind him all the other local rulers and tried to throw the Boers out of the border area. A government force was sent to restore order but there was no attempt at a permanent settlement of the border issue.

The new British government took a different attitude. It wanted to establish the Fish as a defensible frontier, and to settle British farmers on the western side of the river. In 1811 a sizeable force was sent to push Ndlambe and his people back into an already overcrowded Xhosaland and to fortify the boundary and leave it permanently garrisoned. This led to trouble in Xhosaland. Ndlambe made war upon his overlord,

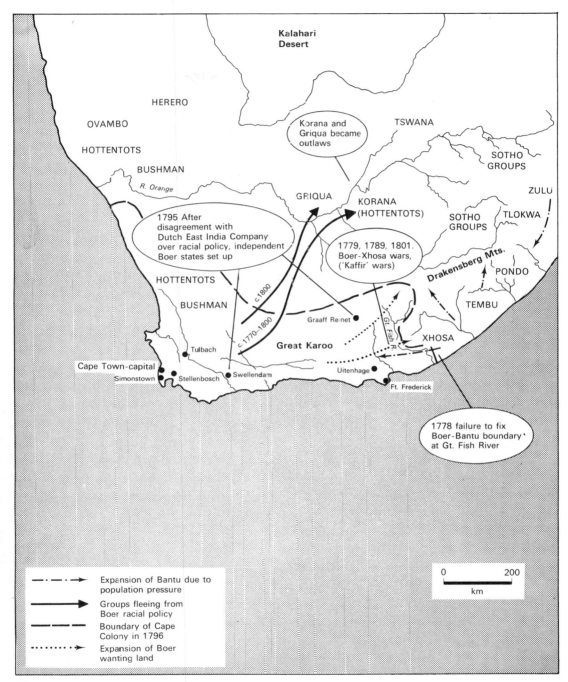

Kalahari Desert

HERERO

OVAMBO

HOTTENTOTS

BUSHMAN

R. Orange

Korana and Griqua became outlaws

GRIQUA

TSWANA

SOTHO GROUPS

ZULU

KORANA (HOTTENTOTS)

SOTHO GROUPS

TLOKWA

1795 After disagreement with Dutch East India Company over racial policy, independent Boer states set up

1779, 1789, 1801. Boer-Xhosa wars, ('Kaffir' wars)

Drakensberg Mts.

PONDO

HOTTENTOTS

BUSHMAN

c.1800

c.1770-1800

Graaff Reinet

Great Karoo

Gt. Fish R.

TEMBU

XHOSA

Tulbach

Cape Town-capital

Simonstown   Stellenbosch   Swellendam

Uitenhage

Ft. Frederick

1778 failure to fix Boer-Bantu boundary at Gt. Fish River

Expansion of Bantu due to population pressure

Groups fleeing from Boer racial policy

Boundary of Cape Colony in 1796

Expansion of Boer wanting land

0   200
km

Xhosa wars

Ngqrika, and seized much land and cattle. Ngqrika called upon the British for help and this led to the Fifth Xhosa War of 1819. For months British forces ranged Xhosaland until famine forced Ndlambe to go into hiding. The settlement reached after the war included two unworkable provisions: all Xhosa were to recognize Ngqrika as paramount chief and the land between the Fish and Keiskamma rivers (known as the Ceded Territory) was to be 'neutral ground', settled by neither black nor white farmers. The pressures resulting from the Mfecane now made the situation in Xhosaland worse. Little attention was paid to the provisions of the 1819 treaty. Many Xhosa leaders did not recognize Ngqrika's right to grant away their land. There were frequent clashes between black and white occupants of the Ceded Territory.

Xhosa with their cattle

It was not until 1834 that this running warfare flared up into another major conflict. Two Xhosa leaders, Tyali and Macomo, gathered a force of 12,000 men in an attempt to restore the Fish river boundary. They raided successfully deep into British territory before reinforcements arrived. Faced with superior weapons and well-disciplined troops the Xhosa were inevitably driven back. The Cape government now tried a new solution to the frontier problem. As well as imposing a huge fine in cattle, it annexed the entire territory between the Fish and Kei rivers under the name Queen Adelaide Province (1835). But the Cape Town politicians had gone too far; the British government refused to approve the annexation and in October 1836 Queen Adelaide Province was abandoned. The frontier returned to its usual chaos.

As time passed and the ownership of border territory was not decided tension increased. British and Boer settlers were clamouring for farmland in the Ceded Territory and for revenge against the Xhosa for cattle raids. Land pressures brought more hardship to the Africans. In this situation groups of young Xhosa men began to urge their elders to take up arms again against the white men. Witch doctors and prophets also appeared promising magical assistance for a new war. Christian missionaries preached peace and tried to break down the divisions between black and white but often they only succeeded in creating divisions within Xhosa society. Then, in the early 1840s, the situation was made worse by a natural disaster. For three years the rains failed. Black and white farmers were desperate for grazing; clashes became frequent.

The situation was now so tense that a minor incident sparked off the seventh and worst of the Xhosa Wars (sometimes known as the 'War of the Axe'). In January 1846 surveyors siting a new British border post on the Keiskamma began work, by mistake, on the Xhosa side of the river. Immediately rumours of a military advance began to spread. Shortly after this a young Xhosa living inside the Cape boundary was accused of stealing an axe and was arrested. A police escort taking the accused to Grahamstown was attacked by a band of Xhosa warriors and the prisoner was freed. Colonel Hare, Lieutenant-Governor of the Eastern Cape, used this as an excuse to teach the 'Kaffirs' a final lesson. He invaded Xhosaland on 1 April.

Soon the ill-equipped Africans were facing a force of 14,000 colonial troops. Despite defeats, loss of men and confiscation of cattle, the Xhosa, knowing what was at stake, fought on desperately. The war dragged on through 1846 and 1847 until it seemed that the Xhosa as a people would disappear. In December 1847 the Cape Governor, Sir Harry Smith, forced a settlement on the remaining Xhosa leaders which involved the annexation of all land as far as the river Kei which was in future to be known as British Kaffraria. Within the new colony the Xhosa were herded into reservations while the best land was given to white settlers. Some chose independence beyond the Kei. Others worked for European farmers, thus becoming servants on their own land.

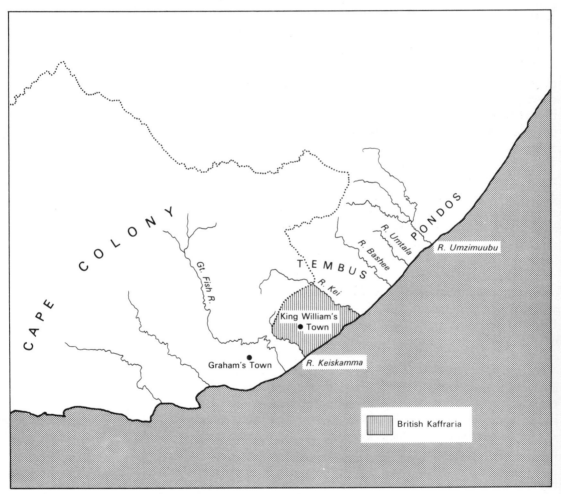

South East Africa during the Xhosa wars

But Xhosa sufferings were not over. Two more wars were fought by bold chiefs anxious to regain their independence. In 1850 the British deposed Chief Sandile of the Ngqrika Xhosa. Thousands of warriors on both sides of the Kei, spurred on by the war-doctor Mlanjeni, rose in support of their leader. This war dragged on until 1853 and resulted in more deaths and stock confiscations for the Africans. Having failed by force to throw out the British the Xhosa turned to the spirits of their ancestors for supernatural support. Mhlakaza, a prophet, persuaded the majority of his people that if they would destroy all their cattle and crops as a sacrifice to the ancestors the land would be freed of white men. Thus began the terrible cattle-killing of 1856–7. Over 200,000 animals were slaughtered and crops were not planted. The people starved but the white men stayed. Death and migration reduced the population of British Kaffraria from 105,000 to 37,600. It was this tragedy rather than government action which finally forced the majority of the Xhosa to submit.

There was still one more Xhosa War to be fought, however. In the Transkei the leading independent Xhosa chief was Kreli. Cape police drove him out of his land (although they had no rights in the Transkei) to stop him making trouble on the border. When Kreli returned to his homeland in 1877 he found that some of the Fingo had been allowed by the British to settle there. When he turned the newcomers out they appealed to their white protectors, and the Ninth Xhosa War began. Conflict soon spread into Kaffraria. By June 1878 many warriors and chiefs had been killed. The remaining leaders made peace with their conquerors. British control was strengthened in Kaffraria, and the Transkei was annexed as Fingoland.

The Great Trek

Long before the final conflict with the Xhosa, thousands of Dutch settlers had decided to move away from the British-ruled Cape to create independent states where there would be no challenge to their beliefs and their way of life. Most of the Boers moved between 1834 and 1839 in large groups with their belongings packed on ox carts. This is still known by the descendants of the settlers as the Great Trek.

The Boers did not like being under the rule of a foreign power but what forced them to leave Cape Colony was basic differences of belief and practice between them and the British.

The Voortrekker Monument, Pretoria

For the government and the increasing number of British settlers did not share the Afrikaners attitude of racial superiority. Though the British often treated Africans badly they believed, in theory, that all men were equal and they opposed slavery. (Slavery was, however, still permitted throughout the British Empire until 1834, although it had been stopped in Britain.) Special courts were set up to protect slaves from their masters. These 'black circuits' were bitterly resented by the Boers. Regulations regarding the treatment of slaves were introduced during the 1820s. Other important changes were also taking place: British settlers were growing in numbers and influence; the legal system was changed; English replaced Dutch as the official language; land became scarce as the number of farmers increased; Christian missionaries were continually complaining to the government about the behaviour of the Boers. Then, in 1833 the British Parliament passed an Act for the total abolition of slavery throughout the Empire. This Act and the problems that arose afterwards about the payment of compensation to ex-slave owners proved too much for many Boers to bear.

The map on page 147 shows the main lines of the Boer advance. Most Boers placed themselves under chosen trek

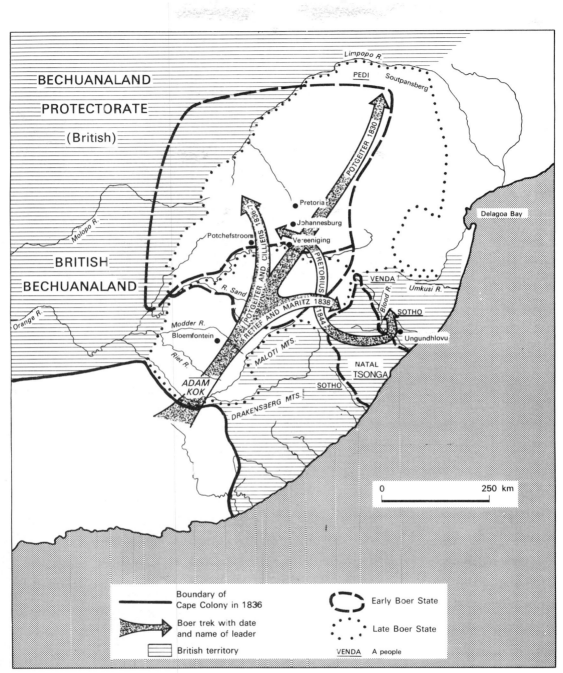

Principal migrations of Boers during the Great Trek

leaders. In 1835 a party led by Janse van Rensburg left the Cape and travelled in the general direction of Delagoa Bay but was too reduced in numbers to set up a new settlement. The survivors sailed to Natal.

In 1836 a party under the leadership of Sarel Cilliers and Andries Potgeiter trekked due north, crossed the Vaal and entered Ndebele country. As we have already seen (page 129), they successfully drove out Mzilikazi's people after a series of battles. Two Boer states were established: Potchefstroom in conquered Ndebele country and Winburg south of the Vaal. Things did not go well in Potchefstroom and Potgeiter was soon leading a new trek. For another ten years his people sought an area of good farming land away from powerful, hostile neighbours. In 1848 they settled in the Soutpansberg, near the Limpopo. For a while all went well but then Boer raids on the Sotho, Venda, Tsonga and Pedi for cattle and

Battle of Vegkop

slaves soon created a typical frontier situation. Years of intermittent warfare with neighbouring peoples followed and eventually, in 1867, the Boers were forced out of Soutpansberg.

Another party led by Piet Retief and Gert Maritz moved eastwards across the Drakensbergs in 1837. They hoped, with the approval of Dingane, the Zulu leader, to settle in what is now Natal. Retief took a small advance party into Zululand. He was received by Dingane in his capital, Ungundhlovu, and negotiations began for the leasing of land to the Boers.

Dingane

But Dingane was uneasy. He doubtless knew something of events on the Xhosa border and was, understandably, afraid that if he let a few Europeans into his territory they would take more and more land from his people. When Retief threatened Dingane with invasion if he would not let the Boers in peacefully Dingane became angry. He had Retief and his companions murdered. A Zulu *impi* was sent to destroy the main Boer party and a further 500 trekkers were killed.

But Dingane had not seen the last of the Boers. A few months later (November 1838) a party led by Andries Pretorius entered Zululand. On 15 December they defeated the Zulus on the banks of the Ncome, ever afterwards known as Blood River. The Boer Republic of Natal was established with a capital at Pietermaritzburg. By 1839, although Boers continued to travel to the newly acquired lands, the Great Trek was over. Three new Afrikaner states existed, free, in theory, from British interference. Matters did not stay like that for long.

Britain and the Boers 1836–80

British leaders in London and Cape Town had no wish to pursue the trekkers into the interior or acquire new and expensive areas of colonial territory. But they were not able to keep themselves detached from the affairs of the trek Boers for long. They were urged by missionaries and their political supporters to defend various African groups from the Boers. They were urged by political groups in Britain and South Africa to prevent the coastline falling into the hands of Afrikaners or other foreigners.

In 1836 the British government made an unsuccessful attempt to control the activities of the trek Boers with the Cape of Good Hope Punishment Act. This stated that all former inhabitants of the Cape living south of the 25th parallel were still British subjects and governed by British law. In theory men who infringed laws concerning slavery and the treatment of Africans could be brought back to Cape Colony for trial. In fact the law proved unenforceable and merely angered the Boers.

The establishment of the Natal Republic brought an immediate reaction from the small British community at Durban. For some years they had been unsuccessfully urging the Cape government to annex Natal. Now matters were more urgent. They did not want to be under Boer rule. They stressed the danger for the Cape of allowing the Natal coast to fall into Boer hands. Missionaries were quick to point out cases of Boer ill-treatment of Africans. The London and Cape Town authorities were reluctant to get involved. It was when Pretorius began to create African reserves in the southern border region—thus creating more population pressure which would affect the situation in Xhosaland—that the Cape Governor took action. He sent government troops to Durban. There were a number of minor clashes as well as protests from all the Boer states' leaders but at last, in 1843, the Afrikaners were forced to negotiate with the British. Natal was annexed by Britain in 1845 and most of the Boers once again packed their belongings onto their ox-waggons.

This settlement did not mark the end of British-Boer hostility. There were, as we shall see, further clashes over Boer treatment of the Basuto and Griqua (see page 159). The story of Boer settlement beyond the Orange river was one of almost continuous conflict with the local peoples. Many African chiefs looked to the British for protection from their new oppressors. In the Cape, opinion was divided on how best to deal with the troubled interior. But in 1847 Sir Harry Smith arrived as Governor, determined to be firm with the Boers and establish, by force if necessary, peaceful British control. After a quick tour of the troubled areas Smith proclaimed a British colony between the Orange and the Vaal in February 1848 and defeated the Boers in a battle at Boomplats. For some months anti-British Boers trekked northwards across the Vaal while others moved in the opposite direction to place themselves under British protection.

The new Orange River Sovereignty was left in the hands of an inadequate staff of administrators and police who soon proved incapable of keeping the peace between Africans and

Boers. The Transvaal Boers were determined to reconquer the lost trekker lands and the disorganized Sovereignty government faced the constant threat of invasion. In London the Colonial Office was anxious to get rid of the troublesome new colony. Representatives were sent out to South Africa in 1851. First they met Pretorius and drew up the Sand River Convention (1852) by which the British renounced all rights over the Transvaal Boers. In the Orange River Sovereignty things were not quite so easy; the majority of settlers wanted to remain under British protection. Not until February 1854 could a group of republican Boers be found ready to sign the Bloemfontein Convention giving the Afrikaners complete freedom in what now became the Orange Free State.

For fourteen years the British largely avoided involvement with the Boer states. The Boer republics were poor farming states whose internal politics were frequently chaotic. As long as they did not attempt to expand to the sea British interests were not at stake and as long as the republics were reliant on Cape Colony for all their supplies they were a source of profit to British traders. What changed the situation was the discovery of diamonds on the banks of the Orange near Hopetown in 1867. Prospectors and adventurers moved into the area and soon discovered important diamond deposits around modern Kimberley. There now arose a dispute over ownership of the diamondiferous territory between the Free State, the South African Republic (Transvaal) and the Griqua leader, Waterboer. Negotiations between the interested parties broke down in 1870, whereupon the Free State leader, J. H. Brand, annexed the area for his country. Waterboer asked for help from Cape Colony and his plea was backed by British prospectors and settlers in the disputed territory.

The Cape High Commissioner, Sir Henry Barkly, entered on a series of negotiations with the Boer governments and Waterboer. Waterboer's territory (which was taken to include the Kimberley region) was annexed to the Cape as the province of Griqualand West. The Boer states were powerless to do more than protest.

The Transvaal in particular was in difficulties. The government was almost bankrupt. The economic development of the land-locked state was at a standstill. Border warfare drained still more money from the exchequer and failure to quell the Pedi drained public support from the government. This came at a time when British politicians were trying to make a

Diamond mine

positive move towards ending the permanent conflict between the two white communities in South Africa. The possibility of a federation was put forward but rejected by the Boers. By 1877 it was obvious that the South African Republic was about to collapse. No one wanted the chaos and warfare that would inevitably result, so the British government offered to annex the Transvaal. There was, of course, opposition to this suggestion but the majority of the Transvaalers were prepared to swallow their pride in the interests of peace and security. A British protectorate was declared in April.

Some South African peoples 1820–80

The Zulus

In 1820 the Zulu nation was at the height of its power. Under Shaka's leadership the borders of Zululand were pushed to their greatest limits. The King, himself, was a tyrant who forced his will on his people and punished with extreme cruelty anyone suspected of disobedience. He was feared by all, even by his *indunas* and close advisers. He extended his protection to the small community of white hunters and traders who settled at Port Natal (Durban) in 1824. About this time Zulu power reached its limits. The warriors were tired after years of ceaseless warfare. They fought with less fervour far from home. Their enemies began to learn how to combat Zulu tactics. Shaka's *impis* began to experience defeat (and were usually punished for it by their enraged King). Discontented people began to plot against Shaka. In 1828 he was murdered by two of his half-brothers, one of whom, Dingane, became the next ruler.

Dingane was less successful than Shaka in maintaining Zulu power and holding together the empire. Subject chiefs broke away from his rule and the army had to be used all the time to maintain the King's authority. The settlement at Port Natal was another cause of growing concern. More and more Europeans were arriving there and travelling throughout Dingane's territory. Disagreements and clashes occurred between them and the Zulus. To prevent this Dingane tried to restrict the freedom of movement Shaka had granted to the Europeans. He found it difficult to enforce his will on the well-armed foreigners. In 1835 the situation improved; Christian missionaries were allowed into Zululand and the Natalians promised not to protect Dingane's enemies. But the agreement was broken the following year and the Zulu leader forbade white men to cross the river Tugela. Not long after this Dingane was faced with a new threat—Retief's trekkers were crossing the Drakensbergs.

Dingane's defeat at Blood River (see page 149) brought complete ruin upon him. His empire began to melt away. His half-brother, Mpande, made an alliance with the Natal Boers and rebelled against the King. In the ensuing conflict Dingane was driven northwards out of Zululand. He was forced to seek refuge among some of his traditional enemies, the Swazi. They lost little time in murdering the Zulu King (1840).

Mpande began his thirty-three year reign as a puppet chief dependent on the support of the Natal Europeans. He re-established control over most of the rebellious parts of the empire and put new heart into the army. He maintained peaceful relations with the Europeans who were gradually encircling his territory. But this policy became more difficult

Dingane

as the Zulu population grew. No longer could the problem be solved by expansion, as in the days of the Mfecane. Now the Zulus' neighbours were well-armed Europeans.

In 1873 Cetshawayo became king. He soon found himself involved in a dispute with the Transvaal leaders over land along Blood River. The dispute was still not resolved when Britain took over the Transvaal in 1877. The following year a settlement was reached giving Cetshawayo possession of the disputed territory but imposing harsh terms in return. The British demanded compensation for dispossessed farmers, fines as punishment for alleged Zulu cattle raids, the stationing

Umpanda, King of the Amazulu

154

of a British Resident in Cetshawayo's capital and the disbanding of the Zulu army. Cetshawayo could not accept these terms so the Cape Governor, Sir Bartle Frere, ordered a British invasion of Zululand. In January 1879 the two armies met at the battle of Isandhlwana and the British force was almost completely destroyed. The shock of this defeat provoked the British government into sending reinforcements to South Africa. Six months after Isandhlwana a second, successful invasion of Zululand was launched. At Ulundi Cetshawayo was defeated and captured and sent into exile. The Zulus were split into thirteen chieftaincies with no paramount chief.

Cetshawayo

Battle of Isandhlwana with Lord Chelmsford's advancing column

A British Resident was appointed. Most of the Blood River lands were given to Boer farmers.

The result was chaos and anarchy. Traditional authority had been taken away and the Resident had no power to enforce British rule. There was indiscriminate cattle-raiding and small wars between African and African and between African and European were common. By 1883, not even Cetshawayo, brought back by the worried British, could restore order. Finally, in 1887, Britain annexed Zululand.

The Basuto   The Basuto were fortunate to have secure mountain strongholds and the wise leadership of Moshweshwe. After the troubles of the 1820s the King tried to live in peace with all his neighbours, black and white. He welcomed to his territory refugees such as the Rolong Chief Moroka and his people. He allowed the trek Boers temporary grazing rights. He sent messages of friendship to the Cape Governor and in 1843 the British at the Cape signed a treaty recognizing Moshweshwe's position and independence.

But Basutoland stood in the way of too many land hungry peoples. Moroka refused to acknowledge himself a vassal of Moshweshwe. The Boers refused to leave their 'temporary' grazing lands. The Basuto clashed with the Griqua over borders. Frequently Moshweshwe appealed to the British for protection only to have his requests turned down by a British government unwilling to take on new commitments. But after the annexation of the Orange River Sovereignty in 1848 Basuto-Boer conflicts became matters of direct British concern. In 1849 the British representative, Henry Warden, tried to solve Basutoland's border disputes (the new border was known as the Warden Line). When this attempt failed Warden tried to impose a settlement by force. He invaded Basutoland only to be crushingly defeated at Viervoet.

In 1852 Governor Cathcart of the Cape made another unsuccessful show of force against the Basuto. Rather than prolong an unnecessary conflict Moshweshwe made peace with Cathcart. The following year Britain withdrew from Transorangia, and Moshweshwe was left to deal as best he could with the Boers and their allies. In 1858 an indecisive war was fought. Years of raiding and petty conflict followed until 1866 when the Boers tried to starve Moshweshwe into submission by surrounding his stronghold. The eighty-year-old King made another desperate appeal to the British and this time they came to his aid. In 1868 a British protectorate was declared over Basutoland. Now the task of fixing the border was once more in British hands. Agreement was reached in 1870, shortly after Moshweshwe's death. The great King had founded a nation and preserved it intact despite great difficulties for nearly half a century.

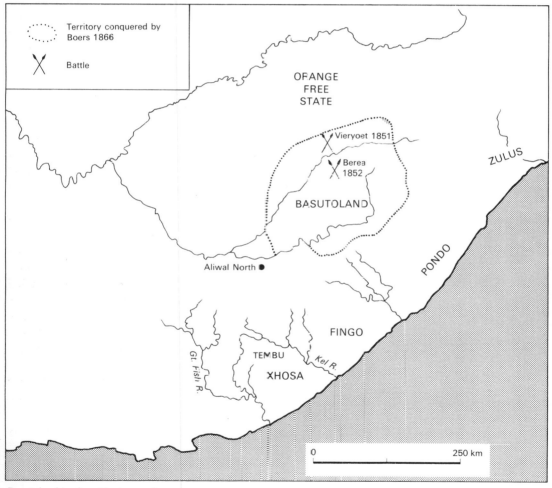

Basutoland in the mid-nineteenth century

Ever since the early years of European settlement in South Africa there had been some racial interbreeding between the European, Khoi and Saan peoples. The result was light-skinned peoples who did not fit happily into either European or African society. Many of them stayed in the Colony and were eventually known as Cape Coloured people. Others left for the borderlands of the white colonies and settled in groups, united only by allegiance to their chosen leaders. They lived by herding, raiding and trade. Such groups were the Griqua and Korana, whose territories are shown on the map below.

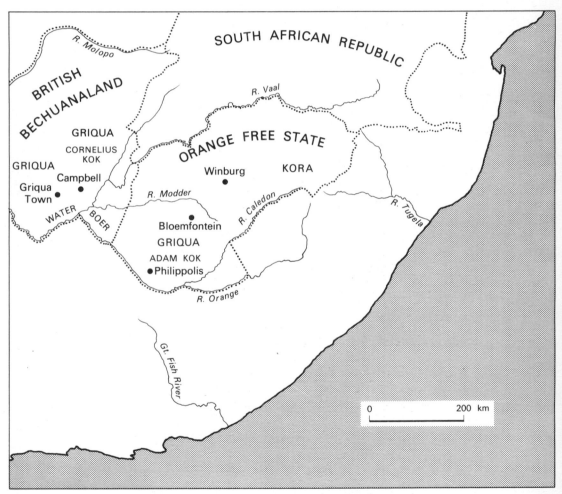

Griqua and Kora lands

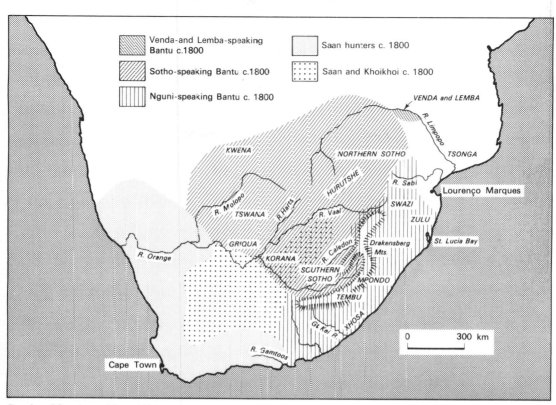

Peoples of Southern Africa 1800

The Griqua and Korana

In the 1830s these communities found their position challenged by the trek Boers, who tried to oust them from their grazing land and water holes. The typical border situation of raids and counter raids developed. Soon Griqua leaders and missionaries were appealing to Cape Town for protection. Treaties of recognition (but not protection) were signed between the British and Waterboer, leader of the West Griqua (1834), and between the British and Adam Kok III, leader of the East Griqua (1843). But conflict between the Griqua and the Boers continued. The East Griqua were within the boundaries of the Orange River Sovereignty when it was annexed by Britain (1848–54) and enjoyed a few years of protection and peace.

After 1854 the Boers overran most of the smaller Griqua and Korana states. In 1861 Adam Kok led his people across the Drakensbergs and established a new homeland (still called

159

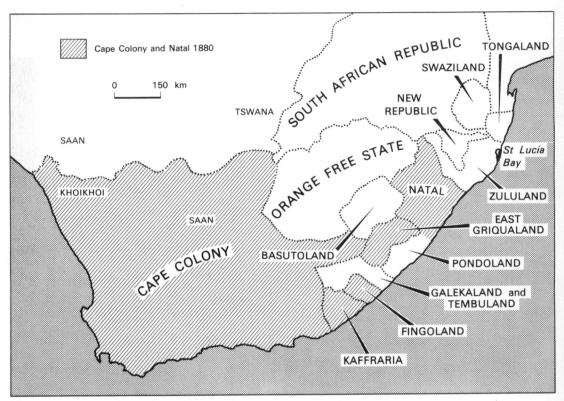

British annexations in South-East Africa

Griqualand East). Waterboer's people enjoyed relative peace and freedom from attack until the late 1860s, when the diamond rush began. Griqualand West contained some of the diamond-bearing rock and it also lay across the main route from Cape Colony to Central Africa. Thus it had economic and political importance for both the British and the Boers. As we have already seen (page 149) the Free State leaders tried by negotiation and force to gain part of Waterboer's territory. The Griqua Chief responded by calling for British protection and Griqualand West was annexed to the Cape in 1871.

The European conquest of southern Africa was a slow and piecemeal affair but it was largely complete by 1880. The African states that had existed in 1800 had either been conquered or were only able to preserve a shaky independence based on British protection.

East Africa is an extremely varied part of the continent. From area to area there are considerable differences of soil, climate, altitude and vegetation. The ways people live are equally varied—settled agriculture among the Baganda and Basoga of southern Uganda, settled agriculture of a different kind among the Kikuyu and Kamba of the Kenya Highlands, pastoralism among the Acholi, Samburu and Maasai, shifting agriculture mixed with herding among the Nyamwezi and Gogo of central Tanzania, etc. We cannot here describe the history of all these peoples. What we shall describe are the most important events that occurred in the nineteenth century—and by 'important events' we mean those that significantly affected the development of East Africa as a whole.

The politics of the area north of Lake Victoria were dominated by two powerful states, Buganda and Bunyoro. For centuries the pastoral Banyoro and the agricultural Baganda had competed for control of this region. Most of the neighbouring chieftaincies were tributary to one or other of the great rivals. Throughout most of the nineteenth century Buganda had the upper hand. Its soil was highly fertile. Work on the land could be left to the women so that the menfolk were free for military service. Banyoro men on the other hand could only be spared at certain seasons from tending the cattle. As they lost more and more valuable pastures to the enemy, economic conditions deteriorated. The Baganda also benefited from foreign trade. Towards the end of the eighteenth century cowries, porcelain and cloth began to reach Buganda along the caravan routes that extended to the coast around the southern end of Lake Victoria. The King (*Kabaka*) sent out hunters and traders to bring back the ivory, copper and slaves that the distant coast merchants wanted. In 1844 the first Swahili and Arab traders from the east coast reached the court of Kabaka Suna II. This was the beginning of a long and profitable relationship

Buganda and Bunyoro

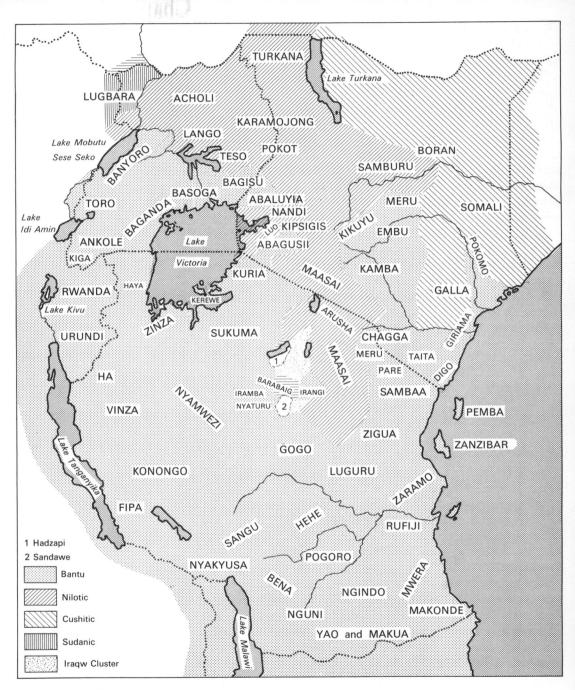

Peoples of East Africa

162

between Buganda and the Zanzibaris. The Kabaka obtained rare trade goods which enhanced his own prestige and with which he could reward faithful service. More important, he obtained guns which enabled him to maintain his hold on vassal states and maintain his country's superiority over Bunyoro. Bunyoro could not benefit from this trade in the same way because the land to the south through which the caravan routes passed was controlled by Buganda.*

Though Bunyoro succeeded in obtaining some guns along the East African trade routes, the Mukama, the leader of the Banyoro, looked increasingly to the north for arms. He made contact with Khartoumer slave and ivory dealers who assisted him in his wars and provided him with guns in return for elephant tusks. The Khartoumers were followed by agents of the Khedive of Egypt, who wanted to incorporate the interlacustrine kingdoms (the states of the Lake area) into Egypt's Equatoria Province. When Kamurasi died in 1869 there was a dispute between two rivals for the throne. Kabarega and Kabagumire. Kabarega obtained the support of Sudanese soldiers from the Equatoria garrisons. Traditional opposition to Bunyoro and fear of growing Egyptian power prompted Kabaka Mutesa of Buganda to support Kabagumire. But the Baganda warriors were no match for well-armed European-trained soldiers.

Buganda's defeat was followed by a period when it seemed that the Khedive must succeed in his aim of conquering Africa as far south as the Great Lakes. Khartoumers overran Langoland and Acholiland. In 1872 Kamurasi fell out with his Sudanese allies, who then destroyed his capital and killed many of his people. The Khedive sent a new Governor of Equatoria to set up his headquarters at Gondokoro and establish strong administration. It was the Englishman, Charles Gordon.

Faced with this threat Mutesa acted with wisdom and caution. He had already had experience of English travellers. In 1862 John Speke and James Grant had arrived in Buganda looking for the source of the White Nile. Though they were weary, ill and totally dependent on Mutesa's hospitality and assistance, they had impressed the Kabaka with their weapons,

---

* When Samuel Baker reached Bunyoro in 1864 he found that the ruler, Mukama Kamurasi, had thousands of pounds worth of ivory that he had been unable to trade.

Mutesa of Buganda

their medicines, their skills and their stories of a distant queen who ruled a vast empire. Mutesa wanted powerful allies and he urged Speke to send more of his countrymen, including missionaries, to Buganda. But the white men went away and Mutesa forged strong links with other powerful strangers, the Zanzibaris. He made a treaty with the Sultan of Zanzibar and in 1865 he became a Muslim. In 1874 Mutesa exchanged messages with Gordon and, the following year, he received a visit from another explorer seeking the Nile source. This was Henry Stanley, who arrived at the head of a larger and more impressive expedition. From what he saw and heard Mutesa decided that the British would make more useful friends than the Arabs. He renounced Islam, implored Stanley to send missionaries to his land and offered friendship to General Gordon. He would like to have remained on good terms with both the British and the Arabs but this was impossible because most Englishmen in Africa at this time were obsessed with one ambition—to stamp out the slave trade.

But Gordon was still under orders from the Khedive. In 1875 he sent an expedition to build forts on the Buganda border and to obtain Mutesa's submission to Egypt. But the Kabaka cleverly tricked the expedition's leaders into coming to his court. There he held them as virtual prisoners until Gordon agreed to withdraw his garrisons from Buganda's border. Shortly afterwards Egypt was forced to withdraw from the southern Sudan and, for the time being, the inter-lacustrine kingdoms were safe from foreign interference.

But Arabs and Europeans now knew much more about the region and their interest was aroused by it. Buganda's hold over the area to the west of the Lake had weakened and from 1877 onwards Zanzibaris were able to reach Bunyoro. When news reached the coast of the cheap ivory to be obtained in Kabarega's kingdom merchants flocked there, taking guns and cloth to exchange for the precious 'white gold'. This led to a revival of Bunyoro's military fortunes. The Europeans had been impressed with Mutesa's power and the stability of his kingdom. Some of them thought Buganda would make a good base for beginning missionary work in the interior. In 1877 the first Christian missionaries arrived. From the beginning they made a great impression on Mutesa and his people. But they created problems. There was hatred and rivalry between them and the Arabs. There was even rivalry between different groups of Christians, for Protestant and Roman Catholic missions both began work in Buganda. Inevitably, as more and more Baganda were converted to the new faith their devotion to many traditional beliefs and customs waned. All these things created problems for the Kabaka and his council (the *Lukiiko*). But Mutesa was clever enough and firm enough to be able to handle the situation.

From a glance at the map it might appear strange that the caravan routes to Uganda from the east coast should pass round the southern end of Lake Victoria; the direct route across what is now southern Kenya is much shorter (and is the route now followed by the railway). But in the nineteenth century, few coast dwellers dared to venture across the territory of the Kamba, Kikuyu and Maasai.

The Maasai, a Nilotic pastoral people, roamed with their cattle over the plains of Kenya and northern Tanzania. Their fierce and highly-trained warriors (*moran*) were greatly feared

The highlands and plains of Kenya

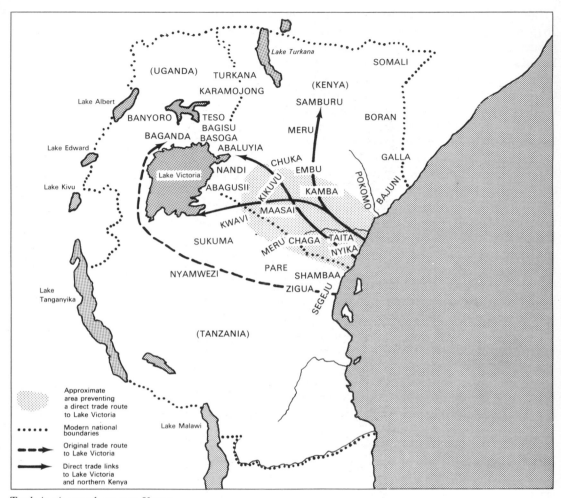

Trade in nineteenth-century Kenya

by their neighbours. At the coast the reputation of the Maasai was exaggerated and very few Zanzibaris dared to venture into their territory. All Maasai raiding was carried out with one aim—the acquisition of cattle. There were very few communities that had not been raided and the farming peoples of the region lived as far as possible outside the range of the tall herdsmen. They preferred the hills and forests of areas like the Kilimanjaro and Mount Kenya foothills.

But the Maasai were not one united tribe; they were not even all pastoralists. They moved about in small groups under the

Maasai moran display their fighting skill

leadership of elders. Though they had no chief they did acknowledge great ritual experts called *laiboni* (singular *laibon*). Before the beginning of the nineteenth century some Maasai had given up the pastoral life and taken to farming. They were despised by the herdsmen, who called them *kwavi* or *ilogolala* ('people with hard teeth'). The two groups frequently raided each other for cattle but during the nineteenth century raiding turned to warfare. There were three main conflicts: 1815, 1840–5, 1870–5. At the end of the wars the Maasai and the Kwavi were much depleted in numbers and military might. The balance of power in the region changed. New forces, such as the Nandi, emerged. The highland peoples were able to move more freely. Traders began to use the short route to Uganda.

Kamba carving

The most active and far-ranging traders were the Kamba. It was trade that had formed the Kamba people out of groups of hunters living in the Kenya Highlands. They began to trade ivory for cattle with the coastal Swahili and Nyika. When they discovered how highly ivory was prized at the coast they organized large hunting and trading caravans to the interior. They carried iron weapons and tools, arrow poison, meat and grain to other dwellers in the highlands and plains. Because of the valuable service they performed the Kamba were allowed to cross territory forbidden to other strangers. By 1850 Kamba caravans were making regular journeys to the Samburu of northern Kenya and they travelled as far south as Uzaramo in eastern Tanzania. By this time also the Kamba had become involved in the slave trade. They raided the Kikuyu and even, sometimes, the Maasai, to obtain slaves either to till their fields or to be sold at the coast. This led to occasional conflict as in 1851 when Kivoi, the wealthiest of all the Kamba merchants, was murdered while leading a caravan through the Mount Kenya forest.

The most numerous people of the Kenya Highlands were the Kikuyu. These Bantu farmers had for many generations been moving into the area from the north-east. From the vicinity of Mount Kenya they spread out through the forest, clearing places for shifting cultivation and pushing further and further southwards. They grew steadily in numbers and were able to overthrow all who opposed them. By the 1870s they were strong enough to take land from the Maasai in the area round modern Nairobi. By 1880 the Kikuyu were a power to be reckoned with. They were trading directly with the coast and cutting out some of the Kamba middlemen.

Central and Southern Tanzania

Inland Tanzania also experienced a long period of disruption due mainly to outside pressures. These pressures came from two directions. There were the Nguni, who arrived about 1840, and the Zanzibaris who, about the same time, began to penetrate deep into the interior in search of ivory and slaves. Many small communities suffered badly as a result of these invaders but the eventual result was that many of Tanzania's people reorganized themselves into more powerful groups able to resist attack.

Long-distance trade grew in importance during the century. The peoples most involved in this were the Nyamwezi and the

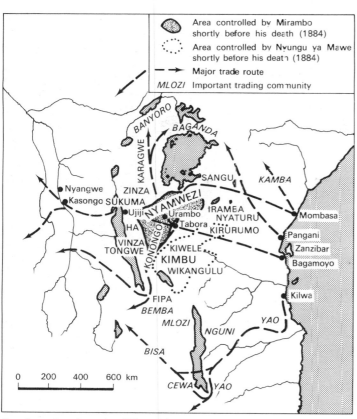

Peoples and trade routes of Tanzania

Yao. The word 'Nyamwezi' means 'people of the moon' and
was applied to the African traders from the far interior who
began to arrive at the coast around 1800. Before that time the
Nyamwezi lived in small scattered communities under the
leadership of *ntemi* chiefs, whose power was often more
ritualistic than political, and who were assisted by lesser
chiefs. However, as some of the chiefs and caravan leaders
began to prosper by carrying ivory, copper (from Katanga),
beeswax, iron hoes, salt, skins and slaves to the coast so they
built up larger followings. Large chieftaincies such as that of
Unyanyembe appeared. By 1830 the main trade routes,
particularly the Ujiji–Unyanyembe–Bagamoyo route, were
well established and Nyamwezi caravans, sometimes comprising more than a thousand men, made frequent journeys to
the coast. In 1839 the ruler of Zanzibar, Sultan Said, had to

Nyamwezi porters

make a treaty with Chief Fundikira of Unyanyembe so that his Arab and Swahili subjects might be allowed to travel through the Chief's territory.

The Yao had been long-distance traders for generations. They occupied much of the area between Lake Nyasa and the east coast. From an early date they had been involved in the mercantile life of the Zambezi valley and the coast. Within their area the Yao dominated trade. Though they were friendly with their Zanzibari colleagues, obtained guns and trade goods from them, copied their styles of dress and building, even adopted their religion, they allowed no Arab or Swahili caravans to cross their territory. Through trading and raiding, some chiefs grew very powerful and rich. Mataka I, who lived until about 1878, lived in great style, ruled over thousands of square kilometres, built a large, walled capital having Arab-type mosques and houses, and had six hundred wives. Much of the merchant princes' power and wealth came from the slave trade. By the time Dr Livingstone crossed Yaoland in the 1860s large tracts of country had been depopulated, hundreds of villages destroyed, and farmland

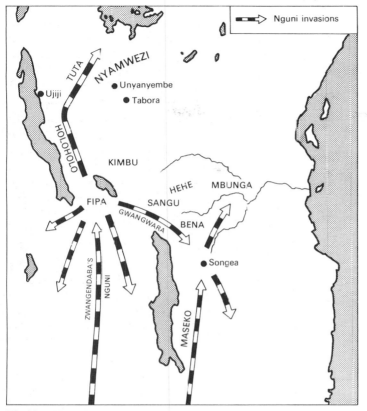

The Nguni invasions

laid waste. Many people voluntarily placed themselves under the protection of great Yao chiefs as this was the only means of obtaining security in troubled times.

The main cause of trouble was the Nguni. Two of these groups from South Africa arrived in the 1840s. The Maseko Nguni settled around Songea, and Zwangendaba's people occupied Ufipa. As we have seen, Zwangendaba died about 1848 and his followers split into five groups. Three of these groups turned back into Central Africa and have already been dealt with (see page 158). The other two sections were the Gwangwara and the Tuta. The Gwangwara moved eastwards under the leadership of Zulu-Gama and caused havoc among the small communities of southern Tanzania. About 1860 they reached Songea and decided to settle there. To do so they had to drive out the Maseko Nguni. After severe clashes between the two groups the Gwangwara triumphed and the

171

Maseko split up, Maputo leading the bulk of his people southwards to the Shiré Highlands. The Gwangwara were not for long able to terrorize their neighbours. After a few years the Sangu, Bena and Hehe had developed Nguni-type battle tactics and regrouped into larger, more powerful units.

Meanwhile the Tuta headed northwards. In battles with groups of Holoholo, Kimbu and Nyamwezi they were by no means always successful. Not until they reached the south-west corner of Lake Victoria were they able to settle in reasonable peace. Even then they could not refrain from attacks on Buganda-bound caravans and Nyamwezi settlements.

By this time Zanzibari activity in the interior had grown considerably. An entire Arab township had grown up alongside Fundikira's capital, Unyanyembe. It was called Tabora. Ujiji and Karonga were other places that attracted colonies of Zanzibaris. At first the coast men got on well with their hosts but as their numbers grew the hosts' attitude changed. They tried to monopolize trade. They raided indiscriminately. They treated African chiefs with contempt. In Unyamwezi war broke out when Mnwa Sele, Fundikira's successor, tried to impose taxes on passing caravans. The Tabora Arabs drove the Chief from his capital and placed a puppet ruler, Mkasiwa, on the throne. Mnwa Sele fought on until he was captured and murdered by the Zanzibaris in 1865.

Other Nyamwezi chiefs followed his lead in resisting the foreigners. The most famous were Mirambo and Nyungu-ya-Mawe. Mirambo inherited the small chieftaincy of Uyowa, north-west of Unyanyembe, and established his capital, Urambo, about 1860. He immediately set about extending his dominion. As a young warrior he had spent some time as a captive of the Tuta and learned the secrets of Nguni success in warfare. Using Nguni methods he built up an empire which covered much of north-western Tanzania. By 1870 Mirambo was in a position to control the caravan routes west of Tabora. When the Arabs refused to pay trade tolls Mirambo did not hesitate to close the routes. This led to an indecisive five-year conflict during which Zanzibari trade came almost to a standstill. In the end the coast men had to meet Mirambo's demands.

The Arabs were forced to respect Mirambo, and his fame extended to the coast and beyond. Early European travellers met him and were impressed by his power. Like his contemporary Mutesa, Mirambo encouraged Europeans to come to his territory and persuaded the London Missionary Society to open a station in his capital because he valued their skills, wanted more guns and enjoyed the prestige their presence gave him. Through trade and through his foreign contacts Mirambo amassed over 20,000 guns. Armed with these weapons his mercenaries, the dreaded *ruga-ruga*, became even more terrible. It was only Mirambo's personality and his army that held the empire together but while it lasted Mirambo's kingdom brought unity and security to a large part of East Africa.

Nyungu-ya-Mawe's kingdom was more firmly based. Nyungu-ya-Mawe (a praise name meaning 'pot of stone') was a prince of the ruling house of Unyanyembe. He was driven out of the capital by the victorious Arabs when they overthrew Mnwa Sele. Nyungu, like Mirambo, was a fearless warrior and it did not take him many years to build up a large band of devoted followers. His bands of *ruga-ruga* roamed the area south of Tabora conquering the small *ntemi* chieftaincies and dominating the commercial life of a large area. By 1880 Nyungu's personal empire extended as far as Lake Rukwa and he ruled it firmly through a number of local governors who enforced his will and collected regular tribute in ivory from local rulers.

The coast

Trade played an important part in the formation and preservation of all the inland states of East Africa but the most important people involved in commerce were the Zanzibaris. They operated from bases in the towns and islands of the east coast, where, for many centuries, a distinct Afro-Arab culture had flourished. Ever since the end of the seventeenth century when their navy had helped to drive the Portuguese out of the coast north of Cape Delgado the rulers of Oman in south-east Arabia had claimed control of the trading centres of the East African coast. However, effective rule depended on the loyalty of the sultans' local representatives. Since Muscat (the capital of Oman) was over 3,500 kilometres away across the Indian Ocean the local governors were virtually free from control. Some took advantage of the situation to renounce Omani overlordship. Chief among these were the Mazrui governors of Mombasa. By 1807 they had extended their personal rule over all the settlements from Pangani to Malindi, including the important islands of Pemba and Pate.

Zanzibar in the nineteenth century

The new ruler of Oman, Sultan Sayid Said, was determined to win back control of his East African dominions. He succeeded but only after thirty years of intermittent warfare. Early in his career Said realized the commercial importance of East Africa. He encouraged trading ventures to the interior. He established a slave market at Zanzibar. He transformed Pemba Island into an agricultural settlement by ordering the plantation owners to grow cloves. He made treaties with some of the world's leading commercial nations and brought merchant ships from Germany, Britain, France and the United States of America to Zanzibar harbour. In 1840 Said moved his capital from Muscat to Zanzibar, where he spent the remaining sixteen years of his life. Those years saw an enormous growth of prosperity. In 1859 Zanzibar's exports (not including slaves, for which no accurate figures are available) were worth over £310,000. Pemba had become the world's leading supplier of cloves, and ships from all over the world called regularly at Zanzibar to take on cargoes of ivory and cloves. Zanzibar had also become one of the main suppliers of slaves to the Muslim world. Coastal traders under the Sultan's protection had travelled to many parts of eastern and central Africa and established a complex commercial network. In some areas men like Tippu Tip had established themselves as 'kings', claiming to rule in the name of the Sultan of Zanzibar. Sayid Said was, therefore, overlord of a large, though undefined, area of inland Africa as well as his coastal possessions.

Sayid Said derived enormous prestige as well as commercial advantages from the presence of European consuls and traders in his territory but like other African rulers he found the presence of Europeans, especially the British, to be a mixed blessing. His contact with the British went back to the beginning of his reign. About that time the British established naval supremacy in the Indian Ocean, and Said had found them to be useful allies in his fight against Arab and Indian pirates and also in his struggle with the Mazrui rebels. (At one time the Mazrui leaders had actually tricked a British captain into establishing a 'protectorate' over Mombasa. They promised to allow Britain to use the port as an anti-slave trade base. All they really wanted was British support against Oman and after eighteen months—1824–6—the 'Mombasa Protectorate' was abandoned.) Said owed his successful reconquest of the East African coast to Britain and he continued to rely on his ally's navy for help in maintaining control of the coastal settlements.

In British eyes influence in foreign ports carried with it an obligation to 'civilize'. This meant spreading Christianity and European culture and abolishing the slave trade. In order to keep on good terms with his allies, the Sultan of Zanzibar assisted European missionaries (the first to arrive was Johann Krapf, who began work at Rabai in 1844), traders and explorers. An increasing number of adventurous white men penetrated the 'Dark Continent' along the east coast trade routes between 1850 and 1880. During those years Livingstone, Burton, Speke, Grant and Stanley solved for the outside world the problem of the source of the Nile and accurately mapped the African lakes system for the first time. These travellers reported their experiences in books, newspaper articles and speeches. The more the Western world heard about the African interior the more appalled it became about the slave trade, the 'heathenism' and the 'backwardness' of these regions. Pressure was placed on missionary societies to send teachers and preachers into Africa. Pressure was placed on politicians to use their influence with African rulers.

British attack on a slaving dhow

Sayid Said was frequently asked by British representatives to put a stop to the slave trade. This placed him in a difficult position: he did not wish to upset his allies yet he knew that any decisive move against the slave trade would anger many of his subjects, who profited greatly from it, and would probably drive them to revolt. Said handled the situation with political skill. He made promises and half promises and he signed treaties which were largely ineffective. By the time of his death the slave trade had, in theory, been confined to the Sultan's East African dominions and the British navy was empowered to patrol coastal waters and search dhows suspected of carrying slaves to other lands. But the volume of the slave trade continued to increase; the slave markets of Zanzibar and other towns were busier than ever (much of the increased demand is explained by the development of the Pemba and Zanzibar clove industry); most slaving dhows successfully evaded the British blockade.

Failure only increased the determination of British inter-ventionists to stamp out the traffic in human bodies. Events in Zanzibar helped them to achieve their aim. After the death of Sultan Said a succession dispute broke out and it was only with the support of the British Consul, Colonel Atkins Hamerton, that the rightful heir, Majid, was able to take the throne. Even then he had to deal with revolutions and attempted revolutions for another five years. In 1870 Sultan Barghash ascended the throne. He had spent several years as an exile in Bombay, where he had seen for himself the colonial might of the British. From the beginning of his reign he found himself under pressure from the British Consul, Dr John Kirk, to act decisively against the slave trade. In 1872 Zanzibar was hit by a terrible hurricane. Faced with the enormous task of reconstruction, Barghash found himself more reliant than ever on his allies. The following year he reluctantly signed a treaty closing all slave markets and abolishing slave trading throughout his dominions. From this point onwards the ruler of Zanzibar was little more than a client ruler of an unofficial British protectorate. His allies encouraged him to make a reality of his rule in the interior, but only so that the provisions of the anti-slave trade treaty could be enforced there. More and more Europeans travelled inland as explorers, mission-aries, technicians, traders and hunters. Increasingly they came into conflict with the Sultan's subjects who, since their coastal outlets were closed to them, became more active as slave and ivory traders in the interior. By 1880 the activities of Egyptian, Sudanese, Khartoumer and Zanzibari agents had established large areas of Islamic control between Khartoum and the Zambezi. It seemed quite possible that this whole, vast area might be brought into the Muslim world and that a series of empires based on slavery might be established there.

Chapter 7   Africa and Europe

For about seventy years most of Africa was under European rule. In this section we shall consider how and why this conquest was achieved. As we have seen, the Portuguese, Dutch, French and British had gained control of some areas but by 1880 only a small part of the continent was in the hands of Europeans. It was not at all clear that the foreigners would maintain control in all areas, let alone extend their authority.

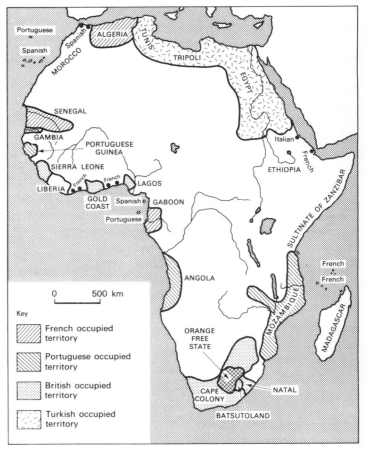

Europeans in Africa in 1800

Africans were resisting European control in most places and most of the white colonies received little support from their governments in Europe. After 1880 this situation changed. European powers took part in a 'scramble' for African territory and within a few years there were few parts of the continent that were not ruled from London, Brussels, Lisbon, Berlin, Paris, Madrid or Rome.

This enormous change was partly the result of events in Africa and partly the result of events in Europe. First, we will consider the events in Africa which led up to the 'scramble'. At this time many European people were developing a new interest in Africa. Africa had always been an almost unknown continent to the rest of the world. Desert, jungle, arid bush-land, disease-bearing insects, wild animals, inhospitable peoples and other real and imaginary difficulties discouraged foreigners from travelling into the interior. But in the nine-teenth century a few brave men—missionaries, explorers and adventurers—did travel far from European settlements deep into the heart of Africa. Many of them wrote books and news-paper articles describing their experiences. For the first time people in Europe could read about the rivers, mountains, animals and peoples of what had always been thought of as the 'Dark Continent'. Some Europeans became interested in and concerned for Africans. Others thought Africa would be a good place to make money.

The most active and adventurous newcomers were Christian missionaries. In Britain and Germany in the late eighteenth century there had been great religious revivals and one result had been a rapid growth of missionary activity. The movement spread to the rest of Europe and to the United States of America so that by the mid-nineteenth century there were many missionary societies working in parts of the world and obeying Christ's command, 'Go into all the world and preach the gospel.' As you can see from the map on page 180, many mission stations had been set up by the end of the century. Because they went far beyond existing white settlement areas to reach the 'heathen' the missionaries also became explorers, discovering and mapping rivers, lakes and mountains pre-viously unknown to the outside world. Some explorers were not inspired by religious zeal. They came to Africa simply to find out about it, driven by a curiosity that their African hosts

Missionaries and explorers

frequently found difficult to understand. We have not the space to describe the travels of all these pioneer travellers so we will consider just two—one missionary and one explorer.

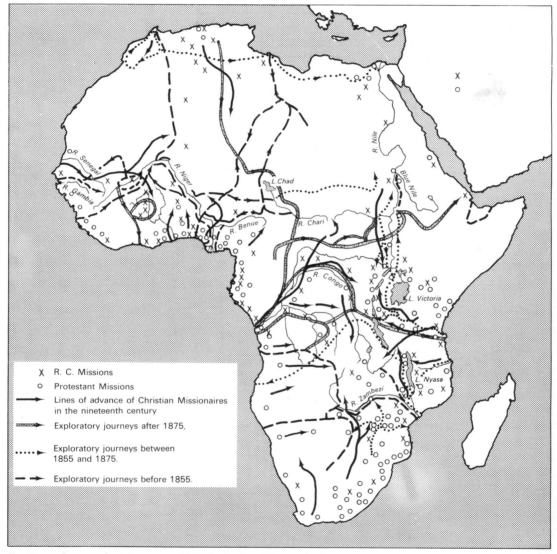

X	R. C. Missions
o	Protestant Missions
→	Lines of advance of Christian Missionaires in the nineteenth century
→	Exploratory journeys after 1875,
···→	Exploratory journeys between 1855 and 1875.
--→	Exploratory journeys before 1855.

Foreign explorers and missionaries until the beginning of the twentieth century

The most famous of all the missionaries was Dr David Livingstone. He was a great missionary traveller whose main concern was to reach new areas and people with the Christian gospel. Livingstone was an eager young man of twenty-eight intent on extending missionary boundaries when he arrived in South Africa in 1841. He devoted the remaining thirty-two years of his life to Africa. Livingstone went straight to Kuruman, the most northerly of all the existing London Missionary Society (LMS) posts. From there he went on into the unknown interior. For the next few years he worked mainly among the Tswana and founded mission stations. In 1847 he established a post at Kolobeng, nearly five hundred kilometres north of Kuruman. From Kolobeng he made expeditions still further afield. He had to head north to avoid the Kalahari desert to the west and hostile Boers to the east.* He also had a strong desire to meet Sebitwane, the Kololo chief. This he achieved in 1851 a few days before Sebitwane's death. On this journey he also reached the Zambezi at Sesheke.

David Livingstone

Lake Ngami is discovered by Oswell, Murray and Livingstone

---

*The Boers refused to allow the LMS to introduce African mission assistants in the areas they controlled. They reacted to Livingstone's rapid penetration with alarm and hostility and in 1852 attacked and burned down his post at Kolobeng.

Livingstone's ideas were becoming more and more unorthodox. He did not believe that the missionary's only task was to make converts. He loved all the peoples he met and therefore wanted the gospel to be spread *rapidly* among them.

Livingstone was excited when he realized that the Zambezi was a large river which flowed more than half way across Africa. He believed the river might prove to be a useful highway along which Europeans could travel, bringing Christianity and 'civilization' right to the heart of the continent. In 1853 Livingstone set off up river from Sesheke with canoes and men provided by Sekeletu, the new Kololo chief. The party reached the headwaters of the great Zambezi and crossed part of the Congo watershed to reach the coast. This meant crossing the area of great commercial activity between the Kasai and the Atlantic. Here Livingstone was angered by the slave trade.

At Luanda he refused to return to his family in Britain. Instead he went back into the interior to take his Kololo porters home. He reached Linyanti, the Kololo capital, in September 1855, almost two years after his departure.

Livingstone now decided to journey down the Zambezi to explore the country to the east. Several Kololo volunteered to accompany the white man and Sekeletu himself even travelled with Livingstone as far as the great falls of *Mosi-o-tunya*, which the missionary called Victoria Falls. In May 1856 Livingstone reached Quelimane and from there made his way to Britain.

In his own country he was recognized as one of the great explorers of the age and given a warm welcome. He wrote an account of his experiences called *Missionary Travels and Researches in South Africa*, which was very soon sold out. His popularity enabled him to travel all over Britain lecturing and preaching. He asked for more missionaries to 'open up' Africa to the civilizing influences of Europe, and many volunteers came forward for mission work and exploration. Businessmen offered to help set up mission stations and keep them supplied with necessary goods. More hunters and adventurers were attracted to Africa by the possibility of obtaining valuable ivory, skins and hunting trophies. The 1850s and 1860s saw many more Europeans travelling into the African interior for a variety of motives, several of them using the 'corridor' between Boer territory and the Kalahari which Livingstone had done much to 'open up'.

In 1858 Livingstone was appointed British Consul at Quelimane and also given the leadership of an official expedition to explore East-Central Africa. He still considered himself a missionary but left the LMS in order to put into practice his own missionary ideas.

The expedition of 1858–64 met with a series of disasters. The lower Zambezi and Shiré region which the explorers wished to examine was a disturbed area of commercial and political rivalry; it was also an area where slave traders were very active. Fierce rapids made long stretches of the Zambezi and the Shiré unnavigable. The steamboat that the expedition carried in sections gave a great deal of trouble and eventually sank in the Zambezi. The hostility of the Yao proved dangerous, and the Europeans were depressed by the signs of the slave trade. Livingstone argued with other members of the expedition, some of whom refused to continue with him. The Universities Mission to Central Africa which Livingstone helped to establish on Lake Nyasa proved a failure. Many of his companions caught tropical diseases and some died. The greatest tragedy for Livingstone came in April 1862 when his wife died of fever. In the following year the expedition was recalled.

But there were some achievements also. Livingstone returned home the Kololo who had accompanied him on his previous expedition and made fresh contact with Sekeletu. A small Kololo community was established in the Shiré valley where it became an important political factor. Livingstone and his companions became the first Europeans to see Lake Nyasa and they were able to add a new region to European maps of Africa. Although the first UMCA venture was a failure, missionary contact was made with the peoples of the Lake Nyasa shore and in the 1870s Christian teachers returned to the lake.

When Livingstone returned to Britain in 1864 he was able to provide his countrymen with yet more information about the 'Dark Continent'. In lectures and in his new book *Narrative of an Expedition to the Zambezi and its Tributaries* he described the geography of the newly explored area, but more than that he described the activities of African, Arab and Portuguese slave traders. Livingstone thought Yao slavers and the Arab and Swahili coastal merchants with whom they worked closely were the most savage and evil men he had met.

Two of the women had been shot the day before for attempting to untie the thongs. This, the rest were told, was to prevent them from attempting to escape. One woman had her infant's brains knocked out, because she could not carry her load and it; and a man was despatched with an axe because he had broken down with fatigue. Self-interest would have set a watch over the whole rather than commit murder; but in this traffic we increasingly find self-interest overcome by contempt of human life and bloodthirstiness. The Yao caravan leaders responsible for these outrages were:

> ... armed with muskets and bedecked with various articles of finery [and] marched jauntily in the front, middle and rear of the line, some of them blowing exultant

The Manyema massacre

notes on long tin horns. They seemed to feel that they were doing a very noble thing.*

Yet what appalled the missionary even more was to find Portuguese officials, the only representatives in the area of so-called European civilization, actively engaged in the evil traffic themselves. His reports angrily attacked Portuguese policy in eastern Africa. Since the problem was so great and the Portuguese obviously unable to tackle it, Livingstone believed that the only way to restore peace and prosperity to this part of Africa was English colonization:

English races cannot compete in manual labour of any kind with the natives, but they can take a leading part in managing the land, improving the quality, creating the quantity, and extending the varieties of the production of the soil; and by taking a lead too in trade and in all public matters the Englishman would be an unmixed advantage to everyone below and around him; for he would fill a place now practically vacant.†

But the British government was not interested in spending taxpayers' money on new colonies that would be expensive to establish and maintain, that would involve clashes with African peoples and, probably, lead to arguments with other European nations. But the ideas of pushing out the Portuguese and of colonizing East-Central Africa had been spread. Not many years later other men, including politicians, took up those ideas.

Dr Livingstone's last African journey began in 1866 when he left the east coast, travelling up the river Rovuma towards Lake Nyasa, in order to explore Lake Tanganyika and beyond, in the hope of discovering the source of the White Nile. He took no white companions and his expedition was a small one. Again he met difficulties as he crossed the troubled lands of the Yao, Cewa, Bemba and Tabwa. Some of his porters deserted; his supplies and medicines were lost or stolen; the battle-scorched earth could not provide his expedition with food; some peoples, whose only experience of non-Africans had been of ivory and slave traders, regarded

---

*Narrative of an Expedition to the Zambezi and its Tributaries, pp. 356–7.

†Letter of Livingstone quoted in R. Coupland, Kirk on the Zambezi, p. 271.

Livingstone with suspicion or hostility. The explorer was frequently ill and always saddened by further evidence of the slave trade. What made matters worse was that he sometimes had to rely on the slavers for supplies, hospitality and protection. For instance, in 1867, Tippu Tip came to Livingstone's assistance when the latter was weak with hunger and disease.

Livingstone visited the Kingdom of Kazembe, which he found in a sad state of decline. He moved northwards through the lands of the Rua and Manyema, where the Zanzibari slavers were now well established. In 1871 he was met at Ujiji by H. M. Stanley, a journalist who had been sent to find him. Stanley brought valuable supplies and medicines but failed to persuade Livingstone to leave Central Africa. After sailing round Lake Tanganyika with Stanley and saying goodbye to the journalist at Tabora, Livingstone turned westwards once more. He explored the Lualaba, which he believed to be part of the Nile system. At Chitambo's village near Lake Bangweulu David Livingstone, weakened by illness, fatigue and lack of food, died on 30 April 1873.

When news of Livingstone's death reached England millions of people were stirred by the great missionary's sacrifice. They felt that this sacrifice must not be in vain. As one newspaper put it, 'The work of England for Africa must henceforth begin in earnest where Livingstone left it off.'

Henry Morton Stanley

H. M. Stanley was, as we have seen, a journalist and was in the pay of British and American newspapers. His backers were wealthy men and when Stanley set out to find Livingstone in 1871 he travelled at the head of a large and well-equipped expedition. Stanley was strong, tough, determined and ruthless. He seldom allowed anything or anyone to stand in his way. In the Congo he earned himself the nickname 'the smasher of rocks'. Stanley was very moved by his meeting with Livingstone and when he heard of the missionary's death he decided to complete the task Livingstone had left uncompleted—the exploration of the Lualaba and its possible connection with the Nile system.

He set out from Bagamoyo on the east coast in November 1874 with a large expedition and reached Lake Victoria in record time. A theory put forward by an earlier explorer (J. H. Speke) had claimed this lake as the source of the White Nile. Stanley travelled right round the lake by boat and proved

Mutesa receives Stanley

that it had only one outlet, the White Nile. As we have seen
(page 164), Stanley visited Kabaka Mutesa of Buganda. He
sent home a message challenging the missionary societies to
respond to Mutesa's request for Christian teachers.

Returning to the old caravan route south of Lake Victoria,
Stanley saw for himself the activities of the slavers. He met
Mirambo, Rumaliza (the Arab slave chief of Ujiji) and Tippu
Tip. He travelled round Lake Tanganyika and proved that it
had no connection with the Nile. He then made for the
Lualaba. By questioning Tippu Tip and other Arabs at
Nyangwe, Stanley learned that the river entered the 'endless'
forest to the north and then turned westwards. He now had to
decide whether to follow the river right through the unhealthy
forest for thousands of kilometres or return to England the way
he had come. Stanley knew his expedition could not make the
westward journey without Arab aid, so he asked Tippu Tip
to help him. Tippu Tip agreed to accompany Stanley part of

King Leopold II

the way. The journey was a terrible one. All Stanley's European companions and many of his African helpers died. As well as smallpox and malaria, treacherous rapids and unfriendly river dwellers all took their toll. But Stanley completed his voyage, proving that the Lualaba was the main tributary of the Congo, and he emerged at the mouth of that river in August 1877.

Stanley was excited by the commercial possibilities of Central Africa. He believed the Congo would be an excellent highway to the distant interior from which ivory and other products could be brought. He wanted the British government to annexe the area, establish posts along the river and build roads to bypass unnavigable stretches of waterway. But the British government was not interested. Someone who was interested was King Leopold II of Belgium. He believed that he could make a personal fortune by exploiting the resources of the Congo basin. He set up the International Congo Association, the declared intention of which was to explore the region and bring to its peoples the benefits of 'civilization'. In fact the Association was just a way of disguising Leopold's personal ambitions. Leopold employed Stanley as his agent and from 1879 to 1884 the explorer spent most of his time on the lower and middle Congo, making treaties in the name of the International Congo Association, establishing trading and administrative posts, setting up a steamer service on the lower river and building roads to bypass the rapids higher up. In effect, Henry Stanley established the Congo Free State.

Stanley's last major exploit was the rescue of Emin Pasha. Emin was a German serving the Egyptian government as Governor of Equatoria Province. In 1886 the Mahdist revolt in the Sudan (see page 195) cut him off from Egypt. Stanley organized an expedition to rescue Emin and his men by way of the Congo. Leopold II saw the venture as a means of pushing the frontiers of his kingdom to the north-east and, perhaps, of gaining control of the Nile. Leaving some of his party at Yambuya, Stanley made an appalling journey through dense forest to Lake Albert, where he was joined by Emin. To his dismay he found the German unwilling to leave. Stanley had to force Emin to accompany him to Bagamoyo (1889).

Other Europeans

As well as missionaries and explorers there was an increasing number of Europeans travelling in various parts of Africa for other reasons. There were hired agents and soldiers of the Egyptian government. There were traders, hunters, prospectors and others who simply wanted a life of adventure far away from all the restrictions of European civilization. They travelled along the trans-Saharan routes, along the slave caravan trails of East and Central Africa and up from the Cape through what is now Botswana. We have already seen how their activities sometimes led directly to colonial intervention and this slow European penetration would probably have continued for many years if events in Europe had not sparked off a 'scramble' for colonial territory.

Throughout most of the nineteenth century Britain had been the most economically advanced country in Europe. She had pioneered the industrial revolution and transformed herself from an agricultural country to a manufacturing nation with the world's first sprawling, grimy, industrial cities. She had the best and biggest merchant navy in the world. British ships carried raw materials from many lands to Britain and manufactured goods from Britain to many lands. The search for materials and markets had led to the building of the British Empire, the biggest empire the world had ever seen. But British governments were always reluctant to add to that empire. It was their experience that colonies cost a great deal to administer. Britain's leaders preferred to encourage traders to establish their own links with other lands. The British navy helped to make the sea routes safe. For this, bases such as Cape Town and Mauritius were important. Occasionally Britain sent military or naval assistance to their subjects who were having difficulties with the natives of a particular locality. Sometimes this intervention led to unofficial political control (as in Zanzibar), sometimes it led to conquest and colonization (as in Lagos). But as long as Britain led the world economically the British government believed that such involvement should be kept to a minimum.

While Britain was establishing her lead, the major European nations were having large political problems. Germany and Italy, for instance, were evolving from a number of small states into new nations, while France experienced between 1814 and 1871 six major changes of government, four revolutions, and two invasions. But by 1871 these upheavals were past. By this time, too, the industrial revolution was having a great effect on the continental powers. They now began to be in need of markets and sources of raw material. Their captains and merchants began to challenge the supremacy of Britain's captains and merchants. Europe also had a population problem. During the second half of the century millions of men and women were driven by poverty or hardship to seek what they hoped would be a better life in another land. But the most powerful forces at work in Europe were nationalism and national rivalry. Germany and Italy, the new nations, were determined to prove their power and glory. France, humiliated by a crushing military defeat in 1870–71, was determined to reassert her ancient greatness. Britain was determined not to yield more of her commercial and maritime supremacy to any rival power. These conflicting nationalisms, as Europe's leading statesmen knew, could lead to diplomatic clashes or even war. No one wanted this, least of all Europe's leading political figure, Otto von Bismark, Chancellor of Germany. He needed peace and stability in Europe so that the new Germany could develop rapidly. As a part of his policy of keeping the peace in Europe he encouraged the nations to turn their ambitions towards other parts of the world, including Africa.

Concern and curiosity about Africa had been growing steadily between 1850 and 1880 but after the latter date there was a great increase of interest in the 'Dark Continent'. In all the leading European countries there were groups of imperialists urging their governments to annex parts of Africa. They urged all sorts of motives for colonization: the wealth to be gained from the exploitation of ivory, gold, diamonds, copper, etc; the need of Africans for Christianity; the urgency of rescuing Africa from the slave trade; the wonderful opportunities for industrious immigrants. But all of them had the same thought in the back of their minds, 'If we don't colonize, someone else will.' Still the statesmen paid little attention to the imperialists.

Clashes in Egypt and the Congo

By 1880 Britain and France had a number of colonies (most of them small) round the coasts of Africa. Portugal, of course, still had her possessions in Angola and Mozambique. The first events in the 'scramble' for Africa occurred when rival colonial ambitions clashed in Egypt and the Congo.

We have seen how the Khedive of Egypt had been deposed in favour of his son Tawfiq as a result of pressure from British and French financiers. Tawfiq was only a puppet ruler con-

190

Charge of Highlanders at Tel-el-Kebir

trolled by the Europeans, and it was not long before angry
Egyptian nationalists rose in a revolt led by Urabi Pasha.
France and Britain decided to crush the revolt, but at the last
moment the French withdrew and it was a British army that
sailed to Egypt to crush Urabi's revolt at the battle of Tel-el-
Kebir (1882). The British government hoped to withdraw its
army quickly but soon discovered that the presence of British
troops was the only means of preserving peace and Tawfiq's
government. The French were furious and accused Britain
of having, in effect, colonized Egypt.

Meanwhile international rivalry was building up in the
Congo basin. In 1882 the French became suspicious of Leopold
II's intentions and concerned for the safety of their trading
interests on the Gabon coast. They sent Count Savorgnan de
Brazza to the Congo and he made a treaty with Makoko, one
of the Bateke chiefs, which he claimed gave France possession
of a large area to the north of the lower Congo. Now it was

Portugal's turn to become alarmed. She saw in all this activity a threat to her interests in Angola. She now claimed to control the mouth of the Congo, which gave her control over the commercial activities of Leopold and the French. Portugal asked Britain to support her claim and a treaty was drawn up whereby Britain guaranteed Portuguese control of the Congo mouth. Once more the French were angry. They asked Bismark to help in their struggle against Britain and Portugal.

Bismarck was delighted to see the other European nations squabbling among themselves, especially in distant Africa, in which he had not the slightest interest. But he did not want these squabbles to become too serious and lead to war in Europe. He therefore suggested a conference to meet in the German capital, Berlin, which would settle existing disagreements and establish the principles on which any further colonization of Africa would be based. Bismarck knew that it would be difficult for him to dominate the coming conference if he had no colonial interests himself and so he encouraged German agents to set up colonies in Africa. This led to German claims being made for Togoland and Cameroon in West Africa, for part of East Africa and for South-West Africa. He also manufactured an argument with Britain about Angra Pequeña.

In 1882 a German merchant, F. Lüderitz, had established a trading post at Angra Pequeña on the coast of South-West Africa. The German government asked whether Britain, as the ruler of Cape Colony, would protect the members of Lüderitz's settlement but received no satisfactory reply. In 1883 Lüderitz acquired more land and declared a German protectorate over it. The following year this protectorate was ratified in Berlin but a startled British government learned that it included, not just Angra Pequeña, but the whole of Namaqualand and Damaraland from the Orange river to the Angolan border. The British feared that the Germans might make an alliance with the Boer states against them. They hastened to lay claim to Bechuanaland, thereby driving a wedge between German and Boer territory and keeping open the way to the north.

The Berlin Conference 1884–5　　Meanwhile the Berlin Conference had begun. Briefly it did two things: it cleared up existing boundary disputes and it established the principles upon which further European

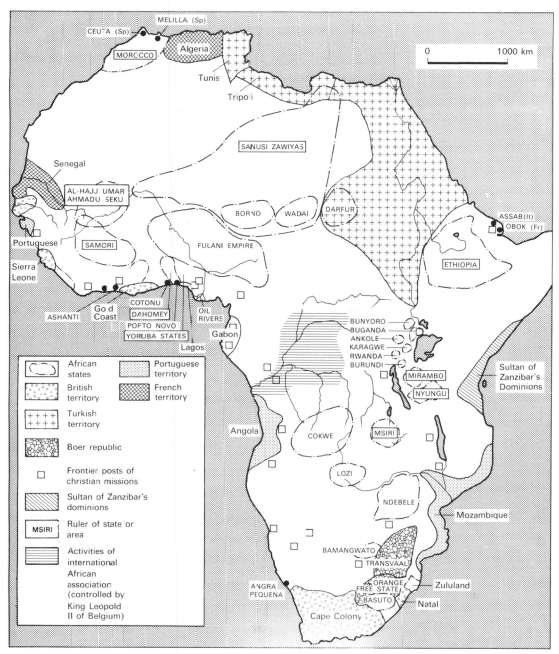

MELILLA (Sp)

CEUTA (Sp)

MOROCCO

Algeria

Tunis

Tripoli

SANUSI ZAWIYAS

Senegal

AL-HAJJ UMAR
AHMADU SEKU

Portuguese

SAMORI

Sierra
Leone

BORNO   WADAI   DARFUR

FULANI EMPIRE

ASSAB (It)
OBOK (Fr)

ETHIOPIA

ASHANTI

Gold
Coast

COTONU
DAHOMEY
PORTO NOVO
YORUBA STATES

OIL
RIVERS

Gabon

Lagos

African
states

British
territory

Turkish
territory

Boer republic

Frontier posts of
christian missions

Sultan of Zanzibar's
dominions

MSIRI

Ruler of state or
area

Activities of
international
African
association
(controlled by
King Leopold
II of Belgium)

Portuguese
territory

French
territory

BUNYORO
BUGANDA
ANKOLE
KARAGWE
RWANDA
BURUNDI

MIRAMBO

NYUNGU

Sultan of
Zanzibar's
Dominions

Angola

COKWE

MSIRI

LOZI

NDEBELE

Mozambique

BAMANGWATO

TRANSVAAL

ANGRA
PEQUENA

ORANGE
FREE STATE

BASUTO

Cape Colony

Zululand

Natal

0   1000 km

Colonial possessions in Africa at the time of the Berlin Conference claims to African territory were to be based. The conference confirmed existing colonial possessions; it rejected Portugal's claim to control the Congo mouth; it established the Congo Free State, under the control of Leopold II, as the administering authority in the Congo basin; and it stated that a vast area of Central Africa was to be a free trade area, open to the commerce and philanthropic exercise of all nations. Many boundaries were left vague and the principles laid down for future colonization were that an area could be claimed only if the claiming nation effectively controlled it and only if the other signatories to the Berlin Act agreed. No longer could colonial powers, like Britain, claim vague, unofficial protectorates. The Berlin Act made it necessary for any power wanting to claim part of Africa to actually send representatives there to 'grab' it. That is exactly what happened in the years after the Berlin Conference.

Chapter 8

The establishment of alien rule in North Africa

When Britain seized control at Cairo in 1882, Egypt's rule of the Sudan was beginning to crumble. In 1881 Muhammad Ahmad, a Muslim teacher from a village near Khartoum, proclaimed himself the *Mahdi*, or saviour. He said he had come to deliver the Sudan from Egyptian rule and to re-establish pure Islam. The peoples of the northern Sudan were tired of Egyptian corruption, heavy taxation and the granting of important administrative positions to Christian Europeans. He quickly gained a following among the nomadic peoples of Kordofan, and two years later his movement had become strong enough to capture the provincial capital of El Obeid. The British rulers of Egypt had to decide whether to resist the Mahdi or withdraw Egyptian personnel from the Sudan. Egypt's finances were still in complete disorder and the British government had no desire to finance the reconquest of the Sudan, since it still hoped to pull out of Egypt altogether. Withdrawal from the Sudan was therefore ordered. Garrisons and administrative posts were closed and many Egyptian staff escaped down the Nile. But at Khartoum General Gordon, who had been sent to organize the evacuation of the town, decided instead to resist the Mahdi. Khartoum fell in 1885 and Gordon was among the dead. With the fall of Khartoum all of the northern Sudan was in Mahdist hands and the new state gradually extended its frontiers southwards. But the Mahdi did not live to see it; he died shortly after the capture of Khartoum. He was succeeded by his general Abdallahi, who took the title Caliph.

In Cairo a British Consul-General (Sir Evelyn Baring) had been appointed and the country's finances were in the hands of an international committee, the *Caisse de la Dette*. The foreigners received little support from the Egyptian people, and though Baring had restored the Egyptian economic balance by 1889 he could not find any local politicians prepared to take over the government. So the British military

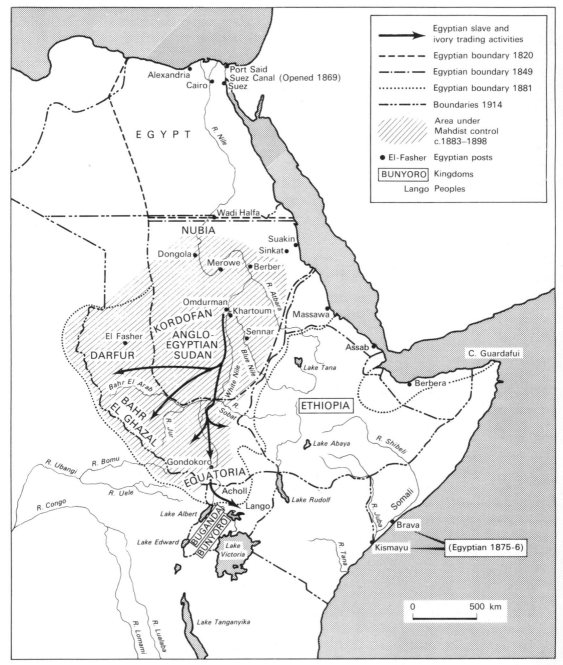

Egyptian expansion in the nineteenth century

The Mahdi's tomb

occupation continued. By this date the Egyptian withdrawal from the Sudan had been completed with Stanley's 'rescue' of the reluctant Emin Pasha from Equatoria Province. There were many British advisers in London and in East Africa who had urged the retention of Equatoria. They wanted to ensure the security of Uganda and they disliked the idea of the upper Nile being controlled by a rival European power. They argued that since Egypt was completely dependent on the Nile, a potential enemy could do the country considerable harm if it had access to the upper waters. In the 1880s and 1890s the Congo Free State and the French in Gabon and the Sudan were both extending their borders eastwards. France and Italy had bases on the Red Sea coast from which penetration inland was possible. The Mahdists occupied Equatoria between 1888 and 1891 but then most of the peoples of the province rose against the conquerors who were forced to withdraw. There was now no political unity in the southern Sudan. Furthermore, the Mahdist state itself seemed to be weakening. There had been revolts in various parts of the caliphate and when, in 1889, Mahdist forces had invaded Egypt they had been soundly defeated. The political chaos

The Mahdi

197

of the Sudan now began to inspire the leading colonial powers of North-East Africa with thoughts of conquest.

By 1890 Baring had realized that there could be no possibility of withdrawal from Egypt in the near future. The harsh taxation and forced labour that had been used to revive the economy had been stopped. New irrigation schemes and other reforms had been introduced. But the peasants still hated their overlords and rebellion was just below the surface of Egyptian society. Nor had the people any respect for the Khedive and the pashas, who lived in luxury and obeyed their foreign masters.

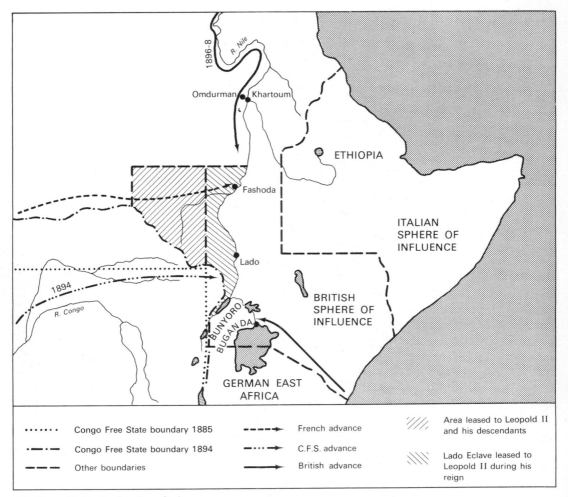

The Scramble for the Southern Sudan

Britain soon had to think about the Sudan. In 1891 the Ethiopians began strongly to resist an attempt by Italy to establish a protectorate over their country. The rulers of Egypt feared that Emperor Menelik of Ethiopia might make an alliance with the Mahdists and, having disposed of the Italians, launch their combined forces against Egypt. When Menelik's forces won the great victory of Adowa in 1896 an Anglo-Egyptian army of occupation marched south. A railway was begun from Wadi Halfa and this made it clear to all that

The defence of the Caliph's standard at the battle of Omdurman

the occupation was intended to be permanent. The main clash with the Mahdists came in 1898 at Omdurman. In this terrible battle 20,000 of the Caliph's subjects were killed.

Meanwhile the French had made a move. Britain had disposed of the claims of other colonial powers by diplomacy. An agreement with Germany in 1890 had removed the German presence from Uganda. In 1894 Leopold II, whose agents had been drawing steadily closer to the upper Nile, was bought off with a lease of land bordering the Nile. But the French proved more difficult. They wanted the British to make territorial concessions in West Africa, so they sent a force from Gabon to Fashoda on the Nile. The British general, Kitchener, hurried from Khartoum with part of his army and camped outside Fashoda. It was only after months of tense diplomatic activity that war was avoided and the French withdrew. The way was now open for the Anglo-Egyptian reoccupation of the whole Sudan.

From 1882 to 1914 Egypt was nominally ruled by the Ottoman Sultan. Throughout this period the British tried to establish an Egyptian government through which they could practise some form of indirect rule but all Egyptian politicians were first and foremost nationalists who wanted the British to get out and take the Khedive with them. Sir Evelyn Baring (later Lord Cromer) did a great deal for the economy of the country during his long term as Consul-General (1883–1907). He reduced the large and expensive Egyptian civil service, built a dam at Aswan (1902) which made possible permanent (as opposed to seasonal) irrigation of the Nile valley, reduced taxation and established a smooth-running, up-to-date administration. But these reforms did nothing to bridge the gap between ruler and ruled, divided as they were by differences of race, religion, culture and language.

The Sudan was officially an Anglo-Egyptian Condominium, i.e. a country ruled jointly by Britain and Egypt. In effect Egypt had little say in the Sudan's affairs. The country was ruled by a Governor-General and his largely British staff. English was the teaching medium in most schools. Economic reforms were based on the needs of the Sudan alone. For instance it was decided to divert some of the Nile waters to irrigate the cotton fields of Gezira district, a scheme that angered the Egyptians who were totally dependent on the Nile. By 1920 the beginnings of a modern road and railway system had been laid linking the Egyptian border, the middle Nile, the Red Sea ports and important centres such as Khartoum and El Fasher.

When the First World War broke out in 1914 Turkey sided with Germany. In Egypt the British declared Ottoman rule ended and established a protectorate. The Sultan organized an invasion of Egypt by Sanusi forces from Libya (1915). The invaders reached Marsa Matruh before being turned back by a large British army. Britain sent large numbers of troops to Egypt in order to protect the Suez Canal and used Egypt as a base for attacking the Ottoman Empire in the Middle East. As a result Egyptian labour, land, crops and houses were taken to help in the war effort. Had it not been for the quarter of a million British troops in the country and a British promise to grant Egyptian independence after the war there would have been a serious rebellion between 1914 and 1918.

Egyptian frontier during the desert campaign, First World War

After the war Britain and France, despite promises made to their Arab allies, divided between them the Arab provinces of the Ottoman Empire. This assured them full control of the route to the East and of the valuable Middle East oilfields. Egyptian nationalists under the leadership of Zaghlul Pasha immediately (1919) organized widespread riots and strikes. As a result Zaghlul was allowed to attend the peace conference meeting in Paris. All he achieved was the sending of a British commission to Egypt to draft a new constitution for the country. In 1920 this committee made its recommendations: Egypt should have independence under a constitutional monarchy and an elected parliament. But there was to be a permanent alliance with Britain, and British troops were to remain in Egypt to guard the Canal Zone. Such a constitution proved unacceptable to the nationalists. Egypt now had a new unity with the rest of the Arab world. The behaviour of Britain and France in the Middle East and the discovery that Britain had promised to give the Jews a national home in Palestine had created a pan-Arab movement aimed at the complete independence of all Arab states. Egypt's nationalists now knew that they were not alone in their anti-colonial struggle.

Ethiopia and Somalia

In 1880 Egypt controlled most of the ports on the Red Sea coast from Suakin to Cape Guardafui. In 1883 the Mahdist revolt forced Egypt to give up most of her possessions. Three foreign powers were now interested in the Somali coast and its hinterland. Britain looked to this area for meat supplies for her garrison at Aden and wished to stop other powers gaining a foothold of the route to India. France, which had a small trading post at Obock, wanted better commercial facilities and also wished to be in a position to check British ambitions. Italy, which had a base at Assab, felt herself falling behind in the colonial race and hoped to extend her control. In 1884 Britain occupied Zeila and Berbera and French representatives moved into Tajoura. The following year the Italians took Massawa and manned it as a base for an advance into the Ethiopian Highlands.

The collapse of Egyptian power in the Sudan had given the Emperor Yohannis IV of Ethiopia a breathing space. But he was not able to relax for long. The Italians played on the rivalry between Yohannis and Menelik of Shoa and they

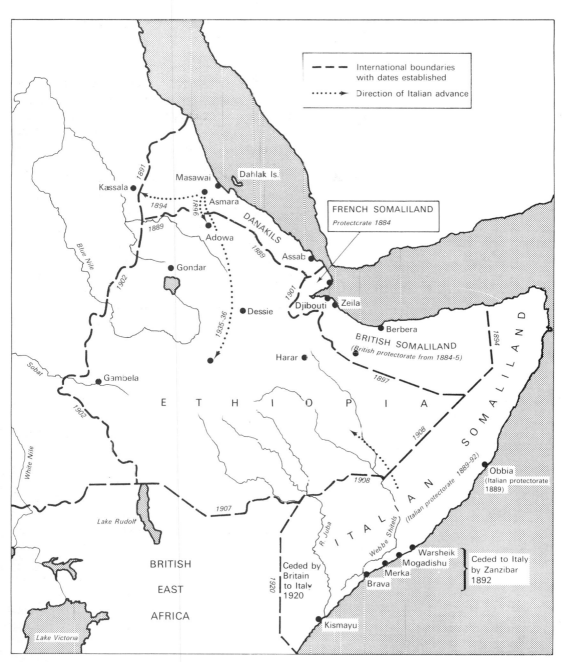

Legend:
– – – International boundaries with dates established
······► Direction of Italian advance

Kassala
Masawai
Dahlak Is.
Asmara
DANAKILS
FRENCH SOMALILAND
Protectcrate 1884
1891
1894
1896
1889
Adowa
1889
Assab
Gondar
1902
1901
Djibouti
Zeila
Dessie
Berbera
1935-36
BRITISH SOMALILAND
(British protectorate from 1884-5)
Blue Nile
Harar
1894
Sobat
Gambela
1897
E T H I O P I A
I T A L I A N   S O M A L I L A N D
1902
White Nile
1908
Obbia
(Italian protectorate 1889)
1908
(Italian protectorate 1889-92)
1907
Lake Rudolf
R. Juba
Webbe Shibeli
Warsheik
Mogadishu
Ceded to Italy by Zanzibar 1892
BRITISH
Merka
EAST
1920
Ceded by Britain to Italy 1920
Brava
AFRICA
Lake Victoria
Kismayu

European intervention in Ethiopia and Somalia

provided Menelik with arms. However the Ras of Shoa gave no practical help to the invaders and when Yohannis was faced with the first Italian thrust in 1887 he was able to stop it at the battle of Dogali. Then trouble reappeared on the Sudanese border. The Caliph declared a jihad against Christian Ethiopia and his followers overran much of Yohannis's territory. It was in battle against the Mahdists at Metemma in 1889 that the Emperor was killed.

By the terms of a recent agreement the Ras of Shoa now succeeded Yohannis as the Emperor Menelik II. He was to prove one of the greatest rulers in the history of Ethiopia. He completed the work of unification begun by his predecessors. He fought off the would-be invaders of his country. He extended Ethiopia's frontiers to the west and the south. He was one of the few African rulers to resist European conquest. To meet the immediate dangers facing Ethiopia Menelik needed guns. He therefore signed the Treaty of Ucciali with the eager Italians which, they believed, gave them protectorate rights over Ethiopia and he recognized their control of Eritrea. In return for his signature Menelik received a large supply of modern weapons. When, in 1891, Italy notified the major colonial powers that she had a protectorate over Ethiopia Menelik wrote to the European governments that the Treaty of Ucciali involved no surrender of sovereignty on his part, and that, moreover, he resented the partition of Africa by foreigners. The Italians realized now that they would have to resort to military conquest. Menelik succeeded in uniting all the provinces of the Empire to face the invasion. It came in 1896. The deciding battle was fought at Adowa where the Italians were devastatingly beaten by an African army using their own guns against them. Italy was forced to recognize Ethiopia's independence and the other European powers treated Menelik with a new respect. In 1896 Britain signed a treaty with Ethiopia recognizing Ethiopia's borders in return for her neutrality in their coming conflict with the Mahdists. Ten years later Britain, France and Italy all signed another treaty giving formal recognition to Ethiopia. Meanwhile, Menelik with his new-found power and prestige extended his country's frontiers to the river Sobat and Lake Rudolf (Turkana) in the south and south-west. To the south-east he successfully claimed a large tract of territory inhabited by the Somali and Galla (formerly ratified in 1908 when the border with Italian Somaliland was fixed). Menelik

Menelik Emperor of Abyssinia

Battle of Adowa

saw his country united, respected, enlarged and enriched from
the increased profits of ivory trading long before his death in
1913.

The Somali coast had, meanwhile, been divided up by the
three European powers operating in the area. Britain and
France, locked in petty and pointless rivalry, declared protectorates over the immediate hinterlands of their ports and
thus British and French Somaliland came into being. Italy
signed treaties with the Majerteyn Somali in 1889 and leased
the ports of Brava, Merka, Mogadishu and Warsheik from

the Sultan of Zanzibar. These became the basis for Italian Somaliland.*

The first serious resistance to colonial rule in Somalia was led by Muhammad Abdile Hassan, known to the British as the 'Mad Mullah' and to his countrymen as the father of Somali nationalism. He was a Muslim scholar and came from the Berbera region. Travelling north-eastern Africa as a wandering teacher, he came to realize that Islamic faith and culture were under attack from the colonial forces of Christian Europe. In 1891 he began to organize resistance to the Europeans. He led his followers inland to Haud and Ogaden, regions to which colonial rule did not extend. From these bases he launched attacks on British and Italian Somaliland and on Ethiopia. Right up to his death in 1920 Muhammad continued to defy his Christian neighbours and to prove a continual nuisance to them. He united many of the Somali tribes and gave them their first feeling of nationhood.

Libya

In 1881 the French occupied Tunisia. This angered the Ottoman Sultan. He could not offer military resistance to the aggressors but he did refuse to recognize the legality of their occupation and he refused for many years to discuss the settlement of the border between Tunisia and Tripolitania. The French for their part were more concerned about linking their North and West African possessions and were unable to bring military pressure to bear on the Sultan. What they did do was encourage Italian colonial ambitions directed towards Tripolitania and Cyrenaica. The Italians had hoped to annexe Tunisia, and, when they were forestalled by the French, national pride forced them to obtain some colonial territory in North Africa.

The major obstacle to an Italian take-over was Turkey's friendship with Germany, a close ally of the Italians. For the time being the government in Rome contented itself with encouraging Italians to settle in Tripolitania and Cyrenaica, buying land and opening businesses. In 1910 a new Ottoman governor, Ibrahim Pasha, arrived in Tripoli determined to check the Italian advance. He concluded a border agreement

---

*The boundary of Italian Somaliland with British East Africa was fixed in 1891 at the River Juba. In 1920 Britain ceded more territory to Italy in a new agreement.

with the French and made new laws prohibiting the sale of land to Italians. At the same time Ibrahim allowed German businesses to acquire territory. Seeing her colonial opportunity slipping from her grasp, Italy declared war on the Ottoman Empire (September 1911) and invaded Tripolitania and Cyrenaica with 60,000 men.

Much to the surprise of the invaders, the Sanusis and the peoples of the coastal area united behind their Turkish leaders. As a result the Italians were restricted to a few coastal footholds. After a year of fighting they had wasted a great deal of money and many young Italian lives but had nothing to show for it. In desperation the Rome government threatened a direct attack on Turkey and this forced the Sultan to make peace (October 1912). The terms were deliberately vague but amounted to Italian sovereignty over Libya while the Sultan remained the spiritual head of the Muslim people.

But the war in Libya was not over. The Sanusi leader Ahmad al-Sharif claimed to rule the country and continued to organize resistance. Unfortunately, some chiefs refused to recognize his authority and fought alone against the invaders. These divisions enabled the Italians to overrun most of the coastal area during the next two years but the Fezzan and most of Sirta resisted European control. When Italy joined in the First World War in 1915 she had to withdraw troops from Libya. The Ottoman Sultan declared a jihad against the European occupiers of North Africa, and Ahmad al-Sharif, supplied with German arms and military advisers, invaded Egypt. After a defeat in 1916 Ahmad retired and his place was taken by Muhammad Idris who made peace with Britain and kept the Sanusi out of the conflict. In 1917 the British succeeded in inducing Italian and Sanusi representatives to sign the Akrama Agreement which recognized the existing Sanusi and Italian areas of control.

In Tripolitania resistance continued, organized by Nuri Bey and Abdul-Rahman Azzam. They persuaded the local chiefs to form a very loose union and, in 1918, declared Tripolitania to be an independent republic. But the new state lacked the strength and unity to survive. The following year a compromise was negotiated with the Italians. Full Italian nationality was granted to the people and the right to share in government through an elected parliament. Azzam now formed the National Reform Party which was to become the spearhead of Libyan nationalism. In 1919 a similar con-

leaders, banned all political organizations and placed the protectorate under martial law.

By 1880 a second generation of settlers was growing up in Algeria and the immigrant community was increasing steadily as a result of natural multiplication and periodic waves of new arrivals. The European population (by 1900 two-thirds were French citizens) developed an aloof, racialist, intolerant attitude. They regarded themselves as a civilized élite upholding high cultural standards amidst a barbaric, heathen people. The Muslim population were a conquered race, enjoying few rights. They could be arrested, imprisoned and

Trooper of the camel corps in Libya

detained without trial by French officials. They were forbidden to leave their districts without permission and their land might be confiscated for real or supposed offences. Foreign travel, including the pilgrimage to Mecca, was almost impossible. Many Muslim law courts were closed and Muslim schools were discouraged. The native Algerian population increased while the amount of land available to the people for cultivation diminished. Some men found work on European farms but for the bulk of the people the results could only be increased poverty and frequent famine.

During the First World War about 173,000 Algerian Muslims served in the French army. In 1918 they expected a grateful French government to reward their community by granting political rights or at least by reducing some of their burdens. A group called the Young Algerians wanted full integration as French citizens on the basis of racial equality. The politicians in Paris moved towards this objective by increasing the Muslim representation on regional councils and by removing certain restrictions. These measures could have been the start of a move towards racial harmony but the settlers threatened to take over the government of the colony unless all the concessions were withdrawn. The French government gave way. In doing so it ensured that Algerian political activity would eventually be led not by the moderate Young Algerians but by more extreme groups.

Morocco in 1880 was still an independent kingdom. The authority of its Sultan was undermined by the activities of European agents and ignored by many of the Moroccan chiefs. But Morocco remained independent largely because the European powers could not agree to any one of their number controlling a territory that was vitally situated at the entrance to the Mediterranean Sea. Sultan Mawlay Hasan (1873–94) did a great deal to restore the authority of the government. He created an efficient, well-equipped army. He made administrative reforms. He improved the taxation system. He led military expeditions against some of the more unruly chiefs. But Mawlay Hasan was succeeded by a minor, Mawlay Abdul-Aziz, and during his reign (1894–1908) most of his father's work collapsed and the European consuls gained still more power.

The young Sultan's subjects refused to pay taxes and

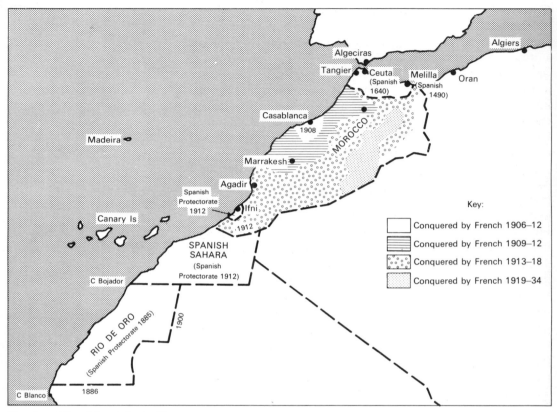

French and Spanish activity in Morocco

Key:

	Conquered by French 1906–12
	Conquered by French 1909–12
	Conquered by French 1913–18
	Conquered by French 1919–34

grumbled about his growing dependence on European advisers. Sanhaja and Jabala tribesmen raided on an unprecedented scale. In 1903 a pretender to the throne, Bu Himara, led a revolt against the Sultan and soon controlled the Middle Atlas and eastern frontier district. France used this breakdown of law and order as an excuse for direct intervention to 'protect her nationals'. In 1904 she made one agreement with Britain, which allowed her a free hand in Morocco in return for recognizing Britain's position in Egypt, and another with Spain, dividing Morocco into spheres of influence. A protest came from the German Emperor, Wilhelm II, who had suddenly developed North African ambitions of his own. He declared his intention of protecting Moroccan independence (1905). A compromise was reached the following year at the

Algeciras Conference when Morocco's independence was formally recognized by the European powers but Spain and France were allowed to 'police' the country in order to restore law and order. The French interpreted this agreement as a licence to conquer and began moving troops into their sphere in 1907.

These activities led to further divisions in Moroccan society. The Sultan's brother Abdul-Hafiz rebelled and forced Abdul-Aziz to flee to the French for protection. In 1908 the Sultan summoned up the courage to face his brother in battle but he was deserted by his own troops and had to be rescued by his French allies. Mawlay Abdul-Aziz now abdicated in favour of his brother. But Abdul-Hafiz was no more able to prevent French and Spanish expansion than his predecessor. Both nations now set out to occupy their respective spheres. Effective resistance came not from the Sultan but from many of the mountain tribes. The European conquest was not completed until 1934. In 1911 Germany made one more attempt to intervene on behalf of the Moroccan government, but in a treaty the following year Germany agreed to recognize a French protectorate over Morocco in return for French Central African territory added to Cameroon. Abdul-Hafiz signed a treaty of protection. Next year he was removed from office by his 'protectors'. A new sultan was appointed but could not make any pretence to authority. In 1912 Spanish protectorates were established over El Rif (Spanish Morocco) and Spanish Sahara, adjoining Rio de Oro (which had become a Spanish protectorate in 1885). Tangier was given the status of an international port.

By 1914 France had added to her colonial conquests the vast areas of French West Africa and French Equatorial Africa. This was the result of thrusts from Gabon, the Niger valley and Algeria. Thwarted by the Royal Niger Company in her attempt to control the lower Niger, the French continued eastwards their colonial expansion which had begun long ago in Senegal. They thus encountered Borno under its new leader, Rabeh. Rabeh was a Sudanese ex-slaver, who had served for many years under Zubeir Pasha. In 1891, at the head of his own private army, he invaded the crumbling empire of Borno. In 1893 he achieved final victory at the battle of Ngala. He had just succeeded in reorganizing the

The Sahara and the Central Sudan

administration and founding a flourishing slave trade when the French appeared on the scene. He offered fierce resistance and was for some time successful. He was finally defeated and killed by the French in 1900. The Sanusi of Wadai and the Saharan oases also offered resistance but after 1900 the French were able to advance on them from the north-west, west and south. One by one the major caravan routes fell under French control. Yet, so vast is this area and so scattered its people, that colonial rule meant very little. French control looked more impressive on the map than it was in practice.

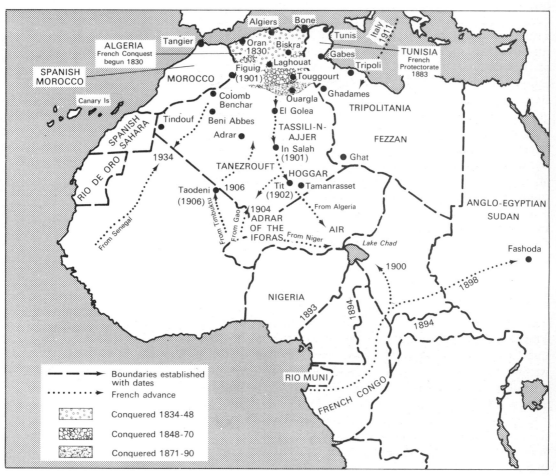

French advance into the Sahara and the Central Sudan

The establishment of alien rule in West Africa   Chapter 9

By 1880 the British and French were well established along the West African coast and had begun to advance inland. Much of Senegambia was under French control and they were penetrating the interior from their forts on the coasts of Dahomey and Ivory Coast. French influence also spread southwards from Algeria. Britain was well established in Gambia, Sierra Leone, Gold Coast and Lagos and had established a large degree of control in the Niger Delta through her consuls. The 'scramble' was largely a contest between the representatives of these two nations to establish claims to the more fertile areas of forest and savannah and the rivers that gave access to the interior. Official expeditions and commercial companies both played their parts in the colonial conquest but when it came to establishing administration the merchants lacked the necessary money and manpower. Then European governments, sometimes reluctantly, took over the responsibility. The colonialists took little interest in the people of West Africa and the new lines they drew on the map cut across African territorial boundaries. Shaded areas on the map did not mean that the Europeans had

Camp of mountain artiilery battery

conquered those areas on the ground. Often colonial claims were based on 'treaties' to which African leaders paid little attention or brief, indecisive military campaigns. Many communities preserved their independence and way of life until well into the colonial era.

The lower Niger

Along the lower Niger the initiative was taken by British merchants. The most powerful company was the United African Company formed in 1879 and led by George Taubman Goldie. Goldie bought out his British rivals and by tough business tactics he soon ruined the French firms in the area. The United African Company was now a powerful commercial monopoly, and Goldie wanted the British government to grant him a charter which would give him the right to administer the whole area of the lower Niger and the Benue. For the moment he was unsuccessful; the government preferred to let him 'pacify' the area without cost to the taxpayer and without causing them diplomatic embarrassment. But the French watched with growing alarm as Goldie's agents pushed further and further inland.

By 1884 Goldie had made about 37 treaties and established a strong fleet of twenty small gunboats. He broke resistance to the Company's activities by ordering attacks on places like Akassa, Brass, Patani and Asaba which were the chief centres of African raids. Nupe had already granted the British a monopoly of trade in 1879 and Goldie saw to it that Umoru, the Etsu (king) of Nupe, was given support against rebels within his state.

While Goldie was expanding British influence in what is now northern Nigeria, Glover was extending his authority steadily eastwards and westwards from Lagos. Alarmed by all this, in 1883 the French annexed Cotonou, Great and Little Popo and Porto Novo, thus preventing Britain linking Lagos with the Gold Coast. However, the activities of Goldie's new National African Company (formed in 1882) made it impossible for France to prevent Britain laying claim to southern Nigeria. During the Berlin Conference the British therefore secured the lower Niger; Germany had Togoland and Cameroon and the French took the upper Niger, Senegal, the Guinea Coast, the Ivory Coast and Porto Novo. Thus after 1885 the stage was set for the carving up of West Africa.

In 1886 the National African Company was granted a charter and was renamed the Royal Niger Company. One of the reasons for the granting of the charter had been the need to stop slave trading in the Niger-Benue region. From the beginning the Niger Company had difficulty in financing military, judicial and administrative systems within its area; the shareholders were not happy at seeing money spent on non-profit-making activities. In order to make as much money as possible the Niger Company exercised a monopoly in violation of the Berlin Treaty which had established the principle of free navigation on the Niger. This monopoly angered other European traders and led to the ruthless exploitation of African suppliers.

As long as trade was satisfactory the company allowed the individual states to be 'ruled through the feudatory princes'. Each king was provided with British advisers whose task was to ensure the complete co-operation of the ruler.

But some rulers were not content to watch their profits dwindle and see their peoples' way of life threatened. Although the Royal Niger Company had signed a treaty with the Sultan of Sokoto in 1885, the emirs of the Hausa states grew restless at the increasing intervention of the Europeans. In 1896 Nupe traders overpowered a Company police patrol. This was only one of a series of acts of defiance and, though the captives were released, Goldie decided to invade Nupe. After many weeks of hard fighting the forces of Nupe collapsed, more as a result of internal squabbles than of the power of the Niger Company. Goldie set up a puppet ruler in Nupe then went on to attack Ilorin. Though defeated in battle the emirates were not conquered. The Niger Company lacked the power to control them and in Nupe the legitimate ruler soon regained his position. Goldie had to agree to the formation of the West African Frontier Force, a colonial army set up by the British government to maintain law and order in the British sphere. The politicians in London were more concerned with the extension of French rule in West Africa than with crushing the resistance of the emirs and so life in Nupe and Ilorin continued much as before.

From their base in Dahomey French agents occupied Borgu and a French Resident was appointed at Ilo with full powers to annexe territory as far south as Bussa. This meant that commerce along a large section of the Niger could now be diverted through the French sphere. Goldie protested that the territory involved had already been ceded to the Niger Company by the King of Bussa. The French replied, correctly, that Borgu belonged not to the ruler of Bussa but to King Baribari of Nikki. Representatives of both rivals rushed to Baribari's court. Because the Company's agent, Captain Frederick Lugard, reached Nikki first, Borgu fell under British control.

The British encountered more opposition from the chiefs of the Niger Delta when, in 1885, they tried to consolidate their position by proclaiming the Oil Rivers Protectorate. Prominent among the Delta chiefs was Jaja, King of Opobo, who, having forged his small state into the leading commercial empire in the area, was determined not to let his position be weakened by the foreigners. His clear mind saw defects in the treaty that Consul Hewitt brought him. He wanted a definition of the term 'protectorate' before he would agree to sign. He wanted to make sure that he was not granting away his kingdom. He made Consul Edward Hewett give him a letter that stated, 'with reference to the word "protection" as used in the proposed Treaty . . . the Queen does not want to take your country or your markets but at the same time is anxious that no other nation should take them. She undertakes to extend her gracious favour and protection which will leave your country still under your government.' Jaja was also determined that there should be no free trade in his sphere of influence. He was a great palm oil and palm kernel trader and, as king, he collected about £30,000 a year as 'comey' (trade tax). He was not prepared to see any European go into the interior to trade directly with the suppliers. Any people who dared to disobey his orders not to trade with the Europeans were severely punished. Thus the terms of the Protectorate Treaty that came into force in 1885 were, on paper, quite favourable to the Niger Delta chiefs.

At first the British merchants of the African Association could do nothing, but when the price of oil went down in the world market they decided to cut Jaja's comey from four puncheons in twenty to three. Jaja made it clear that foreign merchants could only trade on his terms. Miller Brothers of Glasgow backed out of the African Association and paid the usual comey and Jaja granted them a monopoly of all the oil that could be collected. The oil that the Miller Brothers could not buy, Jaja decided to ship to England on his own account.

The members of the African Association and men like

Consuls Hewett and Johnston saw in Jaja a barrier to British ambitions on the Oil Rivers. They decided to use guile and force where persuasion had failed. In 1887 Acting Consul Harry Johnston told King Jaja that he had no right to exact comey since he was then a trader competing with the merchants who paid the comey. Jaja rejected this point of view. He began to fortify his state and to buy ammunition with which to protect his capital. Johnston decided to take a firm stand. He sailed to Opobo in the British warship *Goshawk* and sent an invitation to King Jaja to meet him at the beach of Harrison's factory. Jaja wanted a pledge of safe conduct to which Johnston agreed in these words: 'I hereby assure you that whether you accept or reject my proposals tomorrow, no restraint whatever will be put on you—you will be free to go as soon as you have heard the message of the government'. Jaja took the Consul at his word and went. The whole of the European community was in Harrison's factory waiting. In the improvised court room, Consul Johnston told Jaja that he should either

Expedition to Cameroon mountains

219

surrender himself and go to Accra for trial for all the evils he had done, or he should return to Opobo regarding himself as an enemy of Great Britain, in which case his town would be mercilessly bombarded, his goods seized and he himself outlawed. Jaja had no choice. He allowed himself to be taken to Accra for trial. He was deposed as King of Opobo and banished for five years to the West Indies. He was given a pension of £800 per annum and the right to enjoy all the proceeds from his private income. A Court of Equity was established to take over the administration of the river. It was while he was returning home in 1891 that he died and only his dead body arrived in the kingdom which he had founded.

As soon as Jaja was removed, Consul Johnston decided to go to the Cross River territories to sign various treaties with the chiefs in the interest of free trade. He was not the originator of treaties with the Africans because when Consul Hewett realized that the Germans had proclaimed a protectorate over Cameroon he had undertaken a treaty-making expedition in July and August 1884. Before the end of October the countries in the Delta and along the lower Niger had already been brought under the protection of the British. All these were paper protectorates which had to be converted into 'effective occupation'. This meant either placing them under the administration of the Royal Niger Company or setting up some form of direct colonial rule.

An Imperial Commissioner was sent to study everything connected with the Royal Niger Company's administration and the advisability of placing the Oil Rivers under the Company's administration. Major Claude Macdonald, the Commissioner, reported that the Oil Rivers Protectorate should become a separate administrative unit. Macdonald himself came back as first Commissioner, in 1891. His duties included ensuring that the Royal Niger Company acted within the sphere of its charter. In 1893 the Oil Rivers Protectorate became the Niger Coast Protectorate and its area of jurisdiction included all those areas that had made treaties with Britain but were not included in the Royal Niger Company Protectorate.

The Niger Coast Protectorate administrators were still faced with the existence of powerful Africans who did not like the continued extension of British jurisdiction. One of these Africans was Nana of Ebrohimi who, because of his drive and forceful personality, had become the Governor of the Benin

Chief Nana Olomu of Koko, Governor of Bight of Benin

River, a post that his father Olomu had held before him. The signal rise of Eriomala (known to history as Nana) has tended to make some people think that he was a king of the Itsekiri who are the inhabitants of the Kingdom of Warri. This is not so.

Nana did, however, exercise an almost kingly control over Itsekiri, Urhobo and Ijo territories which covered over 15,000 square kilometres, and imposed a commercial monopoly over this vast area. He made use of his personal lieutenants, most of whom were his senior slaves, as local administrators representing his commercial interests in the various markets. He had a large fleet of well-designed canoes manned by slaves. In all, Nana probably had as many as 20,000 soldiers, 100 war canoes (each manned by 36 paddlers and 40 armed men) and over 200 trade canoes (each pulled by 16 or 20 paddlers and capable of carrying from five to ten tonnes of oil). His powers, derived from trade and force, were so great that he had effective control over the Benin River. Like Jaja of Opobo, he signed the treaty of 1884 with Consul Hewett while excluding the free trade clauses. His war canoes paraded the Benin, Ethiope and Jameson rivers to make sure that new markets were open to his enterprise and that European traders were excluded. The first challenge to his powers came from the Royal Niger Company which in its spree of treaty-gathering had gone to the Ijos of Forcados. Nana quickly sent a protest stating that the whole of that territory was under his jurisdiction, and that, despite the treaty, he was not prepared to tolerate the activities of a company which was his rival in trade. His political and commercial power was so great that the Europeans were unable to resist him.

Once again the merchants resorted to intrigue to achieve their ends. They stirred up some of the Urhobo and Itsekiri traders, who resented Nana's great power. They found discontented elements among Nana's own people who resented the power being wielded by a man who did not belong to the royal family.

When, in 1891, the whole of the Benin River territory came under the new Oil Rivers Protectorate, the Consul could no longer tolerate the over-powerful Nana. As soon as the Oil Rivers Protectorate was proclaimed, Nana's governorship ceased to exist but Nana continued to impose his authority. From 1891 to 1893, Vice-Consul H. L. Gallwey concluded a series of treaties with the Urhobo chiefs thus undermining Nana's authority. Attempts were made to win over the loyalties of many Itsekiris. Consular regulations were introduced, but Nana fought against these regulations and the new customs duties imposed by closing markets to European traders.

Acting Consul-General Ralph Moor decided to take the offensive. When, in 1894, Nana refused to remove his war canoes from the Ethiope, they were seized. Itsekiri chiefs were summoned to Sapele and there they signed a treaty promising free trade. War raged on. Nana placed a bar across the river blocking the entrance to his headquarters, Ebrohimi. The Consul sent a naval detachment. When Nana was confronted with an overwhelming military force he admitted defeat. He fled to Lagos leaving Ebrohimi a deserted village. There he surrendered, was tried and exiled first to Calabar and later to Accra.

In the same year the Brassmen made a last desperate bid to preserve their markets. Since the collapse of the slave trade they had penetrated deep into the palm oil belt to establish contact with the markets of Oguta, Aboh and Onitsha. They did a good trade with some of the European companies until the Royal Niger Company established its monopoly. The Niger Company dealt directly with the producers, and Brass trade dwindled rapidly. In 1894 Koko became King of Brass and immediately complained to Claude Macdonald, the Commissioner to the Niger District, against further restrictions recently introduced by the Company which threatened to ruin his people. Macdonald agreed that the Brassmen were being unfairly treated, but by this time Goldie's power on the lower Niger was complete and even reprimands from London had no effect on him.

When all else had failed Koko ordered a major attack on the Company's depot at Akassa. This was successful. They destroyed the Company's stores and captured about sixty men. Macdonald, now Consul-General, ordered the Brass leaders to hand over the chiefs responsible for the raid. When they refused he ordered the bombardment of Nembe which was captured and burnt and now had to accept the jurisdiction of the Niger Coast Protectorate.

While the British were establishing their authority along the coast and the rivers the Yoruba wars in the interior raged on. Abeokuta had been a scene of missionary activity and the bulwark of Christianity. But the British annexation of Lagos had brought to an end the cordial relations between the British and the Egba who continued to block trade routes.

The Fulani were still on the offensive and had seized Offa. Dahomey continued to stretch her arms from the West and had not only withdrawn her allegiance to Oyo but in fact invaded Oyo, in 1887. On the coast the Ijebus, in an attempt to maintain a monopoly of trade, continued to block the routes to Europeans who wished to go into the interior as well as to Oyo merchants interested in trading directly with the Europeans.

Officials at Lagos involved themselves as little as possible in these troubles until 1885 when colonial rivalry provoked them into positive action. The French had sent a mission to Abeokuta in order to get the chief to sign a treaty which would give the French the right to build a railway to the town from Porto Novo. The Governor in Lagos sent emissaries to Abeokuta and these were informed by the Egba chiefs that they would not give their land either to the British or to the French. Then the Lagos administration heard that the French wanted the Alafin of Oyo to sign a treaty with them which would give them control of all Yorubaland. The Governor of Lagos hurried to Oyo and secured a treaty with Alafin Adeyemi. In this treaty, the Alafin agreed that he would cede no territory to any other power except with the agreement of the British in Lagos. He also promised not to open trade nor levy tolls without the permission of the Lagos administration. The Alafin was to have 200 bags of cowries a year for signing this treaty. At government level Britain reached an agreement with France (1890) which recognized Yorubaland as falling within the British sphere of influence.

As British authority grew so did the need to find solutions to the conflicts within Yorubaland. Ibadan agreed to allow the Alafin and the Governor to settle the extent of her territory but the incessant raids of the Ilorin made a settlement with her difficult. The Egbados who still hoped to break free from Egba control decided to sign a treaty of protection with the British to ward off Egba invasion. At the same time the French, despite their agreement, again showed signs of interest in this side of Yorubaland. To guard British interests a garrison was sent to Ilaro, the Egbado capital, to the annoyance of the Egba.

The Ijebus were not cowed by colonial troop movements. They continued to block the trade routes and refused to sign a treaty of protection with Britain. In 1892 Sir Gilbert Carter, the new Governor, sent a military expedition against Ijebu-Ode. All chiefs fled, leaving only the Awujale.

This military action had an immediate effect on other Yoruba leaders. The Egba invited Governor Carter to Abeokuta in 1893 and signed a treaty which abolished human sacrifice and opened all roads to trade. Carter's next point of call was Oyo where the Alafin also signed a treaty giving the British access to his territories, abolishing human sacrifices, opening Oyo to missionary enterprise and granting the Governor the right of arbitration in all disputes. The only place where there was difficulty was Ibadan where the people objected to a European Resident in their town. It was not until August 1893, after the Ibadan people had received assurances that the Lagos administration had no intention of interfering with the government of the people, that Ibadan formally signed the treaty. The long period of civil war thus came to an end and the whole of Yorubaland came under British jurisdiction.

There now remained only one centre of resistance to British penetration and that was Benin. That great kingdom was ruled by Oba Overami (Ovonramwen) who became Oba (king) in 1888. Benin was a great traditional centre where human sacrifice was still practised. Slavery was also still prevalent. For the British, however, Benin was becoming an important commercial centre. This was because it was the main centre for the production of rubber which was needed for the Dunlop tyre industry. But Oba Overami was an astute businessman and he maintained a personal monopoly over the rubber trade, and he had decreed that no Bini should trade with Europeans.

Benin's commercial importance made it a desirable prize for the Royal Niger Company, and Goldie actually advised the Oba to resist official offers of British protection in the hope that the kingdom would come under the Company's control. This, allied with national pride, inspired some of the Bini chiefs to stand firm against the foreigners. But Overami was more cautious. He knew that hard bargaining would win him more than armed conflict. He could not defeat the British and his own state was weakened by Ishan revolts and Fulani attacks which deprived him of much of his northern territory. Overami kept his kingdom closed to the British as long as possible. In 1897 the Acting Consul-General of the Niger Coast Protectorate, J. R. Phillips, decided to visit Benin City. Despite warnings from royal messengers, he led an unarmed party into the Oba's territory. Against the ruler's wishes the more warlike chiefs ambushed and massacred the party as it neared the city. The event was sufficient excuse for the mounting of a British punitive expedition. Later that year Benin City was captured. Oba Overami was tried by his enemies and deported to Calabar.

During the conflict with Benin agents of the Royal Niger Company had actually been in rivalry with Protectorate officials for control of the Oba's kingdom. In other ways, too, the Company was proving to be an embarrassment to the British government. Campaigns against Nupe and Ilorin in 1897 brought the Company's forces into contact with the French, advancing down the Niger. The British government had to work out a boundary agreement with the French (1898) and provide the Company with money and

King Ejayboo with the Governor of Lagos

officers to maintain a new West African Frontier Force. Since they were now paying for the defence of the Company's territory and, since the Company's record of dealing with Africans and foreign traders was far from good, Britain's leaders decided that the time had come to end its charter. In 1900 the British government took over the administration of all the Royal Niger Company's territory, which now became the Protectorate of Northern Nigeria.

The fate of the Sokoto Sultanate was closely bound up with the decline of the Royal Niger Company. The West African Frontier Force, formed in 1897 and led by Colonel Frederick Lugard, was created to control Hausaland and other areas where the Company was powerless to enforce its rule. In 1900 when Company rule came to an end the Protectorate of Northern Nigeria was formed and Lugard was appointed High Commissioner. By 1906, Lugard, by a mixture of force and diplomacy, had 'pacified' the Sokoto Sultanate. In 1901 he moved against Nupe and Kontagora, conquered them and deposed their rulers. Then he wrote courteously to the Sultan, explaining his action and asked the Sultan to appoint a new emir for Kontagora. While appearing to respect the traditional authorities, Lugard imposed his will by demonstrations of force and by playing on the old divisions between Hausa and Fulani. This prevented the emirs from combining to oppose the British advance. Not until 1903 did the new Sultan, Attahiru I, alarmed by the British conquest of Bauchi and Borno, summon the faithful to resistance and by then it was too late. In February Kano was captured and British forces moved on Sokoto. Attahiru I fled and the British replaced him by Attahiru II. The old Sultan collected his forces round him and made a final stand at the battle of Burmi where he was killed and his army routed.

The Fulani realized that further resistance was pointless. Even if they restricted the area under effective British control the French would have invaded across the boundary agreed by the two imperial powers in 1898. They discussed terms with Lugard. The conqueror lacked the resources to enforce alien rule and had little alternative to the granting of generous terms. Emirs who swore allegiance to the new regime were confirmed in office. They promised to stop the slave trade and to be guided by British Residents. Islamic culture, law and religion were not interfered with. This became the pattern of 'indirect rule' which Britain tried with varying degrees of success in other territories.

The final phase in the colonial conquest of Asante began in 1888. The deposition of Mensa Bonsu had been followed by a period of civil war. Kwaku Dua II held the Golden Stool (the symbol of royal authority) but he could not hold the allegiance of many of the chiefs. The weakness of metropolitan Asante led to rebellions among the subject states. Discord and political collapse were widespread. Among other results this had a disastrous effect upon trade at the coast. It was not difficult for the members of the Chambers of Commerce to demonstrate that unless the Asante menace was removed by imposing a direct administration, British trade would continue to suffer. The problem, however, of getting a stable government in Asante itself was very important. In March 1888 a youth of sixteen came to be installed as Kwaku Dua III. His popular name in history is Agyeman Prempeh. The diverse claims to the throne ever since the deposition of Mensa Bonsu had weakened the central administration of Asante, and Prempeh was far too young for such a post as that of the Asantehene. He could get little respect because he was not traditionally installed. The presence of the British representative made it impossible for the Asante to purify the state with human sacrifice, and until that was done Prempeh could hardly regard himself as a true Asantehene.

Soon after his enstoolment, there was a great rebellion organized by the state of Kokofu and supported by Adansi and Dadiase. This was quelled but before the final battle was over, Owusu Sekyere also organized a rebellion of the Mampong people. Mampong also was defeated and reacted by placing herself under British protection. Nkoranza now asserted her independence. Britain, of course, welcomed this collapse of centralized Asante power and made separate treaties with the chiefs wherever possible. It seemed that the once mighty empire would collapse without the need to send British troops. But the British had reckoned without Prempeh who was growing into a fine political and military leader. The Asantehene sent a letter of protest in which he demanded the return of his former territories. The British Governor rejected this demand. Any weakening of the British position, he knew, would be taken advantage of by the French, who had occupied

King Prempeh and his attendants

the Ivory Coast, or the Germans, who had already occupied Togoland. He was also concerned about the continuing slave traffic between Asante and the neighbouring French occupied territory.

Diplomacy having failed, Prempeh set about regaining all his former territories by force. Nkoranza was completely destroyed and alarm spread through all those territories that had become independent. Attebubu placed herself under the protection of Britain. But other areas including Kokofu, Mampong and Nsuta returned to their traditional allegiance. All this alarmed the British who now asked Prempeh to accept a Resident in Kumasi. The Asantehene refused and sent a delegation to London without heeding the warning of the Governor, Sir Brandford Griffith, who told them that all communications with the British government must be through him. The delegation was not received officially in England

and the new Governor, Mr Maxwell, came with instructions to compel the Asantehene to accept a British Resident. It was only when an expeditionary force was got ready to force submission that the Asante ruler submitted.

This, however, was not enough for the British. Prempeh, thinking he was strong enough, had decided to re-enstool himself in the traditional fashion which included human sacrifice. This was a very good excuse for the Governor as it was a contravention of the Treaty of Fomena. In January 1896, a British army occupied Kumasi. The Asantehene submitted to the inevitable and placed his country under the protection of Britain. He was told to pay a war indemnity of 50,000 ounces of gold leaf. When he said that he could only pay 80 ounces on the spot and the others by instalments, he and his mother, father, two uncles, and many of his relations and chiefs were arrested. They were tried and exiled to the Seychelles. The Asante were horrified by the banishment and what they regarded as British treachery. They did not regard the foreigners as their overlords. The Asantes had respect only for their Golden Stool and the person who was its guardian. Although Kumasi was occupied, the Golden Stool, which was regarded as holding the spirit of the nation, was still hidden away. This meant that Britain was not yet overlord of Asante and the British Resident was a foreign imposter. Nevertheless, the Resident began to exercise in full the Asantehene's authority. He imposed taxes to clear off the indemnity which had to be paid. He pressed people into road building and other public works. Worst of all, he demanded that the Golden Stool be handed over to the Governor so that he could sit on it. The thought of a foreigner sitting on the Golden Stool was sacrilege to the Asante.

Spontaneous resistance broke out. The Asante demanded the return of the hero, Prempeh, the lifting of restrictions on the slave trade and the departure of all the foreigners from Kumasi. From all over West Africa, troops began to pour into the Gold Coast for the British invasion. The military offensive under Colonel Willcocks was so great that Kumasi could no longer resist and accepted defeat. It was in March 1901 that the Kumasi leaders were tried and deported and the whole of Asante disarmed. She was annexed as a Crown Colony. The whole of present-day Ghana thus came under the administration of Britain.

As on the Gold Coast, so in Sierra Leone British authority was extended. There had for some time been a growing demand among administrators and traders for a more permanent jurisdiction in the interior. The pressure became stronger after the Berlin Conference when there was need for effective occupation. There had always been an attempt to introduce the people surrounding the colony to the cultural life of Freetown. Many missionaries who had gone to the interior had brought back to Freetown the children of the chiefs for education. Close links were forged with the colony when these children, like J. K. Mannah-Kpaka, became paramount rulers. Trade with the interior cemented friendship and encouraged closer association. If Britain allowed these areas of trade to be taken away by a rival power then the colony, which could not feed itself, would starve and be cut off from possibilities of further expansion. Therefore, the Sierra Leone administration signed treaties of protection with the paramount chiefs and, in 1896, a protectorate was declared over the whole of the area north of the colony. This would facilitate the building of a railway without which the commercial penetration of the interior would not be possible.

The chiefs themselves did not understand the treaties they had signed. They still wanted to continue the slave trade and other aspects of their traditional way of life. Too late they discovered that they had come under foreign domination. The Governor of Sierra Leone, Sir Frederick Cardew, introduced a hut tax. The people could not understand why they should pay taxes on their houses and, led by the Temne under Bai Bureh, a great soldier, they rose against the government. For months this civil disturbance raged on. Some of the peoples, like the Mende, had not liked the air of superiority of the Creoles and the removal of the powers of their chiefs by the British. The hut tax rising was therefore an opportunity for the strong expression of their grievances. By April 1898, they had massacred many missionaries, alien traders, members of the Frontier Police and government officials. Like all attempts at armed resistance it was in vain. The leaders of the hut tax rising and the Mende were ruthlessly put down. Now the Protectorate started an era of peace, especially when the railway (begun in 1896) began to facilitate trade.

In the interior it was a French advance with which the inhabitants had to contend. The agents of France, continuing their eastwards advance, reached the territory dominated by Samori. The expansion of Samori's empire further west brought it into conflict with the French who, using Senegal as a base, had already conceived a plan for creating a vast empire extending from the Senegal to the Nile. As Samori's empire also extended southward to the forest, it came into the sphere of influence of the British, who were making treaties with the paramount chiefs of the hinterland. But, while the British were just content with extracting a treaty of protection which, to a clever diplomat like Samori, was not worth the paper it was written on, the French were a source of great danger because they continued to undertake military campaigns into the interior. When the French eventually occupied Bamako, in 1883, it became obvious that their further advance into the interior would be halted by this great military empire. At first Samori thought that he could play off the French against the British by signing a treaty of protection with the latter. The British administration of Sierra Leone, however, was not prepared to engage in war and, unfortunately for Samori, neither did Britain have in this area forceful characters with great commercial and industrial interests like Goldie and Rhodes or empire-conscious administrators like Lugard and Glover who could have used a treaty to advantage. France, therefore, took the offensive and because she had better and more modern weapons worked havoc on the empire. At last, in September 1898, Samori was captured and deported. He died in 1900 in exile. France then began to consolidate her position in the western Sudan.

The collapse of Ahmadu's Tucolor Empire occurred at the same time. Many of his subjects resented his rule and this, coupled with the French advance, caused Ahmadu to move his capital from Segu to Nioro, in 1884. In 1887 he signed a treaty with the French by which they promised not to invade his territory. But this was merely a French trick to prevent the leaders of the Sudanese empires uniting against them. In 1891, as soon as they were ready, they marched into Tucolor territory. Ahmadu fled first to Masina, then to Sokoto, where he died in 1898.

The King of Porto Novo

The French drive eastwards was not only hampered by African resistance. As we have seen, rival colonial powers were anxiously watching the French advance and were ready to prevent them threatening their own vital interests. France, therefore, decided to advance inland from her coastal footholds in order to consolidate her position. For many years no colonial power had ventured to challenge Dahomey. Even the British anti-slavery crusaders had been daunted by Dahomey's military reputation. The French had had a foothold on the coast ever since the 1860s when the King of Porto Novo asked for their protection against the British. They also had forts at Whydah, Cotonou and Grand Popo. In 1882 France annexed Porto Novo and soon her traders dominated the coast between Lagos and the German possessions in Togo. Not until 1893 did the French move against Dahomey in order to protect the hinterland from British expansion. King Behanzir was easily overthrown on a manufactured pretext and his more pliant brother was placed on the throne. In 1900 Dahomey became a French colony. Between 1897 and 1906 French colonial boundaries with adjacent British and German territories were agreed.

When the French came to fill in the Ivory Coast 'gap' on the colonial map of West Africa they were confronted by a much more difficult task. Before the 'scramble' began French firms based at Grand Bassam and Assinie traded with the coast and forest peoples and the Mandinka merchants of the interior. The African chiefs and merchants preserved the upper hand in this partnership. In the 1880s commercial and colonial considerations urged the French to establish themselves in the hinterland. They made treaties with forest chiefs as far north as Kong. Immediately the newcomers forced unfavourable trade terms on their allies and tried to involve them in the war against Samori. These affronts were followed, in 1900, by demands for taxation and labour for the railways. This provoked a united resistance which was so successful that, by 1908, the French had been forced back to the coast. Then a new Governor, Angoulvant, arrived and put in hand a ruthless policy of slaughtering opponents and burning villages. Even this policy took seven years to bring some success. By 1915 the country was under military rule which was difficult and expensive to maintain. When the French began to recruit troops for service in the First World War

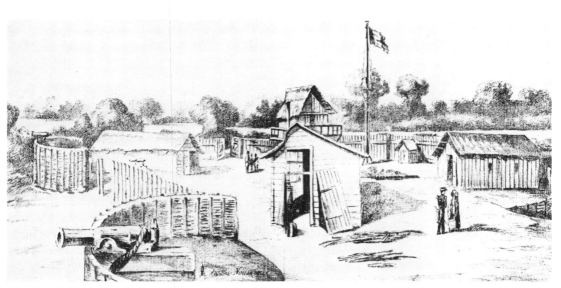

French establishments on the Ivory Coast—Grand Bassam

Assinie—French establishment on the Ivory Coast

the Baoule revolted again (1916) and were only subdued after a further two years' fighting.

By 1907 the partition of West Africa was complete on paper and the boundaries were drawn that were to become the boundaries of today's African nations. The only major change that occurred between 1907 and 1920 was the disappearance of Germany as a colonial power in West Africa. As one result of her defeat by Britain and France in the First World War Germany lost her colonies of Togoland and Cameroon. They were taken over by the League of Nations and each colony was divided into two parts, one part being administered by Britain and the other by France.

The Gold Coast

On the Gold Coast, the administration was in the hands of a Governor who was resident in the capital, Accra. He was assisted by an Executive Council which included the four most senior officials. The Executive Council was an advisory body whose advice the Governor could set aside if he wished.

There was also a Legislative Council which was responsible for discussing public affairs and making the necessary legislation on issues that were brought before it by the Executive Council. This body consisted of four members of the Executive Council, the Chief Justice and three unofficial members. The Legislative Council was further expanded in 1916 when there were eleven official to ten unofficial members. The Bills that were passed by the Legislative Council were not laws until they were ratified by the Governor. The Council was not representative.

The Gold Coast Colony was divided into three provinces, Western, Central and Eastern, each subdivided into districts. Asante was divided into Northern and Southern Provinces and the northern area was divided into Northern and Southern Provinces. In each province the head of administration was the Chief Commissioner who exercised political and judicial functions. The different districts had District Commissioners to administer them. Some of the traditional institutions were retained.

In all Gold Coast societies land was considered as belonging to the community and was held by the chief as guardian. Each man was entitled to a little holding which he enjoyed as a tenant as long as he respected tribal custom. Land could not normally be taken from the individual or the community. At first the British respected this tradition and confiscated very little land. This situation changed as the cultivation of cocoa spread. Cocoa farming grew with great rapidity without European capital and with little government aid. Between 1891 and 1895 five tons of cocoa were exported but this rose between 1901 and 1905 to 3000 tons. After cocoa the next most important export was gold. At first Europeans were content to buy gold from the Africans but as time went by they wanted to increase the production of the Gold Coast mines. At first the government did not regulate mining and so it became easy for mineral prospectors to get land from the chiefs. The government was then forced to take action because it also wanted land for public use. They introduced a bill that made it possible to take land for public needs. Compensation would be paid for lost crops but not for confiscated land. Apart from this, until 1894 the government did nothing about the leases transacted between chiefs and companies. Then the Crown Lands Bill was brought in with the aim of taking over waste lands, forest lands and minerals. Two things provoked controversy. The detribalized men at the coast were afraid that the proposed law would mean that the government could give native land to land speculators. The second point was that there were no waste lands on the Gold Coast. If the Bill had been passed it would have jeopardized the cocoa industry. The opposition against it was very strong so the Bill failed. In 1897 a new Land Bill was brought forward which gave the Crown rights of administration but not of ownership. The opposition, which again was fierce, was based on the term 'Public Land'. This led to the formation of the Gold Coast Aborigines' Rights Protection Society which existed to examine and comment on proposed legislation.

This society launched a great campaign against the Bill and persuaded the Colonial Secretary not to sanction it. The chiefs and the educated classes worked hand in hand to see that the Bill did not go through. The Bill and the protests were sent to England and a Gold Coast Western Province delegation of J. W. Sey, T. F. F. Jones and G. Hughes accompanied it. In the face of all this opposition the 1897 Land Bill was withdrawn, but in 1900 a right to validate concessions by appeal in the High Court was accepted. A Forestry Bill was passed in 1910 to preserve the land so that its fertility might not be destroyed by widespread burning. The Forestry Reserves Bill was introduced. This also met with opposition, so the Belfield Commission was set up in 1912. The Commission did not agree that the colonial government had the right to create forest reserves since it could not claim ownership of the land.

From the work of the Aborigines' Rights Protection Society it is easy to see the part that the educated classes were playing in the history of the Gold Coast. They were increasing and forming a strong, enlightened middle class always prepared to attack any government measure that they thought was against African interests. At first their activities were concentrated on the coast but improved transport and communications enabled them to extend their influence inland.

The need to stimulate the gold industry led to the building of the railway between Sekondi and Tarkwa, the centre of the mining area. It was then extended to Kumasi. As a result, cocoa farming spread to the Asante. As soon as Asante farmers began to produce large crops the government had to construct another railway from Accra to Kumasi (1910–23). At the same time road development was on the increase. By 1919 about 2,000 km of road had been built. The government of the Gold Coast had realized the danger of a one-crop economy and therefore had stimulated the production of timber and rubber. Cattle raising was encouraged in the North.

It was not long before a rift began to develop between the chiefs and the educated classes. The British had introduced a system of indirect rule because they believed it to be the best way of training the people for eventual self-rule. They had their native courts where they enforced the laws which they had helped in making. Their administrative position was increased by the fact that they worked independently of any African institution or public opinion as long as the District Commissioner was pleased. The educated classes saw this system as a retrograde and hypocritical step. They maintained that the chiefs had become agents of the colonialists and did not represent the real wishes of the people.

The educated classes were also dissatisfied with the position of Africans in the civil service. Educated Africans were in fact underpaid clerical employees and the top ranks of the service were retained for British officers. By 1914 a large class of literate Africans had emerged whose training removed them from the farms and prepared them only for white collar jobs which they then found difficult to get. Africans and Englishmen with identical qualifications did not occupy the same position and did not get the same pay. The First World War precipitated matters by pushing up prices. Africans began to suspect that the reason for their exclusion from the top grades of the civil service and from well-paid jobs was their colour. This led directly to the growth of nationalism. Personal relationships between the British and the Africans in the civil service began to deteriorate. This dispute reached its climax in 1919 with the demand by the African civil servants for the immediate recall of the Colonial Secretary, A. R. Slater, who, they said, had no sympathy with African claims for higher wages.

Small as this issue was, it showed an underlying grievance of the people against the administration at a time when Africans were helping Britain to fight against the world tyranny of Germany. The Aborigines' Rights Protection Society had always maintained that as the Gold Coast was not conquered territory Britain had no right to direct administration. The idea of self-rule now began to permeate the whole of nationalist thinking and campaigns were arranged against the administration because it denied representative government to Africans.

Sir Frederick Lugard

237

Governor Hugh Clifford could not concede this but was prepared to amend the Constitution. He was the President of a Legislative Council which had eight members, four of whom were official members of the Executive Council and four unofficial members (two Europeans and two Africans). To provide the means for a fairer assessment of African interests, in 1916 Clifford set up an enlarged Legislative Council of twenty-one members. There were now twelve official members, three unofficial European members, three unofficial African members (chiefs) representing the Twi, Fante and the Ewe-speaking communities and three unofficial educated members representing Cape Coast, Western Province and Accra.

The very fact that the elective principle was not accepted and that officials still predominated made the new changes unsatisfactory to the Africans. A newspaper, the *Gold Coast Nation*, began a series of attacks against the Legislative Council from its inauguration, and the nominated African members: J. P. Brown (Cape Coast), J. E. Casely Hayford (Western Province) and T. Hutton Mills (Accra) carried this campaign to the floor of the Legislative Council itself. The Aborigines' Rights Protection Society wanted to constitute itself into an electoral college for the appointment of the three educated unofficial members. Many petitions were sent to the Colonial Office and met with no response. But suddenly the attention of the African nationalist politicians was diverted towards the creation of a self-governing West African state and all energies were concentrated towards the summoning of the first West African Congress.

Nigeria

In Nigeria, as on the Gold Coast, the problem that faced Britain was that of working out an administrative system for the area of the Niger over which protectorates had been declared. Lagos continued to remain a colony, but its area of jurisdiction was extended after a protectorate had been declared over the Yoruba country and the whole area was designated the Colony and Protectorate of Lagos. Lagos, the Protectorate of Southern Nigeria and the Protectorate of Northern Nigeria constituted three separate administrative units, each under a High Commissioner who was responsible directly to the Colonial Office in England. In the Protectorate of Southern Nigeria, an administration had to be worked out carefully to suit the diversity of the people. It was the duty of the High Commissioner to rule through proclamations and thus provide for the administration of justice, the raising of revenue and the maintenance of law, order and good government. The whole area was divided into four divisions for administration.

Each of these divisions was under the administration of a District Commissioner who was responsible to the High Commissioner. Poor communication and lack of personnel made it impossible for any direct government to be adopted. Traditional institutions had to be encouraged but had to be controlled to make sure that all evil practices were expunged. This was why native councils were established. They provided the means by which the District Commissioners could familiarize themselves with local laws and customs. Native courts were set up in Old Calabar, Opobo, Akwete, Bonny, Sapele and Benin City. Where there were traditional rulers, they became the focal points of local government and they were the presidents of the native courts and the native councils; but where there were none, the District Commissioners appointed important local people as political agents. This was how Chief Dore Numa, who was the great opponent of Nana of Ebrohimi, gained control of the whole of the Itsekiri, Urhobo and Ijo territories.

The only place that still needed disciplining was the territory of the Aros whose people were particularly against the new administration, which, by introducing Christianity, was undermining the religious, political and economic importance of the Arochukwu Long Juju. The Aros were still slave traders and in 1901 the Political Agent reported that they had carried away hundreds of Ibibios to be sold as slaves. A punitive expedition was sent against the Aros, they did not give any resistance, and their territory was incorporated into the new administration.

In the Protectorate of Northern Nigeria the High Commissioner, Frederick Lugard, was faced with the problem of maintaining an administration over a vast territory, part of which had never been under European influence. The Royal Niger Company had not effectively administered the territories gained by treaty, so there was nothing for Lugard to inherit. Lokoja became the headquarters of the new administration. Lugard was soon in difficulties. Most of the emirs were hostile and most of the Royal West African Frontier Force

Chief Dore of Warri

239

had been diverted to the Asante campaign. He moved swiftly against the Emirs of Nupe and Kontagora when he learned that the latter was planning to attack the British garrison in Lokoja. Relations between the British and the Sultan of Sokoto had been strained ever since the Niger Company's attack on Ilorin. After he had conquered Nupe and Kontagora, the High Commissioner asked the Sultan as Lord of Kontagora to nominate a successor to the deposed Emir of Kontagora. But the Sultan's reply was one of defiance. Between 1901 and 1906, therefore, British rule was forced on the Fulani. The Emirs of Yola, Bauchi and Kano, and the Sultan of Sokoto were either expelled or died fighting. The Emirs of Gwandu and Katsina submitted.

Lugard now wanted to establish a system of government that would unite all the various African systems. He allowed the ancient Fulani Council to nominate a new Sultan of Sokoto and allowed the Sultan and emirs to continue ruling in the traditional style. They would, however, come under the overriding control of the Protectorate government and would have to accept the advice of British Residents.

This system of indirect rule through princes was something Lugard believed in. In any case it was virtually impossible with limited finance and personnel to administer the territory directly. He was aided in his scheme by the fact that the Fulani Empire had a good central administrative machinery that could be adopted. Lugard, as High Commissioner, could advise and control the Sultan, and his Residents could exercise the same powers over the emirs as could the District Officers over the district heads.

The first thing that Lugard did was to issue a slavery proclamation which abolished the legal basis of slavery, prohibited slave dealing and proclaimed as free all children born as from 1 January 1901. Domestic slavery was not abolished outright. In respect of slavery and the removal of abuses in the administration Lugard's policy was 'go slow'. In 1902 he drew up a scheme for direct taxation which provided for assessments on land, produce, trade, cattle, sheep, goats, etc. He also reorganized the whole of the judicial system which had degenerated from the purity and impartiality of Koranic law.

Lagos continued to have its old Crown Colony administration with a Governor, an Executive Council and a Legislative Council which had, as in the Gold Coast, an official majority, and when the Colony and Protectorate of Lagos was established, the Protectorate territory was loosely administered from Lagos also. But it became obvious that the cost of administration would be great and the possibilities for economic growth reduced, if all the governments of Nigeria maintained their independent status. In 1906, therefore, the Colony and Protectorate of Lagos was merged with the Protectorate of Southern Nigeria to form the Colony and Protectorate of Southern Nigeria. But this solved only a part of the problem. The system of colonial administration in the North was efficient, but direct taxation alone could not meet the mounting expenditure involved, and the deficit continued to be met by subsidy from the Southern Protectorate and Exchequer grants from Britain of about £300,000 a year. The South was rich because its trade was expanding. The North was dependent on southern ports for its export trade. Amalgamation was the obvious answer but it was not easy to achieve.

One obstacle to closer union was the mutual antagonism between the Northern and the Southern administrations. This was carried to a ridiculous extent in the building of the railway. The South had built the Lagos–Jebba railway to transport the resources of the interior and attract exports to Lagos. The North on the other hand built the Baro–Kano line to send all its produce to the Niger. Obviously transport policy had to be co-ordinated, and by 1911 the two lines had been joined at Minna. In that year construction began of a line from Port Harcourt, first to Enugu, and it was planned to extend it eventually to the North.

In 1912, Sir Frederick Lugard was appointed both Governor-General of the Colony and Protectorate of Southern Nigeria and High Commissioner of the Protectorate of Northern Nigeria with the specific task of amalgamating the North and the South. This was accomplished on 1 January 1914 when he became Governor-General of the Colony and Protectorate of Nigeria. The old administrative boundaries of North and South remained but each unit was now placed under a Lieutenant-Governor whose duty it was to produce an annual budget for incorporation into the national budget and administer his territory. The central government under the Governor-General was responsible for those functions that affected the whole of the state, such as railways, mining, army, audit, treasury, communications and the judiciary. Lagos Colony became a separate administrative unit under an

Administrator and the Legislative Council that had operated for the Southern Protectorate now confined its activities to Lagos only.

Lugard now established a National Council. This had thirty-six members which included the Governor-General as President, members of the Executive Council, the First Class Residents, the Political Secretaries and the Secretaries of the Northern and Southern Provinces. These were the official members. The others were unofficial members and of these seven were Europeans and six were nominated Nigerians. There were two emirs from the North, the Alafin of Oyo and one member each from the educated coastal areas: Lagos, Calabar and the Benin-Warri territory. This Council was only an advisory council to rubber stamp what the Governor-General wanted.

Indirect rule had now to be introduced into the South but while there was some success in its implementation in the Yoruba country, where there were traditional chiefs who became the focus of native authority, indirect rule failed in the East. In the greater part of this region there were no traditional authorities and the people rejected the 'chiefs' imposed on them by the British.

The economy of the territories was growing stronger as communications began to improve. In the early part of the twentieth century, there was great improvement in shipping facilities. The production of cocoa, which was first introduced into Oyo in 1885, had begun to reach great proportions in the West. In the Mid-West and East, palm oil and kernels began also to feature prominently. In the North, groundnuts had been introduced from Brazil at the end of the nineteenth century and plantation agriculture was making phenomenal progress. Cotton was also introduced to the North and rubber production was increased in Ife.

Another economic development that bound Nigeria to the world economy was the discovery, in 1902, of tin deposits on the Jos Plateau. The Royal Niger Company was the pioneer. By 1912 about eighty companies were active in the Plateau area and invested about £3.8 million.

These and other commercial enterprises brought new opportunities for Nigerians. They created opportunities for clerks and petty traders. The expansion of government services also created new openings in the lower ranks which could be filled only by those who were academically qualified and, of course, in the coastal and administrative areas where there were many mission schools the educated classes were on the increase. Wealth and educational facilities began to produce a middle class of educated men who, cut off by the native administration system from a participation in the government of their areas and partly detribalized, sought opportunities in the service of the colonial administration. All of them felt, like their counterparts on the Gold Coast, aggrieved that they could only hold unimportant posts since the higher ranks were reserved mostly for Europeans. The literate population was now influenced greatly by non-Nigerian negroes who were out to attack British policy because it did not place Africans on an equal footing with Europeans. These men like the West Indian, Edward Blyden, and the Liberian, J. P. Jackson, began to spearhead movements that were nationalistic in sentiment since they were aimed at getting the African and the negro a fair share in the profits of administration. Newspapers like the *Lagos Weekly Review*, edited by Jackson, published articles denouncing the British administration. At the same time, the father of Nigerian nationalism, Herbert Macaulay, began his political activities in Lagos campaigning against the water rate which he said only provided money for the maintenance of the European population. But even these internal movements were dwarfed by the greater political movement which culminated in the formation of the National Congress of British West African States.

Immediately after the supression of the hut tax riots in 1898, the British government was in a dilemma over whether or not to break the powers of the chiefs and resort to direct administration. It was, however, at last agreed that the chiefs should retain their positions, but that their administration should be regulated. When, therefore, the Protectorate Ordinance was passed in 1901, supplemented by the Protectorate Native Law Ordinance of 1905, the chiefs in the protectorate continued to be feudatory princes but became, in addition, agents of the central government. The colony on the other hand retained its old Crown Colony administrative system. The colonial administration refused to agree to elections for the Legislative Council.

Sierra Leone

The whole system of taxation and colonial administration came in for attack by the educated Africans. These educated Africans were on the increase in Sierra Leone and most of them were professionals—doctors and lawyers who after good academic performances in England, where they had studied with English students, came back to their country to find that the superior ranks of the administration were closed to them; not because they did not have the requisite qualifications, but because they were Africans.

Joint nationalist endeavour in British West Africa

During the First World War (1914–18) the Royal West African Frontier Force played a great part in Cameroon, Togoland and Tanganyika, which were German colonies. In this war, the West Africans fought side by side with European colleagues in an attempt to put down the tyranny of Germany. The propaganda sent to West Africa claimed that the conflict was a war for the preservation of human liberty. At the end of the war the League of Nations was established and the principle of self-determination became a strong force. This had a great influence on the structure of relations between Britain and her colonies which were gradually evolving into self-governing dominions like Canada and Australia. These political movements had their effect on the thinking of some of the educated classes in West Africa, especially on the Gold Coast. The Gold Coast Aborigines' Society had spearheaded nationalist movements within that territory but had hardly considered the possibility of concerted action by the British West African colonies of the Gold Coast, Sierra Leone, Nigeria and the Gambia for a review of their Crown Colony constitutions. There was a Gold Coast lawyer, however, who saw immense political and constitutional possibilities to be derived from a closer association amongst all British West African intellectuals who were suffering the same political and racial disabilities. He was J. E. Casely Hayford, a man who can be regarded as the architect of the concept of West African nationality.

He contacted Dr R. A. Savage, the Nigerian editor of the newspaper, the *Gold Coast Leader*, and F. W. Dove, a Sierra Leone lawyer practising in Freetown; but the war made it impossible for any solid arrangement to be made. Then the end of the war brought renewed activity from Hayford and his group and, in March 1920, six representatives from Nigeria

An Asante King with one of the newly educated elite showing the conflict of old and new

three from Sierra Leone, one from the Gambia and a large contingent of over forty Gold Coasters met to establish the West African Congress.

The first thing to note about this Congress was that it was the meeting place of the West African intelligentsia who began to assume a position of leadership without seeking the participation and blessing of the traditional rulers. After two weeks of deliberation the following resolutions were made: a British West African university should be set up to reflect a sense of African nationality; all judicial appointments should be opened to suitably qualified Africans; medical posts should, similarly, be available to Africans; Africans were capable of looking after their own interests in the land, and Europeans should no longer exchange and partition countries between them, without reference to, or regard for, the wishes of the people;

and the constitutions of the British colonies should be amended to reflect some element of the representative principle. The Congress decided to send a delegation to London to represent their views.

In September 1920, delegates representing the four British West African colonies went to London to put forward demands based on the Congress resolutions. These demands were rejected by the Secretary of State, Lord Milner, mainly because of the opposition of the governors of the Gold Coast and Nigeria, who stated that the delegates were not representatives of the people of the two colonies. In particular, the Gold Coast Governor, Sir Gordon Guggisberg, was able to use to advantage an attack made by Nana Ofori Atta against the West African Congress. This paramount chief felt that the young intellectuals were despising traditional authority and ignoring the opinions of the chiefs. Despite black divisions and white opposition, the Congress continued to work for self-determination and nationalism.

The Federation of French West Africa

French colonial philosophy differed considerably from that of Britain. France followed a policy of 'assimilation'. This involved turning Africans into 'black Frenchmen'. Everything was done to destroy African culture and to replace it by the 'superior' French culture. The end product would, in theory, be an African province where the way of life would be identical to that of France.

Between 1902 and 1904 all France's West African conquests were amalgamated into one province known as the Federation of French West Africa. It had a Governor-General situated at Dakar. A vast network of local officials was spread over the rest of this enormous colonial territory (the largest single colonial area in Africa). The most important local agent, the *Commandant de cercle*, did not have to learn the local language or respect the customs of the people in order to be regarded as a good administrator. He had to reduce the powers of the chief and appoint a successor without recourse to any native law or custom. Where native institutions were allowed to function at all, they were not native institutions in the sense that they operated native customary practices but native in the sense that they consisted of chiefs and the people and so were allowed to have a say in items that were presented to them for discussion by the responsible officer. The chief was merely an agent of the government officer made to perform certain defined functions and not a native ruler exercising both executive and judicial functions.

The ultimate aim of the French was to bring the West Africans to a standard of French civilization and culture and not to encourage the growth of an independent spirit. In everything there was a great difference between the African French citizen (*citoyen français*) and the French subject

Lady of mixed French and African marriage

(*sujet*). It was possible for a man to be transferred from the position of subject to that of citizen by attaining certain standards which were contained in a decree of 1912. He had to be above the age of twenty-one, have some proficiency in the French language, have shown genuine interest in French life and culture, and have been in French employment for at least ten years. The acquisition of the French way of life became a status symbol. The easiest ways for a subject to become a citizen were for him to marry a French woman and become the father of a child of mixed blood, or to distinguish himself in French military service.

The French educational system encouraged only a few people to attain this status. Education was a government concern and was not left in the hands of missionaries. All education was free and private religious bodies had to get permission to open schools. The language of instruction was French and there was no attempt to develop the indigenous languages side by side with the imperial language. The teaching of French began at a very early age and was considered an important means of encouraging the spirit of loyalty to France. There was also a great emphasis on vocational

The railway from Dakar to St Louis

248

instruction. The aim was not just to produce a literate population with no specific training to fit in with the economic and social growth of the state. The schools in the old towns were modelled on those of France so that it was possible for children from such schools to pass from the primary and secondary schools of French West Africa and go to university in France without any academic disadvantage.

Outside these towns, however, in the French West African Federation popular education ended with the primary school. The number of children who advanced to the three year territorial secondary schools was limited by the government's calculation of estimated demand for future employment. Since there could be few vacancies in administration and commerce, and since the French educational system did not encourage learning for its own sake, competition for entry into secondary schools was great indeed. The pupils who were successful in entering these schools were trained as recruits for subordinate posts in the administration.

When a student in a regional secondary school showed great academic promise, he could be sent after the completion of his course to the teacher training college in Dakar, the Ecole William Ponty, which also provided a three-year medical course. The standard of the Ecole William Ponty was so high that the teachers trained there were sent only to the urban areas to teach, while the teachers for the rural areas were taught in the two normal schools of the Sudan and the Ivory Coast.

Since the Federation was thought of as a part of France, economic development was seen in terms of French interests. To encourage trade and the transport of goods to the coast for shipment, railways were built to link the coastal areas with the Niger. The first railway was built in the 1880s to link Senegal to the Port of Dakar. But this line did not penetrate far enough into the interior so the Dakar–Niger line was constructed from Dakar to Loulikoro, a distance of some 1,200 kilometres. Attempts were then made to link the coastal ports of Conakry in Guinea, Abidjan in the Ivory Coast, and Cotonou in Dahomey with the Niger basin. The result was that a railway between Conakry and Kankan was begun in 1900 and completed in 1914. From Abidjan in the Ivory Coast, a railway line was begun in 1903. After many handicaps it ended in Bobo Dioulasso, a distance of 800 kilometres, while the line from Cotonou stopped at Parakou.

The French were not as lucky as the British in gaining territories that had great agricultural and mineral resources. This made it even more important to have a network of railways and waterways to provide cheap transport from the areas of production to the ports. It is to the credit of the French administration that each railway line opened up economic possibilities both for export production and for new markets ready for imported articles.

The mainstay of the economy, especially in the interior, was agriculture. Groundnuts were the most important cash crop and the centre of production was Senegal. However, cultivation soon began to spread. Palm oil also became a good export commodity from Dahomey. The activities of French planters encouraged the growth of coffee and cocoa in the Ivory Coast and bananas in Guinea. All these products could be exported only to France as there was no free trade system within the French Empire. The French market was open to West African products as the markets of West Africa were also open to French manufactured articles only.

All decisions, whether political, economic or social were made in Paris. This did not mean, however, that decisions were made without recourse to local opinion. Apart from the Governors and Lieutenant-Governors, who were agents of the French government, there was the Deputy of Senegal to the French National Assembly who could press for measures in his people's interest. When Blaise Diagne became, in 1914, the first African to be elected as Deputy to the French National Assembly, he could claim to be a representative of the people of West Africa. During his long service for West Africa, he acted on occasions as Under-Secretary to the Colonies. The Governors also had the services of their advisory councils, which included many Africans.

Many Africans gained personal advantage by accepting the French system. They were educated and trained. They became French citizens and the way to considerable advancement was open for them. But there were always some who opposed the French assumption of cultural superiority. In Senegal the educated class demanded equality before the law and freedom to practise Islam. When Blaise Diagne was elected to the Chamber of Deputies he championed his countrymen's cause and was completely successful. It is not surprising that Senegalese Africans should have taken the lead in early nationalist endeavour, since they had had longer experience of their French masters. By 1920 African intellectuals in other parts of the Federation were following their lead. France was forced to abandon the policy of 'assimilation' and instead evolved the concept of 'association', which had similarities to the British policy of indirect rule.

Chapter 10   The establishment of alien rule in East Africa

1884 was a crucial year for East Africa. Not only was it the year of the Berlin Conference and the arrival of the first colonialists; it was also the year in which three great leaders died. Nyungu-ya-Mawe continued to be an energetic king and warrior to the end. He organized his large territory into six or seven regions each under a *mutwale* (agent) who was completely under his control. Traditional rulers and people who might object to Nyungu's authority were ruthlessly suppressed. As a result Nyungu was able to pass on a well-organized state to his successor. Mirambo, who also died in 1884, did not leave such a legacy. He conquered and controlled a large empire in northern Nyamweziland but his rule was entirely personal. His successor, Mpandashalo, could not hold the state together and Mirambo's great empire collapsed. North of Lake Victoria, in 1884, the great Kabaka Mutesa I came to the end of his long and eventful life. To the end he continued to hold in balance the rival political groups at court. He welcomed foreigners to his country but made sure that they remained there on his terms. The military might of Buganda declined during his last years and the old enemy, Bunyoro, was able to regain much lost land. The future greatness and independence of Buganda would depend largely on the ability of the next Kabaka to continue successfully Mutesa's policies.

Trading companies and imperialists

The activities of the Nguni, Zanzibaris, and rival warlords in some parts of East Africa made easier the establishment of European control. Where the newcomers discovered stable, well-organized African states, conquest was a much slower and more difficult process. As the map on page 253 shows, Christian mission stations were established over a wide area by 1884. By this date also explorers had travelled through East and Central Africa to discover the Nile source and map the Lakes system. Other Europeans came to hunt animals or to help the missionaries, particularly in their fight against the

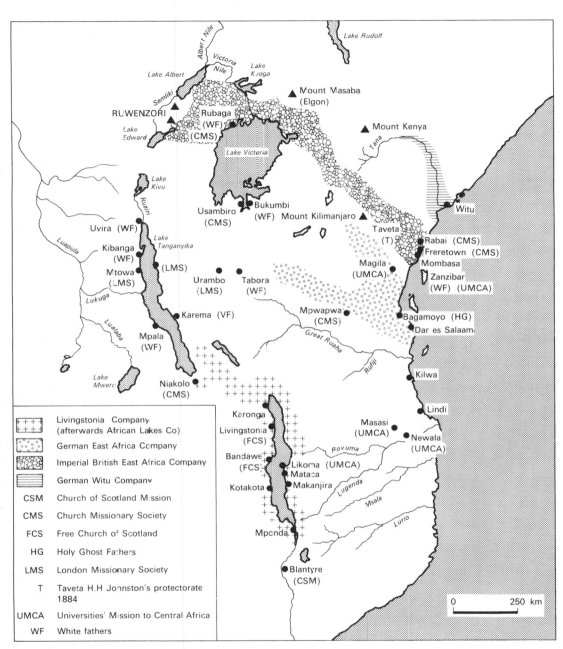

Foreign missionary and commercial activity in East Africa 1884

Arab slave trade. But some Europeans came who had a vision of the commercial and colonial advantages to be found in East Africa. It was these men who were mostly responsible for starting off the 'scramble' in this part of the continent.

In 1856 William Mackinnon founded a shipping company for carrying passengers and goods between Europe and India. It rapidly developed into the British India Steam Navigation Company, the largest steamship line in the world. Zanzibar became an important port of call for Mackinnon's ships, particularly after the opening of the Suez Canal (1869). Three years later he established a regular mail service between Zanzibar and Aden. He established friendly relations with Sultans Majid and Barghash, helped in the development of Dar es Salaam and advised them on the best way of exploiting their mainland possessions. Mackinnon wanted the British government and private companies to invest money in the development of East Africa, as they had in the development of Egypt. With the backing of the British Consul, Sir John Kirk, he persuaded Barghash to lease 1·5 million square kilometres to a development company to be formed for the purpose. But the scheme had to be dropped because Mackinnon failed to get the support of his government.

In 1884 another visitor from Britain, Harry Johnston (see p. 298), arrived to carry out a scientific survey of the animal and vegetable life round Kilimanjaro. During the course of his stay Johnston became convinced that the area was ideally suited for European settlement. He even signed treaties of protection with some of the chiefs at Taveta. But, like Mackinnon, he could not persuade the British government to support his schemes.

Carl Peters, a German, was more successful. He went to Zanzibar as an agent of the Society for German Colonization. He made treaties with many mainland chiefs in the region between the Pangani and Rufiji rivers. Early in 1885 he obtained his government's support for these agreements and was soon back extending German authority into the Kilimanjaro district and over Witu further up the coast. Sultan Barghash was alarmed at what he considered to be an invasion of his territory. He protested to Germany and offered a treaty of protection to Britain. The Germans sent warships to Zanzibar harbour while Barghash's British allies did nothing. The Sultan was forced to recognize the German treaties and allow Peters' Society free access through Dar es Salaam to their new territory. The German East Africa Company and the German Witu Company were set up to develop the new protectorates.

Meanwhile Mackinnon, Johnston and their supporters had brought pressure to bear on the British government. Mackinnon made plans to form a company to administer the Taveta protectorate covered by Johnston's treaties. The British government, faced with a complete German takeover in East Africa, called for a conference. The result of this conference was the Anglo-German Agreement of October 1886. Its main clauses were: (1) the Sultan's territory was defined as the offshore islands and an 18 km wide stretch of territory extending from the river Tana to the river Ruvuma; (2) a line was drawn from the river Umba to Lake Victoria dividing the British 'sphere of interest' to the north from the German sphere to the south; (3) the two European powers were to settle peacefully their rival claims round Kilimanjaro; (4) the German protectorate over Witu was confirmed.

Mackinnon's newly-formed British East Africa Association (it became the Imperial British East Africa Company in 1888) was soon in conflict with its German rivals. The IBEA Company managed to bring most of the northern coast under its control. Then there took place a race with the Germans to see who could reach Buganda first and gain control of the country. We will return to the affairs of Buganda shortly but first we must see how the 'scramble' for territory north of Lake Victoria influenced the overall pattern of partition.

Buganda was seen as the most important part of East Africa, both commercially and strategically. It had good government and a thriving economy. It would, therefore, make a very good trade centre. Strategically it was regarded as a 'back door' to Egypt and the Sudan. Some Europeans even believed that by controlling the headwaters of the Nile they could control the destiny of the lands through which it flowed. As we have seen, most of the colonial powers were interested in the upper Nile region. Matters came to a head in 1886 when the Mahdist uprising cut off Emin Pasha, the German Governor of Egypt's Equatoria Province, in his headquarters at Lado. Several expeditions were organized to rescue Emin in the hope of making fresh colonial conquests in the process and also of obtaining a share of the vast horde of ivory Emin had gathered.

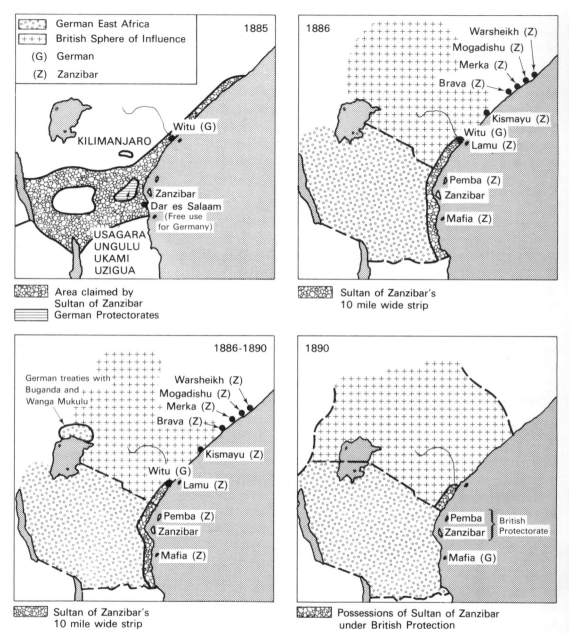

1885

German East Africa
+++ British Sphere of Influence
(G) German
(Z) Zanzibar

Witu (G)

KILIMANJARO

Zanzibar
Dar es Salaam
(Free use for Germany)

USAGARA
UNGULU
UKAMI
UZIGUA

Area claimed by Sultan of Zanzibar

German Protectorates

1886

Warsheikh (Z)
Mogadishu (Z)
Merka (Z)
Brava (Z)
Kismayu (Z)
Witu (G)
Lamu (Z)
Pemba (Z)
Zanzibar
Mafia (Z)

Sultan of Zanzibar's 10 mile wide strip

1886-1890

German treaties with Buganda and Wanga Mukulu

Warsheikh (Z)
Mogadishu (Z)
Merka (Z)
Brava (Z)
Kismayu (Z)
Witu (G)
Lamu (Z)
Pemba (Z)
Zanzibar
Mafia (Z)

Sultan of Zanzibar's 10 mile wide strip

The Partition of East Africa

1890

Pemba (Z)
Zanzibar
British Protectorate
Mafia (G)

Possessions of Sultan of Zanzibar under British Protection

The Emin Pasha relief expedition led by Stanley

It was a Congo Free State expedition led by H. M. Stanley that eventually succeeded in bringing Emin out (1889).

Of more interest for East Africa were two of the expeditions that failed. The IBEA Company sent a party under Frederick Jackson, and Carl Peters led a German group. Peters won the race to Buganda. He signed a protection treaty with Kabaka Mwanga and another with the leader of Wanga Mukulu, an Abaluyia kingdom in north-western Kenya. The IBEA Company, realizing that its sphere of influence might be encircled by German territory, urged the government in London to act. The result was another Anglo-German Agreement (sometimes known as the Heligoland Treaty because Britain gave to Germany the North Sea island of Heligoland as part of the agreement) signed in 1890. Its main terms were: (1) the 1886 boundary line was continued across Lake Victoria to the Congo Free State border along the 1°S line of latitude; (2) Germany gave up all rights north of that line; (3) Britain established a protectorate over Zanzibar and Pemba; (4) Germany bought from the Sultan of Zanzibar all his rights on the mainland. The British and German chartered companies could now settle to the peaceful development of East Africa.

But this did not happen. Both companies were in financial difficulties. The establishment of administrative posts, the payment of troops, the organization of expeditions to the interior took more money than the companies received from trade. The IBEA Company, in addition, had spent large sums on surveying a railway route to Buganda. In 1888, under the leadership of Abushiri, coastal Arabs in the German sphere revolted against alien rule. The German East Africa Company had to send to Germany for troops and money. By November 1890 it became obvious that the Company could not afford to administer the territory. The German government took over all political and administrative functions in what was from that time known as German East Africa.

The fall of Buganda

The future of the British Company was largely influenced by affairs in Buganda. When Kabaka Mutesa died his place was taken by his eighteen-year-old son, Mwanga. The new ruler lacked his father's political skill. He could not hold in balance the ambitions of the Roman Catholic, Protestant and Islamic factions. Confused, he turned against all whose loyalty he doubted. In 1885 he executed a number of Protestant converts and ordered the death of Bishop Hannington of the Church Missionary Society who was on his way to start work in Buganda. The next year Mwanga killed many Christians at court and planned to drive out the missionaries and their principal supporters. But his intended victims struck first. After a successful revolt Mwanga was deposed (1888). Faction struggles gripped the capital and after a year Mwanga was able to win his way back to power. But he could only maintain his position by carefully balancing the rival groups. Another problem for the Kabaka was the revival of Bunyoro which had taken advantage of Buganda's political unrest to strengthen its position.

This was the situation at the end of 1890 when Frederick Lugard arrived in Buganda as the agent of the IBEA Company. Mwanga could not afford to anger this well-armed newcomer who immediately allied himself with the Protestant faction. The two men signed a treaty granting the Company suzerainty over Buganda. Lugard also obtained treaties from the rulers of Toro and Ankole (1891). Inevitably a clash soon occurred between Mwanga and Lugard to settle who was the real ruler of Buganda. Lugard armed his faction and they defeated Mwanga and the Catholics.

But it seemed that the Company's triumph would be short lived. It had no more money left and the British government refused to give any help. In 1893 the Company was ordered to withdraw from Buganda. Missionaries and businessmen argued with the government. While the arguing went on in London, Gerald Portal was sent to Buganda by the Foreign Office on a fact-finding mission. Portal renewed the treaty with Mwanga and in his report urged the continuation of British control. His advice was accepted. In June 1894 a British protectorate was declared over 'Uganda'. Two years later work began on a railway to link the new protectorate with the coast at Mombasa. It was logical that Britain should seek to control the territory through which the railway would eventually pass. In July 1895 the British East Africa Protectorate came into being which gave Britain control over most of what is now Kenya. It was for some years considered to be a worthless, unproductive colonial burden. The railway was completed as far as Kisumu on Lake Victoria by 1901.

African reaction in Uganda

We have seen how the colonial powers divided up East Africa but how did the people of East Africa and their rulers react to this European takeover? Colonial administrators and soldiers penetrated only slowly into the new protectorates, and for many years most Africans had little or no contact with Europeans. Those who did meet the newcomers responded in various ways. As in other parts of the continent some rulers resisted the colonialists, others collaborated with them. Whatever they did, the end result was always the same—the gradual extension of colonial rule.

In Uganda the main opposition came from Bunyoro. Mukama Kabarega regarded the British as allies of Buganda. He resented the Toro Agreement of 1891 since he regarded himself as the overlord of Toro. In 1894 one of the first actions of the new British Commissioner was to launch an attack on Bunyoro. The Bunyoro army was easily defeated and Kabarega

Sir Apollo Kagwa, Katikiiro of Buganda

fled. He was replaced by a ruler whom the British believed they could trust, and Bunyoro lost large tracts of land to Toro and Buganda. A line of forts was built across Bunyoro, and Baganda agents were employed in administering the land of their traditional enemies. Kabarega was later captured and sent into exile. Bunyoro was now effectively subdued although a rebellion of several chiefs in 1907 was successful in forcing the removal of the hated Baganda agents.

In Buganda, Mwanga found it impossible to accept colonial rule. In 1897 he tried unsuccessfully to regain his independence. He was defeated and exiled to Kismayu. His infant son, Daudi Chwa, was named as Kabaka and three regents were appointed to rule on his behalf. In 1900 and 1901 a new series of agreements established the relationships that were to exist between the Protectorate government and the traditional interlacustrine rulers. By the Buganda Agreement (1900) the Kabaka and his ministers were allowed to keep considerable powers and privileges. The co-operation of Buganda was very important to the British who wished to use Baganda agents and soldiers to help them defeat and control neighbouring regions. Prominent among the Baganda who co-operated fully with the British were Apolo Kagwa, Chief Minister, and Semei Kakunguru who helped to establish colonial rule in Busoga and Bugishu.

The rulers of Toro and Ankole accepted colonial rule largely because the agreements left them with considerable power and because the British helped them against their enemies. In Toro British support reinforced the authority of Mukama Kasagama, which had previously been resisted by some of the chiefs, and it was in his interests to maintain friendly relations with the white men. Ankole pastoralists resented the attempts to force unfamiliar political and administrative systems upon them. Their resentment led to the murder of the Provincial Commissioner in 1905. However, the government handled the affair with wisdom, and Ankole soon settled peacefully under the new regime.

Colonial administration spread only slowly throughout the Protectorate. It was not until 1926 that Karamoja in the northeast was brought under effective control from Entebbe, the government headquarters. Because of limited funds and the British belief in indirect rule local chiefs and headmen were, wherever possible, recruited into the administration and Local Native Councils were established.

In the large territory to the east of Uganda there were many examples of more determined resistance to British rule. In 1895 a rising led by an Arab, Mbaruk, was joined by many of the coastal settlements between Kipini and Vanga and some of the African peoples of the coastal plain. Troops had to be brought from India to crush the revolt. For many years effective colonial control only existed at the coast and along the line of the railway. From about 1902 European settlers began to move into the Highlands and administration had to be established there also. In all these areas the British encountered some resistance. Sections of the Abaluyia, Luo, Abagusii, Kikuyu and Nandi had to have the new regime forced upon them. The Nandi were the most persistent and successful opponents of the Europeans. In 1895 they murdered a white trader who ventured into their territory. They did all in their power to prevent the railway crossing their land. They raided depots, attacked track-laying parties, stole equipment and harassed the workers in every possible way. When British and Indian troops were sent against them they disappeared into the wooded hills of western Kenya and continued a successful guerilla war for several years. Their resistance only came to an end in October 1905 when a British official under the pretence of making peace, shot and killed their leader Orkoiyot Koitalel Arap Samoei.

Those African leaders who co-operated with the pioneer European administrators did so for reasons of local politics. Nabongo Mumia of the Wanga Kingdom (the only Abaluyia hereditary kingdom) welcomed the British in the hope that they would help him to reunite his divided state. He valued foreign guns and trade goods. He knew that the presence of white men at his capital, Elureko (Mumias), made him seem important. So Elureko became an administrative centre and Mumia provided warriors to help the British crush local risings. In return, his position in Wanga was secured and he was even nominated Paramount Chief of the Abaluyia.

Lenana, the Laibon of a large section of the Maasai, needed help in his conflict with his brother Sendeyo and his people were suffering greatly from Kikuyu raids. Disease and civil war had much weakened the once mighty Maasai. Lenana, therefore, eagerly made friends with the new rulers. He gave permission for the railway to cross his grazing grounds and he lent his warriors to the British for raids against the Kikuyu and the Nandi. By so doing he won security for his people

Lenana, the Laibon of the Maasai

and considerable gifts of confiscated cattle. He was also given the empty title Paramount Chief of the Maasai. But when the British no longer needed Maasai help they turned against Lenana and his people. They took Maasai land for European settlement and, under the terms of the Maasai Agreements of 1904 and 1911, they moved the people into reserves. Their life of free wandering across the plains thus came to an end.

African reaction in German East Africa

But it was in the German colony that the fiercest opposition to European rule was offered. Abushiri's revolt was followed by other uprisings in the coastal area. The Zaramo and the people of Bagamoyo took up arms against the Germans. Further inland German expansion was resisted by groups of Chagga, Gogo, Yao and Nyamwezi. One of the early heroes of anti-colonialism was Mkwawa, the Hehe Chief. He led his people's resistance against the European occupation of their country and even after his defeat, in 1894, he continued to harass the Germans. He was relentlessly pursued by his enemies and, in 1898 when capture seemed inevitable, Mkwawa committed suicide rather than fall into the hands of the aliens. The Germans did not have to conquer the powerful, centralized state created by Nyungu-ya-Mawe. This passed, in 1884, to his daughter, Mgalula, who ruled wisely and organized successful campaigns against the Hehe and the Unyamyembe Nyamwezi. In 1895 the Germans reached Kiwele, the capital, and offered Mgalula an alliance against Unyanyembe and the Hehe. She accepted and assisted the white men in the conquest of her enemies. It was not long before the Germans had gained real power and appointed their own agents to administer the kingdom.

The Germans provoked opposition by attempting to overrun the land and change the way of life of its people too quickly. It was this unsympathetic and ruthless attitude that sparked off the most serious uprising of all, the Maji Maji Rising of 1905–7. The Germans forced the peoples of the south-east to plant cotton. The scheme was a failure, but this did not prevent the Germans and their agents using brutality against the reluctant workers. The rising began among the Matumbi in July 1905. It rapidly spread to the Pogoro and Gindo whose medicine men urged the warriors on by providing them with magic water which, they claimed, would give protection from German bullets. (This gave the rising its name Maji Maji—

maji is Kiswahili for water.) The coast town of Samanga was destroyed, European houses and settlements burned and many white men were murdered. Before many months had passed the whole of the south-east was involved in the rising. German reinforcements had to be brought from Europe. Even then it took the white men over a year to break the united African resistance. By destroying villages and burning crops the Germans slowly restored their authority. Many leaders were executed and thousands of Africans died in the fighting or as a result of the famine which coincided with it.

When the Sultan of Zanzibar signed the treaty of protection in 1890 he did not intend to sign away all his powers but this was the result of his action. He had to accept the appointment of a Consul-General and a First Minister who gradually assumed more and more authority. There was much discontent among the Arab community, and when the Sultan died in 1896 a member of the royal family, Khalid ibn Barghash, tried to seize power with the help of anti-British forces. It was all too easy for the British, with their command of the sea, to attack Khalid's island stronghold. British ships shelled the royal palace and Khalid fled. The British installed their own Sultan, Hamed ibn Muhammad. In 1902 Hamed died and was succeeded by his seventeen-year-old son, Ali. Because Ali was under age the British were able to assume still more authority in Zanzibar. More white officials were appointed. The traditional system of justice was replaced by British courts. The Sultan became a powerless figurehead respected neither by his people nor by the British.

By about 1910 most East Africans had realized the futility of armed resistance. This does not mean that they meekly accepted every aspect of colonial rule and lost all desire to regain their independence. Those who had ambitions for themselves and their people realized that the best way to fulfil them was to take every opportunity which presented itself to get on equal terms with the white men. They attended mission schools. Some went abroad to complete their education. They took minor administrative positions and, wherever they had the opportunity, they took part in local government. By 1920, as we shall see in chapter 16, they were ready to form their own political organizations.

Zanzibar, the Sultan and the British

White settlement

Between 1900 and 1920 three important events occurred which greatly affected the lives of East Africa's peoples and the future of the three territories. These were the arrival of European settlers, the East African campaign of the First World War and the transfer of Tanganyika (German East Africa) from Germany to Britain. The colonial governments were anxious that their East African territories should as quickly as possible become self-supporting. This largely meant producing cash crops for export and considerable attention was given in the early years of the century to experiments with various products—cotton, coffee, tea, sugar, sisal and others. Most officials thought in terms of teaching Africans to produce and market the new crops, but in the East Africa Protectorate and parts of German East Africa

Hill farm in Kenya

settler farming was seen as the answer to the colonies' economic problems. The main areas of settlement were the Kenya Highlands and the land round Kilimanjaro. These were considered climatically suitable for Europeans and it was believed that the land was good for crops and stock farming.

But these lands were already occupied. The Kikuyu, Kamba and others had for many years practised shifting agriculture in the Kenya Highlands. The Chagga, the Pare and their neighbours farmed the soil of the Kilimanjaro foothills. In the British protectorate the Kikuyu were the people most affected. Some of their best land was taken by white settlers on the grounds that it was unoccupied. The Kikuyu were placed in reserves, usually on inferior land. They now had to pay taxes so many were forced to take jobs on European farms to obtain the necessary money. The white farmers, who were quick to organize themselves and who had by 1906 succeeded in gaining representation on the new Legislative Council, tried to persuade the government to force Africans to work for them. They failed because the government, usually under pressure from missionaries, realized its responsibility to the native population. There developed a three-cornered struggle between the Africans and their representatives, the settlers, and the government which affected Kenyan politics right down to the eve of independence. The settlers aimed at white domination. By 1920 they had gained the right to elect members of the Legislative Council, they had successfully resisted a movement for the settlement of Asians in the Highlands, they had seen more land provided for Europeans after the First World War and they had urged Britain to drop the idea of protectorate government (in 1920 the British East Africa Protectorate became Kenya Colony). It seemed, then, that the settlers might well succeed in establishing total white supremacy.

In the German colony the settlers were not so successful. Unlike the white farmers in Kenya, they were not the main support of the the economy. Von Rechenberg, Governor 1906–12, was a firm believer in preserving African traditional leadership and in encouraging African cash crop production. In vain the settlers urged him to institute forced labour and grant them a share in the political life of the territory. Not until shortly before the First World War did the settlers win representation on the Governor's Advisory Council.

The First World War in East Africa

The Germans, wishing to distract Britain from the main war in Europe, raised an army of almost 3,000 men in German East Africa under the command of General Paul von Lettow-Vorbeck. They attacked Taveta and the railway line in southern Kenya. The British raised forces within the colony and imported soldiers from India, Rhodesia, Nyasaland and South Africa. The Germans were forced back into their own territory but were not defeated. For four years von Lettow-Vorbeck's force remained in the field, moving all the time and engaging the enemy in guerilla warfare. It was still undefeated at the end of the war.

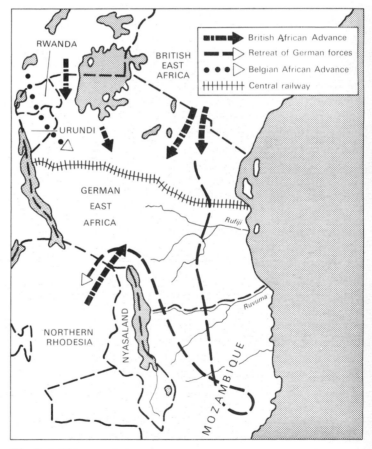

The East African campaign

Nobody won the war in East Africa but everybody lost. In all three colonies farms had been left understaffed while the men were away fighting. Thousands of men were killed and wounded. Others died of diseases caught on campaign. Africans had been forced to take part in the white man's war and this led to widespread discontent and suffering. After the war, when they might have expected that a grateful British government would have paid attention to some of their grievances, the Africans of Kenya found that their oppression continued as before. Many future African political leaders served in the 1914–18 war and they determined to oppose white rule as a result of their experiences at that time. As the colonial governments faced the task of reconstruction they had to deal not only with problems of trade and agriculture but also with politically conscious groups of Africans.

Men of the Nigerian Brigade on their way to German East Africa 1916

The end of German rule in East Africa

As a result of losing the war Germany had to give up her colonies. German East Africa, like other territories, came under the League of Nations mandate. Rwanda and Urundi were administered by Belgium on behalf of the League. The mandatory power for the rest of the colony (at this time known as Tanganyika Territory) was Britain (the mandate was confirmed finally in 1922). The main idea for the granting of a mandate was that the mandatory power's first obligation was to the people of the territory. The mandatory power was a trustee, not an exploiter. It was there to administer the country until its people were able to rule themselves. Thus, in theory at least, the possibility of independence for Tanganyika was acknowledged over forty years before it was achieved.

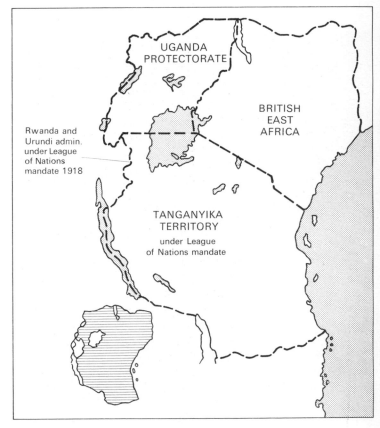

East Africa after World War I

The European take-over of East Africa was a conquest. Whether it was achieved by guns or by diplomacy what happened was that the British and Germans imposed their will on the peoples of East Africa. The Africans lost their freedom. They were forced to give up traditional customs, laws and lands. Their leaders lost their powers. They had to pay taxes to support an administration they did not want. They had to grow cash crops for export to countries of which they knew nothing. They had to accept a new idea of wealth based on pieces of metal or paper instead of cattle or cowries. They had to endure brutality from settlers and imprisonment or fines when they broke laws they did not understand. Colonial officials—even the few who really tried—could not understand African culture and values. Most Europeans assumed that their civilization was superior and that the African could only benefit from having it imposed upon him.

The major difference between white ruler and black ruled was that the white man was more advanced technically. How did he employ this superiority in East Africa? The first major undertaking was the building of a communications system. The Uganda Railway reached Kisumu in 1901 and from there a steamship service operated to Entebbe. One result of the railway was the building of Nairobi which began as a railway depot and later became the capital of Kenya. The Germans took longer to build their Central Railway along the old caravan route to Tabora and Ujiji (completed 1914) but laid shorter lengths of rail from the coast to Kilimanjaro. Railways meant not only easier marketing of goods but the bringing of food to drought-striken areas and the steady supplies of books, medicines, clothes, tools, pots and pans. European farmers applied their skills to the large-scale production of wheat, coffee, maize, beef and dairy products. Government officials helped Africans in Uganda and Tanganyika to grow cotton and coffee and to improve the quality of their stock animals. Very early in the colonial period a battle against epidemic diseases in animals and humans was begun. Dr Albert Cook first diagnosed sleeping sickness at Mengo, Uganda, in 1901. Before long the cause of the disease and a cure had been discovered.

Trade also developed rapidly in these years. It was largely in the hands of Asian settlers. Many of them had come from India to help build the Uganda Railway. When it was completed they stayed as shopkeepers, clerical workers and minor officials. Some prospered rapidly. Aladina Visram, for example, worked in East Africa from *c*. 1875 to 1916. By the time of his death he had a chain of shops stretching from the coast to Kampala and from Lake Victoria along the upper Nile. He built oil mills, furniture workshops, saw mills, soda factories and a cotton ginnery. He was only one example of the wealthy class of Asians (most of whom were British subjects) who were soon demanding privileges similar to those enjoyed by the white settlers. The Indians in Kenya began to organize themselves into political groups in 1904. They wanted political representation and the right to buy farmland in the Highlands. In 1809 the Asian community was granted a single representative on the Legislative Council but all their other demands were resisted by the whites. In 1914 they formed the East African Indian National Congress and continued vigorous political activity. The existence of this active racial minority helped to prevent the white settlers gaining complete control and it encouraged political activity among the Africans.

Constitutional problems in Buganda

Political opposition in Kenya and Tanganyika was not taken very seriously by the British in 1920. In Buganda, however, there was a more difficult problem. Apolo Kagwa, the Chief Minister and one of the Regency Council, had become the effective ruler of Buganda during the minority of Kabaka Daudi Chwa. In 1914 Daudi Chwa came of age and tried to assert his authority but Kagwa continued to ignore the Kabaka. The two men now fought for control of the Council, the Lukiiko. But the Lukiiko had other problems. Since it demanded the right to control the internal administration of the country, it found its work more and more difficult as time went by. The Protectorate government required the Lukiiko to administer taxes, law, currency control, health regulations, veterinary regulations and agricultural reforms. It could not cope with the rising tide of work but refused to give up any of its authority to the British officials. The Lukiiko was supported in its stand by Kagwa and Daudi Chwa. But there were other Baganda who were angered by inefficient government, and what they considered to be unjust laws. The Bataka, clan leaders whose powers had been diminished by the Buganda Agreement, supported by many of the peasants, felt that the Lukiiko only represented the chiefs.

270

The spread of alien rule in South Africa   Chapter 11

By 1880 a large area of South Africa was already under British or Boer control. During the next forty years the few remaining independent or semi-independent African territories were taken over by the colonial powers. The struggle between the Boers and the British came to an end in the formation of the British-controlled Union of South Africa. Germany entered the area by acquiring the colony of South-West Africa (though, along with her other African territories, she lost it in 1918). By 1920 the Pretoria government effectively controlled the entire area and was busy working out the social, political, racial and economic policies on which its administration was to be based. These are the main events with which we shall be concerned in this chapter.

By 1884 the Transvaal (annexed by Britain in 1877) was once more an independent Boer republic (see page 275). What the Transvaal leaders wanted above all things was an outlet eastwards to the sea. None of this territory was effectively occupied by a colonizing power. Swaziland, Tongaland and Zululand were all independent while the southern boundary of Mozambique had not been fixed. The British, particularly those of Natal, were as determined as ever to prevent the Boer republic gaining a stretch of coastline. As we have already seen (page 156), Zululand was in a state of chaos following the Zulu War. In 1887, to quieten the situation and to check Boer ambitions, Britain annexed Zululand. She also warned the Afrikaners off Tongaland. Anglo-Boer rivalry now centred on Swaziland. The King, Mbandzeni, had allowed a number of Boer farmers and British prospectors into his territory. Both factions struggled for control and were supported by officials in Durban and Pretoria (although both sides had recognized Swazi independence in 1884). When, in 1890, Mbandzeni died and was succeeded by a minor, armed conflict threatened Swaziland. Representatives were sent from

The end of independent African states

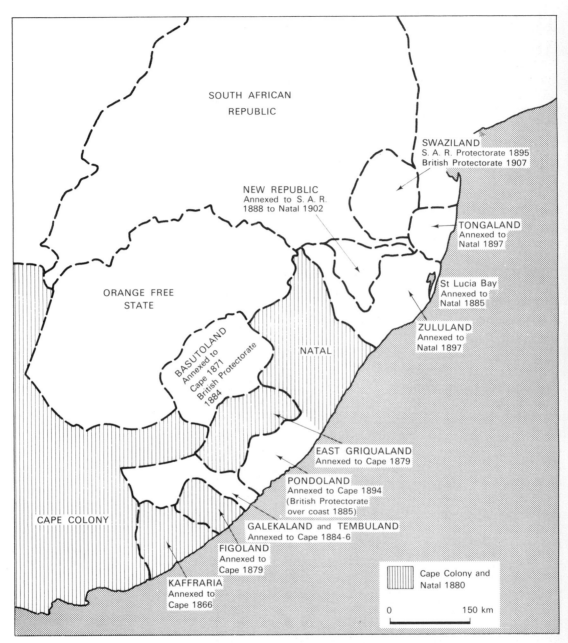

SOUTH AFRICAN
REPUBLIC

SWAZILAND
S. A. R. Protectorate 1895
British Protectorate 1907

NEW REPUBLIC
Annexed to S. A. R.
1888 to Natal 1902

TONGALAND
Annexed to
Natal 1897

ORANGE FREE
STATE

St Lucia Bay
Annexed to
Natal 1885

ZULULAND
Annexed to
Natal 1897

BASUTOLAND
Annexed to
Cape 1871
British Protectorate
1884

NATAL

EAST GRIQUALAND
Annexed to Cape 1879

PONDOLAND
Annexed to Cape 1894
(British Protectorate
over coast 1885)

CAPE COLONY

GALEKALAND and TEMBULAND
Annexed to Cape 1884-6

FIGOLAND
Annexed to
Cape 1879

KAFFRARIA
Annexed to
Cape 1866

Cape Colony and
Natal 1880

0   150 km

South East Africa 1880–1900

Transvaal and the Cape to work out a constitution which would enable the Swazis and the white men to live in harmony. The First Swaziland Convention was a failure. After 1890 the kingdom became a mere pawn in colonial politics. As part of a bargain struck between Britain and the Transvaal, the Second Swaziland Convention of 1893 permitted Transvaal to declare a protectorate over Swaziland. The Swazi Queen Regent totally rejected this and asked instead for a British protectorate to be declared over the land. This request was refused. A Third Swaziland Convention confirmed the terms of the Second. In 1895 Swaziland entered upon seven grim years of Boer 'protection'. The Transvaal leaders were now a large step nearer the desired coastal outlet but in 1897 the British foiled them by annexing Tongaland. Since the southern frontier of Mozambique had been fixed by an Anglo-Portuguese treaty of 1891 the entire coastline was now effectively closed to the Boers. One area of south-eastern Africa largely unconnected with the Anglo-Boer struggle was Pondoland. This untroubled area maintained its independence until 1894 and its leaders were careful to keep friendly relations with the Cape government. But Cecil Rhodes, the Cape Prime Minister, could not tolerate the existence of independent African neighbours. When the Pondo ruler granted trading concessions to some Germans the British used this as an excuse to annexe Pondoland. Thus, by 1897 the whole of south-east Africa had come under European rule.

Inland the large area of Bechuanaland (modern Botswana) was taken over by Britain. The takeover arose out of warfare between various Tlaping, Rolong and Korana settlements (1881). When Boers from the Transvaal intervened on behalf of some of the chiefs they were rewarded with grants of land which became the tiny Boer republics of Goshen and Stella-land. There was now a possibility that the two new territories might be absorbed into the Transvaal. This would enable the Afrikaners to span the British route to the interior. The annexation by Germany of a large area of South-West Africa (see page 192) in 1884 caused further anxiety in the Cape. If the Boers and the Germans were to obtain a common frontier the British colony would be cut off from the interior and the Transvaal might obtain a westward rail link to the sea, which would put an end to its economic dependence on the Cape. The British acted quickly and firmly. High level talks secured the support of the German government while Rhodes went to Pretoria to bargain with President Kruger. Even after agreement had been reached the British still had to send 5,000 troops into the area to force a settlement on the Boers of Goshen and Stellaland. The outcome was the establishment of the Colony of British Bechuanaland south of the Molopo river and the declaration of a British protectorate over the area north of the river as far as 22°N and 20°E. The wishes of the African people and their rulers were given very little attention.

The Anglo-Boer Wars

At the same time the long conflict between the Boers and the British flared up once more into a final trial of strength. The Transvaal under its leader Paul Kruger disliked British rule

Relief for the British during the Boer invasion 1900

274

and sought any pretext to end it. When, in 1880, British officials seized the goods of a Transvaaler who had not paid his taxes the colony revolted. There were a few armed conflicts and one small battle (Majuba Hill) which are sometimes known as the First Anglo-Boer War. Peace was made at the Pretoria Convention (1881) by which the Transvaal achieved self-government under British suzerainty. Three years later the London Convention restored the title 'South African Republic' to the Transvaal and granted it virtual independence. The Republic was poor, encircled by British territory and dependent for most of its supplies on the trade routes up from the Cape. It seemed to pose no threat to British interests. In 1886 all this was changed when a rich goldfield was discovered in the Witwatersrand.

There was an immediate gold rush as European prospectors and adventurers, mainly from the Cape, flocked into the Transvaal. These foreigners, or 'Uitlanders' as the Boers called them, were welcomed by the rulers of the Republic but only on very harsh terms. They were heavily taxed and they were allowed no political rights. All legal, social and economic transactions were carried out in the Afrikaans language and no English schools were allowed. This policy was forced on the small foreign community with unconcealed hatred by Kruger and his supporters. It inspired bitterness among the Uitlanders some of whom, as time passed, turned their thoughts to armed revolt. They were supported by fellow countrymen in the Cape and particularly by Cecil Rhodes.

Rhodes ranks next only to David Livingstone among the famous Europeans connected with Africa. Tough, ruthless and ambitious, he was quite a different type of man to the great missionary. He first arrived at the Cape in 1870 at the age of 17. He rapidly made himself a fortune in diamond mining. He bought up several rival mining companies and formed the mammoth De Beers Consolidated Mines Limited. By 1890 Rhodes was one of the richest men in the world and he was

Cecil Rhodes

determined to use part of his wealth for the imperial expansion of Britain. He wanted his country to dominate as much as possible of Africa 'from the Cape to Cairo'. He played an important part in the acquisition of Bechuanaland and believed passionately that the Boer states should be joined in a federation with Britain's South African territories. He was the leading spirit in Britain's occupation of territory in Central Africa (see chapter 12).

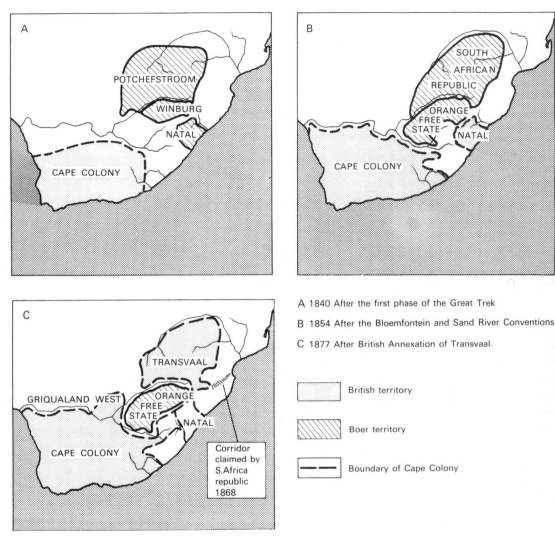

A 1840 After the first phase of the Great Trek

B 1854 After the Bloemfontein and Sand River Conventions

C 1877 After British Annexation of Transvaal.

British territory

Boer territory

——— Boundary of Cape Colony

Boundary of Cape Colony 1800–1880

In 1895 Rhodes sent guns to the Uitlander leaders, encouraged them to revolt and sent a small force of armed men, under the command of his friend, Dr Starr Jameson, to the Transvaal-Bechuanaland border. The rebels disagreed among themselves and eventually called off the rising. But Jameson's raid went ahead as planned, though Rhodes and others tried to stop it. The invasion was soon stopped. Jameson and his colleagues were arrested. Rhodes was forced to resign from the Cape parliament. There was a strong suspicion that the

British Colonial Office was involved and Anglo-Boer relations deteriorated still further. The Transvaal deliberately cultivated good relations with and bought arms from Germany. New laws were introduced which bore even harder on the Uitlanders. Kruger ruled as a dictator and seemed determined on a showdown with Britain. By 1898 any incident could have sparked off another Anglo-Boer War.

That incident was the Edgar case. A Transvaal policeman shot and killed an Uitlander, Tom Edgar. Instead of being tried for murder the policeman only had to face a charge of manslaughter and on this charge he was acquitted by an all-Boer jury. Uitlander society was outraged and petitioned the British government to protect the rights of British citizens in the South African Republic. In response Britain sent troops to the Cape and moved some up to the Transvaal border. The two Boer republics united in the face of a threatened invasion and demanded the withdrawal of British forces. When this ultimatum was ignored war broke out (October 1899).

The Second Anglo-Boer War was a war between one of the most highly trained armies in the world and small groups of fine horsemen and marksmen who knew the country they were fighting over. For most of the war the latter were more successful. The Boers proved to be masters of guerilla warfare. They inflicted heavy losses on the British and made the movement of men and supplies difficult. For months they laid siege to the garrisons of Kimberley, Ladysmith and Mafeking. Only when the British adopted a policy of destroying farms and crops and herding Boer women and children into concentration camps did they manage to make continued resistance impossible for the small Boer fighting units. The war continued until the middle of 1902, by which time over 50,000 people had died in the fighting and the concentration camps and thousands of farms had been destroyed.

Peace was concluded at Vereeniging in May 1902. The main terms of the treaty were: the Boer lands were to become British colonies; Swaziland Protectorate was to be taken over by Britain; the Boers had to swear allegiance to the British King; English was to be the main language throughout South Africa; part of the Transvaal was taken by Natal. But many concessions were made to the defeated Boers in the hope of creating a lasting peace. None of their leaders were to be tried for war crimes. They were to receive £3 million to repair war damage, and interest free loans would be available for restocking. They might keep their own schools, courts and language. They might look forward to eventual self-government and in the meantime Cape Colony's more liberal racial policies would not be forced upon them. Kruger was sent into exile in Switzerland where he died in 1904. Rhodes had already died shortly before the end of the war.

Formation of the Union of South Africa

Peace and unity had obvious advantages and the leaders of both white minority groups were soon agreed on the need to keep South Africa as one political and economic unit. But they could not agree what form that unit should take. The British desired an enlarged Cape Colony. The Boers looked for a republic, practising racial segregation and quite independent of Britain. But there were many moderates who realized that compromise was essential. It was largely due to them that agreement was reached surprisingly quickly. In 1906 and 1907 the Boer states gained internal self-government. In 1908 leaders of the four white states met to work out some kind of federation. Their findings were endorsed by the British government in the South Africa Act (1909). On 31 May 1910 the Union of South Africa came into being. The new state was a part of the British Empire. Its head of state was a Governor-General appointed by the Crown. There was an upper house or Senate and an elected General Assembly. The executive was in the hands of a prime minister and cabinet responsible to the Assembly. In Boer provinces only whites were allowed to vote. In the predominantly British provinces there was a multi-racial franchise.*

The old Boer-British mistrust never died. The two white communities represented different ideals and ways of life. These were soon reflected in the political life of the Union. The National Party, under the leadership of J. M. B. Hertzog, stood for racial separation, Boer domination and the breaking of all ties with Britain. On the opposite side was the Unionist Party. There was a more moderate South African Party and this dominated the political scene until the 1920s, but the forces

---

* The High Commission Territories—Bechuanaland, Basutoland and Swaziland—were ruled directly under the British Crown and did not form part of the Union.

of extremism gained ground steadily. Many of Hertzog's supporters resented Prime Minister Louis Botha's active support for Britain in the First World War. There was a revolt against the war policy which was soon suppressed. South African troops served in the East African campaign and in Europe.

The white minority which was making all the decisions accounted for less than a quarter of the Union's population. The remaining three-quarters, whose feelings and interests were largely ignored, were Cape Coloureds (people of mixed racial origins deriving from Khoi, Saan, immigrant slave and European elements), Bantu and Asians. Their way of life had been completely changed. Their traditional leaders had been deposed, their land had been taken, they were herded into overcrowded reserves, they were forced by economic necessity or direct pressure to take jobs on European farms, in the mines, in factories or in domestic service. Many Africans had been detribalized. They drifted to the cities and built slum settlements known as shanty towns on the outskirts. They received very low wages and even in the British-dominated provinces they had few legal rights.

But from the beginning of the colonial period there were African leaders who rebelled against the system which made Africans exploited and under-privileged citizens of their own land. In 1884 John Tengo Jabavu had begun to publish a liberal newspaper, *Imvo zaba Ntsundu*, in Xhosaland. Dr Abdullah Abdurahman founded a political group, the African People's Organization, at Cape Town in 1902. These made little impact on South Africa's rulers as was shown in 1906. In that year risings occurred in Natal and Zululand. The rebels were angry about pass laws, enforced labour, loss of lands and the imposition of a poll tax. The risings were ruthlessly put down and the leaders executed despite protests from African leaders and white liberals. The Zulu King, Dinizulu, who, in fact, had nothing to do with the revolt, was deposed and imprisoned. With him the royal line founded by Shaka came to an end.

When Union proposals were under discussion in 1909 some educated Africans and Coloureds, realizing the need to protect their people's interests, formed the South African Native National Congress. Two of its members gained seats in the new Cape Province Council but the Congress made no impact on the terms of the Union settlement. The first nationwide radical African organization was the African National Congress (ANC), founded in 1912 under the leadership of Soloman Plaatje, a Tswana journalist. Plaatje vigorously attacked racialist legislation passed by the Union Assembly. Unfortunately his impact was weakened by a split in the African political ranks. The veteran, Jabavu, formed the more moderate South African Races Congress. This organization achieved little, marred African unity at a crucial period, and collapsed on Jabavu's death in 1921.

The first major issue on which the ANC campaigned was the Natives Land Act (1913). White farmers were alarmed at the numbers of Africans leaving the reserves to rent or buy their own farms. The Assembly therefore passed an Act to keep the races apart by forbidding black men to buy land in 'white' areas and vice versa. The ANC protested against this. As a result the Act was not enforced in Cape Province where, because of property qualification, restriction of 'native' land holding would have restricted African voting rights also.

Another issue that contributed to racial tension was employment in the mines. On the gold and diamond fields there was competition for unskilled and semi-skilled jobs by Africans and a growing class of poor whites. Mine owners preferred to employ Africans because they could pay them less. The whites banded together into trade unions to work for better employment prospects. The Africans were not allowed to take united industrial action. The poor whites, therefore, were able to force mine owners to restrict the employment of Africans and the situation was given legal sanction in the Native Labour Regulation Act of 1913.

Many black and coloured citizens took part in the First World War and they believed they deserved fairer treatment from their white masters as a result. In 1917 the Industrial and Commercial Union (ICU) was founded by Clements Kadalie. It was both a trade union and a political organization. The ICU was active in championing African rights throughout the Union. Strikes and protest meetings became frequent as the Africans learned how to obtain concessions by using the strength which comes from united action. But extremist whites feared above all things the unity of the majority population. In 1920 when a large African crowd gathered in Port Elizabeth to demand the release on bail of a recently imprisoned ICU leader, a group of white civilians fired into the crowd, killing 24 protesters and wounding many others. The murderers were never brought to trial. In an attempt to secure better understanding between the races the government did set up a Native Affairs Commission to be a permanent forum for white politicians and black leaders. But, by 1920, nothing had been done to deal with the main African grievances and bitterness was growing.

Slave workers collecting potatoes in South Africa. If they left the line they were whipped

When the German adventurer Herr Lüderitz established a base at Angra Pequeña on the coast of South-West Africa in 1883 no one at the Cape or in Britain took much notice but their attitude changed the following year when Germany used Lüderitz's 'colony' as the basis for a claim to all the land lying between Angola and Cape Colony. As we have seen, Britain immediately secured the interior by proclaiming Bechuanaland a colony and protectorate. In 1890 the two colonial powers agreed their common boundary. Germany gained a sizeable colony and a neck of land (the Caprivi Strip) giving her access to the Zambezi.

When the Germans tried to obtain effective control of the area they ruled in theory, they had no easy task before them. Following the policy of 'divide and rule' they supported the Herero Chief, Maherero, against his enemy Witbooi. When Maherero died they supported the claim of the weak Samuel against Maherero's own nominee, Nikodemus. This split the Herero into rival camps (1891). Meanwhile Witbooi refused to accept German protection. In April 1893 the Germans made a surprise raid on Witbooi's capital at Hornkranz. The Chief escaped but 150 of his people were massacred. It was another eighteen months before Witbooi was captured and forced to accept German rule. In 1895 the Germans persuaded their puppet, Samuel, to alienate land for European settlement. Many Herero did not accept this arrangement, and when Germans seized cattle in the area designated for settlement there was an armed revolt. It was ruthlessly crushed in May 1896 and the 'rebel' leader, Nikodemus, was executed.

Resistance was not yet at an end. As more and more settlers arrived a typical colonial frontier situation was built up. The Germans cheated and abused the Africans. There were raids and counter raids. The attitude of the government towards the two groups was made clear in 1897 when a severe rinderpest epidemic struck the country. Vaccine was rushed from Europe to immunize the Europeans' cattle. Half of the Herero's cattle died in six months. A new law of 1903 actually stated that 'Every coloured person must regard a white person as a superior being.'

In the same year another and more serious anti-colonial rising took place. It began among the Bondelswarts but spread quickly to the Herero and the Ovambo. By the middle of 1904 a large area of central and northern South-West Africa was in revolt. African action mainly took the form of attacks on trading settlements and administrative posts but major battles were fought at Onganjira and Owiumbo. The Germans now decided to mount a large campaign and to impose the maximum possible suffering on the people of their colony. An army of over 7,000 equipped with machine guns and field artillery advanced to meet the Herero at Waterberg. Many Africans were killed. Many more fled eastwards and while some reached sanctuary in Bechuanaland others died of thirst in the Kalahari. Those who remained in the colony were hunted down as part of a ruthless German policy of extermination. But the revolt went on. The eighty-year-old Witbooi rose once more against the Germans and died of battle wounds. Not until 1906 was the last resistance leader captured.

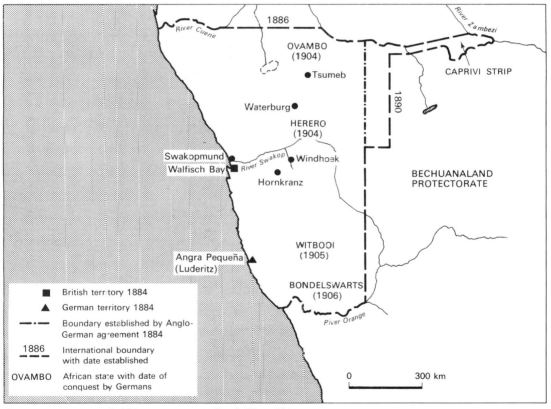

German occupation and African resistance in South West Africa

An enormous amount of land was confiscated during and after the risings and most of it was sold cheaply to settlers. Most of them took up cattle farming. Mineral prospecting revealed deposits of diamonds, copper and lead. Mining centres sprang up rapidly. Railways were built to link the main settlements with the coast. In all this development no regard was paid to the people of the land. They were made to work for their new masters. Their movements were restricted. They had to carry passes. They were forbidden to own land or large herds.

Many Africans must have welcomed the invasion of the Colony in 1915. As part of their support for Britain in the First World War South Africa sent an army of 60,000 to

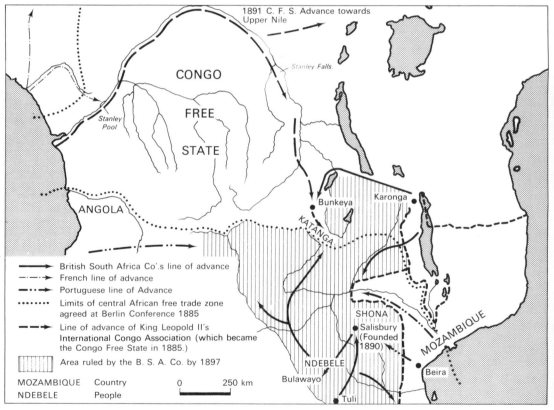

Central Africa 1880–1900

invade the neighbouring territory. The campaign was short and the Germans surrendered. After the war South-West Africa became a mandated territory administered by the Union of South Africa. The League of Nations, as we have already seen, regarded the mandated territories as being held in trust for their peoples with the aim of eventual independence. The Union government did not agree with this. It was contemptuous of the very idea of Africans ever being able to govern themselves. In effect, therefore, the peoples of South-West Africa saw little difference between German and Union rule.

Chapter 12

The establishment of alien rule in Central Africa

Between 1880 and 1900 Central Africa was the scene of many clashes and conflicts. The great Bantu kingdoms continued to decline under pressure from slave traders and powerful rivals such as the Cokwe and Bemba. Then the colonial powers arrived and made an onslaught on the slavers and their allies. At the same time the Europeans were competing among themselves for control of the interior. Portugal tried to link her colonies on both sides of the continent but came up against the agents of the Congo Free State pushing south-eastwards from the Congo Basin and those of Cecil Rhodes's British South Africa Company entering Ndebele and Shona territory from the south.

The End of the slave trade

One of the avowed aims of the Berlin Conference powers was the abolition of Africa's interior slave trade. From 1885 onwards more and more Europeans entered the area beyond the Great Lakes to make good the territorial claims of their governments. African and Arab slavers, many of whom had in the past shown hospitality and friendship to individual European missionaries and explorers now saw their livelihood threatened. As early as 1883 H. M. Stanley had set up at Stanley Falls a frontier post for King Leopold II's International Congo Association. The explorer informed Tippu Tip and his colleagues that they must restrict their activities to the area upstream from Stanley Falls. Tippu Tip, who only six years earlier had helped Stanley to complete his great trans-Africa journey, was enraged. At the Berlin Conference it was decided that the Congo Basin should be administered by the Congo Free State, which took over all the Association's posts. In 1886 the Arabs attacked Stanley Falls and slaughtered the garrison. The leaders of the Congo Free State realized that they had not the resources to defeat the Arabs finally.

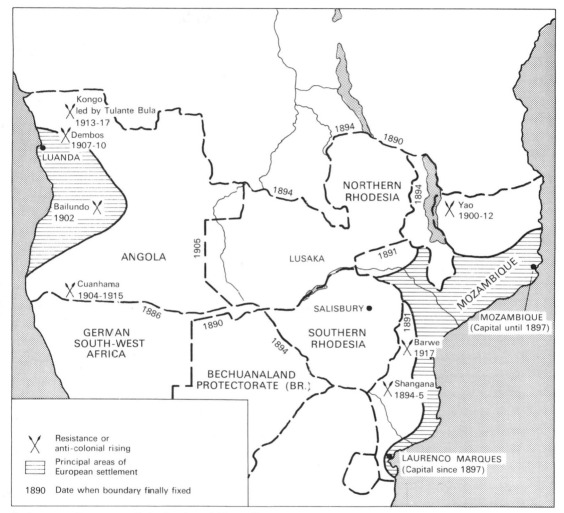

Resistance to Portuguese rule in Angola and Mozambique

They therefore took the unusual step of appointing Tippu Tip as the Free State Governor of Stanley Falls (1887). For three years the notorious slaver continued his activities while posing as a colonial agent. During those years the Congo Free State sent more men to the Congo Basin and sent expeditions to make treaties in remote areas. Thanks largely to Tippu Tip, an uneasy truce existed between the newcomers and the slavers. By 1890 Tippu Tip realized that the slave trade was doomed. As well as pressure from the Congo Free State to the west the appearance of the Germans in East Africa now threatened his caravan routes. He therefore retired to Zanzibar to live in comfort off his profit from slave and ivory trading.

Other Arabs were less foresighted. In 1892, led by Sef, Tippu Tip's son, and Rumaliza, his partner, they rose against the Belgians. The war continued until the end of 1893 when Sef was killed and Rumaliza fled to Zanzibar. This was the only determined attempt to resist the extension of colonial rule in the eastern Congo.

Further south Msiri was all-powerful between the Lualaba and Luapula. But his slaving, the tribute he exacted from subject peoples and his hostility towards Arab traders provoked opposition. In 1886 he failed to crush a Sanga revolt and the following year he was at war with Nsimba. Nsimba was one of the many Arab slavers operating on the Zambian plateau. This area was overrun by groups of Arabs, Bemba and Tabwa who plundered weaker peoples for ivory and slaves and were frequently at war with each other.

Christian missionaries were penetrating steadily deeper into Central Africa (some reached Msiri's capital, Bunkeya, in 1886). They reported back to Europe on the atrocities and chaos they witnessed. They also informed the European world that Katanga, part of Msiri's domain, was rich in copper. This provoked a race for Bunkeya by agents of the Congo Free State and representatives of the British South Africa Company (operating in the area between the Limpopo and Zambezi— see pages 300–2). In 1890 Alfred Sharpe, on behalf of the Company, gained concessions from several African rulers, including Kazembe Kaniembo of the East Lunda. But Msiri refused to sign a treaty. Early the following year he also declined offers of protection from the Congo Free State's representative, A. Delcommune. Delcommune's reaction was to stir revolt among Msiri's subjects. During the widespread conflict which followed Msiri was shot by a Free State agent

(December 1891). The Free State now set about 'pacifying' Katanga and the neighbouring regions. Leopold II's claim to this area was sanctioned by the other colonial powers in 1894.

The agreement of 1894 established on paper the boundary between the Congo Free State and British territory in Central Africa but, as in other areas, it was many years before colonial officials brought these areas under effective occupation. In fact, the occupation of the country between the upper Congo and the Great Lakes was not at all typical of colonial methods. Usually the Europeans worked inland slowly from the coast. The conquest of the eastern Congo Basin had been inspired by the desire for copper and the need to combat the slave trade.

The Congo Free State was a personal kingdom belonging to Leopold II and had no connection with Belgium. Leopold financed it from his own fortune but in 1890 and 1895 he had to obtain money from the Belgian government. The government, disapproving of some of the activities of the Free State's agents, demanded in return the right to annex the Congo to Belgium. This was done in 1908, the year before Leopold's death.

Leopold had financed the exploration and conquest of the Congo Basin because he believed there were rich resources waiting to be tapped. As the occupation of the territory swallowed up more and more money it became increasingly important for Leopold to exploit the land and people to the full. Free State agents therefore acted with great brutality and ruthlessness and, not surprisingly, they provoked considerable resistance.

In the Luba Empire they involved themselves in a succession dispute between the rivals Kasongo Niembo and Kabongo. The resulting war dragged on for fourteen years before the Belgians forced a compromise settlement on the two contenders (1905). Two years later the discontented Kasongo Niembo revolted. It took the Belgians a further ten years to gain effective control of Lubaland.

The Congo Free State had raised a local army, the *force publique*, to control the vast area they were responsible for. Often African soldiers were let loose against traditional tribal enemies. Even these 'loyal' Africans sometimes rebelled. There were mutinies at Luluabourg in 1895 and Boma in 1900.

A group of Tetela mutineers remained at large from 1897 to 1908. There were many other local risings against the policies of the new rulers—especially land-grabbing and forced labour. Exploitation was probably worst on the rubber plantations where men and women were made to work long hours with little food or pay. News of the Free State atrocities reached other countries. After a report on the situation by Roger Casement, British Consul at Stanley Falls, the Congo Reform Association was formed (1904) and the British government urged Leopold to control his agents more firmly.

The situation improved to some extent after the Belgian government assumed responsibility. Forced labour was stopped but people had to pay taxes and therefore they still had to work. The Belgian government invested money in roads, railways, hospitals, schools and towns with modern housing for workers. But no thought was given to the academic and political development of the majority. They received no secondary education. They were not taught French or any other unifying language. They were not encouraged to move outside their own areas. It was believed that Africans would always be workers, supervised by Europeans. No Belgian official thought seriously about the possibility of the Africans becoming independent.

Economic development in the Congo

Communication difficulties prevented the development of Katanga for many years but when these problems were overcome copper rapidly became the Congo's most important product. In 1906 the *Union Minière du Haut-Katanga* was formed to develop the mineral resources of this area. In 1909 Elizabethville was founded as the company's headquarters. The following year a link between Elizabethville and the Rhodesian railway system was completed. The town developed as an important area of European settlement. Immigrant labour from neighbouring countries was encouraged. By 1920 Katangan mines were producing large quantities of copper, tin and gold.

Portuguese advance in Angola

As a result of the bargaining which took place at the Berlin Conference (1884–5) Portugal lost her claim to the lower Congo. In 1886 she had to make an agreement with Germany over the border of South-West Africa and ceded more

Copper train on the Katanga railway line in the Belgian Congo

territory. The eastern frontier of the colony remained undefined for some years and Portugal now attempted to expand eastwards to join up with Mozambique. The people of Angola, who had had long experience of the Portuguese, fiercely resisted this new attempt at domination. In southern Angola the Cuanhama, with the help of German guns from across the border, prevented the Portuguese making good their claim to the land from 1885 to 1915. In 1902 a revolt was started among the Bailundu of the Bie Plateau and soon spread to the neighbouring Ovimbundu peoples. The Portuguese had to fight a bitter and costly war for eighteen months before this area was brought under their control. In the north-west resistance was led by the local Dembo chiefs. Many people flocked to place themselves under the leadership of the Dembos who were well supplied with guns. From 1907 to 1910 this region held out against European domination. On the border with the Congo Free State the

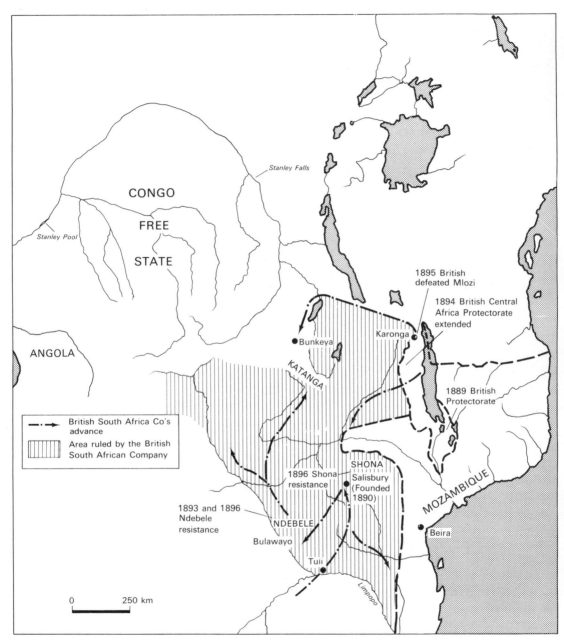

The British advance into Central Africa

mighty Cokwe were all-powerful. It was not until 1917 that the Portuguese were prepared to confront the Cokwe. They then poured men and arms into the area and were able to defeat the Cokwe at the battle of Moxico.

These conflicts slowed down the Portuguese advance into the interior. Meanwhile the British South Africa Company was occupying large areas of what are now Rhodesia and Zambia. The Portuguese plan to link Angola and Mozambique had to be dropped. In 1891 the boundary between Angola and the Company's territory was fixed as the western limit of the Lozi kingdom. But the Europeans could not agree how far Chief Lewanika's dominion extended. In 1903 the issue was decided by an international committee which fixed the Angola boundary where it is today.

Having thus gained by conquest and international agreement a large area of colonial territory Portugal had to administer it. She had an enormous problem arising from shortage of manpower. She could not rule the country properly and there were frequent revolts. What agents there were were of poor quality. Their methods were harsh and, because they received little supervision from the government, they were corrupt. European settlement increased, encouraged by the Portuguese government. Agents, farmers and businessmen all exploited the Africans ruthlessly. Slavery had been abolished but it had been replaced by the contract labour system, which was only slavery in disguise. The worst aspect of this system concerned the provision of labourers for the cocoa plantations of the islands of Saõ Thomé and Principé. The contract workers (*contratados*) were selected in various parts of Angola and marched to the coast under appalling conditions, like the old slave gangs. Village communities were broken up. Thousands of *contratados* died on the journey. They were shipped to the islands where, though their contracts were for a fixed term, they remained for the rest of their days.

This terrible exploitation reflected the fact that Portugal was a poor country. The government needed to make as much money as possible from its colonies in order to compensate for low production from home peasant agriculture. It also needed areas where Portuguese farmers could start a new and more prosperous life. The African colonies were regarded as extensions of the mother country. The African peoples were divided into two categories according to how far they had become 'civilized' (i.e. accepted European culture). There was a small class of *assimilados* who had learned the language and ways of their masters. The remainder were considered uncivilized and the normal rules of human conduct were not believed to apply to them.

Portuguese advance in Mozambique

By 1891 the boundaries of modern Mozambique had been defined, but effective control existed in only a few centres. As one official said: 'We controlled the capital of the province on the island of Mozambique; we also controlled the entire District of Inhambane; we occupied Laurenço Marques and exercised a more nominal than effective authority in the surrounding lands ruled by chiefs who were vassals of the crown; we had forts at various points in the province—Sofala, Tete, Sena, Quelimane, Ibo, Tungue, and a few more . . . in the rest of our possessions in this part of Africa we had no authority of any kind.'

South of the Zambezi the most powerful state was the Gaza (Shangane) Empire, ruled by Gungunyana. But he was under pressure from an Indian adventurer from Portuguese Goa, known as Gouveia. Raiding on his own behalf but receiving some recognition from the government, he had dominated the northern part of Gungunyana's empire and forced the Chief out of his capital. The Portuguese sent agents to make treaties with the weakened Gaza leader but Gungunyana rejected their proposals and sought instead a treaty of protection with Britain (1889). But the British were not interested and the Gaza were left alone to face the Portuguese. But the Portuguese had insufficient forces to face Gungunyana. In 1894 some local chiefs with Gaza support attacked Laurenço Marques and inflicted great damage on this growing port. The Portuguese could ignore the Gaza 'threat' no longer. The following year they sent an army into Gungunyana's territory. A decisive battle was fought near the capital, Manjacaze, and the Gaza were defeated. The Chief was captured and died in exile. Gaza resistance continued for a further two years but without their great leader the people were subdued group by group.

To the north resistance came from the Shona, some of the *prazeros* (Portuguese mercenaries) and their allies. The Portuguese employed Gouveia as their general in this area, but he was murdered by Shona warriors in 1893. Portuguese occupation thereafter proceeded slowly and was not completed until 1902. North of the Zambezi resistance also came from *prazeros* as well as local rulers. In 1884 a large force of Massingere attacked Portuguese posts on the Shiré and raided along the north bank of the lower Zambezi as far as Mopea. The Portuguese had to rely on a force of 4,000 mercenaries in order to suppress the rising but after the army's withdrawal colonial authority lapsed again. In 1892 the Portuguese government had to hand over the Shiré valley to the Zambezia Company which took another five years to subdue the area fully.

In the Zambezia and Niassa Provinces most opposition came from the Nguni and the Yao. Large military campaigns were necessary to subdue the Nguni (1904) and the Makua (1906). The Yao, supplied with arms along the old Kilwa trade route, held out much longer. Their main champion was

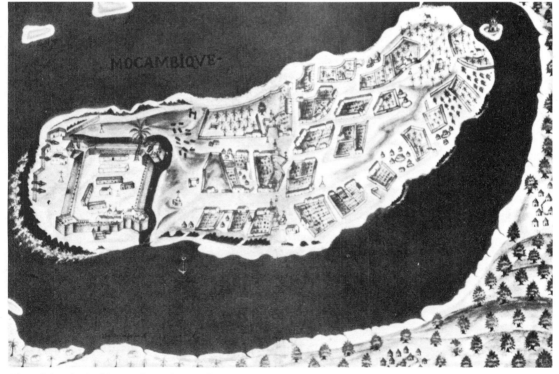

Plan of the island of Mozambique showing fortress

Mataka V Cisonga. Not until 1912 did a Portuguese force succeed in fighting its way to his capital, Mwembe. The Chief fled across the Rovuma into German territory and Yao resistance crumbled.

After the conquest was complete the colonial government (based in Laurenço Marques from 1897) relied heavily on the *prazeros* and the agents of the Mozambique and Niassa companies. Between them, these non-officials ruled vast areas of the colony. There was little effective control of these men or of local government agents from Laurenço Marques. Africans were everywhere forced to work on the plantations which were the mainstay of the colony's economy. They had few rights and very little provision was made for their education or welfare. Occasionally a High Commissioner arrived, who believed in a more liberal attitude towards the majority African population, but intrigue and lack of co-operation on the part of the European minority usually prevented any reforms being carried out.

British Central Africa

British intervention in the affairs of Central Africa came from two directions. Pioneer missionaries worked their way inland from the east. The British South Africa Company, controlled by Cecil Rhodes, penetrated from Cape Colony. During his last two African journeys (1858–64 and 1866–73) the great British missionary David Livingstone travelled along the Zambezi and Shiré, and through the Lake Nyasa region. He wrote vivid reports of what he described as 'one of the dark places of the earth'. He deplored the activities of Arab and African slave traders, and Portuguese administrators. He urged British intervention to bring peace, civilization and sound administration to this troubled area. Although the government paid no attention to his plea, some missionary companies were inspired to start work in the Lake Nyasa area.

In 1875 Scottish missionaries arrived. The Free Church of Scotland Mission established two posts, Livingstonia and Bandawe, on the shores of the lake and used a small steam boat to reach the various communities whose territory bordered it. They were well received by the Tonga and later by some of the Nguni ruled by Mbelwa. By 1890 the Free Church's work was flourishing on the eastern side of the lake. The Church of Scotland Mission concentrated on the Shiré Highlands and established a base called Blantyre. Many local peoples, suffering oppression from powerful enemies, placed themselves under the protection of the missionaries. In almost every instance African chiefs had political motives for welcoming the European teachers. They wanted guns, medicines and the support of the skilled Europeans in their local conflicts. Inevitably the missionaries became involved in politics when they decided to protect some groups from the 'oppression' of others. Inevitably, also, the missionaries found the strain of this political activity too much for them. They appealed to their home government for help. All the London politicians did was to appoint, in 1883, a British consul for the Shiré Highlands. In 1878 the missionaries were joined by businessmen. The Livingstonia Central Africa Company (afterwards renamed the African Lakes Company) was founded to supply the mission stations with necessary goods and to carry on legitimate trade with the Africans. The Company agents hoped (as well as making a profit) to win African merchants away from the slave trade and to show that commerce and Christianity could go hand in hand. In 1881 the Company entered the land of the Arab and Yao slavers when it helped the London Missionary Society to build a road from the north end of Lake Nyasa to the south end of Lake Tanganyika.

During the same period Europeans in increasing numbers had been entering Matabeleland and Mashonaland from the south. Most of them were hunters, adventurers and prospectors hoping to find mineral deposits or large quantities of ivory. But Cecil Rhodes and his supporters had a different interest in the area between the Limpopo and the Zambezi. They wanted to carry out large-scale prospecting in the hope of finding new gold deposits. They also wanted to stop the Boer states expanding into this area. In 1887 Transvaal agents signed a treaty with the Ndebele leader, Lobengula. Under pressure from Rhodes, the British government authorized a missionary, John Moffat, to make another treaty (1888) with the Chief by the terms of which Lobengula agreed not to lease any land without consulting the Cape government. Rhodes followed this up by negotiating mining concessions in Lobengula's territory. In 1890 pioneers of the British South Africa Company moved in to stake out the concessions and begin prospecting.

British activity on both sides of the Zambezi led to conflict with the Portuguese. The missionaries and the Company were both urging their government to stake colonial claims in areas of traditional Portuguese activity. In 1889 Portuguese agents were sent to gain treaties in the Shiré Highlands. The British Consul, Harry Johnston (see page 254), was given similar instructions. The rival parties clashed. Britain demanded Portuguese withdrawal and backed up the demand with a naval patrol off Mozambique. The Portuguese gave way and the upper Shiré valley became the British Central Africa Protectorate. During the next few months Johnston extended the area of his jurisdiction by making treaties with leaders along the western side of Lake Nyasa.

Chief Lobengula

Meanwhile, south of the Zambezi, the Company's pioneers had pushed into Mashonaland. The Portuguese were engaged in their long war with the Shangane. Rhodes's agents stiffened Gungunyana's resistance by offering him money and guns in return for prospecting rights. At this point the governments of Britain and Portugal decided to settle their territorial disputes in the area. By a treaty eventually signed in 1891 Portugal lost most of her claims south of the Zambezi and the area covered by Johnston's treaties west of the lake. She did retain a tongue of land along the Zambezi and as far north as Zomba. By an Anglo-German treaty of 1890 the southern border of German East Africa was fixed along a line just to the north of the missionaries' road from Lake Nyasa to Lake Tanganyika. In 1891 a British protectorate (soon to be called Nyasaland) was proclaimed over the whole area under Johnston's control. The area south of the Zambezi was left for the British South Africa Company to administer and the area west of Nyasaland was also declared to be within the Company's sphere of influence.

Occupation and Resistance
1. Nyasaland

Most of the small chieftaincies of the Shiré Highlands welcomed British protection and strong action against the slave trade. But the Yao and Nguni groups saw their way of life threatened by European rulers. In July 1891 Johnston began a systematic campaign against the Yao slavers. By the end of the year he had defeated most of the principal chiefs one by one and built forts throughout their territory. But Makanjila, the most powerful of all the Yao chiefs, had not been defeated. From his base on the lake shore he defied the commissioner and raided African communities under British protection. This went on for two years before Johnston, with reinforcements, launched a successful attack on Makanjila's base. But the chief escaped into Mozambique, gathered other dissatisfied Yao leaders round him and, for a further two years, organized raids on the Protectorate. In 1895, after all his allies had been killed or captured, Makanjila disappeared over the Mozambique border for the last time.

Johnston now hurried to the north end of the lake to deal with the notorious Arab slaver Mlozi. For many years Mlozi had terrorized the area and held the local people, the Ngonde, in subjection. In November 1895 Johnston launched a surprise attack on Karonga, Mlozi's base. He received willing help from the Ngonde and the town was soon captured. Mlozi was quickly tried and executed. In 1897 and 1898 Johnston's successor, Alfred Sharpe, launched successful campaigns against the Maseko and Mpezeni sections of the Nguni. The Nguni could not adjust to a new way of life in which raiding was forbidden, migration discouraged and in which they were expected to pay taxes and to work for the white man. But their attempts to resist British domination were, of course, futile.

2. Southern Rhodesia

To the south Lobengula had to face the problem of an increasing flow of intruders from the British South Africa Company into Mashonaland. The leaders of the Company aimed to take over the territory of Lobengula, the 'savage tyrant'. As one official said:

... if Lobengula looks on in silence and does nothing [we] will occupy Mashonaland ... If, on the other hand, Lobengula attacks us, then ... he must expect no mercy ... If he attacks us, he is doomed, if he does not, his fangs will be drawn, the pressure of civilization on all his borders will press more and more heavily upon him, and the desired result, the disappearance for ever of the Ndebele as a power, if delayed is yet more certain.

As soon as the prospectors arrived in Mashonaland they began to make treaties with Shona chiefs, completely ignoring their overlord, Lobengula. The Ndebele leader did not want to provoke a clash but he could not see his authority undermined.

There were many clashes between Ndebele warriors and Company men. By mid-1893 the Company's leaders felt themselves ready for a show-down with Lobengula. Their leader, Dr Jameson, provoked an incident and used it as an excuse for war. A force of 1200 Company troops with modern weapons, including Maxim guns, invaded Matabeleland. The Ndebele were defeated in two battles and the survivors retreated, burning their capital behind them. While fleeing, Lobengula died of smallpox (January 1894). The triumphant Company took over his country, herded his people into reserves and divided the best land up into European farms.

For three years the Ndebele accepted defeat. By that time the Shona, many of whom had helped to overthrow Lobengula, were ready to revolt. The two peoples rose simultaneously in March 1896. They raided farms and trading posts, killing and burning. The Europeans fled to the towns and awaited reinforcements from South Africa. The rising, having no united or effective leadership, now collapsed. The Ndebele forces retreated to the Matopo Hills where Cecil Rhodes came in person to discuss peace terms with their leaders. The Shona, inspired by some of their medicine men, continued to resist. From their hilltop strongholds they launched attacks on Company property. The Europeans countered with machine guns and explosives. By the end of 1897 it was all over and the leaders of the Shona rising had been hanged.

3. Northern Rhodesia The Ndebele War had provoked considerable protest in Britain against the British South Africa Company. The government was therefore determined not to allow the Company a free reign in the area which came to be known as Northern Rhodesia. On the other hand the government was not prepared to administer the area directly as a crown colony or protectorate. If British claims to the region west of Nyasaland were to be made good it could only be with Cecil Rhodes's money.

The Company established itself in the western part of this region by agreement with the Lozi King, Lewanika. From his centre in the Barotseland plain Lewanika claimed to rule an empire extending far northwards into the Congo Basin. Yet he was troubled by political divisions within the kingdom and pressures (from traditional and European enemies) without. When, in 1885, a rebellion deposed him he was only able to regain his throne with Portuguese help. Realizing the advisability of obtaining European support for his regime he persuaded F. Coillard, a French missionary, to send a message to Cape Town requesting British protection (1889). Rhodes sent one of his agents, F. Lochner, to negotiate a treaty for the Company while posing as an official representative of the British Queen. The Lochner Treaty was signed in 1890 and was, in fact, later ratified by the British government which sent a Resident to Lealui (Lewanika's capital) in 1897.

The Lochner Treaty gave the Company nominal control of an area far exceeding the limits of Lewanika's real power. Rhodes tried to use this treaty as a basis for gaining control of the copper-rich Katanga area. He sent agents in Nyasaland to visit Katanga to obtain treaties with Msiri and his neighbours. We have seen how Sharpe failed to reach agreement with Msiri and how Katanga was taken over by the Congo Free State. But the Company's agents did obtain treaties with Mambwe and Lungu chiefs and with Kazembe Kaniembo, the East Lunda ruler.

The main obstacle to the extension of British rule in Northern Rhodesia might have been the Bemba but they had by this time passed the peak of their power. They were politically divided, some following the legitimate leader Chitimukulu Sampa and others supporting his rival Mwamba. Mwamba sought the support of the Europeans in his struggle for power and was thus in a strong position when Sampa died and was succeeded by a weakling who could not stand up to Mwamba. Two years later Mwamba himself lay dying. He summoned to his bedside Bishop Dupont, a Roman Catholic missionary. According to Dupont, Mwamba named the bishop as his heir and most of the Bemba accepted him. Almost immediately Dupont handed over Bembaland to the Company, which thus peacefully gained control in 1899.

British rule 1900–20
1. Southern Rhodesia

Most of the Europeans who settled in Southern Rhodesia were either members of the British South Africa Company or farmers. They all assumed that Southern Rhodesia was a 'white man's country' where the minority would eventually exercise complete control without interference from London. The Company was basically a mining company and it found the administration of the colony a growing drain on its resources, especially as the gold they had hoped to find did not exist, although coal and chrome were discovered. Immediately a network of railways was created linking Southern Rhodesia with South Africa, the coast and the Congo Free State. Farming, however, became the mainstay of the economy. On large farms the immigrants produced maize, tobacco and beef for export.

For all this white enterprise black labour was needed. In 1902 a poll tax was introduced which made African men seek work. Where this failed, force was used to press the people into service. Soon thousands of Africans were doing seasonal work on the land and in the mines not only of Southern Rhodesia, but also of Transvaal and the Free State. Further to control the 'blacks' the government introduced the hated pass laws, which obliged all Africans to carry and produce passes on demand. Failure to do so was punishable by fines and imprisonment. As the years went by more and more land passed into European hands while the African population grew and overspilled the crowded reserves.

Political power was shared by the Company, the British government and the settlers. The leading official was the Company Administrator but he had to co-operate with a Resident Commissioner sent from London. The settlers were represented on the Legislative Council and from 1907 onwards they had a majority. All laws were subject to the approval of the South African High Commissioner. African opinion had no political outlet and the franchise was deliberately withheld from the majority population. This political situation was full of tensions which came to a head when the British government, moved by the plight of landless Africans, declared that all unassigned land belonged to the Crown and not to the Company. The Company now asked to be relieved of its administrative responsibilities. All parties concerned now began to work out a new constitution for Southern Rhodesia and this eventually came into operation in 1923.

2. Nyasaland Nyasaland never had the problem of a large, politically active, white settler population. For this reason and because of the educational opportunities provided by mission schools African political consciousness developed rapidly in the Protectorate. By a constitution of 1907 Nyasaland was ruled by a Governor, assisted by Executive and Legislative Councils (Legco) whose members were nominated. Africans were represented on Legco by a missionary. At local level a policy of indirect rule was followed where possible. Many chiefs were paid to administer law and order among their people. In 1912 a new system was introduced which grouped villages together for

John Chilembwe with his wife and child

administration under Principal Headmen. The decision to co-operate with or take office under the colonial regime often created problems for chiefs. It was difficult for them to refuse co-operation yet they were likely to be rejected by their people as colonial 'stooges'.

The first important nationalist leader to emerge in Nyasaland was John Chilembwe. He was a Yao and an ordained Christian minister. He took a university course in the United States of America, then returned (1900) to minister to his people. He grew increasingly dissatisfied with government policies on land and famine relief, and he actively campaigned against Africans being called up to serve in the First World War. In 1915 a European settler involved in a dispute with Chilembwe burned down some of the Yao minister's churches. This provoked Chilembwe's supporters to riot and murder. During the fighting which followed Chilembwe was shot by the police.

African protest also found expression in the Native Associations and the independent church movement. The Associations were groups of educated Africans who met to discuss current problems and to press for government action in solving those problems. They particularly opposed official land policies, forced labour and inadequate education. These Associations were the forerunners of African political parties and when their members travelled to neighbouring countries they spread nationalist politics among people who were not free to discuss matters of common interest. The independent church movement began in northern Nyasaland. There were two main

John Chilembwe's church under construction 1911–1913

reasons for it: missionaries were reluctant to appoint African pastors, even when well-educated candidates were available, and because missionaries imposed European ideas and rejected certain African practices many converts felt that the mission churches did not allow them to express their religious feelings. Such semi-Christian movements as Eliot Kamwana's Watchtower Church sprang up. Many independent religious leaders preached fervently against the colonial regime.

3. Northern Rhodesia

In 1911 the two areas north of the Zambezi which were ruled by the British South Africa Company were united as Northern Rhodesia. Government remained in the hands of the Company but a British Resident Commissioner had ultimate control. In 1917 the small white settler community gained an Advisory Council to central government, to which they elected members. Local government was largely by indirect rule.

The copper deposits of the Copper Belt were not exploited until the 1920s but the Company discovered lead, zinc and some inferior copper ores which were mined from early in the century. Railways were essential for the development of the mining industry and by 1910 the main centres were linked with the Southern Rhodesian Wankie coalfield and Elizabethville (Congo). Settler farming was encouraged and land taken from some of the African peoples (e.g. the Nguni) who were moved into reserves. The government neglected to encourage African agriculture because it wanted to lure more settlers into the country and make plantation production the basis of the economy and also to force Africans to migrate to the mining areas to find work. But no more settlers came.

Meanwhile African traditional life was disrupted. Taxes were imposed. The Lozi were forced to give up domestic slavery and tribute labour. Men had to travel to the centres of European population seeking work. If there was little African political activity it was largely because there were few educational facilities for Africans. In Northern Rhodesia the government, indeed, had no clear policies for African development.

Chapter 13

Colonialism, nationalism and pan-Africanism

The fifty years covered in this last section of the book was probably the most dramatic half century in the history of the continent. In 1920 almost every hectare of African soil was ruled by one or other of the European imperial nations. In 1975 the continent comprised forty-two independent African nations, two colonies and two independent states under white minority rule. It took three major developments to bring about this transformation: the economic exhaustion of the colonial powers, a change in world opinion, and the growth of African nationalism.

Decline of the colonial powers

In 1920 it seemed as if the leading colonial powers had never been stronger. Britain had the largest empire the world had ever seen and France's colonial possessions were extensive. They had recently won a major war and their victory was largely due to the men and goods provided by the loyal colonies. In fact the war had been very costly: commerce and agriculture had been damaged and there had been an appalling loss of life. In 1929, just as Europe seemed to be recovering, the major industrial countries were hit by a world economic depression: banks failed; businessmen went bankrupt; there was massive unemployment. Economic chaos led to political confusion. Governments rose and fell rapidly because no leader could find a solution to his country's problems. One result of the poverty and suffering was the rise to power of fanatical dictators in Germany and Italy. Adolf Hitler in Germany and Benito Mussolini in Italy played on the national pride of the people in order to gain popular support. One of the promises they made their followers was that they would build up large overseas empires. Hitler was determined to regain the territories taken from Germany in 1918. Mussolini was anxious to revenge himself on Ethiopia for the humiliating defeat at Adowa. Italy struck first. In 1935 she invaded Ethiopia and by the middle of 1936 the conquest was complete.

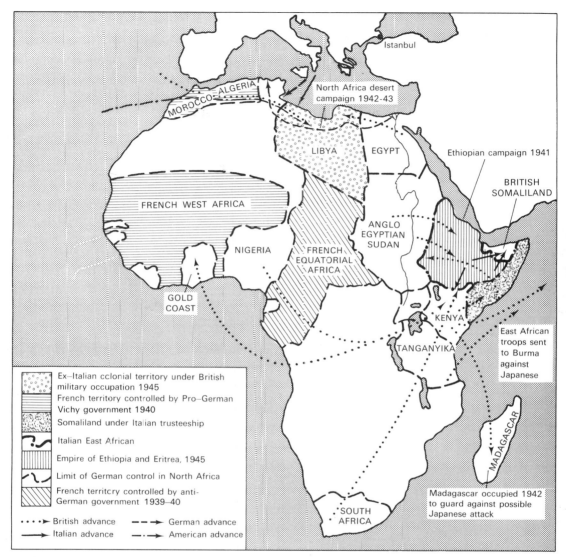

Istanbul

North Africa desert
campaign 1942-43

LIBYA EGYPT

Ethiopian campaign 1941

BRITISH
SOMALILAND

FRENCH WEST AFRICA

NIGERIA

FRENCH
EQUATORIAL
AFRICA

ANGLO
EGYPTIAN
SUDAN

MOROCCO ALGERIA

GOLD
COAST

KENYA

TANGANYIKA

East African
troops sent
to Burma
against
Japanese

MADAGASCAR

Madagascar occupied 1942
to guard against possible
Japanese attack

SOUTH
AFRICA

Ex—Italian colonial territory under British
military occupation 1945

French territory controlled by Pro—German
Vichy government 1940

Somaliland under Italian trusteeship

Italian East African

Empire of Ethiopia and Eritrea, 1945

Limit of German control in North Africa

French territory controlled by anti-
German government 1939—40

• • • •► British advance   – – –► German advance

———► Italian advance   –·–·► American advance

World War II in Africa

The failure to halt Italy's act of aggression was another indication of the weakness of the world's major powers. After the First World War the League of Nations had been set up as an international meeting place where disputes might be settled peacefully and pressure exerted on potential aggressors. The League condemned Italy's invasion of Ethiopia and imposed economic sanctions in an effort to force the withdrawal of the invading army but the sanctions were only half-heartedly imposed and had no effect. The League, and therefore the major western powers supporting the League, had revealed a fatal weakness and lack of resolve, as Ethiopia's Emperor, Haile Selassie, pointed out in a famous speech:

> . . . the problem submitted to the Assembly today is a much wider one than the removal of sanctions. It is not merely a settlement of Italian aggressions. It is collective. It is the very existence of the League of Nations. It is the confidence that each state is to place in international treaties. It is the value of promises made to small states, that their integrity and their independence be respected and ensured. It is the principle of the equality of states on the one hand, or, on the other, the inevitability that they will be forced to accept the bonds of vassalship. In a word it is international morality that is at stake.

Within weeks of that speech being made in 1936 Hitler had begun his career of aggression, and proceeded to take over, one at a time, several small European states. With Mussolini he formed a pact known as the Berlin-Rome Axis and the two leaders laid plans for world conquest. Powerless to stop them and fearful of provoking another major conflict, Britain, France and their allies did nothing until, in 1939, war became inevitable.

At the beginning of the Second World War France was quickly overrun and Britain was attacked from the air. Germany ruled France through the puppet Vichy government. Some of France's African colonies were loyal to the Vichy government but others supported the Free French government in exile. Once again the Free French and the British colonies rallied to the support of their mother countries. From South and West Africa troops were sent to Kenya. From there they invaded Ethiopia while Sudanese forces attacked from the west. In 1941 Ethiopia was liberated and Haile Selassie was restored as leader of his people. The Italians were also thrown out of Somalia. African troops were sent to Madagascar, to guard the island against a possible Japanese invasion (Japan entered the war in 1941), and saw service in India and Burma. In North Africa the famous Desert War took place. Germany and Italy tried to conquer Egypt and gain control of the Suez Canal and the oil-rich Middle East. Until the closing months of the war Egypt remained officially neutral. Her leaders were divided about which side to support but Britain poured in troops and used the country as a base from which, after several defeats, they successfully stopped the German advance on Egypt. In 1942 the United States of America joined in the war. British and American forces landed in the Maghrib and pushed eastwards through Morocco and Algeria. Together with British forces from Egypt and the Free French from French Equatorial Africa they fought a series of hard battles with their enemies. Finally, in 1943, the German and Italian forces were pushed out of North Africa and the Allies were able to carry the war into Italy.

The Desert Campaign 1944

When the war in Europe ended in 1945 France and Britain were exhausted. For several years they had to rely heavily on economic aid from the United States of America to restore their industries and rebuild their towns. There was little effort or money to spare for the colonies and little will left to hold on to overseas possessions in the face of mounting anti-colonialism. There were also divisions within western society. Britain and France were among the world's leading democratic nations. This meant that they stood for the principle of political freedom for men and nations. At the very time in the nineteenth century when they had been building up the world's largest empires they had also been developing at home on the foundations of parliamentary democracies. All previous world empires had been built with the aid of political systems which accepted slavery and supported the principle of rule by right of conquest. These elements were present in the foundations of modern colonial empires but also present in the written legal system of the conquerors were principles such as human equality and the right of all men to pursue their own road to happiness. It is no accident that many African nationalist leaders learned about democracy and human rights while studying in the lands of their colonial oppressors. It was Frederick Lugard, an experienced colonial administrator in East and West Africa, who wrote in 1922, 'For two or three generations we may show the Negro what we are: then we shall be asked to go away. Then we shall leave the land to those it belongs to, with the feeling that they have better business friends in us.' The possibility of eventual independence for the colonies was always recognized, in some circles, at least. White settlers and reactionary officials might believe that the African was incapable of self-government in the forseeable future, but there were always progressives who worked for the advancement of colonial peoples believing that dignified self-government was the only worthy goal that colonial administrators could set themselves. Such views were strongly held in the British Labour Party, which came to power in 1945. In 1947 this government granted independence to India and that act opened the gateway to self-determination for all colonial peoples.

Changing world opinion

The First World War marked the end of a long period of history during which western Europe had been the commercial and

310

political centre of the world. During the next fifty years international economic life became much more complex. In political affairs there were experiments in creating a world assembly. The first, the League of Nations, was not very successful, but the United Nations, founded at the end of the Second World War, has survived many crises and does fulfil a useful function. Real political influence has now come to be held by the 'superpowers', Russia, America and China. These changes meant that, much more than ever before, the actions of the colonial powers came under international discussion. The League of Nations decided that there could be no question of 'sharing out' Germany's colonies which had been confiscated in 1918. These territories were brought directly under the League's control and the League selected nations that were given a 'mandate' to administer them on behalf of the international body. There was to be no question

Fifteenth session of UN General Assembly 1961
Jaja Wachuku, Nigeria's Federal Minister of Economic Development; Demba Diallo, Mali's Technical Adviser

of exploitation by the mandatory power; on the contrary 'the well-being and development of such peoples form a sacred trust of civilization . . . The best method of giving practical effect to this principle is that the tutelage of such peoples should be entrusted to advanced nations who by reason of their resources, their experience or their geographical position can best undertake this responsibility.'

After the Second World War anti-colonialism was widespread. America and Russia, who agreed on virtually nothing else in the 1950s, were united in their insistence that the overseas colonial empires should be broken up as soon as possible. They knew that the newly emerging independent states would be economically weak and they hoped by making friends with the leaders of these states to increase their influence and to create new investment opportunities. In 1956 Egypt nationalized the Suez Canal, without reference to the international company which owned and operated it. Britain and France reacted immediately with a land and air invasion. This provoked an outcry from the superpowers and angry speeches were made in the United Nations Assembly. The attackers were forced to withdraw. Once the tide of independence had begun to roll and new nations took their seats in the United Nations Assembly the pressures on the colonial powers became greater. Anti-colonialism was one of the hallmarks of what came to be called the Afro-Asian Bloc.

The growth of African nationalism

The weakness of the colonial powers and the external pressures put upon them would not alone have resulted in the speedy collapse of the great modern empires. There had to be internal African pressures as well. In the following chapters we shall be considering in detail the growth of nationalism in various colonies. Here we will mention some of the common features that all or most African political movements shared.

In some territories (e.g. the Belgian Congo) there was a continuous history of resistance to colonial rule but in most areas there were distinct phases in the development of nationalism. By 1920 the period of primary resistance had passed because people realized the futility of trying to fight against the superior weapons and better discipline of colonial armies. This was followed by a phase during which Africans tried to improve their position by co-operation and education. Many traditional leaders were incorporated into the colonial administrations. While by no means all of them were 'tools' of the Europeans, they did impress on their people the desirability of making their demands peacefully and constitutionally and of using to the full the educational opportunities open to them, so that they could compete with Europeans on equal terms. Many young men attended mission schools (throughout the colonial era most of the schools were run by missionaries) and some went on to further study in Europe or America. Many of Africa's future leaders learned in this way. Some examples are Kwame Nkrumah, Jomo Kenyatta, Hastings Banda and Nnamdi Azikiwe. Most of the political organizations that existed during the inter-war years were small, tribal or regional societies, seeking to obtain reforms within the colonial system, rather than the overthrow of that system.

But there were some radicals and their numbers grew as the years went by. The two World Wars made a deep impact on many Africans. Those who fought left their own country for the first time. They met peoples of other lands and mixed on terms of equality with soldiers of other races. They were ordered by white men to do what would have been unthinkable before—to kill other white men. They began to realize that Europeans were essentially the same as Africans and that there was no reason why men of one continent should rule the people of another. When they returned home they expected that their sufferings on behalf of their colonial masters would be rewarded in some way. But they discovered that they were still second class citizens in their own country, despised by white settlers and officials who believed themselves to be racially superior. These young men became impatient with the older, moderate political movements and urged more extreme action.

In the period 1945–60 the nationalists organized themselves into larger, more effective groups and demanded independence. This coincided with a cautious policy of constitutional advance which was being put into effect by the colonial rulers. Unfortunately this came too late in some countries. The nationalists demanded a more rapid advance to self-government than the authorities thought appropriate. However, in most colonies the transfer of power from alien to African rule passed off smoothly. The exceptions were those countries with large white settler populations, such as Kenya and Algeria. Here the racial minorities fought hard to retain their privileged position. The result was bloodshed.

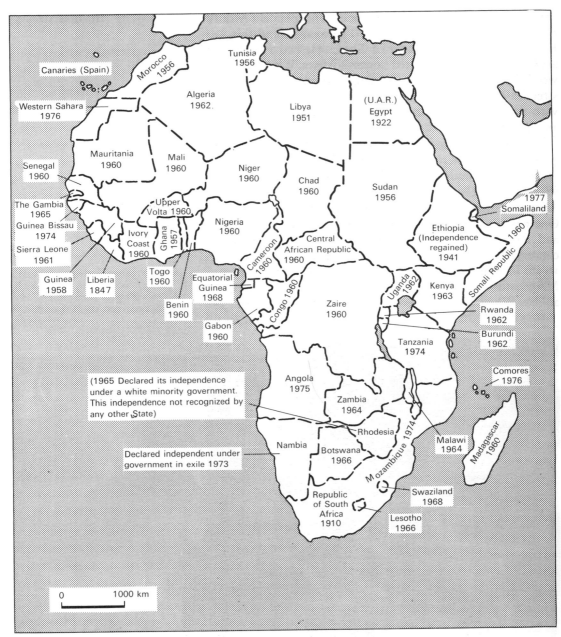

Independence in Africa 1945–75

groups took opposite sides: the Monrovia Group supported President Kasavubu and the United Nations' peace-keeping attempts, the Casablanca Group backed Prime Minister Lumumba and his Communist allies. On the initiative of Emperor Haile Selassie of Ethiopia, delegates from all independent states met at Addis Ababa in May 1963. Despite the many different views expressed the conference produced a very positive result—the signing of the charter of the Organization of African Unity (25 May).

The OAU rapidly became an influential force in African and world politics. Heads of member governments met annually to review all the major issues affecting the continent, and the OAU secretariat held meetings and visits to cope with emergencies and problem which cropped up from time to time. It would be impossible to list all the matters with which the OAU concerned itself in the first decade of its life but the following selection indicates the range and scope of those matters: A commission was set up to try to resolve the civil unrest in Zaire (1965). A long-standing border dispute between Kenya and Somalia was peacefully resolved through OAU intervention (1967–8). A consultative commission was set up to resolve the civil war in Nigeria and recommended the retention of federal government (1969–70). The Organization condemned the sale of arms to South Africa by western powers (1970). It pledged its support for a complete sports boycott of South Africa as a result of which several teams were withdrawn from Commonwealth and Olympic Games (1972–6). The OAU was pledged to ending white rule in Angola, Mozambique, South Africa, Rhodesia (Zimbabwe) and South West Africa (Namibia). Member states were able to win increasing support through their representatives at the United Nations. There they united with other developing countries to form the 'Afro-Asian Bloc' which challenged the political and economic domination of the great powers. But Southern Africa's problems could not be solved entirely by peaceful negotiation. Tanzania and Zambia opened their countries to Rhodesian freedom fighters, and political factions in Zaire and Angola called in foreign troops.

Chapter 14

The re-emergence of self-government in North Africa

In 1920 the whole of North Africa except Ethiopia lay under European control. In this part of the continent colonial rule was even harder to accept than elsewhere for it marked a victory for Christian Europe in her age-old struggle with the Muslim world. As we shall see, nationalist movements began to emerge in all areas but behind them, bringing them strength and unity, was a pan-Islamic movement. It began in Turkey but its main centre became the Al-Azhar University in Cairo. There, students from all over the Arab world learned to found their nationalist plans on Muslim principles and to work for the reassertion of Islamic culture. The pan-Islamic movement later took shape in the Muslim Brotherhood and the Arab League.

Egypt and the Sudan

In 1920 Britain was trying to withdraw from the government of Egypt while at the same time safeguarding her vital interests in the area. Lord Milner headed a mission which aimed at reaching a settlement with the Egyptian politicians but no agreement was reached. Even though the nationalist leader, Zaghlul Pasha, was in exile his followers organized riots and assassinations, and made negotiation impossible. Zaghlul was released and brought into the talks but no compromise agreement could be found. At last, in February 1922, the British government simply announced that Egypt was to have complete independence although four matters were to remain under British control. These were defence, protection of foreign interests and minority groups, security of vital communications with the British Empire (principally the Suez Canal), and the destiny of the Sudan. In 1923 a new constitution was established which provided for a king (Fuad I) as head of state, a Senate and an elected Chamber of Deputies. Zaghlul returned from exile to lead his Wafd Party in the elections of 1924. He won a complete victory and became Prime Minister of Egypt.

There now followed a long period of three-cornered political conflict. The nationalists wanted full independence, which involved the withdrawal of all British troops and the ending of British political interference. They also wanted Egyptian rule in the Sudan. The British were determined to safeguard their interests by preserving a measure of control. The King's party shared some nationalist aspirations but were more moderate and did not want to undermine their own power by making extreme demands of the British. Unrest and outrages against British people and property continued. They culminated, in 1924, in the assassination of Sir Lee Stack, Governor-General of the Sudan, as he was passing through Cairo. Britain retaliated by expelling all Egyptian personnel from the Sudan and ending all pretence of an Egyptian share in the ruling of the Condominium. In Cairo Zaghlul resigned, the nationalists were split and some of them joined the newly formed, moderate, Union Party. The death of Zaghlul Pasha in 1927 gave rise to great demonstrations of national grief. His place as Wafd leader was taken by Mustafa al-Nahas Pasha who proved to be just as determined as Zaghlul. The differences between the political groups in Cairo proved insoluble and, in 1928, King Fuad dissolved parliament and suspended the constitution. It was seven years before democratic institutions were re-established.

1936 was an important year for Egypt. New elections returned Nahas and the Wafd to power. King Fuad died and was succeeded by his son, Faruq. The Italian occupation of Ethiopia brought a new urgency to the resolution of Anglo-Egyptian differences. A treaty was signed in August which made provision for a reduction of British influence and the gradual withdrawal of British troops. The British High Commissioner was replaced by an Ambassador. The Egyptian government became fully responsible for its country's diplomacy and Egypt joined the League of Nations. Many British officials were replaced by Egyptians. But Britain kept a garrison in the Canal Zone and the question of the Sudan was not raised in the treaty negotiations. The next three years were marked by continuing political conflict between the court and the nationalist leadership and between different groups within the ranks of the Wafd Party. A more significant event was the formation of the secret Young Officers Revolutionary Committee by a group of army officers in 1939. One of its leaders was Gamal Abdel Nasser who summed up his

Zaghlul Pasha

319

aims thus: 'We must fight imperialism, monarchy and feudalism, because we are opposed to injustice, oppression and slavery.'

Bound by the terms of the 1936 treaty Egypt assisted Britain in the Second World War. She did not enter the conflict herself but supported British armies garrisoned on her soil to fight the desert and Ethiopian campaigns. The Egyptian political parties were divided in their attitude to the conflict, but there was widespread hatred of the British, whose soldiers were seen to be taking food from the mouths of the people and who virtually dictated to the King and the government. Extreme nationalist groups gained strength. The Muslim Brotherhood (founded in 1928), a politico-religious organization, had accumulated a store of weapons and had a well-trained terrorist wing. In 1944 Nahas Pasha presided over a meeting at Alexandria which was attended by representatives from most Arab countries. The result was the formation of the Arab League.

By this time the war had moved out of North Africa and Egyptian leaders were clamouring for the withdrawal of British forces and a new treaty agreement. In 1946 a draft treaty was drawn up which provided for the withdrawal of all troops by 1949. But the stumbling-block to agreement was still the Sudan. Britain was planning self-government for the Sudan, which meant that Egypt would never be able to exercise sovereignty over her southern neighbour. The government obtained the support of the Arab League and even took the matter to the United Nations. In 1948 the state of Israel was established in Palestine. This was a great blow to the Arab world which immediately took up arms against the tiny nation. The result was a humiliating defeat for the Arabs. The Egyptian people were terribly angry both with their government which they blamed for the defeat and with countries such as Britain which supported Israel. They were determined to sever all ties with the British. The Muslim Brotherhood declared a jihad against the British. Army posts were attacked. Supplies were refused to British personnel.

In January 1952 an incident between British troops and Egyptian police in the Canal Zone led to forty-three Egyptian deaths. This sparked off the worst riots Cairo had ever seen. The Wafd government was quite unable to control the situation and was totally discredited. The Young Officers laid their plans and awaited their opportunity. It came on 23 July. In a

Mustapha Nahas Pasha

Left: Krishna Menon, who led the Indian delegation, and President Gamal Abdel Nasser at the Suez Conference 1959

bloodless coup they overthrew the government and deposed King Faruq. A Revolutionary Command Council was set up under the leadership of General Mohammed Neguib. All political parties except the Muslim Brotherhood were banned. But Nasser was the dominant force in the new government. In 1954 he replaced Neguib and, after an attempt had been made on his life, he banned the Muslim Brotherhood and executed many of its leaders. He made agreements with Britain over the Sudan and the Canal Zone. Realizing the strength of Sudanese nationalism he agreed to British plans for the independence of the Sudan, hoping thereby to win the gratitude and co-operation of the new state. The other agreement provided for the gradual withdrawal of troops from the Canal Zone.

Two years later Egypt faced a severe crisis. The last British troops had gone and Nasser decided to nationalize the Anglo-French Suez Canal Company and take over the organization of the Canal himself. This provoked an immediate attack by Britain and France, aided by Israel. The war lasted only a few days. The post-war world was not prepared to tolerate this neo-imperialist attack. International pressure led by the USA forced the invaders to withdraw.

In 1957 a new constitution came into force with the creation of an elected National Assembly. At the same time, however, negotiations were in hand with Syria for the formation of a united state. In 1958 the two countries were merged in the United Arab Republic. But the union (like other attempts at united Arab action) was short lived. Syria withdrew in 1961. Nasser continued to see himself as the leader of the Arab world and wished to give the Arab League a more concrete form. In 1963 there was a short-lived union of Egypt, Syria and Iraq.

Under Nasser's leadership Egypt became a socialist state. Many industries and businesses were nationalized. Most candidates for elections to the National Assembly had to be farmers or workers. The President and his ministers controlled all executive and legislative functions. Egypt entered a close relationship with the Communist world and the Soviet Union gave the country considerable economic and military aid, particularly helping her with the important Aswan High Dam.

Aswan High Dam

Six Day War

In 1967 Nasser made another bid for the leadership of the Arab world and tried to settle the Palestinian problem. With Jordan he planned a joint invasion of Israel. The war lasted six days and was a crushing defeat for the Arabs. Egypt lost all her land in Sinai and Israeli troops reached the east bank of the Suez Canal. The Canal itself was blocked by sunken shipping and remained unusable until 1975. This brought President Nasser close to political catastrophe but his personal popularity soon recovered and he continued to rule Egypt until his death in 1970.

During these years the Sudan had many problems to face—economic development, whether or not to integrate with Egypt, racial tension between the Arab North and Negro South and the rivalries of many political groups. These problems made difficult the Sudan's journey to independence and have troubled her ever since. During the 1920s and 1930s Britain pursued a policy of indirect rule in the North and was able to introduce improved agriculture, irrigation schemes, new industries and a detailed, workable administration.

Things did not go so smoothly in the South. It was difficult to find among the nomadic and semi-nomadic peoples chiefs who could be incorporated into a colonial administrative system. Many areas were almost inaccessible. Slave raiding and trading continued. Old rivalries and conflicts were more important than the orders of European officials. The most important Europeans in the lives of many Sudanese Africans were the missionaries. But the officials persevered with their policy 'to build up a series of self-contained racial or tribal units with structure and organization based upon indigenous customs, tribal usage and beliefs', and this policy wrought a slow transformation of society in the South.

Sudanese nationalism was complicated by regional and religious differences. Many Muslims followed Abdul Rahman, a son of the Mahdi, who later led the *Umma* (Community) Party. Many educated young Arabs favoured closer union with Egypt, and the expulsion of Egyptian officers in 1924 led to riots, demonstrations and mutiny. Nevertheless, the next fifteen years were for the most part years of quiet protectorate rule and material progress. As we have seen, the Sudan was always a point of disagreement between Britain and Egypt. This meant that the rulers could not avoid thinking about and planning for the political future of the Sudan. They were determined not to hand over the Sudan to Egypt and they wished to establish a strong administrative and political system which would survive pressures from inside and outside the country. The first nationalist group to demand independence for the Sudan was an organization of educated men in Omdurman calling itself the Graduates' General Congress. It claimed to be the voice of the whole people but it certainly was not. One of the misfortunes of Sudanese politics is that no party has ever been able to gain the support of a large majority of the people.

The Second World War strengthened the nationalist movement. Sudanese soldiers fought bravely in the Allied cause, particularly in support of their boundary with Italian-dominated Ethiopia (1940–41). In 1941 the Congress demanded full independence after the war and other nationalist groups joined in the agitation for self-rule. As soon as possible (1944) the British took the next step towards responsible government for the Sudan by setting up regional councils (in the North) and an Advisory Council. The South was not represented on the Advisory Council and southern leaders began agitating to know just what was being planned for the future of their people. Many colonial officials believed the only answer was separation of the two parts of the country but northern nationalists were united in rejecting this. In a meeting at Juba in 1947 southern leaders were persuaded to accept the principle of a united Sudan.

The next constitutional step was the decision to create a Legislative Assembly. The elections for this body took place in 1948. Of the 75 members 52 were elected in the North and 23 in the South. Nine political parties had been formed to contest the elections. The most important were the *Umma* and the *Ashiqqa*, an anti-Mahdist party, which was later renamed the National Unionist Party. While the Assembly continued with its work during the next four years political consciousness spread. There was trouble in many places as Communists and Egyptians spread their ideas in trade unions, schools and colleges.

In 1953 another constitutional change occurred when there were elections for a new kind of parliament. There was a

Legislative Assembly in Khartoum over trouble in Sudan 1951

House of Representatives with 97 members and a Senate of 50. The Anglo-Egyptian Condominium came to an end and it was left to the representatives of the Sudanese people to decide their political future. Now that self-government was so near, the various political groups in the country clashed more violently as they pursued their own interests. Particularly was this true of the South, where the nationalization of mission schools and the establishment of Arabic as the main communication medium provoked hostility.

The real trouble did not, however, occur until after independence. The Sudan became an independent state outside the Commonwealth on 1 January 1956. The announcement, a few months previously, that independence was imminent had been the signal for riots in the South. In August 1955 sections of the army mutinied. Southern politicians tried hard to persuade the Khartoum parliament to formulate a federal constitution. When they failed they walked out (June 1956). The South now collapsed in chaos. Freedom fighters armed themselves and formed guerrilla bands. Government forces carried out a savage repression. Thousands died in the conflict. Tens of thousands fled to neighbouring countries.

The failure of the government to cope with the southern crisis was one reason for a coup in November 1958. The coalition government had been weak from the start. Communist activity, Egyptian pressure (Egypt was backed by the Arab League which was anxious to preserve Arab unity), political and sectarian rivalries all prevented the efficient exercise of democratic government. At last the army seized power and General Ibrahim Abboud assumed the position of President. The coup was followed by the abolition of political parties and trade unions, and the censorship of the press. Abboud promised the people that these were only temporary measures and that there would be a return to democratic government as soon as possible. But the military junta was no more successful in solving the country's problem than its predecessor had been. Repression increased and the situation in the South grew much worse. Laws were passed against Christian missionaries, who were blamed for the conflict. The number of refugees who fled to Uganda and Ethiopia grew to over 75,000. Stories of terrible massacres reached the outside world. And a united army, the *Anya Nya*, was formed by southern nationalists.

In October 1964 there was another coup. It began as a student riot in Khartoum. Quickly other groups, equally appalled at the existing state of affairs, joined in. Abboud was forced to resign. Fresh elections were held in 1965 from which the *Umma* and the National Unionist Party emerged as the strongest parties. A fresh start was made to deal with the problems of the Sudan.

Libya suffered only a short period of full colonial rule. By 1920 the Italians had not established control of the whole country and between 1922 and 1931 they had to face a prolonged and determined military resistance in Cyrenaica and Fezzan. This conflict, sometimes known as the Second Italo-Sanusi War, began when the Sanusi leader, Muhammad Idris, was offered the title of Amir of Libya by a conference of National Reform Party representatives and other Arab leaders held at Sirta. Muhammad Idris reluctantly accepted. His position was made difficult because his authority largely rested on agreements he had already made with the Italians. To escape from the dilemma he sought refuge in Egypt, having appointed deputies to carry on his work in Libya. The responsibility for military leadership fell upon Umar al-Mukhtar, who for nine years organized an effective armed resistance. The Italians quickly overran Cyrenaica by the use of a mechanized army, aerial bombardment and brutality towards the civilian population. But as the Italian soldiers pressed deeper into the desert they proved a poor match for bands of guerrillas who were kept supplied with arms from supporters in Egypt. The nationalists proved to be a prolonged source of irritation to the Italians and the war was costly in men and money. The colonial general, Graziani, eventually broke Libyan resistance by herding thousands of civilians into concentration camps, so that they could not aid the 'rebels', and by building a long barbed-wire barrier to block the Egyptian supply route. The guerrilla bands were defeated one by one and in September 1931, Umar al-Mukhtar was captured and publicly hanged. This brought to an end the Second Italo-Sanusi War.

During and after the war tribal lands were taken away and made available for settlement by Italian peasants. Although Muslim culture was not destroyed, every effort was made

Rodolfo Graziani during the war in Abyssinia 1935

President Bourguiba of Tunisia

of reform, demanding improved health and educational services, full recognition of Muslim customs and laws and an economic system which did not favour only the European settlers. The Destour Party represented principally the traditional religious and civil leaders of Arab society. It had no popular base and did not win the support of the growing class of young intellectuals. It posed no real threat to the Protectorate government. Nevertheless its activities were severely restricted and it had almost disappeared by 1926.

A more active group emerged in 1934. This was the Neo-Destour Party. It was led by Habib Bourguiba and it drew its support from younger Tunisians who had been educated at the Franco-Arab schools. Its programme was much the same as that of the older party but it was more vigorous and it rejected the political leadership of the old chiefly class. The split with the Destour Party originated when Bourguiba and his supporters refused to recognize as true Muslims those who had become naturalized Tunisians. The Neo-Destour Party was declared illegal soon after its formation and Bourguiba experienced the first of his many prison sentences between 1934 and 1936. In 1938 the Neo-Destour Party and the *Confédération Générale des Travailleurs Tunisiens* (a short-lived trade union for Muslim workers) clashed with the police and 174 demonstrators were left dead or wounded in the streets of Tunis. Bourguiba and other leaders were imprisoned in France and the Neo-Destour's activities were ruthlessly suppressed. Then the Second World War broke out, a pro-German French government was established in Tunisia and there was no scope for nationalist activity.

For a brief time in 1942–3 a new nationalist figure dominated the political life of the country. This was Munsif Bey who came to the throne in June 1942. He took advantage of the colonial government's pre-occupation with the war to assert an independence his predecessors had not known for generations. He made himself available to the people, mixed with Neo-Destour members and appointed some of them to his government. Unfortunately he was deposed by the Free French forces as soon as they 'liberated' Tunisia in May 1943. At about the same time Bourguiba returned and urged his followers to support France in her struggle against Germany and Italy. He believed that, after the war, a grateful French government would be sympathetic to Tunisian demands for autonomy.

But the war ended and Tunisia's nationalists soon realized that they would have to fight for their country's freedom. Bourguiba toured foreign countries to win support for his cause. At home the Destour and the Neo-Destour parties and the *Union Générale Tunisienne du Travail* (a newly-formed trade union) held a combined meeting in August 1946 at which they pledged themselves to work together for independence. A campaign of strikes and demonstrations forced some constitutional concessions from the colonial government. In 1950 a new Protectorate government was established which consisted of nine Tunisian and three French ministers under the leadership of Muhammad Shanniq as Prime Minister. On the Grand Council the Tunisians were given the same number of members as the French. These were considerable advances but there was a basic clash of principle between the foreign and indigenous politicians: while the French believed in co-sovereignty, the Tunisians wanted nothing less than complete independence. Shanniq went to Paris to demand freedom for his country. The French response was to arrest Shanniq, Bourguiba and other nationalists and to force the Bey to appoint a new government (1952).

For two years the French tried to achieve a compromise acceptable to the Tunisian people. A series of political and constitutional concessions gave increasing power to Tunisian leaders, but the French still demanded some say in the running of the country. But all this took place against a rising tide of violence and hostility. More Neo-Destour and Union leaders were arrested. Nationalist guerrilla bands appeared and raided European farms and administrative posts. The settlers countered by forming their own guerrilla organization, the Red Hand. There were assassinations and other outrages. At last, in July 1954, the Paris government admitted that the only way to restore peace was to agree to the principle of Tunisian independence.

Negotiations began immediately. At first there was an attempt by the French to do a deal with the Destour Party only which would exclude the Neo-Destour Party from power. But the freedom fighters refused to agree to a cease-fire until Bourguiba was brought into the independence talks. In June 1955 Tunisia gained internal self-government and in the following March France recognized the full independence of her former protectorate. Elections were immediately held for the new Assembly. The Neo-Destour was the only party represented but it won massive support from the voters. The following year the Assembly voted to end the monarchy and in July 1957 Tunisia became a republic with Bourguiba as President and Prime Minister.

Algeria

The struggle for independence in Tunisia was as nothing compared with the bloody conflict that took place in the neighbouring French colony of Algeria. There were two underlying reasons for Algeria's problems: the rising Muslim population and the power of the European settlers. The rate of population expansion can best be shown by the following figures:

Muslim Population, 1872, 2,125,000; 1931, 5,588,000; 1954, 8,450,000

At the same time as their numbers were increasing, the land available to Algerian peasants was decreasing. More and more was taken over by the colonial government for distribution to settlers. Poverty was deep and widespread. Men were forced to seek work on settler farms at extremely low wages. Some travelled abroad—mainly to France—in search of employment. The settlers always felt slightly afraid of this growing majority population and used their influence to keep the Muslims in a subservient position. We have already seen how, in 1919, they forced the French government to drop planned political concessions to the Algerians. In 1924 they obtained new laws restricting the migration of Algerian workers because this was putting up the price of farm labour.

It was among Muslim workers in France that a popular nationalist movement began. The French-educated Young Algerians continued to press for moderate and gradual reform within the colonial framework but they were not representative of the people. In 1926 Muslim workers in France formed the North African Star, a semi-Communist organization aimed at uniting French-speaking, North African nationalists. Its leader was Messali al-Hajj and, like other nationalist leaders, he spent a great deal of his time in prison. He was allowed, however, to return to Algeria in 1936, where he formed the *Parti du Peuple Algérien* (PPA) the following year.

But for the moment nationalist initiative lay with the moderates. A movement for Islamic revival, the Association

332

Messali al-Hajj, leader of Algerian Nationalist Party

of the Ulama, was founded in 1931. It sought, through opening schools, to strengthen Islamic culture and prevent it being swamped by European culture. The Young Algerians continued to press for the full integration of Algeria and France and the extension of French citizenship. In 1936 an Islamic Congress was held in Algiers. It was dominated by both of these moderate groups. They pledged their loyalty to France at the same time that they demanded new rights and privileges. Later that year some of these demands were included in a Bill before the French parliament. When this Bill was rejected as a result of pressure from the settlers some of the moderates began to change their political attitudes. One of the Young

Algerian leaders, Farhat Abbas, parted company with his pro-French colleagues and formed the *Union Populaire Algérienne*.

During most of the Second World War Messali was in prison or under house arrest but his supporters spread PPA ideas among the Algerian people with considerable success. Abbas remained at liberty and he negotiated with the leading European groups in the country—first the Vichy government, then the American liberators, then the Free French administration—for various concessions. Towards the end of the conflict he formed a new party, the *Amis du Manifeste de la Liberté* (AML), whose main aim was the establishment of an Algerian republic federated with France. But when he called an AML Congress, in March 1945, the meeting was dominated by PPA men, and resolutions were passed demanding the release of Messali and Algerian autonomy. Two months later there were nationalist demonstrations in Sitif which led to terrible riots and police brutality. Trouble spread to much of the Constantine and Oran regions. Race hatred ran high. Innocent people on both sides were killed but Muslim deaths numbered many thousands. The AML was banned. Abbas and 4,560 of his supporters were imprisoned.

The French government realized the need to deal with Algerian grievances. It introduced projects to help with agrarian and social problems and it provided for the election of a number of Algerian representatives to the Constituent Assembly equal to the number representing settlers. It released Abbas from prison and allowed him to form a new party, the *Union Démocratique du Manifeste Algérien*, to contest fresh elections in 1946. There being no serious rivals, the UDMA won all but two of the seats contested. After his success Abbas made fresh demands but these were ignored by the French government. An Algerian statute, introduced in 1947, sanctioned a new Algerian assembly but it was still to be dominated by the settlers and its decisions were subject to approval in Paris.

Algerian nationalists were by now disillusioned with political action. In 1948 the first guerrilla army, the *Organization Secrète*, was formed. Its leading spirit was Ahmad Ben Bella and under his leadership the OS gained support and carried out several daring raids. In 1954 the movement was reorganized as the *Front de Libération National*. The FLN organized widespread revolution. By isolated military strikes and the support of the mass of the people the leadership hoped

Parade of FLN on 14 July

to force France to negotiate. Had it been left to the politicians in Paris the two sides might well have met to sort out a peaceful solution but the settlers were determined to wipe out the 'terrorists' and to make no concession to nationalism. French troops were poured into Algeria (they numbered 150,000 by 1956). Many settlers enlisted. Many others took the law into their own hands and organized private wars against Muslims suspected of being FLN members. In Algiers authority was in the hands of the army and the settlers' leaders. The Paris government had little influence. The first phase of the war ended at the end of 1957. A year earlier Ben Bella and other leaders had been captured. After that the fighting gradually died down.

But the FLN was only pausing for re-organization. In April 1958 representatives of all shades of Algerian nationalist opinion met at Tangier. They formed an Algerian government-in-exile. Furthermore, the newly independent states of Morocco and Tunisia pledged their support to the ideal of

Ben Bella

Algerian freedom. By this time the French were under considerable international pressure to reach a political settlement of the Algerian issue. The settlers refused to tolerate any political discussions with the 'terrorists' and in May 1958 they and the army came close to rebellion over the issue. In the following October the French President, de Gaulle, offered a compromise solution which included massive economic aid, pardon for FLN members who surrendered, and discussion of all problems with Algeria's elected representatives. De Gaulle refused to talk with the nationalist government-in-exile and, therefore, the FLN rejected the peace proposals. Acts of violence were resumed by both sides.

But de Gaulle had travelled to Algeria in person and seen, for himself, the state of affairs there. He realized that it was only the stubborn racialism of the settlers which was standing in the way of a settlement. He moved steadily towards the idea of discussions with the nationalist government. The settlers and army leaders reacted by riots and political action aimed at bringing about de Gaulle's downfall. In 1961 they formed the *Organisation de l'Armée Secrète* (OAS), a terrorist organization designed to smash the nationalists and to bring pressure to bear on the French government. All it succeeded in doing was a vast amount of damage to property and frightening thousands of settlers into returning to France.

De Gaulle starts tour–then screaming mobs run wild in the streets of the capital

TANKS FACE RIOTERS

Police tear down the barricades

From RICHARD KILIAN: Algiers, Friday

BARRICADES were torn down by police in Algiers tonight after a day of bloody rioting by thousands of

Headline from Daily Express *10 December 1960*

In May 1961 discussions began between the French government and the Algerian government-in-exile. In the following March Algeria gained her independence and Ben Bella became the first president of the new republic. But he never commanded the support of all the people. Many former FLN soldiers were reluctant to accept the leadership of one who had been absent (in a foreign jail) during most of the fighting. Ben Bella's government proved to be autocratic and too socialist for some Algerians. The President ruthlessly suppressed all opposition until 1965, when his government was overthrown by a coup headed by Colonel Boumedienne.

In French Morocco the Sultan remained the head of state but real power lay with the French Resident-General. In the regions traditional forms of administration and justice were maintained but all the Sultan's officials were subject to French control. Most of the best land was taken for European settlement but the number of European farmers was never as great as in neighbouring Algeria. Mining rights were all in the hands of French companies and between the two World Wars production of lead, cobalt, phosphates, coal, manganese and oil began. There existed a Council of Government, which was an advisory body, but only Frenchmen could elect members to it. In the interests of building up an economy based on the output of European farms and industries, Morocco's roads, railways and harbours were rapidly developed; electricity and irrigation schemes were introduced. These improvements were paid for out of taxation, the burden of which fell heaviest on the people who derived least benefit from them—the Moroccans.

Spanish Morocco was a much poorer country. Iron ore was discovered and exploited at Kalata but apart from that no industry of note was developed. Spanish settlement was not encouraged and native agriculture remained the mainstay of the economy. The head of government was the Caliph, appointed by the Sultan of Morocco, but real power lay with the Spanish High Commissioner.

Though smaller, the Spanish Protectorate proved more difficult to control because of the mountainous country and the fierce independence of the people. It was here that the first effective nationalist resistance emerged. In 1921 Abdul-Karim, a chief from the Rif, launched a rebellion against

Spanish rule. He quickly increased the territory under his control and the following year announced an Islamic republic. With the help of foreign arms Abdul-Karim overran most of the Rif and occupied many of its leading towns. In 1925 he moved into French territory and soon penetrated as far as twenty-five kilometres north of Fez. But the French were not so easy to defeat as the Spaniards. Colonial reinforcements and efficient generalship turned the tables on Abdul-Karim, who was defeated and captured in May 1926.

Yet Abdul-Karim's defeat proved to be a triumph for Moroccan nationalism. He became a popular hero, and later politicians were able to conjure up support by using his name. In the mid-1920s groups of educated Moroccans began to meet in secret to discuss the need for reform. In 1930 some of them formed the National Group. It was still a small society of intellectuals and, in any case, the need for secrecy prevented its members from seeking a wide, popular membership. However, numbers continued to grow and in 1932 the organization came to be known as the National Action Bloc.

The turning point for the nationalist movement came in 1936–7. By this time the sense of grievance was widespread among Moroccans. Population growth had forced thousands to leave home and seek employment on European farms or in the towns. Poverty and ill treatment led to protest and, when the government refused to allow Moroccans to join trade unions, the people realized the nationalist movement was the only outlet for the expression of their grievances. Membership of the National Action Bloc grew so alarmingly that the French authorities were forced to ban it in 1937. But its leaders simply reorganized themselves under a new name, the National Party for Realizing the Reforms (NPRR). At the same time bad harvests had led to extreme hardship which in turn provoked demonstrations and, in some places, clashes with the police. The NPRR took up the cause of those threatened with starvation. The results were threefold: most of the NPRR leaders were arrested; the party received an influx of new members; and the NPRR had taken the decisive step from a discussion group to an action group.

There was a lull during the Second World War in North Africa, but in 1943 the NPRR returned to the attack. First of all the name of the party was changed to the Independence Party to show that its members were no longer concerned simply with reform. Secondly, the party emerged as a national party, drawing support from all areas. Thirdly, there was a move to involve Sultan Muhammad V (who, in order to preserve his position, had hitherto held aloof from politics) in the nationalist movement.

In 1947 the growing determination of the Independence Party forced the first important concession from the French. Moroccans were admitted to the Council of Government, although the franchise was restricted to *evolués*. Independence Party members gained seats on the Council and used their position to oppose unpopular government policies and to strengthen the resolve of Sultan Muhammad. In 1950 the Independence Party members walked out of the Council. A few months later the Resident-General told the Sultan that he must choose between keeping his throne and supporting the nationalists. Muhammad V decided to retain his throne.

Once again an apparent defeat turned into victory for the nationalists. The French threat to their Sultan enraged the Moroccan people and led to increased support for the Independence Party. In March 1952 the Sultan showed that he was not a tool of the colonial power by demanding full sovereignty over his people. France now tried to control Morocco by dividing its people. They encouraged some mountain chiefs who rejected Muhammad's leadership. In 1953 the Resident-General 'gave way' to the rebels' demands and the Sultan was exiled to Corsica (and, later, Madagascar). This action united all the people against the French. There were terrorist attacks all over Morocco. Muhammad V was brought back in 1955, a popular hero, and appointed a new government. France and Spain could not now deny independence to a populace united under the leadership of its traditional ruler, and Morocco regained its freedom on 2 March 1956.

King Muhammad V of Morocco

Muhammad V took the title of King and made it clear that he was not to be a mere figurehead when he also assumed the office of Prime Minister. He remained in full control of Morocco until his death in 1961. He was succeeded by his son, King Hassan II. Early in the reign plans were set afoot for the creation of a more democratic constitution. New political parties were formed to contest elections to the new parliament (1963). The new constitution established a directly elected Chamber of Representatives (144 members) and a Chamber of Counsellors (120 members, indirectly elected). The government, formed from the leading party, assumed many executive powers formerly reserved to the King, but Hassan retained considerable authority.

Ethiopia and Somalia

When Menelik the Great died in 1913 the crown of Ethiopia descended to his seventeen-year-old grandson, Yasu. The task of keeping the regions united under growing pressure from Turkey and the colonial powers proved too much for the young man and in 1916 he fell from power. For the next fourteen years power was shared between Zewditu, Menelik's daughter, who became Empress, and Ras Tafari (the future Emperor Haile Selassie) who was Regent and heir to the throne. During this period Ethiopia's standing in the world increased. She joined the League of Nations in 1923 and Tafari, during his many visits abroad, made a considerable impression on foreign governments. In order to develop the country's resources as rapidly as possible agreements were signed with various European industrial concerns and in 1928 a treaty of friendship was made with Italy which provided for the improvement of roads from Ethiopia to the Eritrean coast. Education and other social services were improved as government revenue permitted.

The Emperor Haile Selassie

In 1930, on the death of Zewditu, Ras Tafari was crowned as Emperor Haile Selassie I. With full power in his hands he forged ahead with the modernization of the country. A two-chamber parliament was introduced in 1931, with one chamber elected by Ethiopia's leading men. More foreign advisers arrived in Addis Ababa and more young Ethiopians went abroad to gain higher education and technical qualifications.

But Ethiopia's steady progress was halted by the Italian Fascist Dictator, Benito Mussolini. He decided that national pride demanded the reversal of the battle of Adowa and the colonial occupation of Ethiopia. The invasion began in October 1935 and was accomplished within seven months. Haile Selassie appealed, in vain, to the League of Nations whose leading statesmen were too frightened of war in Europe to risk provoking Mussolini. Haile Selassie then went into exile in Britain while bands of his countrymen kept up a determined guerrilla resistance in their native hills and valleys.

The outbreak of the Second World War brought the Emperor that foreign support which persuasion had failed to bring. Britain and British colonial forces helped him and his

An Abyssinian feudal levy assembled near Addis Ababa

people to drive out the Italians. The Emperor led a liberation army gathered in the Sudan and British forces invaded Eritrea and Italian Somaliland (1940). The only major battle was fought at Keren and in May 1941 the Italians surrendered. Haile Selassie quickly re-established his government, though for some years he received help from British advisers and administrators.

After the war the problem of the future of Eritrea and Italian Somaliland had to be decided. Since 1941 they had been under British control. Eritrea was claimed by Ethiopia but this was opposed by the Muslim world on account of the considerable Muslim population of the country. The issue was considered at many sessions of the United Nations, which in 1950 decided that Eritrea should be federated with Ethiopia. This came into effect in 1952. Ten years later Eritrea was fully incorporated into Ethiopia.

Haile Selassie had also laid claim to Italian Somaliland but this was rejected by the United Nations which returned it to Italy as a Trust Territory in 1950 for a period of ten years. The Italians took seriously their task of decolonization. An intensive programme of education and training was set up.

50,000 ITALIANS INVADE
ABYSSINIA: EMPEROR CABLES GENEVA

LEAGUE COUNCIL SUMMONED
TO MEET TO-MORROW

"WAR ABOUT TO
BEGIN,"
MUSSOLINI'S CRY
TO NATION

Headline from Daily Herald *Thursday 3 October 1935*

As a result the country was soon well provided with technicians and civil servants. By 1960 all senior administrative posts were held by Somalis and there was an elected Legislative Council. Even before independence the people decided to join with their brothers in British Somaliland, and in 1960 the two territories joined together as the Republic of Somalia. A new democratic constitution came into force in 1964. Between 1963 and 1967 Somalia was at war with her neighbour, Kenya, over a territorial dispute. This quarrel was eventually resolved by negotiation within the framework of the Organization of African Unity.

Haile Selassie played a very important part in international and Pan-African affairs in the post-war period. He gave practical support to the United Nations by sending Ethiopian contingents to join United Nations' peace-keeping forces in Korea and the Congo (Zaire). He was a leading founder member of the Organization of African Unity, which came into being at a meeting held in Addis Ababa in May 1963. At home, while maintaining executive power, he widened the democratic base of his government. A new constitution came into force in 1957 which provided for an elected Chamber of Deputies. The members of the Senate continued to be appointed by the Emperor. In 1975, army officers, dissatisfied with the pace of constitutional reform, deposed the emperor, who died shortly afterwards. Within a few years Ethiopia's peace was shattered by war with Eritrean secessionists and a territorial conflict with Somalia.

The re-emergence of self-government in West Africa

Chapter 15

Before the Second World War the British West African dependencies were at various levels of constitutional, economic and social growth. In the Gold Coast, Nigeria and Sierra Leone, the limited elective system in their Crown Colony administration had provided political opportunities for Africans in the towns along the coast. In Lagos, in particular, Herbert Macaulay's Nigerian National Democratic Party had gained successes in the Lagos Town Council elections and had captured the three seats in the Legislative Council. On the Gold Coast, political activities were concentrated in Accra, Cape Coast and Sekondi, but at the same time the paramount chiefs were beginning to become politically educated enough to identify themselves with the aspirations of the educated nationalists. In Sierra Leone, the centre of political activity was the Colony. There continued to grow up in the territories an educated élite who continued to see in the British administration a barrier to their ambitions. The establishment of Achimota College on the Gold Coast and the Yaba Higher College in Nigeria posed their different problems, which began to engage the minds of nationalists and create a band of frustrated youths who, although they had passed their London Matriculation Examination, entered these institutions which had no university status.

On the Gold Coast the youths were gradually becoming more alive to political and economic considerations as they came under the influence of Dr J. B. Danquah and his professional colleagues who in the 1930s had already formed the Gold Coast Youth Conference as an association for the discussion of political, social and economic problems. In 1939 Achimota College staff began the Achimota Discussion Group and opened the society to all educated people. In Nigeria, on the other hand, the staff of Yaba Higher College did not show such initiative. It became clear that the College fell short of the status which the West African National Congress had aimed at when in their resolution in 1920 they

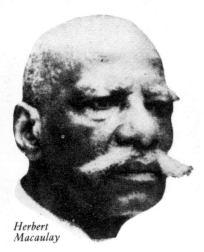

Herbert Macaulay

had stated that 'the time has come to found a British West African University on such lines as would preserve in the student a sense of African Nationality'. The result was that in 1934 a Lagos Youth Movement was formed by Ernest Ikoli, Dr J. C. Vaughan, Samuel Akisanya and Hezekiah Oladipo Davies. The main aim of this organization, which in 1936 changed its name to the Nigerian Youth Movement, was at first to attack the government's educational policy, especially insofar as it dealt with the Yaba Higher College. Contemporary events, however, turned the movement into a political party. It superseded Herbert Macaulay's Nigerian National Democratic Party in political scope when it gained the Lagos Town Council and the three Lagos seats in the Legislative Council from the older party.

British West Africa 1939–45

But these were minor events when compared with the great influence of the Second World War. Britain had suffered defeat at the hands of Germany and Japan at the beginning of the war and this showed Africans that Britain after all was not as formidable and invincible as Empire Loyalists had led the world to believe. In order that the people of the colonies might make their contributions to the war effort, it became fashionable to nominate some of those Africans who were loyal to the empire to executive positions. This was how two unofficial nominated members—Nana Sir Ofori Atta and Arku Korsah —became members of the Gold Coast Executive in 1942 and two African unofficial members entered the Nigerian Executive in 1943. In Sierra Leone, too, Africans were allowed to play some part in government. When the war started, three Africans joined five officials of the government and two European commercial members of the Legislative Council to consider ways of raising more taxation. All these marked some political advance for Africans.

It was in the economic field, however, that the effect of the Second World War was particularly marked. Increased economic growth resulted from Britain's reliance on the production of raw materials in West Africa. Although in 1929 the first Colonial Development Act had been passed, which was to provide £1 million per annum for capital projects in the colonies, it was not until 1940, when a new Colonial Development and Welfare Act was passed providing a maximum expenditure of £5 million a year for ten years, that the colonies began to gain substantially from British generosity. Each colony was asked to draw up a scheme of economic and social development and raise its own local revenue to supplement this British ex gratia grant. This grant was increased in 1945 to a maximum of £17.5 million in any one year. The implementation of this Act meant that West Africa began to experience a great economic change. Telecommunications, medical, educational and capital projects began to open up the different colonies and this increased the production of raw materials.

The British government had decided to buy all the cocoa produced by both the Gold Coast and Nigeria and this had a stimulating influence on production, bringing money into the hands of the farmers. There were also vast opportunities for other produce from West Africa.

The increase in personal wealth of the farmers and the professional classes enabled the various governments to introduce and increase direct taxation on income without much difficulty, while at the same time the growth of towns made the necessity for democratic local government institutions a matter of urgency.

The new wealth was unfortunately not spread equally over the African community. Farmers grew rich because they concentrated on the production of cash crops. The young men who could have helped on the farms had been sent to the war front. Prices of foodstuffs began to soar and the governments had to impose some form of control in order to eliminate black-marketing. The wages of the workers had not been increased while those of the European administrative staff continued to rise.

The British government had encouraged the formation of trade unions. On the Gold Coast a Labour Department had been established as far back as 1938, and in 1939 a labour exchange was opened which prepared legislation on juvenile employment, trade unionism and collective bargaining. In 1942 a Labour Department was opened in Nigeria which gave expression to the Labour Ordinances of 1941, establishing provident funds for employed persons and providing an arbitration tribunal and a board of enquiry to examine economic and industrial disputes. The encouragement given to the growth of trade unions led to the creation, in 1942, of the Federated Trades Union of Nigeria and the Nigeria Trades Union Congress. In Sierra Leone, trade unionism had started just before the outbreak of the War. When the Trade Union Ordinance was enacted in 1939 there were already as many as seven registered unions in the colony and, as in Nigeria, attempts were made to amalgamate these unions to establish larger and more consolidated unions. The basic aims of the unions were the extracting of higher wages, the elimination of the disparity between European and African earnings and the provision of better employment opportunities for the indigenous staff.

In order to force the hands of employers, the trade unions resorted to strike action and in this they were supported by nationalist politicians who saw in the process the means by which to achieve a greater political objective. Between 1940 and 1945 industrial action was on the increase in Sierra Leone. The most important strikes were the Marampa Iron Mines strike in February 1942, the Air Ministry strike in 1944, and the Diamond Mines strike in 1945, which were partially successful. But in the whole of British West Africa, the most serious strike was that in Nigeria, led by a forceful Ishan trade unionist and nationalist, Michael Imoudu, and aided by the growing nationalist press and politicians who placed their full weight behind the struggle. While European salaries continued to rise, the cost-of-living allowance which was granted in 1942 to the African workers did not keep pace with rising prices. The African Civil Service Technical Workers Union had demanded an increase of 50 per cent in the cost-of-living allowance and a minimum daily wage of 2/6d. for each employed labourer. The government, hard-pressed by military and economic commitments, refused to grant this. A strike was called and was joined by railway workers, post and telegraph workers and all the technical officers of the government departments. For thirty-seven days Nigeria was paralysed by this action. The government set up the Tudor Davies Commission of Enquiry which recommended increased salaries. This strike proved that the hand of the government could be forced by concerted action.

Another result of the war was that it gave the West African a great opportunity to see the world and its peoples and to imbibe new ideas and cultures. 176,000 soldiers of the Royal West Africa Frontier Force had been engaged in services in many parts of Africa and had distinguished themselves in Kenya, Italian Somaliland and Ethiopia. Two divisions of the Force were sent to Burma and there again they gave a good account of themselves. At the end of the war, most of these soldiers returned to West Africa to be faced with unemployment. They posed a great social problem. During their military training and service they had seen that the idea of white superiority was a mistake, and they now came back to the old status of second class citizenship from which they had hoped they would be emancipated, especially when they remembered that they had fought and sacrificed a great deal. These, then, formed another militant nationalist group.

During the war West African students in England had formed the West African Students' Union which now began to organize meetings, arrange campaigns, draw up memoranda for constitutional reform and lobby members of the British parliament. The Students' Union became a training ground for the new nationalists who were no longer confining themselves to the demand for reforms and were calling for self-government. It seemed, however, that Britain's constitutional practice did not give her African students that political radicalism and bitterness that conditions in the United States of America produced in her African graduates. Probably American negro mass demonstrations and the prevalence of the colour bar produced a stronger nationalist political bias among West Africans studying in America.

The most important American educational product was Dr Nnamdi Azikiwe (known as 'Zik' by his supporters) who, having obtained his Master of Arts and Master of Science degrees and having been instructor of political science at Lincoln University, was denied a post at King's College, Lagos, possibly because he was a journalist and therefore might be a political agitator. Azikiwe was to lead a new political movement where his academic ability, genuine nationalism, forceful oratory and knowledge of American big business methods, made him the foremost Nigerian political figure. He became an inspiration to the young. His radicalism was unacceptable to the older political parties which favoured gradual constitutional change. After a dispute with the Nigerian Youth Movement he left and with his two Lagos papers, the *West African Pilot* and the *Comet*, awakened the people to their national heritage. He also worked through the trade unions. In 1944 he helped in the formation of the National Council of Nigeria and the Cameroons (NCNC) of which he was General Secretary and Herbert Macaulay the President.

Dr Nnamdi Azikiwe

Dr Kwame Nkrumah

Another West African who studied in America and came back to the Gold Coast to fulfil the same political functions as Dr Azikiwe was performing in Nigeria was Dr Kwame Nkrumah, who obtained a Bachelor of Divinity degree from Lincoln University and a Master of Arts degree from the University of Pennsylvania. When he returned in 1947 he became the General Secretary of the United Gold Coast Convention led by Dr Danquah. The constitutional gradualism of the party did not suit his forceful and radical character and he afterwards left to form the Convention People's Party.

British West Africa 1946–54

The various forces making for change in West Africa influenced the various colonial administrations. On the Gold Coast the Governor, Sir Alan Burns, who had seen that there was not only greater collaboration between the chiefs and the educated element in the demand for constitutional change, but also that there was a great awakening of a sense of unity between the Colony and Asante, decided to draft a constitution to meet with the increasing political consciousness. In 1946 he established a new Legislative Council of 31 members, and for the first time there was an unofficial African majority. There were in this Council five elected members from the municipalities as well as nine others elected from the Provincial Council. One of the significant provisions in this constitution was that there were at the same time four members who were elected from the Asante Confederacy Council thus bringing the number of elected members to eighteen as against six official members. The introduction of members from Asante was important because for the first time the Colony and Asante could now work together in a cordial atmosphere for the growth of one country. There was now more emphasis on one national identity. The Northern territories and Togoland, however, had not got representation, but the Burns Constitution, although it did not give the legislators responsibility and enough authority in the control of policy, represented a welcome constitutional concession.

In Nigeria, on the other hand, the tendency was towards regionalism. This was mainly because each region had a distinct political and constitutional identity. At the same time, the theory of indirect rule which had permeated the whole of the northern administration had to be incorporated into the new constitutional system for the whole of Nigeria. There had been the prevailing fear that the North, with its traditional feudal emirates and its Muslim practices, would find it difficult to work with the South, which had been under the influence of Western civilization. Even between the East and the West, there were great differences in the traditional political systems. While it had been possible to adopt a certain pattern of indirect rule in the North, in Southern Nigeria the system had had to be modified, particularly in the East. Educationally, the North was more backward than the South. It was important that allowance should be made for the slow political growth of the North. The British administrators of the North were themselves very suspicious of the South and were inclined to preserve the North in its system of benevolent autocracy and its blind obedience to authority. However, constitutional change was necessary. There was agitation for it and the state of social and economic growth demanded it. The guiding political thought that dominated the minds of both Sir Bernard Bourdillon (Governor 1935–43) and his successor, Sir Arthur Richards, was 'unity in diversity' and this became the distinctive feature of the Richards Constitution which was introduced in 1946. Richards also advocated that Africans should have 'greater participation in the discussion of their own affairs'. This constitution provided for a Nigerian Legislative Council of sixteen nominated members, four elected municipal members and twenty-four nominated or indirectly elected members. There were Regional Councils which in the North consisted of a House of Chiefs and a House of Assembly but in the West and East only a House of Assembly. These were not just collections of chiefs, but regional deliberative bodies which could consider and advise on any matters referred to them by the Governor or introduced by a member.

The Gold Coast and Nigerian constitutions did not meet the demands of the nationalists. The elective system was too restricted and the Executive Councils which were the Governor's advisory bodies were still distinctly official. The Governors were still the single supreme authorities responsible to and representative of the British Crown. The introduction of the constitutions led to intensive political action. Soon differences emerged in the methods used by the nationalists in different countries as they organized their parties and programmes in order to achieve self-government. The

United Gold Coast Convention (UGCC) organized demonstrations and undertook political agitation. But it continued to be a middle class movement with no direct appeal to the masses. What gave the nationalists their opportunity for political agitation was the fact, as has been discussed, that the war had brought dislocation within the country. The problems of resettling soldiers, unemployment, inflation and the swollen shoot cocoa disease, for which the government could not find any answer, brought more criticism of the administration. In disturbances which took place on 28 and 29 February 1948, there was such destruction and looting that the leaders of the UGCC were arrested. They included Danquah, Nkrumah, William Ofori Atta, Akufo Addo, Ako Adjei and E. Obetsebi Lamptey.

The British government set up the Watson Commission of enquiry whose proposals were closely studied by an all-African committee under the chairmanship of Henley Coussey, an African judge. But the radicals, including Kwame Nkrumah, were excluded. This made the whole of the Coussey proposals suspect.

The committee produced a new constitution. It was agreed to give some responsibility to Africans in the formulation and implementation of policy by creating a cabinet that would merge officialdom and nationalism and thus provide a training ground for responsible government. In the cabinet there were to be three unofficial members and eight African ministers chosen from the Legislative Council. Of the 75 elected African members, 19 each were to come from Asante and the Northern Territories. There was no uniform electoral procedure and only the five municipal members were popularly elected. It was during this period that Nkrumah showed his extreme radical and nationalist bent. He broke away from the UGCC and began his militant party, the Convention People's Party (CPP). Nkrumah's positive action was supposed to include 'strikes, boycotts, and non-co-operation based on a principle of non-violence' but his adherents could not confine themselves to these limits and civil disturbances were the outcome. Nkrumah's seditious articles and the civil disturbances led to the arrest of himself and other CPP leaders in January 1950 but his oratory and organization had so fired the imagination of the young and the masses that even though he was in prison, his lieutenant, K. A. Gbedemah, did not have much difficulty in leading the CPP to success in the general election in February 1951. The CPP won 34 out of the 38 seats contested and the Governor, Sir Charles Arden-Clarke, wisely released Kwame Nkrumah to lead his party in this experiment in African responsible government.

In Nigeria, on the other hand, the fact that there was no consultation with the people before Sir Arthur Richards imposed his constitution annoyed the National Council of Nigeria and the Cameroons (NCNC). The Richards Constitution was, however, the foundation on which all future constitutional development was laid. While some vocal nationalists who had criticized the constitution were prepared to give it a trial, the NCNC decided to appeal to the people whom they claimed to represent. Azikiwe's political stature had been enhanced by the outcome of the strike action which had identified him with the workers all over the country and this had a great psychological effect on the fortunes of the NCNC. Its leaders toured the country. The inclusion of Herbert Macaulay, the father of Nigerian nationalism, Dr Azikiwe, the foremost nationalist of the new age, and Michael Imoudu, the trade union leader who had so ably fought on behalf of the workers, made the NCNC tour popular and, even though Herbert Macaulay died in Kano, the momentum was maintained. The NCNC won the three Lagos seats in the Richards Legislative Council, thus enabling Nnamdi Azikiwe, Adeleke Adedoyin and Olorun Nimbe to take their places as elected representatives of the people of Lagos. Armed with this popular support, the three NCNC leaders went to London in 1947 to ask the Colonial Secretary to revoke the Richards Constitution. They were told to go back and give the constitution a fair trial. The delegates, who themselves had quarrelled in England, came back to face great criticism about the way in which they had spent the £13,000 that they had collected from the public; but this was a temporary setback for the party.

The 1940s marked the emergence of tribalism in Nigerian politics. The Yorubas had as a result of early contact with the Europeans produced an educated élite and for some time they had dominated Lagos politics. By the time Dr Azikiwe returned from America, his chain of academic qualifications made him the most important Ibo representative and he inspired various Ibo youths who, learning from his adventurous spirit, also went to study in America. When he broke away from the Nigerian Youth Movement, he was followed by the people of his ethnic group. He particularly disliked the Yoruba

Chief Abafemi Awolowo

Malam Aminu Kano

351

Sir Ahmadu Bello, the Sardauna of Sokoto

domination of Lagos politics. Various tribal unions were formed of which the Ibibio State Union was important. As a result, the Pan-Ibo Federal Union was formed and in 1948 Azikiwe became its president. When he stated that 'It would appear that the God of Africa has created the Ibo nation to lead the children of Africa from the bondage of ages', he made suspect to other Nigerians his political party, the NCNC, of which the Ibo Union had been one of the founder unions. It was at this time also that the Yorubas, probably afraid of the magic personality of Zik, inaugurated the Conference of the Egbe Omo Oduduwa 'to create and actively foster the idea of a single nationalism throughout Yorubaland'. Many of the leaders of this organization were those whom Dr Azikiwe in his series of articles had called imperialist stooges because they maintained good relations with the British administration. But the secretary of the Egbe, Obafemi Awolowo, was a Yoruba lawyer with political ambition and a clearcut approach to the realization of his ambition. Since the leadership of the Ibo Union and the NCNC were the same, the Egbe Owo Oduduwa became an organized weapon to dwarf the image of Dr Azikiwe and things degenerated to such an extent that there was almost bloodshed in Lagos.

The initiative for the review of the constitution came from the new Governor, Sir John Macpherson. He started at the local level by bringing democratic processes into the Eastern Region's local government and making arrangements for the recruitment of Nigerians into the senior sector of the civil service. He not only appointed four Nigerians into the Executive Council but for the first time a Nigerian, Dr S. L. Manuwa, became head of a department as Director of Medical Services.

Sir John made arrangements for local conferences, regional conferences and a general conference to deal with the new constitutional proposals before a final drafting of the constitution itself. During these discussions, the various tribal groupings emerged as distinct political parties. Most Ibos backed the NCNC proposals. Many Yorubas were still solidly behind the NCNC, but their intellectuals and their natural rulers backed the Egbe Omo Oduduwa, whose political wing, under the direction of Obafemi Awolowo, in March 1951 became the Action Group. In the north the Jami'yyar Mutanen Arewa, founded in 1949 by Aminu Kano and Abubakar Tafawa Balewa with the intention of helping the natural rulers in the proper discharge of their duties, was becoming a great conservative and moderating political force. Its more ebullient and progressive sections led by Aminu Kano, finding that the Jami'yyar or Northern People's Congress (NPC) was not radical enough for them, formed a splinter group, the Northern Elements Progressive Union (NEPU), which started agitation for radical reforms.

Some members of the Zikist Movement were responsible for some nasty incidents. Despite its name the movement was not led by Azikiwe. The worst was the Enugu Coal Mine incident in 1949. The colonial administration, not knowing the peaceful nature of the 'sit down' strike and erroneously coming to the conclusion that the miners, directed in their action by the radical members of the movement, might seize the explosives in the mine, sent a contingent of police. The miners, on the other hand, mistaking the police arrival as an attempt to break up the strike decided to riot. The European Assistant Superintendent of Police committed an error of judgment by telling his men to open fire on the defenceless horde of rioters. Twenty-one of them were killed. This incident caused a frenzy in the country. There were attempts at reprisals and it seemed as if law and order had broken down. There were riots and looting in the East. Radical leaders demanded that the Assistant Superintendent of Police who had ordered the shooting should be brought to trial. Because of this outrage, Nigerian nationalists decided for once to work together. This gave birth to the National Emergency Committee which organized a series of protest actions. A member of the Zikist Movement attempted to assassinate the Chief Secretary, H. M. Foot, on 18 February 1950. As a result, in April the movement was banned.

But the consultations that were going on for the drafting of the new constitution continued. As soon as the Drafting Committee had completed its work, the General Conference met in Ibadan and accepted certain proposals which were then embodied in the Macpherson Constitution, which was agreed in 1954 and introduced three years later. Nigeria was to have a federal constitution with the boundaries of the Northern, Western and Eastern Regions unchanged. There was to be a strong central legislature called the House of Representatives, comprising a President, 6 unofficial members, 148 members elected from the Regional Houses (half of this number was to come from the North) and 6 special members nominated by the Governor to represent various interests. The Executive, presided over by the Governor, was to be a Council of Ministers consisting of 6 unofficial members and 12 Nigerian ministers, 4 nominated by each regional government.

Each region was to have a Lieutenant-Governor, a Legislature and an Executive. The Legislature in the North and West consisted of a House of Assembly and a House of Chiefs whilst that of the East was a House of Assembly only. Lagos, although the federal capital, was to be administered as a part of the Western Region. All the laws that were made by the Legislature had to be referred to the Governor. The final constitution with which Nigeria was to go into independence was agreed in 1957. Governor's powers were abolished in the Eastern and Western Regions. Self-government in the North was planned for 1959. The House of Representatives was increased and a second chamber established. The office of Federal Prime Minister was created.

As soon as the constitutional proposals were known there was intense political action all over the country. Obafemi Awolowo formed the Action Group. The Northern People's Congress, now led by Ahmadu Bello, the Sardauna of Sokoto, did not have any national ambition and so confined its activities to the Northern Region.

In the election that followed the introduction of the constitution, the NPC won in the Northern, the Action Group in the Western and the NCNC in the Eastern Regions. The President of the NCNC won the election with the two other NCNC candidates, Adeleke Adedoyin and Olorun Nimbe. Only one Lagos member could go to the Federal Legislature from the West. It was thought that the other two NCNC delegates for Lagos would step down but, after some undefined manoeuvres, the two men went against the NCNC decision and contested individually with the National President. The Action Group made sure that they did not vote for Dr Azikiwe who thus lost and became the Leader of the Opposition in the West. The structure of the Federal Cabinet was such that the Northern People's Congress as the party in power in the North provided four Federal ministers, and the NCNC in power in the Eastern Region and the Action Group in the Western also provided four each. The leaders of the various political parties thus remained in the regions while they sent their subordinates to the Federal Legislature. The main flaw in this constitution was that there was no clear division of functions between the Federal Legislature and the regional ones and, as the leaders of the parties were in the regions, it became clear that residual powers were with the regions.

The political activities and the economic and social changes that affected constitutional growth in British West Africa and brought in the 1946 constitutions in the Gold Coast and Nigeria, replacing the official majority with a majority of elected members, also resulted in Sierra Leone taking a further step in 1951 and the Gambia in 1954. In the 1951 constitution the Sierra Leone Executive Council consisted of four unofficial members and not less than four appointed members who were selected and appointed from among the members of the Legislative Council. This constitution and that of The Gambia in 1954 had the same flaws as those of Nigeria and the Gold Coast in 1946. The Gold Coast and Nigeria had gone a stage further than this in 1951 when there was greater African representation and participation in the formulation and implementation of policy. But even then there were still conflicts which had to be resolved, and the nationalists were only prepared to operate the constitutions as interim measures for the realization of their political objective, 'self-government'. But British administration had been the cementing factor in inter-tribal and inter-party relations. As the common enemy the British administration began to fade into the distance, while the old tribal animosities, fear and distrust began to rear their heads providing great difficulties in the constitutions which had not carefully defined the authorities of the different institutions of government.

When the Convention People's Party won the Gold Coast elections to the Legislative Assembly in 1951 it had become a highly organized party with certain objectives in view, of which the main ones were the immediate achievement of independence, the fostering of a united West African nationalist movement, the achievement of a socialist state and the eradication of white imperialism in Africa.

When Kwame Nkrumah was released from jail the Governor, Sir Charles Arden-Clarke, asked him to submit the names of his ministers. He had no difficulty in nominating his most loyal supporters—K. A. Gbedemah, Kojo Botsio, Dr Ansa Koi, A. Caseley Hayford and T. Hutton Mills. Both of the latter were sons of prominent nationalists of an earlier generation. In the interests of national unity he agreed that E. Asafu-Adjaye of Asante and J. Braimah of the Northern Territories who were not members of his party should be appointed ministers. There were at the same time three European officials in the Executive Council, which was presided over by the Governor. The CPP took the opportunity of this administration to democratize the local government system of the Gold Coast by establishing local councils with two-thirds elected members and one-third nominated by the traditional rulers. But the chiefs ceased to perform any distinctive administrative function in local government. They were only allowed to preside over ceremonial occasions. Each council had an elected chairman.

At first, opposition to the government was poorly organized, but in 1952 when Kwame Nkrumah became Prime Minister it became clear that the British were receding more and more into the background, and fears began to be expressed by the Provincial Council members and the opposition party, the Ghana Congress Party led by Dr K. S. Busia, who saw in Nkrumah's 'showman' methods a tendency to personal dictatorship. Nkrumah was only prepared to work the 1951 constitution for a short time because he was not happy with the retention of officials in the Executive Council which he wanted transformed into a cabinet controlled only by the elected representatives of the people.

Independence achieved 1954–65   The British Government agreed in 1954 to an amendment of the 1951 constitution. There was now to be an all-African cabinet and a Legislative Assembly consisting of 104 members elected directly. In the election that was held on 15 June 1954, the Convention People's Party again swept the polls gaining 71 out of the 104 seats. But greater constitutional concessions brought in more opposition to Dr Nkrumah's government. There were two sources of opposition—Asante and the Northern Territories. The Northern Territories, still educationally backward and with greater attachment to traditional systems, were beginning to fear southern domination. This area supported Mr Braimah, leader of the Northern People's Party, which won 12 seats out of the 17 allotted to the North in the National Assembly and, as the single largest Opposition Party, was accepted by the Speaker as the official formal opposition in the House. There was also a great opposition from Asante

356

where the CPP was unpopular. The old animosity between the Colony and Asante had not died out, and since most of the CPP supporters came from the southern towns, the Asante people feared a new kind of colonial domination. They had some reason for their fears: the government increased the export duty on cocoa so that cocoa merchants had to pay more for exporting their produce. Then the money paid to the cocoa farmers was reduced to 72 shillings per load at a time when the price of cocoa in world markets was rising. The Asante farmers, thinking that they were being defrauded, grouped round the National Liberation Movement which not only campaigned against the pegged price of cocoa, but also urged a federal system of government. The National Liberation Movement had the support of the Asantehene and his chiefs, who, themselves afraid for the security of their territory, had sent a petition to the Queen for a commission of enquiry to settle the problem of a federal system for the Gold Coast. The demand for the federal structure both by the Northern People's Party and the National Liberation Movement, now led by Dr Busia, caused complications for Nkrumah as he prepared to take the next constitutional step.

When the CPP decided to ask for independence the British Colonial Secretary, Lennox Boyd, made clear that the constitutional issue had first to be settled by elections. The CPP again won, which meant a popular endorsement of the CPP's constitutional proposals, but safeguards had to be injected into the constitution against possible dictatorship. So the stage was set for Ghana's independence on 6 March 1957.

In Nigeria, the 1957 constitution bristled with difficulties. This was the first time that Nigerians were taking part in the administration of their country. The leaders of the various political parties remained in the regions. This made their subordinates in the centre refer back most decisions to their regions of origin. There was no all-embracing party in the country and since the representatives of the regions in the Federal Legislature were at the same time members of the regional legislatures, they had divided loyalties. Then again there was considerable overlapping of functions between the central and regional legislatures.

But the regions, especially the Western, could not wait for fuller responsibility in a distant future. Obafemi Awolowo wanted more legislative competence for this region in order to transform it into a model state, and he wanted a clear demarcation of functions. When the Governor refused to consider further constitutional amendment, the Action Group declared a policy of non-co-operation.

Meanwhile, the different departments of government now had African ministers as their political heads. British officers now found themselves receiving orders from Africans. Some of them could not change their outlook and some even stooped to writing confidential reports on ministers. The leader of the Action Group quickly put a stop to this in the West and compelled expatriate officers to accept the new dispensation.

It was not only in the Western Region that there was a demand for constitutional change. The defeat of the NCNC leader in his attempt to gain a place in the central government had brought confusion to the NCNC ranks. On the one hand, Eyo Ita by leading the NCNC government in the East was virtually party leader there. At the centre, the NCNC ministers were carving out positions of power for themselves. It did not seem that in the scheme of things, Dr Azikiwe, who was leader of the opposition in the West and still president of the NCNC, had a place. The *West African Pilot*, one of the Zik group of papers, and chief organ of the NCNC, saw in the failure of Azikiwe to get to the centre of power one of the reasons why the party should not give its support to the new constitution. The truth was that there was already in the NCNC a conflict between the parliamentary and the national leadership. There was a growing movement within the party demanding that Azikiwe should resign his position as opposition leader in the West and seek election to the Eastern House of Assembly. Others suggested that the whole constitution should be cast overboard. The NCNC Parliamentary Party did not like this idea especially since, at the Port Harcourt Convention of the Party in 1952, it had been agreed that the constitution should be given a fair trial.

The leading African politicians in the central government realized that if Nigeria was to achieve full independence and harmony there would have to be compromise. The squabbles among the main parties were leading to demands for autonomy from almost every ethnic group in the country. Nigeria was in danger of disintegrating into dozens of small states. In 1959 the Prime Minister, Alhaji Abubakar Tafawa Balewa (deputy leader of the NPC), managed to obtain the support of NCNC politicians and formed a coalition government of NPC and NCNC members. It was this coalition that led

Nigeria to independence in 1960. Dr Azikiwe's supporters were pacified when he was appointed the first African Governor-General of Nigeria

The remaining British colonies could not long be denied their freedom. In Sierra Leone African political development was hampered by conflict between the Creoles of the Colony and the hinterland peoples until Sir Milton Margai, a man respected by both sides, formed the Sierra Leone People's Party. This party was overwhelmingly successful at the election of 1958 and Margai became the Prime Minister. In 1960 he led a delegation to London to ask for independence and this was at last granted in April 1961, leaving The Gambia as the last British dependency in West Africa. The Gambia did not have to wait long because the rivalry between the Colony and the Protectorate was bridged by the emergence of the Progressive People's Party which was able to claim independence in 1965.

French West Africa

The French colonial system, unlike that of Britain, gave no scope for intensive nationalist movements. This, however, did not mean that there was no political activity among French West Africans. In fact there was even an earlier political consciousness in some of the French colonies than in the British ones. In the Old Towns of Senegal, at the beginning of the twentieth century, there were already elections and, as has been stated above (page 250), an African, Blaise Diagne, had been elected to the French National Assembly in Paris. Even before Blaize died in 1934, a more extremist group of younger Africans, like Lamine Guèye, had emerged. This group campaigned for the enfranchisement of all Africans as opposed to those of the four *communes* — Dakar, Gorée, St Louis and Rufisque. Lamine Guèye was from a Muslim family of St Louis in Senegal and had gone to a Koranic school at the age of six. Then he went to the William Ponty School in Dakar where he afterwards taught before going to Paris to study law. As early as the 1930s he had campaigned for Senegalese representation by two members in the French National Assembly. Nationalist activity during this period was directed towards greater representation in Paris and not for any establishment of institutions in West Africa.

For one thing, it was difficult for any French West African to engage in any activity that could be regarded as nationalistic.

Political opposition to French administration could hardly develop in an atmosphere in which the colonial officials had the arbitrary power to impose fines and terms of imprisonment on all those who were engaged in radical political activities or refused to obey orders given by an official or chief.

But the Second World War dislocated the administration of the territories. Most of the regulations that came directly from the Ministry of the Colonies in Paris ceased when France was overrun by Germany. The governors, faced with the problem of maintaining a resistance movement against Germany, were forced to seek the aid of the indigenous leaders in order to get enough African forces. The leaders responded by asking for political concessions such as the abolition of the *indigénat* (Naturalization laws) and forced labour. General de Gaulle, the chief representative of Free France, realized the importance of the French West African colonies, especially the strategic port of Dakar. The most powerful French battleship was stationed there.

In January 1943 General de Gaulle summoned a conference of all colonial governors at Brazzaville to discuss the type of colonial policy to be adopted during the war. It was agreed that as soon as the war was over, certain social reforms would be implemented. These included the removal of the much-hated *indigénat* and forced labour. There were already French nationalists like Mamadou Dia of Senegal and Sekou Touré of Guinea who were campaigning for an 'equal and special' association between France and the colonies as Britain had with her dominions, but the Brazzaville Conference refused this proposal. The only concessions which were granted were that some powers formerly exercised in Paris were to be transferred and more rapid assimilation would be encouraged. General de Gaulle promised to grant representation to the colonies at the French Constituent Assembly which would be summoned at the end of the war to frame a constitution for France and her empire.

It was as a result of this promise that delegates from Senegal went to the National Constituent Assembly in October 1945. Prominent among these delegates were Lamine Guèye and Leopold Sedar Senghor. Both men took part in the drafting of the constitution of the Fourth French Republic and the law which has immortalized the name of Guèye—the Loi Lamine Guèye which granted French citizenship to all African citizens of the French Union. Forced labour was abolished and the *indigénat* was eliminated. The colonists were given the right to vote. The French West Africans were thus provided with greater opportunities to become Frenchmen, rather than Africans, and encouraged to take their seats in the French National Assembly rather than in an assembly of their own.

To many Frenchmen the proposed constitution was unacceptable and in the Second Constituent Assembly, elected in June 1946, any idea of autonomy was rejected. The First and Second Constituent Assemblies had provided an opportunity for the Africans to maintain close association with political parties in France who were interested in some form of colonial reform. The Africans gained a few more seats in the French National Assembly and the expansion of the Senegalese Territorial Assembly system to cover other colonies in West Africa. It is important to note this last concession because, although these assemblies had limited powers, this constitutional provision was the beginning of some form of decentralization which was to have a great effect on the development of political parties.

The establishment of the Territorial Assemblies awakened great political activity. The only party in France that was interested in colonial reform was the French Communist Party whose mass appeal and organization suited some of the African leaders. In order to have concerted action in this fight, it was agreed that all enlightened organizations, including trade unions, study groups and political groups, should send delegates to Bamako in October 1946 for a conference. This was the origin of the single federation-wide party called the *Rassemblement Democratique Africain* (African Democratic Convention or RDA) which had communist backing.

The Bamako Conference might have succeeded in bringing all the French West African political groups together but for the opposition of the French Socialist Minister of Colonies who persuaded all those politicians who were members of the Socialist Party not to attend the Communist indoctrinated and controlled conference. Apart from this, there were some politicians who, because of their former political associations, were not prepared to associate themselves with younger elements who were making more radical moves. The older politicians like Lamine Guèye and Leopold Senghor of Senegal, who had experience in French politics because they had been consistently elected into the French National

Assembly, saw great danger in a closer association with the Communists, who were becoming more and more unpopular in France itself. They probably thought that if the French colonists were to gain any further political and social concessions it would only be through an association with the parties that were in control of the government. The Senegalese leaders therefore did not join the RDA. The deputies of Sudan, Guinea and Dahomey also refused to join the party. The most outstanding leader of the party therefore was Félix Houphouet-Boigny of the Ivory Coast, a very intelligent and adaptable leader. On the other hand, Leopold Senghor of Senegal tried to collect all those French Senegalese leaders who were not prepared to go into the RDA to form a new independent party, the *Bloc Democratique Senegalais* (Senegalese Democratic Bloc or BDS). Then he tried to get in touch with other African leaders who refused to work with the RDA.

The real period of test for the popularity of the various parties came when there was an election to the new French National Assembly. The RDA gained many seats. The next month, December 1946, also marked the elections to the territorial assemblies. Here the RDA did not do very well. It was only in the Ivory Coast, the colony to which Houphouet-Boigny belonged, that the party had a strong majority. But its initial success was enough to cause alarm to the Socialist administration. Unless its actions were curtailed, the Communist bloc in the French National Assembly would continue to increase. But at the same time, it was the only party that was organized enough to press for self-government.

It therefore became the policy of the French administration to suppress the RDA movement in West Africa. The leaders were accused of subversion and of generating anti-French ideas. They were harassed, and in the Ivory Coast the conflict between the Socialist Governor and the RDA supporters reached such a peak that some Africans were shot at Dimbokro when an attempt was made to arrest Houphouet-Boigny. There was also an attempt to ban the party in all the territories. Houphouet-Boigny now found that the alliance with the Communist Party was hindering the realization of his aims. Senghor, because he had the political advantage of associating with the party in charge of the administration, tried to achieve more in this political struggle by allying his party with the other independent nationalist parties that had been established in the various colonies. This was immediately before his well-organized regional party, the BDS, campaigned in Senegal and got the support of the masses against Lamine Guèye and his supporters. Leopold Senghor called together all the independent African deputies in the National Assembly in Paris, in 1948, and formed the *Indépendents d'Outre Mer* (Overseas Independents or IOM). The RDA, therefore, finding that it was at a political disadvantage, severed its association with the Communist Party and tried to work with the Socialist administration from which Senghor and his group came to be divorced when it defeated Guèye and the Socialist-controlled Governor-General. The policy of Senghor in advocating federalism with the ultimate aim of forming one or at most two very powerful African republics within the French Union could hardly have met with the approval of the administration but old friends were more easily trusted than new and so, for some time, although the RDA was supposed to be on the government side, it was still kept under observation. Even then, there was not much the parties could do to achieve any new constitutional concession until 1956.

What influenced French colonial policy was not the activities of the French West African politicians but the militant nationalism that was displayed in North Africa and Indo-China. After severe defeats in these areas, Guy Mollet's Socialist government wisely decided that some political concessions would have to be granted to the French colonies in West and Equatorial Africa if they were not to adopt militant methods. The RDA now gained from its earlier policy of support for the administration. It was allowed to campaign unfettered during the 1956 elections for the French National Assembly. The results were so encouraging and the popularity of the party was so distinctly shown at the expense of Senghor's IOM that the Socialists had no alternative but to appoint its leader, Houphouet-Boigny, a minister in the French government in Paris. As he had a post in the cabinet, he helped in the framing of the *Loi-Cadre* of 1956 which showed a great change in French colonial policy.

The *Loi-Cadre* first granted universal suffrage to all the French colonies. Each French colony could draft a constitution which would give the territorial assemblies considerable legislative autonomy comparable to the 1951 constitutions of both the Gold Coast and Nigeria. The law also empowered the colonies to establish Executive Councils with African ministers who were responsible to the Assemblies. Each territory could now maintain its own direct link with France and so the legislative and executive functions of the Governor-General were curtailed. Each colony could now develop along its own lines. This law made the operation of an inter-territorial party unnecessary. Each branch of the RDA in the different colonies began to operate as a separate entity. The fact that Houphouet-Boigny had compromised himself and the party by association with the administration had already caused dissention within the party itself. The greatest opponent to this new policy of gradualism and association with the government was Sekou Touré of Guinea, the dynamic rebel trained in Marxism and descended from Samori. He was not prepared to accept any solution short of independence and the 'equal and special' association which he had advocated before. He had organized a strong inter-territorial trade union movement. He saw that the excessive decentralization which had been achieved would create small states that would have no effective voice in the association with France. He was interested in the creation of a very strong state large enough to make its presence felt in the struggle for complete elimination of imperialism in Africa. However, it was the former conservative, Leopold Senghor, who, with his IOM, now took a very radical line advocating a greater independence in federation.

An attempt was made to bridge the gap between the nationalist leaders by creating an all-embracing party but this did not meet with the approval of the RDA leaders who had succeeded in gaining control of Ivory Coast, French Sudan and Guinea during elections to the territorial assemblies of 1957. Senghor then got the leaders to form a broadly based party, the *Parti de Regroupement Africaine* (PRA), with the object of achieving independence in federation. The movement towards independence was further stimulated by the self-government which Kwame Nkrumah had achieved for Ghana. The infection had caught the whole of dependent Africa and there was now great agitation for autonomy. This wind of change which was stirring the whole of Africa did not fail to make an impression on the mind of General de Gaulle who, in 1958, was popularly swept to power in France. He had made up his mind that he had to come to terms with modern African nationalism. In his grand tour of Africa with Houphouet-Boigny, he posed as the emancipator of all Africa with the exception of Algeria. He was anxious to transform the French Union into a French 'Community' on the same model as, but different from, the British Commonwealth. He therefore gave all the twelve colonies of West Africa and Equatorial Africa the choice, at a referendum, of domestic autonomy within the French Community, or total and complete independence which would mean the loss of all French financial and technical assistance. The Community was to be a confederation of states holding power over foreign affairs, defence and many common services. There was to be an Executive Council composed of the President of the Community, some French Cabinet Ministers and the heads of government of the various autonomous states of the Community.

When this constitution was presented to the West African states in a referendum which was held in September 1958 only Guinea under its leader Sekou Touré voted 'no', and so that small and poor state became the first of France's West African colonies to gain independence. The presumption of Guinea caused consternation in Paris, and General de Gaulle decided immediately to take action. The attitude of the President was that Guinea had seceded from the Community and should be penalized for it. All French aid was stopped immediately. French officials were withdrawn. All this, however, did not affect the young rebel and make him change his mind. Sekou Touré had to look elsewhere for aid in order to transform Guinea into a Socialist state.

The other French colonies remained as self-governing states in the French Community. It was, however, obvious to many of the African politicians that the states were too small to remain by themselves. The very fact that Guinea did not remain in the French Community ruled out any possibility of a federation of states such as Leopold Senghor had advocated. Guinea in its bid for external aid had made terms with Ghana for the formation of a union of the two states and as a result Ghana was prepared to grant a loan of £10 million to the smaller state. But there were difficulties that the union of the two states had to face. A constitution had to be found which would be acceptable to the two peoples and which would take into account the many geographical, linguistic and racial differences between the two territories. These problems could not be solved and the idea of union was dropped.

The great advocate of federation, Leopold Senghor, finding that a federation of all the states was not possible, decided that Senegal should walk hand in hand with the neighbouring republic of Sudan to form the Federation of Mali which could be used as a base for the incorporation of some other states. This Federation, however, was doomed not to last long because the two leaders, Senghor of Senegal and Modibo Keita of Sudan, could not work out a suitable constitution acceptable to both countries. Also Leopold Senghor and Mamadou Dia were becoming afraid that there was growing up a close relationship between Modibo Keita and Lamine Guèye which might give Guèye the political leadership of Senegal. But these difficulties came only after the Mali Federation had, in 1960, gained independence within the Community. This success of Mali strengthened Houphouet-Boigny's resolve. He wanted the territories that he could influence to seek independence first before undertaking any negotiations on the terms of association with France. It was on the basis of this that Houphouet-Boigny, Hubert Maga, and Hamani Diori gained independence for their territories of the Ivory Coast, Dahomey and Niger, respectively, in 1960. With the attainment also of independence by Upper Volta at the same time, the whole system of the French Community collapsed as far as West Africa was concerned.

There remained the trustee territories which had been administered by Britain and France since the end of the First World War. These were Togoland and the Cameroons. Togoland was divided and part of it was being administered by Britain with the Gold Coast while the other part was under French administration. The Cameroons were also divided and while the part under Britain was administered with Nigeria, the French maintained their own, much larger part independently. When it became clear that Gold Coast and Nigeria were becoming independent, the United Nations Trusteeship Council organized a plebiscite to determine whether the British sectors wanted to remain with the countries with which they were administered. The sector governed with the Gold Coast chose to remain with Ghana while, under the leadership of Sylvanus Olympio, the French sector became independent in 1960 as the Republic of Togo but refused to join any of the former French West African blocs. Olympio also refused to join the independent state of Ghana. In the British area of the Cameroons, the northern section, which was administered with Northern Nigeria, elected to merge fully with Nigeria, while the southern part joined the independent state of Cameroon (1961).

Independence was not an automatic guarantee of peaceful progress and development. Some West African countries passed through a decade of political change and occasional violence. In Nigeria regional and tribal jealousies undermined the federal constitution which collapsed under Major-General Ironsi's military coup in 1966. Ironsi was overthrown by Lieutenant-Colonel Gowon in 1967 but within months the Ibos of the Eastern Region had seceded to form the state of Biafra. Civil war only ended after three years of bitter bloodshed with the defeat of the Ibos. In Ghana, Nkrumah became President in 1960 and head of a one-party state in 1964. His dictatorial measures and ruthless suppression of political opponents led to his overthrow in a military coup in 1966. Civilian government was restored in 1970 but two years later Colonel Acheampong became head of state after another army-led revolt. Dahomey in the 1960s saw seven changes of government most of which were brought about by political and military leaders seizing power. In 1970 authority was vested in a presidential council of three men.

Not all countries, of course, experienced such troubles. In Senegal, President Senghor's government remained secure. In Gambia, Guinea, Ivory Coast, Chad and Cameroon political change came gradually and peacefully. But all the new states were in a process of change. The political systems set up by the colonial powers before independence were based on European democratic models which were not suited to African society. They were replaced by one-party states or authoritarian, military control. Throughout the 1970s the process of change and experiment continued. The last West African state to achieve independence was Guinea-Bissau, where Portugal finally gave up control in 1974.

Chapter 16

The re-emergence of self-government in East Africa

When, in 1919, Britain accepted responsibility for the administration of Tanganyika (the League of Nations mandate was confirmed in 1922) the three East African mainland territories and the offshore possessions of the Sultan of Zanzibar all came under British control. But each of the territories had its own peculiar problems, so we shall consider them separately.

Kenya

In 1920 the East African Protectorate was renamed Kenya Colony. For most of the white settlers and many of the officials this seemed to indicate that the future of Kenya as a 'white man's country' was assured. The small European community dominated the economic life of Kenya and was enjoying a steadily greater share in political affairs. But three factors combined to undermine the position of the white minority: Asian agitation; the development of the trusteeship principle; and the growth of African nationalism.

The Asians, who dominated the business world and many of whom were richer than the average European, demanded equality of status with them, greater representation on the Legislative Council and the right to own land in the Kenya Highlands. In 1922 the British government decided that most of the Asian complaints were justified. It made many concessions, only standing firm on the issue of the allocation to Asians of land in the so-called 'white highlands'. The settlers sent representatives to London to demand a change of attitude. The end result of all these wranglings was a policy document issued by the Colonial Secretary, the Duke of Devonshire, and known as the Devonshire White Paper (1923). It clarified the government's attitude towards relations between the three races in Kenya. The most important statement was 'Kenya is an African territory, and . . . the interests of the African native must be paramount . . . if and when those interests and the interests of the immigrant races should conflict, the former should prevail'.

Apart from that basic statement of intent the Devonshire White Paper did very little for the cause of political or social progress for the African. It confirmed that the Kenya Highlands were to stay 'white' but rejected racial segregation in other areas. It provided for five Indian members to be elected to the Legislative Council and one missionary to be appointed to represent African interests. It dashed the political hopes of the white minority by informing them that they would not be allowed a dominant share in the government.

Kipande or metal container which Africans were forced to wear round their necks

The racial conflict was far from over in Kenya; much worse was to follow, but this early clash helped to establish the idea of 'trusteeship' in the minds of British politicians. It was an idea put forward by Sir Frederick Lugard (later Lord Lugard) in his book *The Dual Mandate in British Tropical Africa*. No colonial officer or settler thought in the 1920s that African self-government would be achieved for decades, perhaps centuries, but at least the principle was accepted.

Kenyan nationalists had other ideas. Political activity began among the peoples of the Highlands who came into closest contact with the white men. Their land had been taken for settlement, they had been forced into reserves, they were made to work on European farms, they were physically ill-treated and they had to carry the hated identity pass—the *kipande*. In 1920 a Kikuyu chief formed the Kikuyu Association which aimed to be a mouthpiece to the government on land and labour abuses. But a year later a more radical organization appeared. This was the Young Kikuyu Association (YKA), whose secretary was Harry Thuku. Its members were mainly young men who had received some education at mission schools. Some of them had served in the army and auxiliary corps during the First World War. The YKA made use of public meetings, newspaper articles, strikes and deputations to air their grievances. In 1922 Thuku was arrested. This led to violent scenes in Nairobi. Police and settlers opened fire on the crowd, killing many. The first blood in Kenya's fight for freedom had been shed.

Thuku was kept in detention for eight years but his supporters carried on the struggle. The YKA was reformed in 1925 as the Kikuyu Central Association (KCA) and men such as Jomo Kenyatta, destined for a prominent place in the history of Kenya, were among its leadership. In 1927 when a British government commission arrived in East Africa to consider the possibility of closer union between the three territories the

Harry Thuku as a student

KCA took the opportunity of making their grievances known. As well as demanding the redress of many ills they also called for direct African representation on the Legislative Council. The commissioners were sympathetic and their report in many regards favoured the Africans. But whatever was said or decided in London made little practical difference in settler-dominated Nairobi. In 1929 fresh disturbances occurred after a clash between the KCA and Church of Scotland missionaries, who disapproved of the Kikuyu practice of female circumcision. Demands were made for the banning of KCA. Its president was imprisoned and there was a permanent breach between young Africans and the Christian missionaries who had, until then, exercised some restraining influence on them.

Land grievances were aroused again in 1932 when gold was discovered on one of the African reserves. Despite the Native Lands Trust Ordinance which had declared reserve land inviolable and only to be taken by white men after the provision of full compensation, the farmland of the people of Kavirondo was violated by prospectors. The people formed an organization, the North Kavirondo Central Association, to protest. They succeeded in getting another commission sent from London. It was to look into the whole problem of land ownership in the colony. Inevitably its detailed report (1934) recommended a series of compromises which pleased none of the contestants, but once again African representatives had clearly and forcefully presented their case and their views were respected by the officials.

The number of educated Africans was growing steadily and more and more discontented young men were joining the ranks of the nationalist associations. The Kikuyu, who were at the centre of the land and labour struggle, were the most politically active community but other peoples also had their political groups. In the mid-1930s the Kikuyu nationalist ranks became divided. Thuku was dissatisfied with the KCA tendency towards more extreme action. He broke away to form the Kikuyu Provincial Association, pledged to obtain reform by constitutional means. Another breakaway moderate group was the Kikuyu Loyal Patriots of Chief Koinange.

In the years immediately before the Second World War the pace of nationalist activity quickened. Kenyans returned from years of study abroad with fresh ideas about democracy and techniques of political agitation. Peter Mbiyu was one such and he founded the Kenya Teacher's Training College in 1938. As well as providing education, this college, and other independent establishments, stirred a new generation to nationalist aspirations. Government actions over issues such as cattle destocking provoked resentment which in turn led to the founding of new political organizations. In 1939 living and working conditions at the port of Mombasa led the Labour Trade Union to organize a strike, which was supported by the KCA. At the same time the leading nationalist groups united to demand direct African representation on the Legislative Council. This matter was still unresolved on the outbreak of the Second World War when all African political groups were banned. But the nationalist movement had reached an important stage by 1939. Membership was increasing and the need had been realized for a truly national party which cut across tribal barriers.

During the Second World War attitudes hardened. The banning of African political groups drove the nationalist movement underground where it became more extreme. As in the conflict of 1914–18, Kenyans were pressed into war service and underwent experiences which left them embittered. Soldiers returning from the war found no improvement in conditions at home. Though the first African, Eliud Mathu, was admitted to the Legislative Council in 1945, African grievances and political aspirations were still not taken seriously. The British government encouraged fresh white settlement and even the most progressive British politicians thought of Kenya's future in terms of a multi-racial society, and not one in which the African would be in control of his own destiny. Political grievances, social and economic injustices led to demonstrations, strikes and riots.

Once again protest was spearheaded by the Kikuyu. In 1946 a group of Kikuyu ex-soldiers formed the Forty Group, which rapidly grew into the Kenya Land and Freedom Army. They used their military training to seize weapons and organize a guerrilla style resistance from bases in the Mount Kenya Forest. Thus began the Mau Mau emergency which lasted from 1952 until 1960. Bands of guerrillas ranged the Highlands attacking European farms and 'loyalist' villages. Troops were brought in from Britain, but it was 1956 before the principal leaders, Dedan Kimathi and 'General China', were captured and another four years before the last pockets of resistance had been cleared out. During the fighting atrocities

Anti-Mau Mau drive in Nairobi 1954. Thousands were questioned and if they could not satisfy the interrogators they were taken to a camp

were committed on both sides and over twelve thousand African lives were lost.

Meanwhile other nationalists confined themselves to political action. When Eliud Mathu was admitted to the Legislative Council, an unofficial committee of Africans from various communities gathered to advise him and keep him informed of events in the rural areas. In 1946 this grew into the Kenya African Union (KAU). The following year Jomo Kenyatta, newly returned from several years of study in Britain, was appointed Chairman of KAU. Its membership was predominantly Kikuyu but it was, nevertheless, the first really national political movement. When the Mau Mau emergency broke out, splits occurred in KAU ranks between those who supported the Freedom Fighters and those who rejected violence. White politicians accused KAU of being the political wing of the Mau Mau movement. All African

Eliud Mathu with members of his Consultative Committee

political organizations were banned; Kenyatta and other leaders were imprisoned.

But constitutional gains were being made. Britain realized how determined the people of Kenya were. Though the settlers became even more extreme in their demands for white supremacy it was obvious to the British government that the existing political situation could not be maintained against the rising tide of nationalism. KAU demands for increased representation on the Legislative Council had led by 1951 to the presence of five African members on that council. In 1955 the ban on African political activity was lifted but organizations could only operate at a local level. This situation threw up more potential leaders in various parts of the country. The following year the Executive Council was reconstituted as the Council of Ministers and included two African members. In 1957 Africans were for the first time allowed to elect members to the Legislative Council.

With eight members on the Legislative Council the nationalists now had the nucleus of a parliamentary party capable of bringing pressure to bear on the government. In 1959 they boycotted Council meetings, demanding the release of Kenyatta and a constitutional conference to determine Kenya's future. The main opponents in the political arena now were the nationalists, who were pledged to common roll elections and Kenyan autonomy, and the settlers who wanted a multi-racial constitution which would guarantee the immigrant races a place in the political life of the country out of all proportion to their numbers. There were some European 'hard-liners' who refused to make any concessions to the 'blacks' but their numbers steadily dwindled.

The destiny of Kenya as an independent nation was decided at two conferences held at Lancaster House, in London (1960 and 1962). At the first an interim constitution was devised which gave African elected members a majority on the Legislative Council. In preparation for elections to be held in 1961 two African political parties were founded, the Kenya African National Union (KANU) and the Kenya African Democratic Union (KADU). Most of the leading nationalists gave their support to KANU but others, who feared domination by the Kikuyu and Luo and who wanted a constitution which would devolve real power on regional assemblies, formed KADU. Although KANU won the elections its leaders refused to take office until Jomo Kenyatta was released. Ronald Ngala therefore headed a KADU administration. Kenyatta was released a few months later and became President of KANU. The second Lancaster House Conference attempted to reconcile the two African parties without success. It did manage to establish a coalition government and this, with the help of British advisers, worked out an independence constitution for Kenya.

It was decided that Kenya should have full, internal self government in June 1963 after fresh elections had been held. The elections gave KANU a large overall majority and thus Jomo Kenyatta became Prime Minister of Kenya. Almost immediately most of the KADU opposition crossed the floor of the House of Representatives. In December 1963 Kenyatta led his country into full independence. One year later Kenya became a republic with Kenyatta as first President. In 1965 KADU was disbanded, the upper house—the Senate—was dissolved, and Kenya became a one-party state.

Uganda reached its present geographical shape in 1926 when Turkana District in the north-east was transferred to Kenya. Administration had never been easy among the nomadic and semi-nomadic peoples in the northern half of the Protectorate and the Entebbe government was delighted to relinquish part of its burden. In the outlying districts colonial administrators interfered as little as possible with the traditional life of the people, though wherever possible chiefs became paid agents of the government. Political and economic activities were centred in the South and particularly in Buganda.

In 1921 a Legislative Council was established. The small European settler community was well represented and provision was made for one Asian member. The Asians regarded as an insult anything less than equal representation with the British and until 1926 they boycotted the Council. Africans, it was thought, were adequately represented in their own tribal councils. For their part African leaders had little interest in the Legislative Council. Land alienation to Europeans and forced labour were never serious problems in Uganda. Traditional values and patterns of life were only changed slowly. Therefore there was no early development of an aspiring group of young nationalists coming into conflict with the government.

Political development sprang from the relationships between the colonial government, traditional African ruling bodies and young men impatient with their own leaders. In Buganda it was the Lukiiko that was at the centre of controversy. It could not handle efficiently the growing volume of administrative business but would not relinquish any of its authority. This led to difficulties with the colonial government. The Kabaka, Daudi Chwa, believed that the Lukiiko had usurped some of his powers. Within Bugandan society various groups existed which believed that the Lukiiko was a conspiracy of chiefs who had made an agreement with the foreign rulers for their own interests.

In 1920 the Protectorate government ordered the Lukiiko to repeal certain laws which, according to the British, were unjust. The Lukiiko successfully resisted this demand but had to submit to a close scrutiny of their laws by government officials. Shortly after this the Buganda National Federation of Bataka took to the Governor their grievances over clan lands which, they claimed, had been stolen and re-allocated by the Lukiiko. The Lukiiko had refused to consider the Bataka case and Daudi Chwa had proved powerless to help. The govern-

The infant Kabaka, Daudi Chwa

ment, though sympathetic to the Bataka Federation, found it impossible to give them practical assistance. It did, however, take action to protect the Baganda peasants who, in 1925, complained of exploitation by the Lukiiko. The following year the powerful Katikiiro (Lukiiko President), Apolo Kagwa, was forced to resign after a clash with the Provincial Commissioner. In the early 1930s a constitutional conflict developed when Daudi Chwa refused to approve legislation introduced by the Lukiiko. This difference had to be sorted out by the colonial overlords. This troublesome and politically unproductive era ended in 1939, a year which saw not only the outbreak of the Second World War but also the accession of a new Kabaka, Mutesa II, who was only fifteen years old.

During the war years the well-meaning Governor, Sir Charles Dundas, reinforced the authority of the Lukiiko. This increased the frustration of those Baganda who believed themselves to be exploited and unjustly treated. It also increased the hostility of neighbouring regions which did not enjoy such a degree of autonomy. Demonstrations were organized against Lukiiko policies by the Young Baganda, the Bataka Federation and the Uganda Farmers' Union, but achieved nothing. In 1945 matters came to a head in a series of riots, some of which had to be put down by Protectorate troops. The Katikiiro, Wamala, was forced by his enemies to resign. This was followed by a government purge of the Lukiiko and the installation of Nsibirwa as Katikiiro. But in September Nsibirwa was gunned down on the steps of Namirembe Cathedral. The assassins were caught and punished and the political affairs of Buganda came under closer control by the colonial power. Far from stopping agitation this move only directed it against the British and created in Buganda the beginnings of a genuinely nationalist movement. Even the introduction of elections to the Lukiiko and the appointment of three Africans to the Legislative Council did not pacify the Baganda agitators. In 1949 there was a fresh outbreak of anti-Lukiiko agitation led by the Bataka Federation and the African Farmers' Union, which ended in both organizations being banned.

By this time African and European political thinkers were beginning seriously to consider the future of the country. Self-government now seemed a possibility some time in the not too distant future. African participation in central government was increased by stages. But no degree of autonomy could

Mutesa II, Kabaka of Buganda

be achieved without Ugandan unity and the attitude of
Buganda's rulers seemed to stand in the way of that unity. In
1950 the Lukiiko, fearing that constitutional change would
impair Buganda's special status, refused to nominate a
member to the Legislative Council. Lukiiko fears were
enhanced two years later with the foundation by I. K. Mosaazi
—a Muganda—of the first all-Ugandan political party, the
Uganda National Congress. In 1953 another reorganization
of the Legislative Council increased African representation
to twenty. Again the Lukiiko refused its co-operation. It
seemed that the Buganda council would be forced to give in
sooner or later.

Then occurred a crisis that strengthened the Lukiiko's position. The British Colonial Secretary raised the possibility of creating a federation of East African states. This raised considerable protest in Uganda, whose people did not want to be tied to settler-dominated Kenya. The Baganda united behind their Kabaka and the Lukiiko in demanding, not only reassurance on the federation issue, but independence for Buganda as a separate state. This led to the deposition and exile of Mutesa II and heated discussions between colonial and Baganda representatives. In 1955 Mutesa was allowed to return but the Governor's attitude towards the Kabaka was seen by many Africans as an affront and the demand for independence now became insistent.

In 1958 there were for the first time elections to the Legislative Council. These elections were direct elections in all areas except Buganda where the Lukiiko was still making difficulties. More political parties had now come into being, the main one being the Democratic Party. After the election some members broke away from the Uganda National Congress to form the specifically anti-Bugandan Uganda People's Union (soon to be reconstituted as the Uganda People's Congress). A committee was now set up to decide the next stage towards independence. This work continued steadily despite the continued open defiance of the Lukiiko and political differences in Buganda which led to some of the worst riots the country had seen.

By 1961 Uganda was ready to elect its first predominantly African parliament. The Lukiiko was only partially successful in organizing a boycott in Buganda. In that province most of the Uganda People's Congress's supporters were frightened off from voting, but the Democratic Party was better organized and it was the winning of the Buganda seats that gave it the victory. Now it only remained for the details of the independence constitution to be worked out and a date for the handover to be fixed. At last the Baganda leaders realized that they would have to take part in the political game. They were represented at the discussions in London which worked out Uganda's independence constitution. Then they formed a new political party, *Kabaka Yekka* (King Alone), to fight the election which would precede independence. This election took place in April 1962. The intervention of *Kabaka Yekka* led to the defeat of the Democratic Party in Buganda and so Dr Milton Obote's Uganda People's Congress formed the

Prime Minister Milton Obote takes the oath of office at Uganda's Independence Ceremony

government which led Uganda to independence in October 1962.

The position of Buganda had been temporarily solved by linking it in a federal relation with the rest of the country. It was fully represented on the National Assembly but maintained control over many internal affairs. While Dr Obote became Prime Minister of Buganda, Kabaka Mutesa was given the position of non-executive President (1963). But Uganda's political problems had been concealed rather than removed. Early in 1966 differences within the ruling party led to the arrest of five ministers on the order of the Prime Minister. Obote now suspended the 1962 constitution and declared himself President. Political meetings were forbidden and

Kabaka Yekka was banned. It only remained for the final show-down between the Baganda leaders and the central government to take place. In May 1966 government troops attacked the Kabaka's palace. Mutesa escaped and fled to Britain, where he later died. In 1967 a new constitution came into effect naming Uganda a republic. But still further repressive measures were to be introduced and by 1970 Uganda was a one-party state under the iron control of Dr Milton Obote.

Tanganyika

Almost from the beginning of their period of rule in Tanganyika the British instituted the policy of indirect rule. This system was particularly associated with the governorship of Sir Donald Cameron (1925–31). His aim was, as he said, 'to administer Africans as far as possible through the instrument of their own indigenous systems instead of directly through the administrative officer'. The territory was divided into provinces and every effort was made to find African leaders capable of incorporation into a colonial system. By the Native Authority Ordinance of 1926 these men were empowered to collect taxes and carry out administrative tasks. The Native Courts Ordinance of 1929 incorporated local courts within the framework of colonial law. Where no suitable traditional leaders could be found, other educated Africans were appointed as local officials. In 1926 a Legislative Council was established. As in other areas it was only the immigrant races that were represented on this council. Thus the pattern emerged of an African controlled system of local government and a foreign dominated central administration.

For all practical purposes this system worked well but it had the effect of hindering the formation of a sense of nationhood among Tanganyika Africans. There were no political groups in the early years. Such African organizations as did exist were of two types. First of all there were local groups, such as the Bukoba Bahaya Union. This was founded in 1924 by Klemens Kiiza, a Haya businessman. He wanted to unite his people for their better social and economic progress. He disapproved of the policies pursued by the local chiefs with the sanction of the government in distant Dar es Salaam. There were others like Kiiza who were frustrated by lack of power and who regarded the African administrators as tools of the colonial regime. The other kind of African organization was that organized by educated Africans in the towns. This united the élite and recognized no tribal barriers. Such an organization was the Tanganyika Territory African Civil Service Association, founded in 1922. There was nothing political about such an association but it did bring together for the first time men who were destined to play an important part in the nationalist movement later on. A more important organization was the Tanganyika African Association (TAA) formed in 1929 largely by educated Africans frustrated by unemployment and by exclusion from administrative posts for which they believed themselves to be qualified.

Only very slowly did conditions become favourable for the development of a nationalist movement. Probably the most important development was the gradual realization by the people that the chiefly class of paid administrators was a barrier between them and government. They felt that self-interest prevented the chiefs initiating reforms or making known to the Governor the wishes of their people. Educated Tanganyikans believed that the continuance of indirect rule was a plot to keep them out of the administration. Matters came to a head in some localities when unpopular government economic policies were enforced by the chiefs. Thus, in 1955, the Luguru resisted attempts to make them terrace their hillsides.

Only after the Second World War did the various strands of African political activity and thought come together. In 1945 the TAA decided that an effort should be made 'to enrol all Africans, women and men, in the African Association'. At the same time the colonial rulers began to involve Africans in the work of central government; two African members were appointed to the Legislative Council in 1945 and this number was steadily increased over the next ten years. In 1953 the Governor accepted the growing criticism of Indirect Rule. A local government ordinance of that year provided for the gradual replacement of traditional authorities by elected councils. As far as central government was concerned, the administration was now committed to an experiment in a multi-racial society. The Legislative Council was to maintain its official majority but the unofficial side would be equally representative of all three races. In 1954 African and Asian membership of the Executive Council was increased and they began to be trained in ministerial responsibility. The following year Legislative Council elections were held for the first time. The Governor no longer presided over Council meetings; his place was taken by a Speaker.

This steady constitutional advance owed little to the African nationalist movement but that movement was, by now, gathering momentum. In 1953 Julius Nyerere, a teacher who had been to university in Britain, was elected President of the TAA. He immediately began to give the Association a more political flavour and in the following year it was completely reconstituted as the Tanganyika African National Union (TANU). TANU's main policy was the achievement of independence as soon as possible. Membership grew rapidly and Nyerere himself made several visits to the United Nations' headquarters to urge the justice of his people's aspirations. A United Nations' mission visited Tanganyika in 1954 and in its report urged that the mandatory power (Britain) should

Headlines from Daily Sketch *13 January 1964*

establish a timetable for the movement towards the country's independence.

But the government was becoming worried about the 'undue haste' being urged by TANU. Some more outspoken members of the Union were imprisoned, branches were closed and Nyerere was forbidden (1957) to address public meetings. In 1956 African and European opponents of TANU formed the United Tanganyika Party (UTP), pledged to the idea of multi-racialism. The UTP did not last long; it was disbanded after its failure in the elections of 1958. TANU's obvious support throughout the country and the growing pressure of the United Nations impressed on Britain the need to accelerate the pace of constitutional change. When Sir Richard Turnbull was sent out in 1958 it was with instructions to preside over the transfer of power to an independent administration. In 1959 the Executive Council was replaced by a Council of Ministers which included five TANU leaders. In the following year elections were held on a wide suffrage to an enlarged Legislative Council. TANU won all but one of the seats and Dr Nyerere formed a government. On 1 May 1961 Tanganyika gained internal self-government and on 9 December full independence. A year later Tanganyika adopted a republican constitution and Nyerere became first President.

In 1963 Zanzibar also became independent but conflict between Arabs and Africans and the mismanagement of the transference of power soon wrecked the new constitution. A bloody revolution in January 1964 overthrew the Arab Sultan and his government in favour of an African Revolutionary Council. Tanganyika gave the new Republic valuable assistance in its early days and in April 1964 the two states were united as the Republic of Tanzania. From the beginning the new nation pursued Socialist policies. Many foreign companies were nationalized and laws were passed that prevented the development of a class of African capitalists. Tanzania forged strong links with the Communist world, especially China, who helped with the building of the Tanzam railway.

In 1967 the East African Community was established to organize joint services such as railways, posts and telecommunications and East African Airways, and to foster close economic links between the three nations. Unfortunately in less than a decade the EAC had become the victim of divergent politics in East Africa. Kenya, which became a one-party state (KANU) in 1967, remained united under the leadership of Mzee Jomo Kenyatta. It pursued a policy of gradual economic and social reform within a basically capitalist framework. By contrast President Nyerere of Tanzania declared a radical programme of socialist reform in the Arusha Declaration (1967). This involved the nationalization of foreign-owned businesses and industries and restrictions on private ownership of land and property.

Uganda's political progress was destined to be violent. There was mounting discontent at Obote's harsh rule, and in 1971 he was deposed by a coup d'état under the leadership of Major-General Idi Amin. Rejoicing at Obote's downfall proved premature. Within a few years the whole world was shocked to hear of religious and political persecution, assassination, and large scale massacres carried out on Amin's orders. He was condemned by many African leaders, and all close links with Kenya and Tanzania were broken.

Chapter 17

The continuing struggle in South and Central Africa

In Africa south of the Congo forest nationalist movements had only been partially successful by 1975. The former colonies of the Belgian Congo, Northern Rhodesia and Nyasaland, the Belgian Trust territory of Rwanda-Urundi, and the High Commission Territories (Swaziland, Basutoland and Bechuanaland) had all gained independence under African governments. Portugal had relinquished control of her colonial possessions but South Africa and Southern Rhodesia, though they had broken their ties with Britain, remained firmly under white minority rule.

The Belgian Congo

In the vast territory of the Belgian Congo most Africans had little contact with Europeans. Apart from Katanga and the areas round Leopoldville (the capital from 1929) and Boma there was no European settlement and the foreigners were only to be found in scattered administrative posts, plantations and

Congolese Housing Estate

mission stations. Thus, though many Africans availed themselves of primary education and medical facilities, their lives were little changed. Certainly they developed no national consciousness. The government actively encouraged regionalism by decreeing that administrators should learn the languages of the people in their care and by ensuring that the educational medium was the local language.

Life was very different in the towns, especially in the industrial towns of Katanga. Industrial development depended on a large, permanent force of cheap African labour. There thus grew up a class of detribalized urban Africans. Most employers provided adequate housing for their workers and materially these urban Africans were better off than their counterparts in other colonies. But they suffered the perpetual indignity of racial segregation. They were not allowed to use the same facilities as the Europeans and they were despised by the Belgians who often referred to them as *macaques* (apes). This was particularly resented by the growing class of *evolués*, Africans who, by a combination of increased wealth and education, had become a sort of middle class. They were frustrated because certain positions which they were qualified to fill were available to 'whites only'.

The Belgian regime was paternalistic. The rulers believed that their only responsibility to the African population was to cater for its material needs. They were able to do this quite well because the Congo prospered enormously in the interwar years. Katangan mines came into full production, more roads and railways were built, the rubber industry boomed and plantation crops such as palm oil, cotton, sugar, tobacco, cocoa and sisal found ready markets. Peasant agriculture was also encouraged and in 1933 the National Institute for Agronomic Study in the Congo was established to make modern knowledge and techniques available to Africans. But in the political field there was no question of African advancement. Native councils were set up in a few areas but there were very few exceptions to the practice of direct rule and any organizations that appeared to have a political flavour were banned. Belgian officials boasted of their attitude: 'It is true that no one votes in the Congo; they work. The Belgians prefer administration to politics.'

The sensitiveness of the Belgians towards African 'politics' can be seen in the history of the Kimbanguist Movement. In April 1921 Simon Kimbangu established a separatist religious movement. It was essentially an attempt (one of many through-out Africa) to find a specifically African form of Christianity. Kimbangu preached for five brief months in the lower Congo regions, gaining many converts especially among the Kongo. In September 1921 he was arrested and his movement was banned. He was kept in prison for thirty years and died there in 1951. But his movement survived as a secret society and came into the open again in 1956 when the ban was lifted.

A more successful religious movement was the Kitawala, which was strongest in Katanga. In 1923 it arrived from Nyasa-land and Northern Rhodesia and by 1939 it had thousands of members. Considering that its teaching had a distinctly political flavour it was lucky not to be banned:

> The Bible makes no distinction between whites and blacks
> ... it is only here in the Congo that the government
> considers the natives as slaves. We are fed up with this and
> the new God of the Kitawalist doctrine is here to help us . . . .

Apart from such separatist religious groups the only associa-tions which can be seen as precursors of later nationalist organizations were certain tribal cultural societies such as ABAKO (a Kongo tribal society) and a few *evolué* clubs.

It is not surprising, then, that there was no real nationalist pressure from within the Congo until the mid-1950s. Then the spread of nationalism in other parts of the continent, the attainment of self-determination by ex-colonies and pressure on Belgium from the United Nations caused a sudden upsurge of nationalist feeling in the Congo and an equally sudden change of attitude by the Brussels government. The result was a disastrous rush to independence which led to the most terrible consequences.

In 1955 a Belgian university professor published a suggested plan for the emancipation of the Congo in thirty years. Though this horrified most administrators and settlers it drew forth a response from the nationalists. An *evolué* group in Leopoldville countered with the demand for a more rapid schedule for independence and the formation of a national African political party. In the lower Congo region a more extreme voice was raised. It belonged to Joseph Kasavubu, who had become President of ABAKO and was transforming it into a political organization. At Stanleyville another important political figure appeared. This was Patrice Lumumba, a nationalist with strong anti-colonial feelings. New leaders appeared in other areas. They were all regionalists, with the exception of

Moise Tschombe, President of Katanga

Patrice Lumumba, first Prime Minister of Congo

Joseph Kasavubu leader of Abako Party in Congo

Lumumba. Belgian policies had prevented the emergence of a large group of nationalists with a vision of a free Congolese nation; most of the new politicians represented tribal and regional interests. Lumumba alone worked for the foundation of a national political party.

In 1957 the government took the first step towards African political representation. The *Statut des villes* provided for the election of Africans to town councils. This was immediately put into effect in the major towns and Kasavubu and Lumumba were among those elected. Now political parties sprang up all over the Congo; by early 1960 there were over a hundred and twenty parties, most of them small and representing local interests. The prospect of independence had renewed old tribal rivalries. African leaders, fearing that their traditional enemies might become too powerful or make territorial gains under a new constitution, took to arms in an attempt to achieve a position of strength. But Lumumba did found a party aimed at attracting support from all peoples, the *Mouvement National Congolais* (MNC). Kasavubu rapidly emerged as the leader of a federalist movement. In 1959 delegates from several parties met at Kisantu and accepted Kasavubu's plans for a federal constitution. In fact, Kasavubu won much more support than Lumumba but the Belgians would not agree to the splitting up of the Congo into a number of small, federated states.

The sudden unleashing of political aspirations and the renewal of old rivalries had a disastrous effect. 1959 was a year of demonstrations, strikes, riots and violence. In Kasai, war broke out between the Luba and Lulua. There were attacks on isolated plantations and mission stations. Frightened settlers began to leave the country. In many areas Belgian police and troops completely failed to restore order. Many political leaders, including Lumumba and Kasavubu. were imprisoned, only to be released after a few months in response to the demands of their supporters.

Through the mounting chaos the Belgian government tried to maintain a policy of cautious development leading to majority rule. The situation in the Congo made it impossible for the leading politicians to accept this. The populace had become so excited by irresponsible public speakers who promised a 'golden age' after independence, that politicians could only bid for support by demanding immediate independence. No one who urged cautious constitutional advance would have gained many votes. A conference was held in Brussels in January 1960 at which the Belgians gave way completely. They promised independence within six months. The new state was to be a united republic. Elections were held in May. Predictably the resulting Assembly contained members from a variety of parties. The MNC with 35 seats (out of 137) was the largest party but could only form a government by combining with other parties in a coalition. At length agreement was reached. Kasavubu became President and Lumumba as Prime Minister headed a very insecure coalition government. Thus the Congo entered independence on 30 June 1960.

The new constitution lasted six days. Then the army garrison in Leopoldville, dissatisfied at the rate of Africanization in the upper ranks, mutinied. Law and order collapsed completely. Without consulting the new government, Belgium sent troops to protect European interests. Lumumba was furious at what he regarded as an attempt at recolonization. On 11 July the mineral-rich Katanga seceded under the leadership of Moïse Tshombe, who had much local support and was backed by Belgian capitalist interests. The Luba-Lulua conflict in Kasai worsened. Other regions followed Katanga's example in breaking away from the new state. In desperation Lumumba turned for help to the United Nations, which sent a peace-keeping force. When this army made no attempt to enforce the allegiance of the seceding regions Lumumba sought military aid from Russia. For many months the Congo gained international importance as a battle ground of Communist and anti-Communist ideologies.

During the conflict Lumumba had assumed dictatorial powers and resentment against him now grew. Early in 1961 Kasavubu managed, with army support, to remove the Prime Minister from office. When he tried to whip up support for a return to power Lumumba was arrested and sent to Elizabethville. There he was assassinated by some of Tshombe's soldiers. With the collapse of effective government, the army assumed increasing importance. Under its new Commander-in-Chief, General Mobutu, it cleared the country of foreign troops and brought most regions back under central government control. By August 1961 the situation had quietened sufficiently for a new government, under the leadership of Cyrille Adoula, to be appointed.

Still Katanga refused to be reconciled. In September 1961

United Nations' troops were ordered to invade the secessionist state. There followed a year of appalling warfare before Katanga was forced back into the Republic (January 1963). In order to reconcile the Katangese completely a new Congolese government was formed in 1964 under the premiership of Tshombe. Still the Congo could not find peace. Fighting continued in various parts of the country. Tshombe called in foreign mercenary soldiers to help with the trouble. The behaviour of these European professionals only served to make Tshombe unpopular. In August 1965 he was dismissed from office. But there was now no politician who could command sufficient support to take over. In November General Mobutu headed a coup and became President. Under his strong leadership the exhausted Congolese Republic (later renamed Zaire) began to settle to a more peaceful future.

A patrol in Leopoldville

LUMUMBA'S INVADERS

Belgians fly to stop them

From DANIEL McGEACHIE

ELISABETHVILLE,
Friday.

LUMUMBA'S invasion troops —300 strong— have advanced 10 miles into the breakaway province of Katanga tonight.

Rifles above their heads, they waded the Luika River near the border a few hours

Headlines from the Daily Express

Rwanda-Urundi

General Mobutu

Belgian lack of control also allowed Rwanda-Urundi to slide into strife and bloodshed. The trouble here arose because the aristocratic Batutsi minority had established control over the Bahutu peasantry. When the independence issue was raised in the neighbouring Congo the Batutsi urged the Belgians to grant immediate independence to Rwanda-Urundi. This would have enabled them to retain their ascendancy over the Bahutu. When the Belgians insisted on granting independence to a majority government only, the Bahutu rose against their oppressors (1959). There was an appalling loss of life, especially in the north. It soon became clear that Rwanda-Urundi could not attain independence as one state; the two peoples, as far as possible, would have to be separated. Plans for independence were made under United Nations' control. In 1961 the people of Rwanda voted by referendum to end the Batutsi monarchy and elections for a Legislative Assembly were held. Gregoire Kayibanda was elected executive President and the state became independent under his leadership in July 1962. Many Batutsi fled to Burundi where the King, Mwambutsa IV, remained in power. Constitutional changes before independence led to certain limitations being placed on the monarchy. A Legislative Assembly was elected and an executive Prime Minister appointed. Burundi achieved

392

independence in July 1962. The early years of both independent states continued to be marred by conflict between the two races. Hundreds of thousands of refugees from Rwanda fled to neighbouring states.

Nyasaland and the Rhodesias

Though each of the three British possessions in Central Africa pursued a different path to independence, their destinies were, for a time at least, closely bound together. By 1925 both the Rhodesias had come under direct control from London. The British South Africa Company had experienced growing difficulties in administering the colonies, and European settlers were dissatisfied with control by a commercial company which did not, in their opinion, put the needs of the people above the desire for commercial gain. In 1921 a British government commission was sent to examine the position of the Company and recommended that it should be relieved of administrative responsibilities. A serious attempt was made to unite Southern Rhodesia with South Africa but this was rejected by the white population at a referendum (1922). A new constitution which came into force in 1924 provided for a British Governor with overall responsibility and complete control of legislation concerning Africans. There was also an elected parliament of thirty members representing the European minority. It was competent in all internal matters. With this large measure of control the settlers set about organizing the social, economic and political life of Southern Rhodesia for their own advantage. The United Party, which was in power from 1934 to 1939, set the colony on the path of racial segregation and permanent subordination of the African with its policy of 'parallel areas', and excluded Africans from the possibility of obtaining the top positions in commerce and administration.

In Northern Rhodesia the settlers were never so powerful and the administration which replaced Company rule was a typical kind of protectorate government. The Governor was assisted by Executive and Legislative Councils. Though settlers were represented on the latter their elected members never had a majority over the officials. In 1929 a move towards Indirect Rule was made when local chiefs and other local authorities were given administrative functions including presidency of Native Courts. In 1936 the powers of these African officials were extended to cover finance.

Nyasaland was also moving in the same direction. By 1920 it already had a typical protectorate government and in most areas local rulers had some power and responsibility. In 1929 some judicial powers were returned to the chiefs. In 1933 new Native Authorities were appointed with wider powers, including some control of local finance.

The Nyasaland Protectorate was ahead of its neighbours in the development of nationalism. After the death of John Chilembwe (see page 303) political activity continued through the Native Authorities and the Native Associations. Not all the authorities were tools of the colonialists; some used their position to urge new policies on the government and to present the grievances of their people. They kept up a steady demand for educational improvements and an increased share in central and local government. Native Associations had been set up in most areas by 1930 and they continued to press for reforms. In 1924 the Associations of the Northern Province united to form the Representative Committee of Northern Province Native Associations, which was the first large and important African political organization in Central Africa. This largely reflected the work done by the Scottish missionaries in the field of education. A class of educated Africans emerged rapidly in Nyasaland. Some went abroad to complete their studies. Others went to work, for shorter or longer periods, in other colonies. Their experience was widened and they were in a better position to champion reform at home.

In Northern Rhodesia African education was not so far advanced and there was little evidence of real nationalist or reformist energy before the Second World War. In 1923 a small group of educated young men formed the Mwenzo Association in the north-east of the Protectorate. But its membership never grew and it disappeared in 1928. 1930 saw the foundation of a number of welfare associations in towns along the railway. Their activities seldom ventured into politics and an attempt to form a United African Welfare Association of Northern Rhodesia (1933) failed. It was on the Copperbelt that African protest first became organized. Racial discrimination was practised in matters of pay and employment in the mines and the white mineworkers' union in 1936 forced the employers to agree to the exclusion of black workers from skilled jobs. Housing and working conditions for Africans were generally poor. These factors mattered little

The Moffat Institution

when African industrial labour was seasonal but during the 1930s more and more workers took up residence on the Copper Belt with their families. In 1935 workers at several mines came out on strike over a suspected tax increase. The protest was answered with police and guns. Seven Africans were killed. In 1940 another strike called by workers demanding better pay and an end to racial discrimination was answered in the same way. This time seventeen strikers lost their lives.

Nationalist activity in Southern Rhodesia was largely due to the infiltration of men and ideas from South Africa. In 1923 Abraham Twala, a South African, formed the Rhodesia Bantu Voters' Association. By uniting the small class of educated, property-owning Africans who had the vote, it aimed to do a deal with one of the major political parties in order to gain more rights for Africans. It failed to make any political impact and represented only a tiny African minority. Two years later the land issue created a focus for African political activity. Thousands of people came forward to protest at the government's land policy when a British government commission arrived to enquire into the matter. They achieved little. The process of keeping Africans in reserves and increasing territorial segregation continued. In 1927 Robert Sambo arrived from South Africa to form branches of the Industrial and Commercial Workers' Union. His success was immediate in Salisbury and Bulawayo. The government deported him and tried to break the movement. But it spread rapidly and

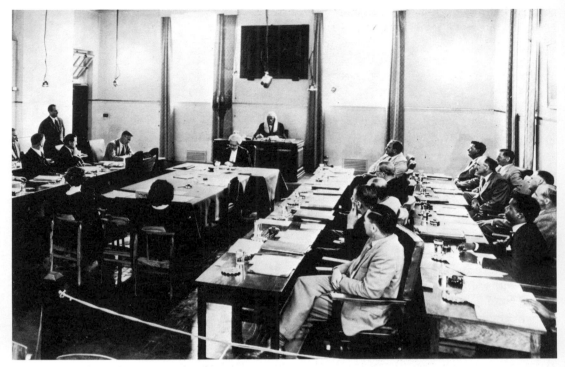

The Legislative Council in session at Lusaka

became an important mouthpiece of African discontent. In 1934 another important organization appeared—the Southern Rhodesia African National Congress.

After the Second World War Britain began to introduce greater political responsibility for Africans in its colonies. This led to gradual constitutional change in Nyasaland and Northern Rhodesia but not in Southern Rhodesia where any move towards African advancement was squashed. African representation on the Nyasaland and Northern Rhodesia Legislative Councils began in 1948, and by 1953 there were three African members on the Nyasaland Council and four on the Northern Rhodesia Council. African share in local government was also increasing. Between 1944 and 1946 a system of Provincial Councils supervised by a Protectorate Council was introduced in Nyasaland. In 1950 Urban Advisory Councils came into being to help with town government. Africans played an important part in all these bodies. In Northern Rhodesia the powers of Native Authorities increased. Urban Advisory Councils were created and, in 1947, all-African Town Management Boards were set up on the Copper Belt. African Provincial Councils were set up, on which sat leading Africans in the regions. At the centre a purely advisory African Representative Council was formed in 1946.

Nationalism really 'got off the ground' in Northern Rhodesia in 1946. In that year a conference was held in Lusaka for representatives of workers' welfare societies. The result was the Federation of Welfare Societies, which was concerned not only with urban and industrial grievances but also wider political issues. In 1948 the Federation reformed itself as the Northern Rhodesia Congress, the first political party for Africans. Similar developments took place in Nyasaland, where the Nyasaland African Congress was founded in 1944. Both these bodies concerned themselves largely with reforms and the redress of grievances within the framework of the colonial system—until 1950. Then something happened which gave nationalists in British Central Africa a new and quite clear political goal.

The European minority in British Central Africa grew increasingly concerned about their future as time went by. It was obvious that Britain wanted to move the colonies to greater autonomy and possibly even independence. It was also obvious that she had no intention of handing over power to minority governments. Some European politicians, foremost among whom was Roy Welensky, leader of the unofficial group of the Northern Rhodesian legislature, wanted the whites of the Rhodesias to combine to preserve European rule. They urged amalgamation of the two colonies on the British government. When this was turned down they suggested a federation of all three territories. The idea, first put forward at a settler conference at Victoria Falls in 1949, was attractive to Britain. It seemed to be a way of creating an economically strong state with a multi-racial constitution. Its advantages to the settlers were obvious and Southern Rhodesia particularly looked forward to sharing the profits of the Copper Belt.

African leaders opposed federation from the start. They saw it for what it was, a means of preserving European domination indefinitely. They also resented the suggestion that Britain could consider giving away African sovereignty in the two Protectorates. In 1949 Harry Nkumbula (for Northern

Rhodesia) and Hastings Banda (for Nyasaland) sent a memorandum to London condemning the Victoria Falls Conference proposals. In 1950 a group of young men in Ndola published a pamphlet called *A Case Against Federation* which was adopted by the Northern Rhodesia Congress. Under the leadership of Nkumbula the Congress became much more active in organizing opposition to federation. The Congress changed its name in 1951 to the Northern Rhodesia African National Congress. In 1952 a Supreme Action Council was set up to organize anti-federation protests and demonstrations. The Nyasaland Congress was equally active.

But plans for the Federation went ahead. In 1951 it was discussed by colonial officials in London. Another Victoria Falls Conference was called by the Colonial Secretary. African representatives were invited but boycotted the meeting, preferring instead to make known their opposition to the whole idea by deputations and demonstrations. The

Left: Clement Kumbikano and Pascal Sokoto who opposed the white settlers scheme to federate the three central African territories

Conference worked out a constitution. In 1953 it was put to the Legislative Councils of the protectorates and to the European electorate of Southern Rhodesia. It was enthusiastically accepted, and in October 1953 the Federation of Rhodesia and Nyasaland came into being.

The constitution of the Federation was designed to preserve racial imbalance in political affairs. Of the 35 member parliament 6 seats were reserved for Africans. There was no extension of the franchise to include more Africans. During the ten years the Federation was in being, the African majority gained little from it. The colour bar remained. Improvements in educational facilities and job opportunities were few. Another result of federation was a fresh influx of European settlers.

But it was not only Africans who began to feel frustrated with the Federation. As time went by it became clear that Southern Rhodesia was benefiting more from the new arrangement than her partners. Large grants from Federation funds went to the setting up of new industries in the South. The

Kariba Dam

federal capital was established at Salisbury, which was good for Southern Rhodesia's prestige and also good for business. After a long wrangle with her partners Southern Rhodesia succeeded in getting the new Zambezi hydro-electric plant sited at Kariba on her side of the river. Leaders of Northern Rhodesia and Nyasaland began to have second thoughts about the Federation.

However, for the time being it seemed that the Federation was moving inevitably towards independence. In 1956 Welensky became Federal Prime Minister. All who knew him realized that Africans could not hope for political advancement at his hand. In 1957 Britain devolved more powers upon the Federation parliament. African representation on the parliament and in the regional councils increased but African majorities were never considered. The African Congresses had to continue to fight for every advance—relaxation of the colour bar, more schools, land reform, etc. Nationalist leaders became more militant as the possibility of independence became stronger. When a British government white paper outlining moderate changes to the Northern Rhodesia Legislative Council was issued Harry Nkumbula treated it to a public burning (1958). Shortly after this the Northern Rhodesia Congress split into two groups, Kenneth Kaunda leading the more extreme Zambia African National Congress (ZANC). There was also an upsurge of nationalist politics in Southern Rhodesia. For a while African leaders had been content to support the moderate Prime Minister, Garfield Todd, in his attempts to extend African political freedom and create a multi-racial society. But time passed and there was little change in African rights. In 1957 the African National Congress was formed. The following year Garfield Todd was forced from office by his more extreme opponents. Sir Edgar Whitehead became Prime Minister and one of his first acts was to ban the African National Congress.

In Nyasaland frustration and impatience boiled over in extremism and violence. From 1955 the Nyasaland African National Congress (NANC) came under the influence of more radical leaders, such as Henry Chipembere and Kanyama Chiume. In 1958 Dr Hastings Banda returned to Nyasaland after many years of work and study abroad. In the same year he attended the first Pan-African Congress at Accra (see page 315) where he and Kenneth Kaunda made a pact to break up the Federation. Meanwhile irresponsible members of NANC had turned to violence. As a result the Congress was banned and Banda and many of his colleagues were imprisoned. Similar events in Northern Rhodesia led to the banning of ZANC and the detention of Kaunda (March 1959).

Feelings were now running too high for these moves to be effective. The banned parties reformed under new names, the Malawi Congress Party in Nyasaland, the National Democratic Party in Southern Rhodesia and the United National Independence Party in Northern Rhodesia. Most of the imprisoned nationalists were released in 1960 and immediately resumed the battle for majority rule and independence. Banda led a Nyasaland delegation to London demanding elections to the Legislative Council on a wide franchise. His demands were for the most part granted. In 1961 elections were held which gave the Malawi Congress Party a majority. Banda formed a government which, over the next three years, took over more and more responsibility. On 6 July 1964 Nyasaland attained independence as the Republic of Malawi.

President Hastings Banda

Northern Rhodesia's progress to independence was not so peaceful. Any move towards greater political freedom for the majority was fiercely opposed by Welensky and the settlers. Thus when, in 1961, under pressure from the United National Independence Party (UNIP), Britain proposed a new, liberal constitution Welensky and his colleagues forced the British government to drop the idea. Inevitably this clash of opposing interests led to violence and bloodshed. The British government sought anxiously for some compromise solution, but there could be none. When the strength of African opposition north of the Zambezi had made it obvious that the Federation was doomed, the European minority was forced to accede to the demand for political reform. In 1963 a new constitution was devised. Elections in January 1964 gave UNIP a comfortable majority in the Legislative Council. Kaunda and his ministers lost no time in negotiating the details of independence with Britain. In October 1964 Northern Rhodesia became the Republic of Zambia.

President Kenneth Kaunda

By then the Federation was dead. How did this come about? A Royal Commission was sent to Central Africa in 1960 to examine the workings of the Federation and make recommendations for its future. It decided that the Federation could continue only if Africans in the northern territories received more political power and could be persuaded to drop their opposition and if Southern Rhodesia dropped its racial policies. Neither of these conditions could be met as a Federal Review Conference in December 1960 made quite clear. Britain was soon committed to the principle of majority rule in the northern states and Banda and Kaunda made it clear that they would lead their people out of the Federation as soon as they had the opportunity. For their part Southern Rhodesian politicians did not like the idea of mixing with black African leaders on equal terms, so enthusiasm for the Federation cooled there also. Therefore the British government accepted the inevitable and the Federation came to an end on 31 December 1963.

African triumph in the two other colonies caused grave anxiety in Southern Rhodesia. In order to save the Federation and minimize black-white conflict, Whitehead, between 1960 and 1963, tried to find a constitutional compromise acceptable to his own people and the nationalists. The National Democratic Party rejected a constitution proposed in 1961 and was, as a consequence, banned. It simply reformed under the

British Prime Minister, Harold Wilson (right) with Ian Smith at talks aimed at settling the constitutional crisis in Rhodesia

name of the Zimbabwe African People's Union (ZAPU). The failure of compromise hardened racial prejudices and there were outbreaks of violence in many areas. ZAPU was banned, only to re-emerge with even more radical policies, as the Zimbabwe African National Union (ZANU). By now the white minority had rejected Whitehead. At elections in 1962 they gave their allegiance to the extremist Rhodesia Front led by W. Field. The new government demanded independence—independence under minority rule. This was quite unacceptable to Britain. For nearly three years negotiations went on to try to discover a compromise solution. They all broke down because of Britain's insistence on the principle of 'no independence before majority rule'. Then, in November 1965, Ian Smith, the Rhodesian Prime Minister, made a unilateral declaration of independence (UDI), i.e. Southern Rhodesia seceded from the British Commonwealth. No other state gave formal recognition to the new Rhodesia, and the United Nations enforced economic sanctions against it, but with the support of South Africa and the Portuguese territories Rhodesia survived. It was able to put its racial policies into full effect for over ten years. Only when neighbouring Mozambique gained independence were the Rhodesian leaders forced to negotiate.

Portugal's poverty and her changes of government resulted, for her colonies, in continued exploitation, determination to maintain control, fear of African political progress and a lack of consistent, constructive development planning. In 1920 the government gave its African territories a greater degree of autonomy in the hope that the administrators on the spot would use their increased freedom of action to ensure rapid economic development. But the very opposite happened. World economic depression and inefficient administration brought the territories to the verge of bankruptcy. The Lisbon government had to intervene with advice and financial aid. Eventually it took direct control back in its own hands by the terms of the Colonial Act (1930).

Official policy became even more harsh after the appointment of Dr Antonio Salazar as Prime Minister in 1932. He remained in power throughout the period to 1973. His position was always quite clear: 'We are in Africa and it is our duty to stay there, for ourselves, for the West to which we belong, for

Angola and Mozambique

the peoples who have been entrusted to us . . .' Africans continued to be regarded, basically, as a source of labour. Every adult male had to work for at least six months a year and wages were low. Large numbers of Africans obtained better pay from seasonal labour in the Rhodesias and South Africa. The colonial governments tried in vain to stop this migration which brought Portuguese subjects into contact with more fortunate Africans in neighbouring territories. The governments of Mozambique and Angola had very little money available for social services. African education, health and housing were almost ignored by the Treasury. For example, in 1959 the total number of Mozambique Africans entering secondary schools was forty-one.

The official racial and cultural policy of the Portuguese government was 'assimilation'. The overseas territories were regarded as extensions of Portugal and citizens of all races were to move towards complete cultural unity. No racial discrimination was to be practised, all people were to mix freely. In practice Angola and Mozambique were segregated societies and became ever more so as European immigration increased. A very small class of *assimilados* gradually appeared. These were Africans who had bought full citizenship by gaining education, learning Portuguese and assimilating the white man's culture. By 1960 out of a population of over 10 million Africans in the two territories there were about 35,000 *assimilados*.

Portugal was a dictatorship. In Africa her officials brought to bear, not only the usual techniques of colonial repression but the methods of the modern totalitarian regime, including the secret police and the paid informer. This made it difficult for nationalist groups to build up a following. In 1923 the Liga Africana was formed to operate in both states as a body for bringing African grievances to the attention of the government. But it was a government-approved body and was pledged to non-violence and the use of constitutional means to further its ends. Its activities were closely watched, its recommendations largely ignored and any of its members who looked dangerous were 'removed'. A number of other small societies of a semi-nationalist character did spring up in the inter-war years but were swiftly crushed. The growth of towns in the 1930s was accompanied by the growth of African slums. These became potential centres of protest. In some towns papers and broadsheets were circulated and these frequently carried anti-government statements.

Though effectively suppressed and controlled, nationalism was never destroyed. It emerged clearly in the 1950s and 1960s, drawing inspiration from the successes of nationalists in other parts of the continent. In Angola trouble began in the northern part of the country in 1955. In that year a group of Kongo leaders opposed the government over the installation of Dom Antonio III, the official candidate for the Kongo throne. They formed a political party, the *União do Populacões de Angola* (UPA). Some of them formed a rival Kongo government and directed anti-Portuguese activities from across the border in Congo. Not far away a separatist religious leader Simão Toco was gathering a large following by prophesying the overthrow of Portuguese domination. Both these movements stirred a new courage among the people. A crisis was brought closer in 1960 when, as a result of poor coffee prices, northern Angola plantation owners decided not to pay their workers.

In 1956 a nationalist movement was formed among the *assimilados* of Luanda. This was the *Movimento de Libertacão de Angola* (MPLA). It had to operate in secret but it worked out a programme of reform and began to train people in the techniques of agitation. In 1960 the secret police swooped and arrested the MPLA leader, Agostinho Neto. He was detained without trial in Lisbon. In a clash with the police thirty MPLA supporters were killed.

In southern Angola the frustrations of the Ovimbundu led, in 1954, to the foundation of the *Associacão Africana do Sul de Angola*. The Association, inspired by the resistance movement of 1885–1915, gathered weapons and prepared for revolution and guerrilla warfare.

The storm broke in 1961. First of all there was a strike among Ovimbundu cotton workers. Troops were called in and a brief, bloody war ensued. While the fighting was at its height an MPLA revolt broke out in Luanda. The streets of the town became the scene of violent clashes between nationalists and police. At the same time the North burst into flames. Bands of uncontrolled rioters attacked European plantations, killing many of their oppressors. The government was taken by surprise but recovered quickly, sending in massive land and air forces to reassert control with great brutality. In the North alone twenty thousand men, women and children were killed in three months. Thousands fled into neighbouring states.

Things could not be the same after the 1961 troubles. The nationalists had acted, had gained martyrs, had given the people some hope and had provoked support abroad. At the United Nations Portugal was called to account for its colonial policies and unnecessary violence. MPLA leaders fled to Brazzaville. There they were joined by Neto who had escaped from Portugal (1962). From then on the Congo was used as a training ground for guerrillas who were sent on raids into Angola.

The first nationalist movement to emerge in Mozambique was the *União Democratico Nacional de Mozambique* (UDENAMO). It was founded by Uria Simango, a priest who had been in trouble with the police for his criticisms of government officials. In 1959 he moved to Rhodesia to escape police surveillance and there he founded UDENAMO among migrant workers from Mozambique. But the Rhodesian police became suspicious of his activities, so he fled to Dar es Salaam (Tanganyika) in 1961. At about the same time the Makonde African National Union (MANU) was formed as a cultural and political organization among the Makonde of north-east Mozambique by Lazaro Nkavandame. MANU also had to take refuge on the other side of the border and in 1960 Nkavandame made Dar es Salaam his headquarters.

In 1962 the leaders of the two groups, together with other Mozambique nationalists, held a conference in Dar es Salaam. They decided to unite into one organization, the *Frente de Libertacão de Mozambique* (FRELIMO), and to work for the liberation of their country. The first President was Eduardo Mondlane, who had studied in the United States and had worked on the United Nations' secretariat. FRELIMO armed and trained guerrillas to make raids into Mozambique. It infiltrated nationalists into various regions, there to build up cells of supporters and organize resistance in readiness for an eventual revolution. It chose young men to be the future leaders of independent Mozambique and sent them abroad for education. Despite tragedies such as the loss of many men on active service and the assassination of Mondlane by a Portuguese agent, FRELIMO made steady progress towards its aims.

The struggle in both territories continued for another five years. It was only after the death of the Portuguese dictator, Salazar, and the overthrow of the undemocratic government in Lisbon, that a new official attitude was adopted towards

TROOPS FIRE ON ANGOLA CROWD

Rioters Try to Free Political Prisoners

7 KILLED, 10 WOUNDED & 20 ARRESTED

From RONALD PAYNE

Sunday Telegraph Special Correspondent

LISBON, Saturday.

PORTUGUESE forces opened fire on armed Africans rioting against the Salazar regime early

Headlines from Sunday Telegraph, 12 February 1961

Portugal's overseas territories. In 1974 Mozambique gained its independence and the following year Portuguese officials withdrew hastily from Angola. In neither country had the way been carefully prepared for majority rule. As a result the two new states began their existence with considerable problems to overcome.

South Africa's continuing commercial prosperity was the background to a continuing struggle between Afrikaner racialism and British liberalism. Eventually the extremists won and South Africa moved towards complete racial separation and the denial of African political rights. The idea of racial separation—*apartheid*—was first urged by J. M. B. Hertzog, leader of the Nationalist Party. He became Prime Minister in 1924 after the defeat of J. C. Smuts in the elections. Smuts had spoken out against white workers who had gone on

South Africa

407

General Smuts

General Hertzog

strike to force the mine owners not to employ black skilled labour. The issue of employment was causing great unrest and Smuts eventually had to send troops to restore law and order. This cost him the support of many voters and allowed Hertzog, in alliance with the Labour Party, to form the first extremist administration in South Africa.

Hertzog believed that to separate the white and black races as far as possible into different territorial areas would be to the advantage of both. In 1926 he introduced the Mines and Works Amendment Act which excluded Africans and Asians from all skilled and some semi-skilled jobs in the mines. Other Acts restricted the movements of Africans in towns and on the reserves. In 1931 the franchise was extended to white women and a larger section of men in order to maintain a white voting majority in the face of the growing number of Africans qualified to vote. Hertzog saw the growing political influence of the majority as the real stumbling block to his policies. In 1936 he resolved to settle this problem by the Natives Representation Act. This removed Cape Province African voters from the common roll. They were to vote in all-black constituencies for white candidates. Hertzog's original draft had been even more extreme but he now headed a coalition government which included Smuts's South African Party and he was forced to modify his demands. Liberal pressures within the Assembly prevented Hertzog carrying out other racial measures. In 1939 the Second World War broke out and the issue was raised whether or not South Africa should go to Britain's aid. Hertzog violently opposed committing the country to war but he did not carry the Assembly with him and he was forced to resign. South Africa was not yet ready for an Afrikaner take-over.

Although the plight of the Africans was growing steadily worse there was little attempt at effective protest in the inter-war period. The industrial situation of the early 1920s led to a considerable increase in the membership of the Industrial and Commercial Union. However, the work of police spies and Communists, who tried to take over the Union, caused disruption and the organization collapsed when Clements Kadale resigned in 1929. Many ICU members joined the Communist-led Non-European Trade Union Federation. The Natives Representation Act (1936) took away what little effective political influence Africans had. They thus had no real constitutional channels through which to seek redress of

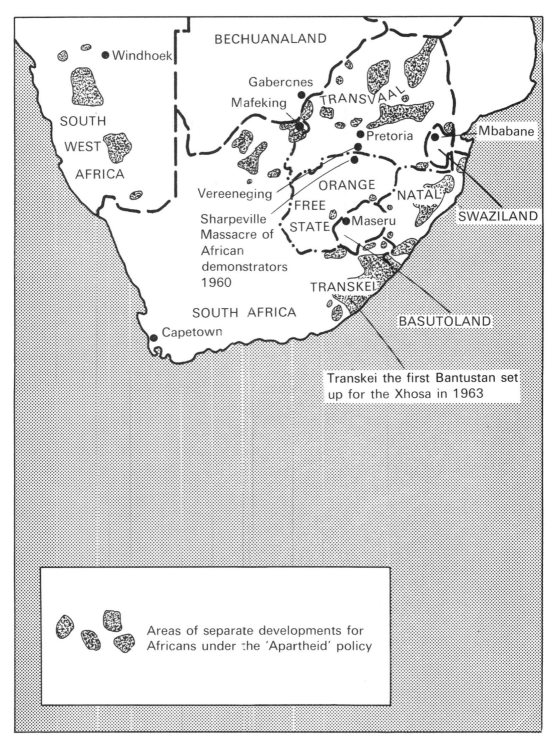

BECHUANALAND

Windhoek

SOUTH
WEST
AFRICA

Gaberones

Mafeking

TRANSVAAL

Pretoria

Mbabane

ORANGE

NATAL

Vereeneging

FREE

SWAZILAND

Sharpeville
Massacre of
African
demonstrators
1960

STATE

Maseru

TRANSKEI

SOUTH AFRICA

BASUTOLAND

Capetown

Transkei the first Bantustan set
up for the Xhosa in 1963

Areas of separate developments for
Africans under the 'Apartheid' policy

Areas of separate development for Africans

their growing grievances. Apart from the colour bar and the contempt in which they were held by most Europeans, the Africans had to suffer many injustices. They were harshly treated by employers. Their movements were restricted by the pass laws. They were excluded from many jobs. Their wages were much lower than those of white workers. Despite the fact that Africans and Coloureds made up over four-fifths of the population (1960 census) they occupied about one ninth of the land of South Africa. One reason why this situation did not lead to serious conflict in the inter-war years was the comparatively high standard of living enjoyed by black citizens of the Union. The country was rich and, though Africans only came in for a small share of this wealth, they were better off than their counterparts in most other parts of the continent.

In South-West Africa there was some attempt to resist the repressive Cape Town administration after the confirmation of the League of Nations mandate (1920). The Union government encouraged white settlement and provided cheap farmland. In 1925 a new constitution was established which gave the settlers an elected majority on the Legislative Council. From then on South-West Africa was in reality a province of the Union though Hertzog's attempt at formal incorporation in the late 1930s was unsuccessful. The first Africans to revolt were the Bondelswarts. In 1922 they refused to give up one of their leaders, Abraham Morris, who had returned to his people without permission. Instead they took up a defensive position and prepared to fight it out with Union forces. They were ruthlessly bombed and machine-gunned into submission. Protests from the League of Nations led to some redress of the Bondelswarts' grievances. In 1925 the Rehobothers made a bid for independence. Having failed with diplomatic appeals to the League of Nations and the Union government, they began to organize themselves for armed resistance. Once again a large force despatched from Cape Town put an end to the revolt. By 1939 white settlers had taken all the best land and the Africans were forced to live in reserves or work for white employers.

After the Second World War changes in the political parties left Smuts's United Party and the Afrikaner HNP (*Herenidge Nasionale Party*) the main contenders for power. The HNP was under the leadership of D. F. Malan, a thoroughgoing racialist whose avowed aim was the preservation of 'white civilization'. Afrikaner values seemed doomed by the influx of British settlers after the war, the spread of liberalism and the trend towards self-determination and majority rule in British colonies. In the 1948 elections Malan's supporters played on the fears of the white electorate and pledged themselves to the implementation of full *apartheid*. The HNP won a narrow majority. The new government used every means to increase its majority. It stopped British immigration. It insisted on Afrikaans as the only medium of instruction in predominantly Boer regions. It incorporated South-West Africa into the Union by the South-West Africa Affairs Amendment Act (1949). This Act was put into effect despite the protests of the United Nations and the decision of the International Court of Justice (1950) that the South African government had exceeded its authority.

South Africa now fell increasingly under the spell of Afrikaner racialism and grew increasingly out of touch and out of sympathy with the rest of the world. The government became almost fanatical in its devotion to *apartheid* and its determination to force extreme measures on the country by every possible means. In 1949 inter-marriage between people of different races was prohibited. The Group Areas Act of 1950 forcibly separated the races. In towns and in the country, areas were designated as exclusively for 'whites' or 'others'. Considerable hardship and, often, violence were experienced by people who were moved under the terms of the Act. Following legislation introduced in 1953, education was segregated. African and Coloured children were not allowed to study alongside white children and could only embark on syllabuses designed to fit them for an inferior station in life. Later, universities were brought under similar regulations. From 1951 to 1956 the government fought a long battle to remove Cape Coloured voters from the common roll. When government intentions were successfully challenged in the courts the government changed the law to bring the judiciary under the control of the executive. After this removal of a fully independent judiciary (a cornerstone of any democratic state) the government was unassailable. It could make and enforce whatever laws it chose. Whenever opposition looked like becoming effective the government could, and frequently did, impose its will either by force or by changing the constitution. One example of this is the Suppression of Communism Act (1950). By this Act the government took powers of arrest,

Father Huddleston, a champion of African civil rights, addressing a meeting on Nyasaland 1959

censorship, detention without trial, dispersal of public meetings and exclusion from parliament of persons suspected of Communism. But 'Communism' was never defined and the government simply used the Act as a justification for proceeding against any opponent or critic of the regime. The spectre of international Communism was used to frighten the white population into supporting the government. The secret police was extensively used in ferreting out 'Communist' agents. Behind the Nationalist government was the secret *Broederbond*, aimed at Afrikaner domination. Its activities ensured that more and more important posts were filled by Afrikaners and that symbols of the British connection (such as the British flag and national anthem) gradually disappeared.

The full implementation of *apartheid* involved the creation of separate territories for the black population. The Nationalist government was pledged to this but found it difficult to carry out. South African industry depended on African labour, and European families refused to do without African servants. However, the Nationalist dream was carried some way towards reality. In 1951 the Bantu Authorities Act made provision for the establishment of separate internally self-governing territories under African control. In 1959 the areas of Bantu administration were clearly defined and in 1963 the first such area, the Transkei, came into being. It was a Xhosa homeland in which the people could elect some of the members of legislature. It was, however, still under the strict control of the Nationalist government as was shown when Chief Kaizer Matanzima was appointed Chief Minister, although he did not have the support of a majority of his people.

The policies of the HNP provoked considerable opposition both inside and outside South Africa. Other countries have been powerless to do more than protest. In 1966 the United Nations' Assembly put an end to South Africa's trusteeship over South-West Africa (Namibia) but could do nothing to enforce its decision. In 1961 South African racialism threatened to destroy the Commonwealth when newly independent states refused to join. The dilemma was resolved by a referendum in South Africa which approved, by a narrow margin, the withdrawal of South Africa from the Commonwealth and the creation of a republic. This was a triumph for Afrikanerdom. South Africa was excluded from many world bodies, and sporting organizations, such as the International Olympic Committee, having refused to select teams on a basis of racial equality.

Within the country resistance was made very difficult by the powers held by the government. Parliamentary opposition to the Nationalists split into a number of small parties. Considerable opposition came from white liberals, particularly missionaries and church leaders. Such men were watched carefully and detained, imprisoned or deported if their activities or utterances proved too unpalatable to the authorities. Frustration led even some whites to violent action. An assassination attempt was made on the Prime Minister, Dr Verwoerd, in 1960. Another attempt on 6 September 1966 was successful. Both attackers were Europeans. Sporadic African riots and demonstrations were easily put down by the police and were used by government propagandists as evidence of the need for strict control of the majority population.

South Africa

The time has come for bursting out. People are going to get more organised. If the whites think they can get away with their system, they are mistaken.

—A MOTOR MECHANIC, aged 17, talking to British reporters in Soweto last Thursday.

130 MURDERED – BUT THE FIGHT FOR FREEDOM GROWS

THE RISEN PEOPLE —Pages 8 & 9

Chief Albert Luthuli

The first serious widespread campaign was led by the African National Congress (ANC). In 1952 it organized passive resistance against the colour bar and the pass laws. Thousands of demonstrators were arrested and there was no change in government policy. The leader of the ANC was Chief Albert Luthuli who was widely accepted as the leader of African nationalism, even by Europeans, because of his moderation and opposition to violence. But Luthuli was not moderate enough for the government; he was banned from his home area and his activities were severely limited. In 1961 he drew the world's attention to African grievances in his book *Let My People Go* and in the same year he became

the first African to win the Nobel Peace Prize for his attempt
to win African rights by peaceful means.

But peaceful means made no impression on a determined,
racialist government. Robert Sobukwe formed, in 1958, the
Pan-Africanist Congress. He aimed to force the government's
hand by mobilizing the whole African majority in nationwide protest. The first mass protest, in March 1960, was also
the last. A demonstration of 50,000 people in Cape Town was
dispersed by troops. A similar demonstration at Sharpeville,
near Johannesburg, provoked a violent reply by the police.
The killing of 69 unarmed demonstrators and the wounding
of another 180 shocked the world. Sobukwe and others were
arrested and detained indefinitely at the penal settlement on
Robben Island. Another ANC member, Nelson Mandela,
decided that only violence would win justice for the black
citizens of South Africa. He organized secret guerrilla and
sabotage groups. But the secret police were thorough and
efficient. Mandela eventually ended up on Robben Island
(1964). At the same time the ANC was banned. By 1975 South
African prisons were full of political detainees, many of whom
had never been convicted in a court of law.

Robert Sobukwe

The High Commission Territories

Despite many attempts by the Pretoria government to
bring the High Commission Territories under its control,
Swaziland, Bechuanaland and Basutoland remained under
British authority and eventually achieved complete independence. All of the territories were closely bound to South Africa
by economic ties. Many of their menfolk worked in the Rand
mines and there were white settlers within their borders. The
South Africa Act of 1910 had made provision for the possible
transfer of the territories to the Union. In 1921 white settlers
in Swaziland succeeded in getting an elective Advisory
Council formed. In 1933 the Bechuanaland ruler, Tshekedi
Khama, was deposed and it seemed that Britain might impose
direct rule as a prelude to a hand-over to South Africa. It was
the emergence of Hertzog and the Nationalists which prompted Britain to resist any such move.

After the Second World War the South African government
renewed its claim to the Territories. This posed a problem for
Britain. The three protectorates had small populations and
were poor. They would probably find it difficult to exist as
independent nations and would always be partly dependent

Nelson Mandela

415

King Sobhuza II

on the Union. On the other hand Britain did not want to administer them indefinitely and knew that they would never consent to being handed over to the Afrikaners. The British government delayed making a decision but seriously undertook the economic development of the territories.

As time went by and the Nationalist government of South Africa became more and more racialist it became obvious to the British government that complete independence was the only answer for the territories. Constitutional changes were planned. In 1959 Basutoland received a National Council which was partially elective. The following year provision was made for elected regional councils. In 1961 Bechuanaland received a Legislative Council with an elected, unofficial majority. In 1964 Swaziland followed suit. Complete internal self-government swiftly followed. In 1966 Basutoland and Bechuanaland became independent under the names of Lesotho and Botswana respectively. In 1968 Swaziland became the last British protectorate to obtain its freedom. In 1976 two new Bantustans were formed: the Transkei and Kwa Zulu.

One of the most important events in Southern and Central Africa during the 1970s was the achievement of independence by the Portuguese colonies. In 1973 political changes in Portugal led to the election of a democratic government. This was followed by Portuguese demands for an end to the fighting against nationalist forces in Africa, which was claiming the lives of many Portuguese soldiers and settlers. The government announced its intention of handing over independence as rapidly as possible. This was achieved peacefully in Mozambique (1974) when Samora Machel became the first President. In Angola the colonial forces withdrew before arrangements had been made for a transfer of power. Only after months of bitter fighting between rival groups did the MPLA succeed in establishing a government (1975).

Index

Prepared by V. Howard-Vyse